An Overflow from Hockley Brook

by Ron 'Smudge' Smith

This third book I dedicate to two wonderful people. The first my wife Edythe, or 'Cuddles' as she is now known.

The second is a man whom I met only a short while ago, but feel I have known a lifetime, Mac Joseph of "Good Morning Ladywood" fame.

Foreword

I have known Ron for several years and this is his 'hat-trick' of books.

It is a great honour for me to be asked to write this foreword for a very dear friend who has helped me over the last few years.

Ron, affectionately known as 'Smudge' has given great pleasure to many, many Brummies, and adopted Brummies, with his entertaining talks, books and paintings depicting the suburbs of old Birmingham.

Ron shares his memories of sad and happy times of his life in Birmingham through the words and paintings in this book and I am sure many people will reflect on these memories and say 'Yes, that happened to me' or 'Yes, I remember that'.

I feel privileged to know Ron and Edythe and I wish them every success with this book.

Mac Joseph

Like many more people of Hockley and elsewhere, life was hard for the Moms and Dads in the thirties. Children were children in a life of dreams whatever class.

It was in 1934 that I decided "I wanted to draw like mi Dad" after he showed me a rather worn piece of paper with the most wonderful pencil sketch of a horses head he did whilst serving in the Royal Artillery in the 1914-1918 Great War.

I find in life if you can laugh at yourself you can laugh at the world.

I'm sure Dad would be proud of my efforts.

They had "Perfect Milk", which was according to them "Perfectly Bottled"

September 1943 to August 1945

"CUM-ON-SON". It was my Dad shaking my left shoulder gently, and whispering softly, presumably so that he wouldn't waken the other members of the family. "Yo'll 'ave to gerrup now if yome gunna get ta ya' nu job on time, so cum on now, I'll gu down fust an' mek yarra cuppa tea, w'ile yo' getcha self dressed, an' don' mek a noise or yo'll werken the othas, oright Son?" "A-r-r-roright Dad, o wunt mek a noise", although I silently chuckled to myself as I thought what I'd like to do, and that was jump out of bed and run round the bedrooms blowing a trumpet, "tharred bloody sherk 'em, an' werken the lazy sods up", I thought. I answered Dad's question sleepily, and off he went down the stairs. I listened as he made his way slowly down the wooden stairs, the creaking as he trod on each wooden strip, trying to be as quiet as he possibly could, but as always never being completely successful in the attempt. I thought as I heard this creaking, "O bet that wunt do the othas sleepin' any bloody good", and at this thought I turned slightly to the right, looking at "Our Kid" seeking confirmation of this thought, but the scene I witnessed devastated any thought in that direction completely, for he was snoring away contentedly in a deep sleep.

I had gone to bed pretty early on the Saturday night, due to the fact that I had now fully accepted the change of jobs as the right decision to make, resulting consequently in a free and happy mind, which in turn made me very excited indeed. Unfortunately for me this also had an adverse effect, for when I did get into bed I found it very difficult to get off to sleep. I lay there mulling over the events of the past weeks, and all kinds of thoughts came flashing through my mind, also hypothetical answers to them. Eventually I did drop off to sleep, but it was a restless sleep, full of God knows what fantasies.

Climbing out of bed quietly I dressed and went downstairs, where I found Dad in the middle room having a 'fag' and a cup of tea. He had lit the fire, but it hadn't reached the point where it was giving off heat of any significance yet. Prince and Smut had disregarded this fact, and were snuggled up together as though the fire was blazing halfway up the chimney, they stirred slightly on my entrance into the room, opening one eye each to find out who had so rudely interrupted their slumbers.

Dad poured me a cup of tea, put sugar and milk in, then gave it a vigorous stir, of which I was glad as I didn't want any sugar caked at the bottom of the cup when I had finished, did I? I drank the first cup in complete silence; Dad just sat there enjoying another "Gold Flake", and another cup of tea. I looked hard at him for a moment and thought how at "peace with the world" he seemed. His blue watery eyes staring through the grey-blue haze of the smoke from the cigarette at God knows what; his gentle face, although lined with the ravages of this hard life, still gave me a great deal of comfort and security. Yes, I loved Dad; I loved him very much.

I poured my second cup of tea and Dad broke the silence. "O cudda dun that fer ya' Ron, yowed on'y gorra arsk". "Nah it's oright Dad, yo' wuz enjoyin' ya' fag, so o wudden disturb ya'". Everything went quiet again, momentarily. Dad "nipped" his fag and put the nub end into his waistcoat pocket and took another swallow from his cup. I was half way through my second cup when he spoke again. "Yer Mutha tol' me aboutcha changin' ya' job las' night, w'en we wuz down the "Turk", Son. She sez yome gunna be a milkmon up at 'an'sworth Dairies?" "Ar-r-r-r tha's right Dad, an' w'en ov bin thaya ferra bit they'm gunna gi me a round ov miyone, an' if odda stopped w'ere o wuz, at Rowlan's, they wuddna gid me a round ov miyone until o wuz twenny one, I yeard Wally Mason say so, o did 'onist."

I made a big deal of informing Dad of this just in case he was annoyed at the move I made, but I needn't have really made such a big thing of it, or worried regarding that aspect of things. Dad confirmed this when he replied "It's soright Son o worn't queryin' w'y yo' left Rolan's, cuz yo've gorra please yaself about that, nah don' worry about tharrat all, as a marra a fact I admire ya' fer standin' on yarrown two feet, an' doin' w'at chow think is best fer yaself, an' no' ralways thinkin' abouruthas, as lung as yome 'appy, an' yo' ain' 'urtin' anybody in w'at yome doin', or w'at yome gunna do, then ev'rythin's oright, we-l-ll, as fer as I'm concerned any road up."

At this point, before I could make any kind of answer, Dad looked at the clock on the mantlepiece and said, "W'at time 'ave ya' gorra be thaya Son?" "Between 'alf five an' six a clock Dad", I replied, a feeling of apprehension rising in me, which was confirmed with his swift reply, "Well yowed berra getcha skerts on adden ya'? It's ten ta five now, an' yo' don' know w'at time the buzzis run on a Sundee do ya'?"

"Nah, o don' Dad, any way I'll finish mi tea an' gerroorff down ta "The Brook" sharpish, o don' wanna bi lert, o could a used mi bike, burr I ain' cert'in w'ere ro cun purrit w'en o get thaya, so I ain' gunna tek any chancis's, o don' wan mi bike pinched, I'll 'ave ta see 'ow the land lies w'en ov bin thay ra bit." "Ar-r-r-r ro think yome wise ta do that Son, yo' don' know w'at thay'm like at a nu plerce do ya', an' ya' bike cost a lorra munnee din it", Dad replied.

I finished my tea hurriedly, put my "wick day" best coat on, and said "tarrar" quickly to Dad who was by now putting some newspaper up to the front of the fire to attempt to draw it up quicker, which normally resulted in the newspaper catching fire and being thrown onto the fire itself, with Smut and Prince running for their lives until the incident had been coped with, and things returned to normality. He turned and said "Tarrar Son", and whilst in the act of turning the newspaper *did* catch fire, and I left Dad coping with the situation, with Smut and Prince no help at all and me being even less help.

I ran down the entry tittering to myself, naturally I daren't let Dad see me doing this, it might have inflamed(!) the situation, and I couldn't see him enjoying the joke one bit – could you?

Off I went down New John Street West, passing Bull's, Beddoes, Belchers, and Nash's before reaching "The Brook" by Elsie and Violet Colemans. As I passed Elsie was getting the papers in off the front doorstep, and I wished her "Good

Morning", and she gave me a brief "Allo Ronnie". I crossed over by Izons straight across to Shakespears without any trouble; well at that time on a Sunday morning there was no traffic to speak of, only the occasional Wathes Cattel and Gurdon, Co-op, Shaws, Holt's, Marsdens, or Ravenscrofts milk carts to worry about, and even they weren't too evident. Like the Sunday previous it was cold, but the sun was already coming up giving a wonderful cheerfulness to the day, and making it altogether more like I was going on a trip out for the day instead of going to work, but then as I discovered in later years, this was one of my characteristics; to me everything is an adventure, and I confront each situation, whatever it may be, with wholehearted energy and happiness.

I passed the Co-op, over the bridge where underneath "The Brook" ran merrily, then the Florist's and Gills the newsagents next door, which in turn was adjacent to "The Watt". The papers were still on the doorstep of "Gills", as was the milk from "Midland Counties". I thought they must 'ave said "Sod it we'll 'ave a lie in this mornin', bugga the perpers", and I smiled to myself at this thought. I looked into "Gills" window, noting all the different magazines, toys, and weekly papers they had on show. After what appeared to be a lifetime, although in reality it could have been only a few seconds, I got bored with this and started to get anxious regarding the buses, but more particularly the one that was going to convey me from here to "The New Inns" and get me to work on time. The bus shelters were deserted, not a soul in sight, I looked up towards Claremont Road and admired the logo of "Martins", just inside the road, it was a Martin in flight. I saw an old fellow starting to hose the frontage of "The Watt" down in preparation for the Sunday lunchtime crowd.

Getting a little agitated now, I searched for any sign of life up towards town, hoping that I would spot a bus coming down from the "Duke of York" at the junction of Key Hill, but nothing. I thought to myself as I stared across at "The Palladium", "It'll bi jus' like me ta bi bloody lert on mi fust mornin' at a nu job". Suddenly I heard the unmistakable throb of a "Leyland Cub" and I turned my attention again in the direction of Hockley Hill, but nothing was descending the steep hill. But just poking his nose out of Whitmore Street was indeed a bus. I watched as little by little it emerged into "The Brook" and turned in my direction. I was very anxious, hoping that this bus would not be a number 70, Oxhill Road, which of course would be of no use to me. As it approached, however, I was overjoyed to find that it was a number 74. I rushed to the shelter under the sign indicating that this part of several sections was for the Dudley and Wednesbury buses, and waited for the bus to draw up.

I boarded it and said "Allo" to the conductor who was busy preparing his ticket rack for the day's work. He replied, "Warrow Son, nice mornin' innit? Ar-r-rit's great innit? It's too nice ta bi werkin' though innit?" "Ar-r-rit is that". I then made my way upstairs, right to the front of the saloon. (I still liked to pretend that I was driving, although I wuz a werkin' mon now.)

I waited for the bell to sound, indicating the driver to move off, almost urging this to take place, but nothing. I went back down the upper saloon to see what was holding us up, and I saw through the rear window a man running from "the gulley" by "The Municipal Bank", towards the bus. He boarded the bus and the conductor gave the driver his bell, and off we went up Soho Hill at rather a rapid pace. I heard the conductor say to the man "Blimey, yo' left it a bit fine this mornin' dain' ya' Fred?"

"Ar-r-rom eva sa sorry Chas, me an' the ol' gel stopped ova at "The Swan" las' night. We 'ad some pals come, an' o couldn' very well not stay could o? Warra bleedin' night we 'ad though, one o the best night's ov eva rad, a bloke come with 'is accordion, an' we 'ad a right ol' sing song, Christ om mekkin' up forrit this mornin' though, o feel as though mi bleedin' 'ead's gunna blow up". "Bloody 'ell yome right Fred o cun still smell it on ya' bloody breath, yo' smell like a bleedin' brewery; still as lung as yo' enjoyed it. Mind yo', o wuz nearly ready fer the off, we couldna werted much lunga, cuz the bloody Inspecta' was due ta come out on the next buzz". The conversation became rather muffled then, but I'd lost interest anyway, so I went back to my seat at the front of the bus. I heard this bloke who had delayed us come up the stairs and although I didn't turn around to see, presumed that he had made himself comfortable on one of the back seats.

The bus went at quite a fast pace and it being a Sunday morning he didn't have to pull up at too many stops, for they were deserted. So in next to no time we had passed Soho Hill into Soho Road, and then on very swiftly up towards "The Regal" and the junction of Holyhead Road, Soho Road, and Booth Street. At the stop outside "The Regal" we had to stop for some passengers. I looked up Booth Street and thought "Blimey it's bin agis since o wen' an' sin mi Gran an' Grandad, o mus gu an' see 'em w'en o get the chance", and I made a mental note to do this soon, for they had indeed been very good to all us "Smith kids".

The bus started off from the stop, and we entered Holyhead Road on the final leg to "The New Inns", passing Milestone Lane, Brewery Street and Church Terrace, where in the first garden up the terrace was the largest greenhouse I'd ever seen. All these locations were to prove a big part in my life later on.

At last the bus arrived at the stop I was to alight at, just outside Mallins the "Cooked Meat Shop", just above "Pococks the Chemist" and right opposite "The Albion Cinema". I jumped off the bus behind another man, and by the smell of beer wafting from him I could only assume this was Fred, who had kept the bus waiting at "The Brook". I was proved right when the conductor (Chas) raced from the inside saloon where he had been collecting fares and shouted after the man, "I'll se ya' ternight in "The Vine" Fred, okay?" The bloke in front of me turned and shouted back, as the bus continued on its way up Holyhead Road towards "The Baggies Ground" and its final destination "Dudley", "ar-r-rokay Chas, about eight in the snug, cuz I'll 'ave the Missis with me, w-e-e-ell, ferra w'ile any way".

The bus disappeared out of sight as Fred and I made our way in the same direction along Sandwell Road, and I thought at the time, I wonder if he works at Handsworth Dairies, I can't think of any other place along here that he could possibly be going to at this time on a Sunday morning, because other than the dairy the whole area was made up of great big "posh 'ouses".

We moved on further along the road, passing first Regent, and then Westbourne Road. As we neared the junction with Island Road this bloke suddenly turned left up a narrow dirt lane, so, when I reached the lane I had a look up, and I could see a number of horse and carts with the brown and cream livery of Handsworth Dairies lined up apparently loading crates of milk onto the carts. I thought about following this Fred up to this loading bay, just outside Mr Davies's house, but then I thought "nah, 'e told me ta gu ta the blokes od sin w'en o come fer the job, so od berra do as o wuz told, o dain' wanna gerrin ta trouble affowa o started, an' any road up o knew that od see eitha Jim, Tom, or Vic, orevan all three if o wuz lucky". So I ran round the corner into Island Road up past the new part of the dairy and into the gates I had entered on the Sunday that I attended to apply for the job.

As I walked across the yard towards the shed like buildings which housed the three Supervisors I could hear someone inside the dairy itself singing in a very loud voice, and apparently he was trying to compete with the many other noises surrounding him, the clanking of metal milk crates, the sound of bottled milk being put into these cases, the steam hissing from the sterilising plant, the shouting, and laughing from the dairy staff whilst going about their daily tasks. The singer was trying, but I don't think he was winning.

I knocked on the open door, although I could not see any sign of life from within, I knocked just in case someone was in the back part of the building, which was very dark indeed, and I didn't want to go "barging in", for that would have been an intrusion of privacy, with the vast amount of paperwork I could see around. I waited patiently with my cards (P45) clutched tightly in my hand, and when I was thinking about going further into the dairy to try to find someone, a big fellow emerged from the dairy itself, and in a very pronounced Irish voice said "If ya' hang on a minnit oil go an' fetch sombody for ya' me old Son", and with that he disappeared back into the steam filled area that he had come from. This was my first sight of a very dear friend of future times, JIMMY LEE.

After a while it was Jim who came out of the same entrance that the big "fella" had gone into. He came across the yard at a casual pace, looking at the clip board he had in his hands, studying it rather closely. It wasn't until he was right near me that he actually saw me. " 'Allo nip, o see yo' got the job then. Jimmy come across an' told Vic, burr'e's busy at this minnit checkin' the rounds out on the otha deck, so 'e's told me ta see ta yo' ", and with that he put his arm around my shoulder and guided me into the shed. Once inside he said "gu an 'elp yaself to a cuppa tea Son, yo'll find ev'ry thin' ova thaya", and he pointed to a long table right at the back of the "office". I did as I was told and whilst pouring the tea from a huge tin teapot I said "D' yo wan' one?" "Ar-r-r yo' mirras well powa me a cup, I ain' 'ad one fer ten minnits", and he started to laugh, the joke being, and I fully understood by now, it was an occupational part of any job like this to drink tea at the slightest excuse.

I poured the tea and took it across to where he stood, looking over some figures. I placed his down, and he said "Thanks, o wunt be a minnit", so I went to the other side and sat down on an upturned wooden "Willan's" pop case, which had an herden sack over it to make it a little more comfortable for the person who did put their "bum" down on it.

I drank my tea watching Jim pour over his figures silently, and suddenly he said "ah-h that's w'ere yove bin ya' bugga, now I've gorrit strert", from which I could only assume that he had solved the particular problem he had had with his notes. He wrote some figures down briefly and then said "tha's it" to himself, put his clipboard down and drank the tea in one long swallow. On completion he put the tin mug down and said "right nip, now let's get yo' sorted out".

He looked at some more clipboards hanging in a line on nails driven into the wooden structure of the shed, and after a few seconds he said, again to himself "a-h-h-h, 'ere we are", took the particular clipboard he had selected, and put it down on the bench. He studied it for a moment, then he looked across at me and said "Cyril's left a note 'ere, yove gorra gu with (and he mentioned the name of the lady, but I'm afraid I've forgotten now), she's cumin' back ta werk this mornin', she's bin orff bad fer ra bit now, so Cyril said fer yo' ta gu with "a" fer this wick any road up, an' 'elp 'er get back inta 'arniss". There was a pause and Jim looked skywards, as if he was appealing to some greater power for an answer to this particular problem he appeared to have.

"O think the best thing fer yo' ta do is wait fer 'er in the tack room, cuz o don' know which way she'll bloody come in, an' she's gorra gu in thaya ta gerr 'er 'arniss for 'er ross, so come on nip an' I'll show ya' w'ere the tack room is, an' intraduce ya' ta Mrs Thomas".

Jim put his clipboard under his arm and went out into the yard, with me closely following. We passed piles of crates containing empty bottles, waiting their turn to be taken into the dairy, washed, and then re-filled with milk. Turning left we passed a couple of old 1934-5 Fords, one was a twelve c.w.t. boxed van, and the other one had the most peculiar driver's cab I had ever seen on any vehicle. It must have gone a good six feet higher than it was in its original state, and I imagined it would be like our assembly hall at school, with its very high ceiling. This added structure was made of wood, and I thought there wasn't a good deal of imagination put into it by whoever did the job. It was as though they had chopped the original roof off, and put four pieces of two-by-two inside, secured them, and then added a wooden surround of some kind. It looked most odd.

Jim must have seen me looking at this monstrosity and started to laugh. "She's a beaut int she? We call 'er "The Green'ouse". The reason they built the cab like that wuz so uz they could stack the crates 'ighya an' so get more ov 'em on board, an' the funny thing is it bloody well werks. Mindyo' " he went on, "it might look a bloody mess, burr it's a gua-a-a, it ain' very offen that this one causes any trouble". I was to see a lot of "The Greenhouse" in my stay at Handsworth Dairies.

I looked over to the left and saw Mr. Davies's house, well what I thought was Mr Davies's house, although I learned later that it actually belonged to "The Whites", and they rented the house to whoever was the current Manager, which was the position held by "Cyril". When I saw the house and the drive in front of it leading down to Sandwell Road, on my previous visit for the interview, I naturally thought that that was the drive for the house alone, but looking at the drive now, I knew that this was indeed not the case. For, going down the drive as far as I could see was a long line of Handsworth Dairies floats, flat wagons, and box carts, in their cream and brown livery, all horse drawn, of course. Standing round these different vehicles were the roundsmen, and roundswomen, chatting away to one another, whilst waiting for the cart in front to move on, when they would then pull their vehicle forward.

Around the corner, obviously out of sight, I could hear the thump of full milk cases being loaded onto these various carts, and the clink of milk bottles, and the general light hearted banter between people, the occasional "tarrar then, don' bi lert in taday", "don' ferget warr I tol' ya', an' cum an' see me w'en yo' cum in"; the click from the roundsmen or women as they urged their horses forward, the rumble of the metal rims on the drive, and the muffled squeal of the hand-operated brake, as they made their way down the steep hill to its exit into Sandwell Road. Jim and I walked into a huge, long wood and brick building, passing the long line of vehicles in the process, which extended far into this structure. Jim chatted to some of the roundspeople as we went by, and I was filled with excitement by this general happy atmosphere, that appeared to exist between these people, and decided there and then that I was going to enjoy very much the prospect of working for this firm.

We entered this building and I could see, further down, more carts of different descriptions lined up either side. Some just stood there, whilst others were having a horse put into the shafts in preparation of the day's work. On the left-hand side was a long wooden type fence, which divided this large structure in two, with two gaps at measured intervals, which I noted horses being brought out of, so I assumed, naturally, that the other side of this wooden fence, was where they stabled the horses, which proved me correct a little later.

In front of this wooden fence was a deep drain channel, and this was for the drainage of water when the stablemen had finished cleaning out the stalls, which was done when all the roundspeople had gone out on their various rounds. This information I found out, again a little later.

"Ayup nip, w'ere ya' guin"? Cum on in 'ere." It was Jim, of course. I had been so concerned about what was going on inside this building that I had forgotten I was with him. We turned right into a sectioned-off room which was full to capacity with horses' harnesses. There, on separate hooks, hanging from strong wooden frames, were sets of beautiful, clean bridles, collars and saddles. The brassware on the leather items shining brightly. Oh..., the smell of the leather, mingled with dubbin, brasso, and the old sweat from the horses themselves, it was heaven. Just inside this aperture of the main structure, on the right was a long bench with pieces of harness on it, being cleaned by a small but very handsome lady. She had a brown cowgown on, covering quite a petite figure. Her face was small, but beautiful; her hair was fair, and cut close to her head, with a fringe in front, big, light-blue eyes, twinkling and smiling; a small and pretty nose, largish mouth, with slightly thick lips that nevertheless fitted in with everything else. She smiled at us when we entered, revealing large tombstone teeth, sparkling white. The lady was in the process of applying some sort of oil to a collar, but she looked up and said in a quiet and charming voice, "Hello Jim, brought a new boy friend for me, have you?", then started to laugh, which reminded me of a set of tinkling bells. It really was wonderful to hear.

"Nah luv" replied Jim, "unless ya' like 'em young like this". He was going to continue but the lady interrupted, "You cheeky thing you, and me only just eighteen and all", and another burst of tinkling laughter.

"O wunda if you'll look arta Ronnie 'ere, and keep 'im with ya' until Mrs .... comes in, cuz 'e's gorra gu with 'er, an' ge' 'er ra birr ov an 'and arta rer bein' bad an' ev'rythin', ya' don' mind do ya' love?"

"No, of course I don't mind, as far as I'm concerned he can stay here all day and help me, if he would like that" and she turned to me and gave me one of her beautiful smiles. I went all bashful and started to blush, and sweat. I wanted to say "O-o-o-o yes maam please, od like ta stay with yo' fereva" but the words would just not come out.

"Look yo've med 'im gu red now, with all that talk, now don' gu tekkin' advantage on 'im arta rime gone" said Jim with a big grin on his face. Then he started to leave this room and go about his normal duties, I suppose, with the lady calling after him "Once you've gone Jim he's my responsibility, so I'll do what

I like with him, so mind your own business" followed by another peel of her wonderful laughter.

"Well young man, and what's your name then, eh?"

"Mo nerm's Ronnie Smith maam, an' ov jus' started werk 'ere, this mornin'."

"My name is Mrs Thomas, and I'm very pleased to meet you, you'll probably be seeing an awful lot of me whilst you are working here Ronnie. Now you go and sit over there and I'll make us a nice cup of tea; I bet you could manage one, couldn't you?"

"O-o-o tar maam, ov jus' 'ad one with Jim, burr I like tea, so thank ya', thank ya' very much".

"I don't suppose Mrs .... will be here very early; she didn't come till late before her illness, so I don't suppose she will change her habits now, there's a paper over there if you want to have a read for a while, whilst I make the tea".

"O-o-o tar maam, od like that very much", and I went across the room and picked up the paper "The Sunday Pictorial", the paper "Our Dad" read. I sat down by the table on which lay all the horses' tackle, and turned to the cartoon section. Mrs Thomas eventually returned with a tray filled with tea in a pot, sugar in a bowl, and milk in a jug, "proper posh" I thought. She placed the tray on the table, then reached up to a cupboard over the top of it, undid the door by the wooden latch, held in place by a screw, and took out two tin mugs. Pouring the tea in she said, "Help yourself to milk and sugar, Ronnie, then you won't be able to blame me if it's not to your liking".

I drank my tea and read the paper, but not with any great depth because, naturally, I was expecting this lady whom I was going to assist. I kept looking up, watching Mrs Thomas carrying out her work cleaning harnesses. People kept coming and going: "'mornin' Mrs Thomas"; "'allo luv; 'ow are ya' this mornin'?" "Yo' ain' gorra drop left in the pot 'ave ya' luv?" "Go on you cheeky devil, go and get the milk delivered to all those nice customers of yours". (Laughter and quiet words were exchanged at times between these different women and men who came in to collect the harness for their particular horse. I waited for what seemed an eternity for this lady to arrive; I waited so long that I began to think that she would never come, and her supervisor would have to go out on the round. It seemed I would never be delivering milk for Handsworth Dairies when, all of a sudden, whilst I was deep in reading a particular piece in the paper, I heard Mrs Thomas say, "Hello ...., how nice to see you back again; how are you love?"

I didn't look up because I thought it was another person just passing through, and then I heard the reply to Mrs Thomas's question, in a broad Lancashire accent.

"E-e-e om nay betta for seein' this plerce agen, still ar suppose I musn' grumble, thay's a lot werse off than me". "Well .... I have got a nice young man here for you, he'll be helping you until you feel able to cope again, so that's a blessing anyway".

"A-a-a ol' Jim torld mi there were a lad wertin' fer mi' (then there was a pause), "but 'e dern't tell mi 'e wos such a big 'ansome lad, if that's 'im over thaya".

This caused me to look up, naturally, because there was no one else in the room beside Mrs Thomas and myself, so I had to assume that they were talking about me, and on looking up I was met with the funniest sight I had ever seen – well, it was funny to me, any road up. I couldn't believe my eyes at this vision, I wanted to laugh, but I knew that I daren't. I had seen quite a few people come into this "tack room" in the short space of time I had been there; quite a few nice looking girls, and handsome men, and some not quite so beautiful, and not quite so handsome, but this was on the verge of being ridiculous.

She was short and stocky. A black beret covered her hair, but what bits I could see, sticking out from beneath the beret wasn't very enhancing. It was a straggly, nondescript colour. The face beneath the beret and straggly hair was a mixture of Terry Thomas (she had a gap right in the middle of rather large teeth) and Arthur Askey (she wore horn rimmed glasses). Her face was podgy and pale, the eyes brown and dull, not a sight of a twinkle, it was like looking into a muddy pool. The stocky figure was covered by a long, black leather motorcyclist's coat, and just showing was a pair of black trousers, and showing beneath these were a pair of black boots.

I thought to myself, "well she ain' no Betty Grable, Ann Sheridan, Alice Faye, Margaret Lockwood, Patricia Rock, Jean Kent or any o' the otha filum stars like that. In fact she worn evan as 'an'sum as some o' the blokes, like Michael Dennison, John Payne, John Wayne an' the like – but she *was* very friendly. As was proven later, she was like Beth at Rowlands, she was a very caring woman, and although she did not actually tell me – I heard it from another source later – she had what appeared to be insurmountable problems in her private life. Her husband was in the army, and something had happened, although I never did find out what, but on hearsay, he was captured and was indeed a prisoner of war.

" 'Allor love", she said, and came across to see me, "my nerm's .... an' yome Ronnie ernt cha?"

"A-r-r-r tha's sright maam, tha's mi nerm". I stood up ready to start work, waiting for this lady to tell me what to do. "E-e-e-e w'a's ya' rush love, we'em gunna 'ave a neece cuppa before we start werk. We alwis do dorn't we Mrs Thomas?" she shouted to her, as I saw her disappear with the tray and pots once again. "Sit ya' down lad, an' tell me w'at cha know about this job".

I sat down and revealed all the experience I had had over the past few years; not only delivering milk, but bread and papers, too. On completion of this answer she said, "Well lad, yo' wunt need much tellin' will ya'?" "I yope not maam". "An' dorn't keep callin' mi maam, mo nerms .... It'll make it easy all roun' wun it?"

"A-r-r rit will" I replied.

Mrs Thomas came back with the tea and said to me, "We always have a cup of tea before.......... goes out on her round, don't we?" "I-i-i-i- it's 'abit o dorn't wannta chernge, an' o worn't if ar can 'elp it". At this reply both ladies had a laugh, but I'm afraid it was beyond my scope of thoughts, so I just gave a weak grin.

On completion of this latest tea break .... got up and said, looking at me through her thick "Arthur Askey" glasses, "Well lad we'd best mek a move, else we'll 'ave Cyril think I ain't come, so if yo' gor an' get Mary's (the mare) 'arness orff peg numba ten, an' I'll show yer w'ere t' ol' gel is, an' we'll gerr 'er ready fer the road oright Ronnie?"

"Ar-r-r-r, tha's oright bi me, ma...." I said, suddenly remembering that she had told me to call her by her first name and not "maam", so I finished up with "........".

I got up from where I was sitting and walked down the rows of wooden frames, each with a number in black paint showing above the hook. Finally I came to number ten. First I got the bridle down and placed it on the bench below that ran the whole length of each frame, then the collar, and finally the saddle with the reins buckled to it. I put the collar and saddle over my shoulders and carried the bridle, walking back towards the exit, and to my lady who was waiting for me.

"Tarrar, Mrs T, I'll see yer lerta ron, an' 'opefully it'll bi earlier wi' owa Ronnie 'elpin' mi". "Tata love, and you just mind how you go," replied Mrs Thomas. We walked out of the tack room and entered the stables themselves through one of the apertures in the long wooden fence dividing the huge structure.

"'Allo love, 'ow are ya', I yope yome a lot berra now. Mary's all ready fer ya' love, all brushed, and combed, o bet she'll bi glad ta see yarran all." This greeting came from a stocky fresh faced lad. He came towards us to have a further conversation with my lady. His face was handsome in a rugged kind of way, his hair fair and curly. His eyes blue, but rather squinty, as if the sun was continually shining into them. The nose was just as though he had spent some time in the boxing ring with adverse effects, but it gave an impression of toughness, which I found out later was quite true. His mouth small, and when he spoke he revealed small, but very white teeth. The body build was that of an athlete, although a bit on the small side. This lad was to sum it all up, the guy I would like on my side if a scrap looked imminent.

"'ellor love,'ow niece ta see yo' to, om glad yove looked arfta mi yorse", my lady started, and then the two of them went into a quiet conversation, but I didn't think it was the type of conversation between two people in love, due to the fact that this lad was only just a little older than myself, sixteen, maybe seventeen. The reason I mention two people in love, was simply because that was the way I felt at this particular time.

It was a time for love all around, with all the American films coming in, about Joe going off to the war, and returning with difficulties of one kind or another, but naturally it all came right in the end. The British films, like *In Which We Serve* and *The Cruel Sea* sparked off a very sensitive feeling to all of us, and rubbed off on some of the service men and women when leaving their loved ones, even though they may only be going to Chatham, Devonport, or Portsmouth.

Of course there were real heartbreaking times when a soldier, sailor, or airman had got a good idea that he was going abroad somewhere, although he didn't know for sure, and of course it must have been very difficult for him to put it off telling his loved ones. Yes, it was a very dramatic, and soul tearing time, and in a lot of cases ultimately tragic.

I stood there in the middle of the stables with the saddle over my shoulder, the collar over the other one, and the bridle in my right hand. I couldn't go and harness the mare up, because I didn't know the horse, so I just stood there whilst they chatted on, feeling like a "right narna".

Eventually my lady broke away and started to come back to me, and whilst she was in the process of doing this, the chap she had been talking to shouted over, "It's a good job yome guin back to 'im love, if 'e'd a bin thaya any lunga with all tharr 'arniss on 'im somebody y'da grabbed 'old on 'im an' purrim in the shafts ov thaya wagons an' driven 'im orff". He burst out laughing, and so did my lady.

13

Naturally I didn't take to this joke lightly, I felt like going up to him and "bostin' 'im one", but three things deterred me. Number one I didn't want to upset my lady on this my first day at Handsworth Dairies, secondly I didn't want to blot my copy book with this bloke, and thirdly, and I must say, most important, I reckon that if I did approach him in this manner, and with his physical attributions, he'd have "knocked eight bells ov S..t, ourov me", so I just grinned sickly, and remained "schtum".

The lady led the way to the stall where Mary was stabled, and I walked to the right hand side of the horse, talking to her quietly, hopefully gaining her confidence. I stroked her and whispered sweet nothings to her, and to my surprise it really worked, for she snickered, and responded when I stroked her nose, and kissed her. I love horses, I love all animals, but horses are a bit special.

After gaining this lovely chesnut's confidence, I placed the saddle over her back gently, and then lengthened the britches strap, put the britches around her hind quarters. Then very slowly I brushed her long tail downwards four or five times standing well away from her hind legs, just in case she changed her mind about me, and decided to have a little kick out. But she didn't move, so I lifted her tail up, an held it there whilst I placed the crup around it, and then I gently let her tail down again once the crup was in position. Having made sure that the crup was comfortable for Mary, I then pulled the saddle forward a little more towards her shoulders, and when satisfied that all was well, I reached under her "tummy" and buckled the body strap up, which secured the whole of the saddle.

Next I picked the collar up off the floor of the stall, and holding it upside down, so that I could put it over the mare's head comfortably, I placed it onto the feeding trough, whilst I undid the canvas halter holding this lovely horse in her stall for the night. After releasing the canvas halter, I put it aside, to hang it up later, and then I placed the collar over her head, and she never murmured. Once in position over her head, I then turned the collar around to its proper position, with the traces hanging down from the metal forks inserted into the collar.

I then pushed the collar firmly onto her shoulders, and made sure that she was comfortable, before picking the last item to be put on her, the bridle. Stroking Mary's nose gently I put the thumb and second finger either side of her mouth and softly prised it open, she did reject this part of the proceedings momentarily, but then gave in to it. I slipped the bit between her open mouth, and when it was settled as comfortably as a metal bar in one's mouth could be, I pulled the rest of the bridle upwards, and placed the top part over her long ears. After straightening her mane up, so that it would not fall into her eyes, I buckled the strap under her chin up first, and then the one lower down, just above her mouth last, and there she was all ready for the road. Giving her another kiss, and a hug I backed her gently out of the stall and took her back down towards the exit from the stables into the main body of this building ready to be put into the shafts of her cart, or float.

Whilst leading Mary down towards the exit the chap who had been talking to my lady appeared from one of the stalls he was apparently clearing out, and he waited for me to go by. On reaching him he said, "I yope yo' dain get shirty wi worr I said a birra gu, o dain' mean anythin' 'onist o dain't, it wuz on'y a joke". "Na-a-ah" I lied, because I *had* taken offence, but I thought if he's apologising he must have wanted to make friends with me, and who am I to refuse the hand of friendship? Besides that, if I had have argued with him, or "cut up rough" he might have "bosted mi roun' the bloody ear'ole any road up".

"Mi nerm's 'orace Willetts" he said and stuck his huge right hand out towards me in an offer of friendship, so I took it, and shook his hand warmly. "I'm Ronnie Smith, "I replied, "ov jus' started 'ere taday, so I spect I'll bi seein' a lorr ov ya' frum now on wun I?". "A-r-r-r yo' will, I live in Murdock Road, d' ya' know w'ere tharris?" "N-a-a-ah om afrerd o don', is it roun' 'ere anywhere?" "Well not really it ain't, d' ya' know Boulton Road d' ya'?" "A-r-r-ro know w'er Boulton Road is, is it by thaya then?" "A-r-r-rit's the fust on the left afowa yo' get ta Boulton Road if yome guin tawards 'ockley Brook, Boots the Chemist is on one corna rov owa road, an' Dalton's the charabang people are ron the othar". "A-r-r-r I know it now, o know w'ere yo' live." "Ar-r-r live at numba twen'y three down on the right 'and side, yo'll 'ave ta come down some time oright. W'ere da yo' live?"

"O-o-o no w'ere as bleedin' posh as w'ere yo' live", I replied "o live in Nu John Street West just orff "The Brook", if yo' gu up Nu John Street on the left 'and side an' gu past Frankie Anderton's op'nin, w'er Mr Belcher the wallpapera lives on the right 'and side at the beginnin' ov the op'nin, if yo' jus' gu past thaya yo'll cum ta some 'ousis w'ere they ain 'gorreny frunt dowas, cuz the dowas are rup the entry, an' it's the fust lorra these 'ousis w'ere ri live, on the right 'and side ov the entry, numba two twenny eight". "Ar-r-r I know it, ov bin up thaya ra lot w'en a mate o mine usta tek mi in 'is lorry w'en we wuz guin ta Aston, or somew'ere like that, are ro know it well, any way yode berra get guin or .... will bi lookin' fer ya' an' you'll neva get finisht terday, so I'll see yarra agen okay Ron?" Ar-r-rokay 'orice, I'll see ya' lerta tarrar then". "Tarrar then Ron".

With that Horace went back to his work, and I led Mary out into the yard where the carts and floats were kept, and on looking up the ranks of these vehicles I saw my lady waiting by a flat cart, and she beckoned me to her.

I led Mary up to the lady, and I positioned the horse in front of the flat cart, ready for her to be secured into the shafts. She stood perfectly still whilst I undid the shafts which were held by a thick leather strap, from around the shaft itself and buckled round the metal rod of the brake handle. The braking system on these type of carts was antiquated, but never the less quite efficient for what was required of it. It consisted of a metal rod, the one I have just mentioned, with an iron wheel screwed to the top of this, which the driver of the vehicle would turn either clockwise, to apply the brake, or anti-clockwise to release it. This rod descended from the driver's right hand side of the bench seat, to the small platform on which she or he rested their feet. Through this platform the rod would continue for about an inch, when another rod going from the front to the rear of the cart was joined by a type of cotter pin, which allowed freedom of movement at this joint. Half way down this second rod were two threaded wheels, one attached to the rod, and the other attached to an extension rod the other side, but this wasn't a straight piece of metal, this too was threaded for a certain length, and then it went back to a plain piece of metal, which extended to either side of the cart just in front of the rear wheels. At the end of these rods was a block of wood, and the part of this wood that faced the metal rim of the rear wheels a piece of thick rubber was adhered. Now when the driver turned his little handle clockwise this block of wood moved inwards to the wheel, and eventually clamped onto it, thereby stopping the cart, or if applied moderately, it slowed the cart down. The braking system was applied in this fashion when the cart was going downhill, but the driver didn't want to stop completely, but wanted to take the strain off his horse, who was naturally in this position completely holding the cart back. That then was the braking system, well a rough explanation anyway.

Of course, this braking system was not applicable to the two wheel carts, or floats, because the simple answer was, it wouldn't work, would it?

On completion of undoing the leather strap I lowered the shafts gently from the right hand side. When I had done this I found that Mary was too far back for me to place the point of the shaft through the thick leather body band which ran around the outside of the saddle. The shafts fitted into a thick circle of leather attached to this external body band, which was similar to one of those liquorice winds we bought, with an aniseed sweet inserted into the hole, "on'y wi the aniseed ball norrin o course!" I clicked Mary forward a little and then I put the shaft through the hole. Then I went to the other side, and did the same thing.

Once both the shafts were situated, I then drew the loose end of the body band itself towards me and buckled it up securely, ensuring that it wasn't too tight for the horse.

When I had done this I went to the collar and undid the folded traces, situated on the brass band fitting snugly into a recess in the collar itself. I extended the one and ran it the length of the shaft and then I called out to the lady, " 'ow many links o' chain d' ya' wanner purrup to?" "Oi-i-i" the lady called back to me, looking up from the roundsbook she was studying quite closely. "If thee put's 'er on the fourth link thile bi about reet Ronnie", and she then returned to her study of the roundsbook once more.

I hooked the fourth link of the chain extending from the leather trace, and then I secured the hanging leather of the trace by the britches strap, through an eyehole piece of metal fixed to the under part of the shaft itself. Having buckled the left side up I then went round and carried out the same operation to the righthand side.

Finally I undid the reins from the two brass loops on top of the saddle. I buckled the one end to the bit rings, and then I ran the reins back through the brass loops, and looped the other end around the metal rod of the brake handle.

"She's all ready fer the road", I called to the lady, who looked up from the book, and then carefully put it under the bench seat. She gave a quick look around the horse to check that everything was indeed alright, and said "I-i-i-i ev'rythin's oreet lad, thank ya', o supporse we'd best bi yoff or else the cusamers'll think we ain't cumin' worn't they Ronnie?" I didn't answer, because quite candidly I didn't know what to say.

The lady took the horse by the reins and led her quietly out of the stables, and joined the tail end of the queue, leading down past Mr Davies's house.

I looked back at the amount of carts still in the building and I thought to myself "Christ if weem gunna bi lert with the bloody milk, warrabout the poor sods tharr 'ave gorra 'ave the milk orff that lot then?"

We moved behind the other carts slowly, and as we went around the corner I could see that I had been right in supposing earlier that this was indeed the loading deck.

Suddenly it was our turn to start loading. A few pleasantries were passed between Vic, who was the retail loading supervisor, and then he told her how many cases of sterilised, pasteurised, and tuberculin tested milk she was allowed. We had no sundries like, butter, eggs, and the like, due to the milk being rationed, and it would have been a little too complicated for the roundsperson to cope with. So all sundries were re-allocated to grocery shops, or if you really wanted to deal with the particular dairy of your choice, and the prerogative was yours, you could always call at the dairy's shop.

Vic said to me "'ello nip, yo' soon startid 'ere din ya', now yo' watch 'ow ya' gu wi' this lady, cuz she'll 'ave ya' runnin' abou' rall ova the bloody plerce, she will", and he started to laugh, and the lady spoke up "O tell thee w'at Vic o'll 'ave thee runnin' abou' rall ova the bloody plerce if yo' keep on like that. I'll 'ave thee runnin' sa bloody fast ya' feet worn't touch the ground", and they both had a good laugh. But me as usual didn't see anything funny, so I just gave a sickly grin.

"E yar lad, start purrin' these on th' cart fer .... , an' purrem up the frunt end, an' then werk back'ards wi' ya' load, tha's 'ow ya' like it innit.....?" "Thi knors 'ow o like it Vic we out askin' all an' sundree, thi knors dorn't thi?" Another outburst of laughter, and a further sickly grin, and I thought to myself "o 'ope this ain' gunna gu on all bloody day, there mus' bi summat funny, burr I don' know warrit is, an' o don' wann them ta think om soddin' thick."

Vic had pointed to the huge stacks of sterilised milk when he had instructed me to start loading the cart for the lady, so I walked across to the stack and lifted the first metal crate containing the two dozen bottles of milk with a devil may care attitude. But on lifting it I found that it was a lot heavier than I had thought, which slowed me down immediately. I thought to myself "bloody 'ell they'm 'eavia than the tray's o' soddin' bread at Rowlan's these are." They weren't a great deal heavier of course, but they were more concentrated in weight due to the bulk of weight being reduced to a smaller capacity container. I mean the trays that Rowland's used were massive.

After loading four or five of these crates of milk onto the cart as instructed by Vic, they did seem to get lighter, and by the time I had completed loading the cart I wondered what all the fuss was about. Of course this was entirely due to the fact that my arms, and legs for that matter were starting to become accustomed to this new type of action to my body.

"Tha's it then mi love" said Vic to the lady, "yome loadid an' checked, an' yove checked it no doubt, so orff ya' gu then, tarrar see ya' lerta." The lady climbed onto the bench seat, turned to Vic and said "tarrar love, an' thanks a lot, o'll see thee w'en we'em finisht, i an' that'll bi soona than lerta if mar mate 'ere 'as anythin' ta do we it, worn't it Ronnie?" "O o-o ar-r-r-r .... it will".

The lady clicked Mary into motion and we moved off down the steep dirt drive leading to Sandwell Road, and on arrival at the bottom, she looked to the right, released the brake on seeing that nothing was approaching from that direction, and turned left toward Island Road. I hadn't got a clue as to where the lady's round was, and she hadn't said anything, up till now, so I thought "yo"ll 'ave ta wert an' see wuntcha?" So I just sat there and waited.

We turned left at the junction with Island Road, and started to climb the slight incline, without too much difficulty for Mary.

Passing Lawnswood Grove and the front of the dairy I began to think where the round might be, West Bromwich, Smethwick, or maybe farther than that. My mind was in a whirl. The lady talked to me asking me different things about myself, and did I enjoy this type of work, and I chatted back and told her about my drawings, and then she said she would like to see them, and the conversation went on in this vein generally.

The lady turned Mary into Austin Road, where the hill was a little steeper, but again it didn't seem to bother Mary too much. Over the crest of the hill we went and down the other side to the junction with Holyhead Road, with the lady applying the brake partially. On reaching the junction, she made sure the road was clear and then we went across this main road into Wattville Road, and my thoughts ran back to my footballing career at Farm Street, and I decided to keep a look out for the school itself. I did see it, but later on the right hand side of Wattville Road.

The cart was stopped just inside Wattville Road, and the lady turned to me and said, "This is w'ere we start then lad". So the brake was applied partially again because the descent was not too steep at this point, and we both jumped down off the cart. She looked at her roundsbook, and told me the amount of milk, and the number of the house I was to deliver it to, and I was off like a shot, firstly to please this lady and secondly so that we should get finished as quickly as possible.

We moved on very efficiently taking in, Belmont, Paddington, and Malvern Roads, before returning to Wattville Road, down where we went again, and then we turned into Kentish Road on the right hand side, up the left hand side we delivered until we reached the junction with Belmont Road, then we turned around and delivered down the other half until we reached Wattville Road again.

Off we went down this road delivering either side, until we reached Downing Street. We passed "The Phoenix", at the junction where Downing Street veered to the left leading back down to Booth Street. On the right hand side in between William Street West and Mornington Road were a row of shops, and just about in the middle of these was a coffee house, and this is where the lady pulled Mary up. The aroma of cooking from this cafe was enough to drive anyone mad with hunger, it was absolutely beautiful. We served all around this cafe and then the lady said "put norse bag on Mary Ronnie, there's a good lad, an' we'll gor an' get some brekfust, eh?" "A-r-r-rokay .... , o wunt bi ya minnit".

The lady then walked across to the coffee house and went inside, whilst I carried out the task she had set me. Whilst doing this I reflected on the day so far. There was no doubt about this lady, the customers really loved her, according to the amount that had enquired about her, and when I informed them that she was indeed back on the round again they gave me all kinds of lovely, and compassionate messages to pass on to her. "Tella' ta come an' si me w'en she's got time Son". Tella 'ow nice it is ta 'ave a back agen." "Ge 'er mi love, an' tella Mrs .... arst aboura'. W'en shis got time tella ta come an' 'ave a cuppa tea wi' me". I could go on for ever, but that was a general description of the messages given to me to convey to her. I in turn went all out to relieve her of any kind of hard work, I moved the crates around when they were empty, and I rushed to the customers as quick as I could, so that I was always ready to deliver to more than she did, remembering what had been said earlier at the dairy "She 'ad bin away bad forra lung time".

Finally I went across to the coffee house, after making sure that Mary had got her nose bag buckled securely around her neck, but, not too tight. I entered the cafe, and at first I couldn't see my lady. The "bloke" behind the counter saw me and said "o yo' lookin' fer the milk lerdy nip?" "Ar-r-ri yam, w'ere ris she?" "Soright we ain' run orff wi" ya' she's jus' gon out the back fer summat, shi wun bi lung, gu an' sitcha self down, an' she'll bi wi" ya' rin a minnit, gu on now, gu an' sit ova thaya, tha's w'ere she's purr 'er book an' things" and he pointed to a part of the long bench situated beneath the front window. "Ar-r-rokay thanks" I replied, and did as I had been told.

This "bloke" who I assumed was the owner of the cafe was a shortish thick set man, with a shock of thick black curly hair, which looked as if it had a mind of it's own, it went over this man's head in a most unruly way, and yet was quite nice really.

His pallor was yellowish, and his face generally seemed to hang loose, finishing up at the bottom in a very hanging treble chin. Eyes brown, big, with a cheeky glint in them, very much alive, and black bushy eyebrows hanging low over the top. His eyelashes were long and curled, more, one would say befitting a women, but again they looked quite in place on this man. His face was broad, and so was his short nose, the mouth small, and sticking out of the right side was a "fag" which I was to learn later, seemed to be part of him, for each time I saw him he was never without one. When he did blow the ash from this continual "fag", and his mouth opened slightly to the left, it showed to all concerned a set of yellowing dentures. A white apron, spotlessly clean covered an equally white shirt, rolled up at the sleeves, revealing a pair of thick muscular arms. The rest I never did set eyes on because he was always behind the counter. All in all though he was a very pleasant, and happy man, and one other thing about him which was predominant with all the customers I had served up till now, he certainly thought a lot of my lady.

I sat there quietly reflecting what I should do about paying for this breakfast. I mean I was "a mon" now, wasn't I? And it was always the man that paid wasn't it? The only thing with this man was that he'd on'y gorra couple a bob in his pocket, and that would hardly pay for two breakfasts and four cups of tea, would it?

It certainly was a quandary, and quite candidly I couldn't see a way clear, and then it suddenly came to me, I would explain to the lady that I had "come ourra thi 'ouse in mi werkin' clo'es, an' od lef' all mi munnee in mi bes' clo'es, arta rod bin out las' night". Yes, I thought, trying to convince myself that I was right, that's what I would do, I would tell her that, and I then settled down a little more comfortably, accepting the situation. I mean I could ask "Our Mom" for some money, or if she hadn't got any "Our Kid", or even "Our Dad" if I could get hold of him, and pay the lady back tomorrow. I was still lost in thought with this highly technical situation, and worrying once again if it would indeed turn out all right when a plate of bacon, eggs, sausage, and tomatoes was placed in front of me. I looked up to see my lady returning to the counter for her breakfast, and a plate of thick "doorsteps" of bread and butter, and two very large mugs of tea (oh it wasn't all "spam sandwiches, and powdered eggs" during the War). I mentally squirmed at the thought of the money I would have to find for this lot, and once again I started to sweat, so I had to revert to the situation I had experienced with "Beth" at Rowlands when we went into the coffee house in Woodland Road, Erdington, by the "cooling towers" of Salford Bridge. Om eva sa sorry ....., o dain' orda this, o 'ad mi brekfust afowa ro come out the 'ouse this mornin' I lied. "E-e-e tha's soright love" replied my lady when she had put all the items on the table in front of us, and then sat down. "A big chap like thee can manage another brekfus' can't cha?" I had no answer to that. I just couldn think of a reply, so I must have shown this in my face for the next thing my lady went on, "e-e-e an if yor're bothered about anythin' else lad, dorn't botha, cuz o 'ave all mi grub 'ere fer nuthin', cuz o look after them wi' milk, so gu on lad an' gerrit down ya'" Now whether this story was true or not I had no way of finding out, but I would think that it wasn't, and like Beth, this lady was helping me out of a very difficult situation. In both cases they must have thought in much the same way, I thought I was a man, and I'd got to be allowed the freedom of thinking I was a man. Of course I wasn't, and as it proved for not only me, but for lads like me, this was a very difficult period to go through, and it was through people like Beth and this lady, and may I add, in my particular case, a good many more, that helped us through it.

After I had finished this huge breakfast the lady ordered some toast, and another two mugs of tea, and placed them in front of me. I didn't say anything, but I thought well if she says we gerrit fer nuthin', o mirras well gerrit down mi yole, mighten I?" So I got "stuck in" and demolished the lot, although in fairness I was never completely taken in by this statement of the lady's that the food was free, but the second thought was, well if that's what she want's, who am I to argue.?

"O y' oreet fer milk 'arry" said the lady after we had finished our meal. "Tha's nice on ya' mar wench, o could do wi' some, if yove got some ta spare?" "'erf a dozen sterra, en erf a dozen pas do ya' lad" replied my lady. "Ar-r-r tharr'll do bostin' mar love, but don' put yasef short, will ya? Nor-r-r lad yer orreet, o'll get Ronnie ter nip across ta cart an' bring 'em in fer ya', orreet 'arry?" "Ar-r tharr'll bi grert love ta" the bloke said. I was already on my way out of the shop, wishing to please the lady after such a sumptuous meal. I shot across the road, and put the six bottles of sterilised, and the six bottles of pasteurised into an empty crate, and returned to the shop with them. "'E yar Son purrem 'ere, an' I'll gerrem roun' lerteron, okay?" I put the crate where I had been told right by the little door, and flap situated to the right hand side of the counter, and then we both said "tarrar" to the man, and went back across the road to the wagon and Mary. I unbuckled the nose bag, and hung it on the hook situated at the rear of the cart, underneath just in front of the back axle.

The rest of the round took in Mornington, Lewisham, Oxford, Cambridge, Sydenham, Melbourne, Whitehall, Carlton, and part of Middlemore roads. Part of Halfords Lane, Lewis Avenue, Middlemore Avenue, before we finally finished at about twelve o'clock, which according to the lady was a lot earlier than she normally completed the round. We actually finished at the bottom of Mornington Road just around the corner from the coffee house, and whilst I straightened the load up on the back of the cart, my lady completed her booking.

Back up Wattville Road we travelled, retracing our journey back to the dairy This time we entered the front gates in Island Road, and pulled up by the shed like building on the right hand side, which housed the supervisors, Vic, Tom, and Jim.

Tom checked the empties and returned milk, suitably noted all this on the printed form Vic had used that morning whilst checking us out, and when this was completed we moved off round the corner to the left and I told the lady I would unload the empties, and stable Mary. I didn't say anything but I thought she did look a little tired."Thanks Ronnie thase a good lad, I'll gu an' see Mrs Thomas orkay, an' I'll see thee in a bit".

"Ar-r-rokay then love" I replied, and with that she went off into the large building where Mrs Thomas worked.

I unloaded in double quick time, then led Mary into the building, unharnessed her, putting the tackle onto the back of the cart momentarily, and led the horse back to her stall. Well I say led her back to the stall, she just went on her own, with a bit of coaxing this way and that from me. The stall was beautiful and clean, feed and water were readily available, so I put the canvass halter back over her head, and tied the girl up for the night. I patted her and wished her "tarrar" before going back to the cart to collect the harness for return to the tack room.

When I arrived back at the room I found my lady, Mrs Thomas, and Horace Willetts, the stable hand. I put the tack onto No. 10 hook, and then I went back to the trio, and I said to the lady "Is there anythin' else o cun do?" "Nor-r-r Ronnie, wi normally gor up ta office ta 'and owa books in, an' pay any munnee we've collected, but tha's ornee int wick, corse th' office dorn't orpen on a Sundee, so yad best bi orff ta ya Sundee dinna, 'adn't thee, an' I'll see thee tomorra eh?" "A-r-rokay" I replied, and went out of the door with a "tarrar" to everyone."

I hadn't gone far however when the lady came out after me. "'ang on a minnit lad, ov somethin' fer thee" I couldn't think what it could possibly be, I hadn't left anything behind, that was certain, because I hadn't brought anything with me, so I was naturally very curious.

"E-e-e ya' are lad, 'ere's summat for thee, fer bein' a good lad, an' 'elpin' mi so much, on mi first day back, gu on tek it, an' gu ta the pictures, with it or summat, o really am grertful love, o really am". With that she put a coin into my hand.

"Nah-h-h..., o don' wannit, om bein' perd ta 'elp ya', it ain' as if I wuz a kid yowed picked up on the street ta 'elp ya', onist... o don' wannit, 'onist o don', ov loved 'elpin' ya', an' om lookin' forward ta tamarra, as well. I attempted to push the coin back at her, but she wasn't having anything of that.

"Now dorn't upset mi lad, ov med up mi mind that yowell 'ave it an' yo' don' want ta see a full grorn lady cry do ya? So gu on lad an' terk it an' enjoy thiself, gu on!"

I blushed, and looked down at the floor to try and hide this, and I mumbled ... "Thank ya', thank ya' eva sa much, o wish that there wuz summat else o could do fer ya', fer this munnee, o wish there wuz.

"Thee's done enough fer mi terday love, an' om really grertful fer that, so yo' jus' gu an' enjoy thiself, an' think nay more about it, an' I'll see thee tamarra, about sevenish, no earlier okay?" "Ar-r-rokay, an' thanks, thanks eva sa much."

I wandered off down the path in front of Mr Davies's house, which I now knew was a thoroughfare, and not private, which also was the nearest way for me to catch the bus home, from "The New Inns".

Just as I was passing Regent Road I heard someone shouting "Ron, ay Ron, wert fer me, om cumin' yowa way, I'll walk down wi ya' away's" I turned thinking "w'o the 'ell knows mi, ov on'y jus' come ta werk 'ere, o don know anybody". but my name had been mentioned so I was obliged to turn, to see whether the caller was actually shouting to me. On turning I saw Horace running down Sandwell Road at quite a pace, and when he reached me after all that running I expected him to be a little out of breath, but no he was breathing normally, he must have been really fit I thought. "O wuz wertin' fer yo' in the tack room, o thought yo' wuz comin' back, an' then Mrs .... tol' mi yowed gone, so o 'ad ta rush an' get mi gear, which od left in the sterble spare stall, an' then come 'arin' arta ya', cuz o thought od walk down ta the New Inns with ya' an' wi could 'ave a birrova natta".

"I'm sorry 'orice, o thought yo' wuz still werkin', so o dain' think anythin' onnit, burr I'm glad yove come any road up, I'll walk down 'um'. with ya' an' o cun cop the buz by "The Red Lion" can' I?"

"Nah-h-h there's no need fer that Ron, yo' gerron the buz at the New Inns, an' gerrum ta ya' dinna, o cun see ya' tammarra". I interrupted him quickly "Nah-h-h it's a nice day 'orice, on o cun do wi" a walk". We both laughed at that, considering the amount of walking I'd done on the round that morning, "an' wi cun 'ave a birrov a natta ras well can' we?" "Ar-r-r we cun an' all, it'll bi nice".

We both set off down Holyhead Road nattering away like a "couple of old washer women". passing Farcroft Avenue on the left, and St James Road on the right. As we were passing Holyhead Road Police Station with the vast greenhouse running from the side of it right up to Church Terrace, Horace said "one ov owa blokes lives up thaya, 'e's about yowa rage Ron, an' 'e's duin a round somew'ere in 'an'swerth, o don' know jus' w'ere but somew'ere in 'an'swerth, an' 'is nerms Bob, Bob Jones. 'e's a big lanky bloke, spect yo'll meet 'im soon enough though". We passed Brewery Street where I knew "The South Staffordshire Laundry" was, then Milestone Lane. Running from Milestone Lane right up to Booth Street, and going up a parallel line with the end of Milestone Lane was a big house in it's own vast grounds. The residents of this place were the owners of "The Albion Cinema". Horace and I nattered on quite content, passing Rookery, Queens Head, Alfred, and Babbington roads without even noticing when suddenly Horace said "Well, 'ere we am then, 'ere's w'ere ri live, od berra 'urry up an' gu an' get mi dinna, cuz o gorra gu back ta the dairy this arta to mek sure the 'osse's am all right, tain' like some on ya'" he said, smiling "got the rest o the day all ta yaselves, soright fer some innit?" "Ar r-ros suppose so 'orice, still yo' could allis gerra job on th"roun's couldn" ya'?" "Nah-h-h it wouldn' suit mi, I like mi 'osse's too much, an' it giz mi a wick end orff ev'ry so offen, so in the lung run om berra orff than some o yo' blokes, anyway Ron od berra gerrorff else owa ol' lady'll bi creatin at me fer bein' lert".

"Oh-h jus' one thin 'orice affowa ya' gu, cun ya' tell mi if there's anyw'ere ro cun park mi bike, cuz it'll bi much berra ta cum on mi bike than the buz, on'y o don' wanna leave it anyw'ere it might get knackered, an' it ain' very old it ain't". "Ar-r-r don' worry about that Ron yo' cum on ya' bike tammara an' bring it inta the sterbles. I'll look arta rit fer, ya owill, an' ge it a clean w'en I ain' busy". "W-o-o thas' grat tharris 'orace, an' then if there's anyw'ere ya' wanna gu w'ile I'm out, yo' cun use it if ya' wanna?"

"Ar-r-r tha's great tharris Ron, cuz o cun come um ta mi brekfust then can' I?"

"Ar-r-r cors yo' cun, thanks eva sa much 'orice, thanks".

"Nah-h-h, it's mi that is thankin yo' Ron. I'll 'ave ta gerrorff now, okay, I'll see ya' tammara then okay?"

"Ar-r-rokay 'orice, o'll see ya' tammara."

With that he ran down Murdock Road, and I carried on down Soho Road towards "The Brook".In all the excitement of talking to Horace on our journey from the dairy to Murdock Road, I had forgotten to look at the coin which was still tightly clenched in my right hand.I opened it up slowly and to my joy, and amazement I found that it was a "'alf dolla". I stood there momentarily and thought how good this lady was to me, and I had regrets about my first thoughts of her.I didn't know how to ask God to forgive me for this sin because I was ignorant, but one thing I do know and that's as God's my final judge, I felt the most funny sensation when I was thinking of how I had had these first mental feelings of this very kind lady. On reflection of this sensation I can now assume that it was the feeling of guilt, a spasm of unworthiness inside an ignorant body. Maybe it was God punishing me for those thoughts that morning, who knows?

I looked at the half a crown and contemplated what I was going to do with it, I could hardly go to the shops with it could I? Most shops were closed on a Sunday, and especially Sunday afternoon. But even if they were open, what could I buy? Hardly a great selection in this time of War, so in the end I decided on a trip to "The Palladium", a couple of ice creams, and some popcorn. One thing I wasn't going to do was to tell "you know who", for old habits die hard don't they? I rather expect she would still want "'er 'alf" even though I was a "werkin' mon" now, so "Our Mom" was the last person I was going to tell about this inheritance of mine, and "ya' could betcha boots on tharran all".

I put the large silver coin into my trouser pocket, along with the other few coins already there and I felt very happy, very happy indeed.

A number 74 pulled away from the stop by "The Red Lion", and I didn't even try to run for it. I thought it's such a nice warm day, and I'm really in no rush I'll walk it home. Further thoughts made me even happier. These thoughts were that I would be riding to work on my "Kingsway" tomorrow, that would be better than waiting around for buses, and more important, I had made a very good friend in Horace Willetts.

Off I went down this most pleasant, quiet, respectable long road, which as far as I knew then ran from "The Fanny Brown" right out to "The Baggies Ground" and beyond.It was a beautiful clean thoroughfare, with gentlemen in bowler hats, and deep blue suits going in and out of the various "posh pubs", it was so graceful, and I had thoughts on being like them one day. Nice smart blue suit, spotless white shirt, stiff collar, and a neatly tied tie. Bowler set at a jaunty angle on my head, the creases in my trousers razor sharp, and patent leather shoes gleaming from beneath them. O' what dreams. Mind you, I thought, "owa Uncle Alf lived up 'ere rin the posh quarta. He lived in Douglas Road" so why shouldn't I later on?

I passed Boulton Road, "Kelly's" and "The Little Red Shop" "Pendry's" "Norman's" the fresh fish shop, and "Rose's" the butchers before it, and just after it on the right was first an ironmongers, and then "Darlington's" before reaching "Barn Lane" and the "Cross Guns" On I went taking in "The Pump Tavern" on the left, and "The Grand" cinema on the right, and just past the cinema "The Handsworth Open Market" "Hawkins" and then the "Post Office" lying back off the main road.

Linwood Road, with Baker Street further on down, and right opposite "The Barrell" with the narrow alley running alongside it leading into Louise Road, and Victoria Road.I crossed over Grove Lane with "Dudley's" on the one corner and

"The Municipal Bank" on the other, and just up Grove Lane on the right was Union Row, which lead from the lane right into Stafford Road, and the gates of the "Fire Station" with its spotless red doors, and the equally spotless engines behind them. Ninevah Road, on the right, and then the "beer house" I believe it was called. "The Star" right opposite "The Frighted Horse". Going alongside the motor cycle shop "Vale Onslow's" next door to "The Star" was a very narrow lane, running down to the lower part of Holliday Road, the rear entrances to houses in Waverley Road being housed there, and also in that lane "Burrows and Jennings bakery" The name of this lane ? Well I don't know where it originated from, but it is one of the most unusual names for a thoroughfare that I have heard of, and I've heard of a few. It must have an originating factor, and in all probability it's recorded in some bibliographical department somewhere, but I'm not aware of its fact, so I won't dwell on that aspect. The name of this lane ? ? ?, MARROWFAT LANE.

I passed "Handsworth Library", What a beautiful building it was, the same as the Fire Station, and the "School" and "Police Station" in Golds Hill Road, although the Police Station was named "Thornhill Road", all in Victorian architecture. Next to the Library was "The Elite", a picture house I was to visit quite frequently, and so on to Handsworth Railway Station, which brought back memories, although only a short time ago of my early morning start to my paper round for Elsie and Violet Coleman on "The Brook".

Belgrave Terrace at the end of the beautiful alms houses, and the couple of shops just before the station, and then just over Ivy Road "The Ivy House", and right "bang" next door to that Mottershead and Smith, motor engineers.

I had a quick look in at the new cars in the showroom window, and I thought "one day ......, one day, I'll get one o' these, an' I'll gu up ta mi Grandad Smith's in Market Street, an' say ta 'im, 'eyar Grandad ov brought mi car ta purrup ya' shed at the top o the gardin'", and I visualised him looking at me with those big blue watery eyes of his and saying "ah-h-h-h nu ya' do it ol' mon, o nu yad do it, gu on an' purrit away then".

I passed "The Labour Exchange" and saw the signs informing all men how good the Army, Navy, and Air Force was, and now was the time to join and defeat our common enemy, Adolf Hitler. I gave this some thought and I knew what service I wanted to get into, when I was old enough, and that was the "Royal Navy" like "Our Joe" was in, and "Billy Langley" ourrov Nursery Road, by Brougham Street. "Mind yo" I thought" yove gorra w'ile ta gu yet yo 'ave", all of two years I had, still it would soon go by.

On I went passing "Dennison's" "The Beehive" "Philip Mist's Car Showrooms" "The Roebuck", just after "The R.S.P.C.A.", and at last the long steep descent of Soho Hill which returned me back to "The Brook".

Stopping for a quick look at what was on at "The Palladium", I then saw "Dinkie Phelps"and said "worrow Dink, 'ow's ya' Dad?". He was stood in the doorway, where usually Elsie Coleman stood during the week, selling morning papers to people alighting from buses, or making their way down to "Lucas's" or some other factory for their day's work. That was in the last doorway before the six ways of "The Brook" itself, of "Tippers"

"Oh-h-h 'im, 'e's sova rat the Benyon, washin' the dust down, from 'is werk, or tha's warr 'e sez any road up", and he started to laugh. "Tell 'im I arst abourrim

24

wunn ya' Dink? "Ar-r-rile tell 'im Ron, an' don' ferget, if yove gorra spare Sundee one o th times, cum an' geus a lift will ya', the ol' mon'll mek it wuth ya' w'ile 'e will?"

At this last question I had to go back to Dinkie and tell him that I would really like to help out, but that I had started a new job at Handsworth Dairies, and I would naturally be working every Sunday now "spechly as o wuz gunna 'ave a roun' o mi yone". I finished sticking my chest out with pride. "Oh-h-h om sorry about that Ron, wi coulda done with ya wi could 'ave, cuz anutha rov our blokes 'ad ta gu in the nervy las' wick, and it's really lef' us short it 'as. still neva mind, it can' bi 'elped can it?"

"Om eva sa sorry Dink, o really yam, od a Iiked ta 'elp ya' Dad, an' yo', cuz 'e wuz always good ta mi ya' Dad wuz, 'e wuz really good 'e wuz.Still like ya' say it can" bi.yelped, well od berra gerrorff an' get mi dinna, else the ol' lady "ll bi yarfta mi, an' o don' wanna upset 'er, cuz om bloody sure she would still gi me a bost roun' the bleedin' earole, an' think nothin' onnit, so tarrar Dink". "Tarrar Ron, all the best in ya' nu job, tarrar".

I saw Mr Phelps emerge from "The Benyon" as I made my way across from "Tippers" towards "Izons the Chemist's". I waved, but I don't think he noticed me, or he might have noticed me, but had had too much medication from Dr's Mitchell and Butler. Anyway he certainly looked happy enough to me.

I passed "Hardy's Outdoor", and had a quick peep to see if I could see Joan, and thought I bet she would like me a bit better now that I might "bi doin' a roun' ov mi yone at 'andsworth Dairies", but then I didn't hold too much hope out for that. She would be going out with somebody "posh" like a grammar school, "kid", or even "abloke w'at werked in nan office or sommat Still o could dream couldn' I?"

Shrugging these romantic thoughts off I looked across at "The Turk" to see if I could see Dad. Outside the pub was quite a crowd standing on the corner of Icknield Street having a natter after their Sunday lunchtime drink, but Dad was not one of them, so I could only assume that he had gone up home to his dinner.

Running up New John Street West I saw Dad talking to Mr Belcher, and two other "blokes" I didn't recognise so I stopped and said "allo", and Dad turned to me and said "'ow's ya' fust day gone down Ronnie?" "Oh-h-h okay Dad, o wen' with a smashin' lady, an' o think o gorra gu with 'er fer the rest o the wick, jus' ta pick up a few things until o 'ave a roun' o mi yown, tharris, burrit's great Dad, it's great". "Now gu on up 'ome an' tell ya' Mutha om cumin up in a minnit, so shi cun get the dinna ron the terble, tell 'er o wunt be ya minnit there's a good lad". "Ar-r-rokay Dad o'll gu strert up an' tell a, tarrar Mr Belcha, tarrar". I looked at the other two men, and they all wished me "tarrar", and as I ran off to 228, I caught the first part of Dad's conversation with them. "Ar-r-r 'e's jus' started a nu job up at 'an'sworth Dairies 'e 'as, an' 'e's opin ta 'ave a roun' ov 'is own in the near future. Then Mr Belcher in his deep gruff voice, "ar-r-ris a bright young lad is Ronnie, if it ain' a success though Arthur, tell 'im —— " I didn't hear any more of the conversation then, because I was on the move away from them, but Dad did tell me when he finally came up for his dinner. Mr Belcher had said, that if I didn't make a go of it at the dairy, then I was to go down to him, and he would see what he could do for me.

Really, I wasn't interested in being a painter and decorator, I wanted a round of my own. I would have preferred a bread round, but of course I was too young for that, although at the time I reasoned with myself, what was the difference between me doing a bread round or a milk round? I couldn't fathom it out. Obviously there was a reason, and probable it was quite viable, but it still didn't satisfy me.

We had our dinner when Dad did finally arrive from his "gasbagging" with Mr Belcher and the other two blokes, and then I went off down to "The Palladium".

Mom served the "Bubble and Squeak" up on the night time, Dad had already gone off to "Bradfords", and on completion of this evening meal, I decided to stop in.

The comings and goings in 'The Smith' household were enough however to compete with anything on the radio, for there was hardly ever a dull moment. The three big wenches' mates would call, and inevitably bring their mates with them before going out for the night. 228 never seemed to be empty for any length of time. There always seemed to be someone calling in for one thing or the other, the house never seemed to be unoccupied.

Ruby Coney, our "'ildas" mate was a frequent caller, she was without doubt the most bubbly girl I had ever met in my life, to date, that is. She never stopped laughing, she was to use the modern parlance "a very much fun girl". Our Hilda was married to Joe and Ruby was either courting, or married to another sailor. The girls would go out with one another, for company, although most of them were married, or courting someone in the armed services. The tales they used to come back with were if I had understood them would have no doubt been a comedy programme on its own. Warrabow rim the cheeky bugga, o soon tol' 'im ta sod orff". "I tol' 'im mi yusband's meetin' me, an' if 'e gorrolt ov 'im, 'e'd sort 'im out". "Warra bourrim, 'e wuz nice 'e wuz, o would a liked ta 'ave gone out wi' 'im, pity 'e wuz on'y sixteen though a-a-a". A burst of laughter followed these comments. They would play me up sometimes. "O betchove gorra girl friend somew'ere ain'tcha Ronnie?" "'E's too good lookin' ta be withourra girl friend 'e is". Plenty of blushing from me, and another burst of laughter from the girls "'ow's Joan 'ardy then Ronnie, am yo' still sweet on 'er, o berr 'e is, jus' look arrim guin' red".

"Ain 'ya' gorra date ternight Ronnie, on'y some wenchis on "The Brook" 'ave jus' arst us w'ere yo' live, an' wiv told them, an' they'm cumin up 'ere arta ya', they said tha yowed promist ta meet 'em, an' yo' ain "turned up". "I ain' promist ta meet any girls Ruby 'onist I ain't". "Well yowed berra watchout, cuz they'm on their way up 'ere, we 'ad ta ge 'em yer raddress, cuz they sed they wuz guuna folla rus up 'um' if we dain't. This would result in my going red, and making some excuse to go upstairs, even though I knew that I hadn't made any such arrangements with anyone. As I attempted to go through the middle room door, they would say something like "don' worry Ronnie, we wunt lerr 'em come in the 'ouse we wunt, we'll stop 'em wunt we 'ild?". Consequently that would be sufficient for me to remain downstairs, until they decided on another way of having a bit of fun with me. It was all good clean, honest fun, and no doubt at all, it was a lovely time, for all of us, because it made us all realise what a wonderful thing it was to have real friends, which in later years proved to be true.

All that week, and the following week I stayed with the lady, my friendship with Horace Willetts strengthened, and l got to know his Sister, Rita, who was doing a round. Lot's of other people, including chaps about my age were also doing rounds. These lads had confirmed that it would not be long before the dairy had a round for me, for they were so desperately short of roundsmen and roundswomen.

On the second Saturday of my employment with the dairy, and still assisting my lady, we returned to the dairy on completion of the round. I as usual put Mary into her stall. After completing this task, I did not as was usual in the week collect my bike, and go off home, I had to go up to the Office to collect my wages. The entrance to this Office was situated in Island Road, just to the left of the main entrance. It was beautifully clean, with grey concrete steps leading to the upper floor, and on the right hand tiled wall was a wooden hand rail with brass fittings, all highly polished. Arriving at the top of these steps you would walk along a narrow passage, and enter a smallish room, where all the roundspeople would be "paying in". This room had a shelf about four foot off the floor, running around three of the four walls. This shelf enabled the women and men to empty the leather satchels of the day's takings, and then separate and count them.

First the silver, and the coppers would be sorted, and then counted out into pound piles for the silver, and shilling piles for the copper. The pound and ten bob notes would be counted, coloured green, and red respectively, and placed onto a wooden board about a foot square. Then the silver, and copper would be placed on top of the notes, to keep them in place, and also to prevent them blowing away should anyone come in through the door whilst you were transferring the money from the shelf to the cashier behind one of the four apertures situated in the fourth wall of the room. I made my way up to the office as usual on this second Saturday, hoping the lady would cease in her generosity towards me this time. She had given me another half a crown on the Saturday previous and I was to say the least, feeling slightly embarrassed by the whole affair. But, looking at it from another point of view, which I had done, I was very grateful.

Arriving in the room, my lady spotted me. She had obviously already paid her day's takings in, and was busy talking to one of the men.

"Ova 'ere Ronnie, ard lark ta see ya' ra minnit." I went over to her, and she turned away from the man with whom she was having a conversation. When I reached her the first thing she did was to push a coin into my hand, and thank me for the help I had been during the week. I was going to protest, but didn't, for I knew that it would be useless, so, I saved my breath, and said, "Thank yareva sa much......." then I went to move off across the room to one of the apertures to collect my 27/6d wages, but my lady spoke up again. Ar-r an' bar th' werr Ronnie, Mr Davies wants ter see yer before y" gor 'orm, oright Son?". Ar r-r-rokay ...., o'll gu down ta 'is 'ouse as soon as ov got mi wergis, okay?" "Ar-r oreet Ronnie, now dorn't ferget will thee?" "Nah o wunt ferget". With that I went and collected my wages and rushed off down the wooden steps, shouting "tarrar" in the process, back into Island Road wondering what Mr Davies could possibly want with me. Perhaps a change of round, or more sinister, perhaps I didn't suit him, and he was going to give me my cards? I started to sweat at this prospect, and also this thought put "the wind up me proper". Still I thought, Tom, Vic, or Jim, would have given me some idea as to what was going on, so, temporarily I put these fantasies to the back of my mind. Nevertheless I ran even quicker to Mr Davies' office, which was situated in a kind of conservatory attached to the side of his house. I knocked on the small green painted door, which had two elongated pieces of glass running from the top of the door to half way down, and a voice in a deep Welsh accent bade me enter.

"Come in lad" he said. He was sat behind his big polished desk attending to some documents, and it looked all very efficient to me. I went to the opposite side of the desk, and stood in front of him. "Sit down lad", which I did, and then he stared at me for what seemed an eternity, with his very light blue eyes, watering slightly. "Do you know West Bromwich much lad", suddenly breaking the silence with the question. My mind was in a whirl momentarily, I thought I wonder if he has got a round up West Bromwich he wants me to do, and then I dismissed that idea. I mean you couldn't run a pony and float all over to West Bromwich, do the round, and then return to Handsworth in one day could you? On the other hand Scribbans', and Grant's, did rounds in the Black Country, and Birmingham with horse and carts respectively, so I supposed, that discounted both my ideas. I thought I might as well leave all these bright ideas to other people, and listen to what Mr Davies had to say. I looked straight at him, and then realised I'd forgotten what he had asked me in the first place. I was about to ask him to repeat the question when he said, misunderstanding my silence to be that of shyness, thank God". "Come on now son I only asked if you knew West Bromwich?", to which I replied rather hastily in case I wandered off into another of my day dreams "Nah-h-h Mr Davies, o don'know it at all, 'cept the "Baggies" ground, om sorry". "Well never mind you're a bright lad, I've been told, I've no doubt you will soon pick the area up, eh?" Ar-r-rit'll bi no trouble Mr Davies, "I replied, not wishing to throw an opportunity like this away. "That's a good lad, so tomorrow I want you to go to our depot in Trinity Street, and the depot Manager Mr Harold Haynes will instruct you on what you are to do. Is that understood?" "Yes, Mr Davies, but what time do you want me to be there?" "The same time as you attend here, between half past five, and six o'clock, why is there any problem son?" "Well, yes there is Sir, I'm afraid the buzis don' run till about six o'clock from 'ockley," I lied, giving myself a little time to spare "an' that wunt get mi ta Trinity Street fer 'alf five will it, an' it's too far fer mi ta gu on mi bike". "Yes-s-s, I see your point, now let's see where do you live?" He wasn't asking me the question, he was in fact talking to himself, for as he asked the question he began sorting through some papers and then he suddenly said, before I had time to say anything, "ar-r-r you live at 228 New John Street West, that's just off Hockley Brook isn't it, just past Icknield Street on the opposite side?"

"Ar-r-r tha's right Sir, tha's 'sactly right, an' our 'rouse is just up from "The Brook" on the left hand side". "Never mind Son, I'll find it, you just be ready for me in the morning at about quarter past five, and I'll pick you up and take you to the depot for the first time, but then you're on you're own after that, I'll explain to Mr Haynes about the difficulties of the buses on a Sunday, and I'm sure that he will understand, and make allowances, now do you understand all I've said son?" "Ar-r-r Sir, you'll pick me up at quar're past five tamarra, o'll get mi Mom ta mek sure rime up, so don' worry, I'll bi thaya". "Right, off you go son, I'll see you in the morning alright?" "Ar-r-rile bi thaya, don' worry Mr Davies". With that I left the office, and raced back to the stables, to get my bike, and tell my lady if I could find her, and also Horace. I found Horace, and I told him what was happening, and he said "well od gorran idea yo' wuz guin' up Wes' Brom'ige Depo' Ron, burr I worn't absolut'ly sure, but don' worry any road up, cuz I'll still bi seein' ya' wun I, yo'll bi comin' up the Monkey run wun' ya'? Ar-r-ra course o will, burr I know w'ere ta fin' ya' anyway, an' by the way 'ave yo' sin mo lerdy arrall?" "Ar r-ro think she wen' 'um' Ron, o think she's gorra do 'er roun' on 'er roan tammarra, an' o don' think she'll like tharrat all, cuz she's got ta depend on yo' she 'as, still she can" expect ta 'ave ya' rall the time can she, else yoad neva rave a roun' ov yarrown would ya?"

"Nah-h-h o suppose not, burr I would da liked ta 'ave sin 'a an' said tarrar, any road up, will yo' tell a tammarra 'orice, will yo' tell a tarrar fer mi tammarra please?'

"Ar-r-ro course o will, o wun ferget Ron, an' now o mus' gerron else o wunt bi finisht in time ta meet mi mates tonight o wunt, so tarrar Ron an' I'll bi seein' ya' soon".

With that Horace went back to his chores, and I got my "Kingsway" from the stall and rode my way back to "The Brook". I wasn't to use my bike for some time after that due to the distance I was going to have to travel, but I was to see a lot more of Horace and we were to have some nice times together, but the one thing that really made me sorry more than I can say, is that I never saw my lady again, never.

I was out of bed, and ready when Mr Davies called the next morning, for I didn't wan to keep "The Gaffa" waiting did I?, and more to the point "You know who" didn't want me to keep him waiting either. I can hear her now "Ya' Gaffa's gunna pick ya' rup in 'is car our Ronnie, bloody 'ell yo' mus' bi doin' oright, mussen ya', ya' Fertha's on'y 'ad 'is Gaffa pick 'im up once, an' tha's w'en 'e wannid 'im ta do 'im a ferva, an' gu in ferra couple a night's on 'is 'olidees, so yo' gerrup fus' thing tammarra, an' no lyin' in bed fer five minnit's, yo' getcha self down 'ere, an' bi ready fer ya' Gaffa, we don' wanna keep 'im wertin' do we?" I thought to myself", shis talkin' as though she's comin' with mi ta bloody werk, WE this an' WE bloody that". I had a titter to myself thinking of "Our Mom" trying to get into the back of Mr Davies's 1936 Ford Eight. If she did manage to get in, what then? I'll tell you what then, the bloody thing would have collapsed, that's what, and when.

Mr Davies knocked on the entry door, and "Our Mom" went and answered the knock. She invited him in, and asked if he would like a cup of tea, but he refused both saying "I would like to Mrs Smith, but I am very busy at the moment, maybe another time, when I have more time, is young Ronnie ready?" "Yes Sir 'e's comin' now, 'e wunt keep ya' wertin' wunt our Ronnie, 'e's a good lad 'e is" I had been out back to the "lavvy; funny how you want to go to the lavatory at the last minute when you are doing something a little out of the ordinary, like, going on holidays, going for an interview, or starting a new job, you nearly always want "ta gu ta lavvy jus' afowa ya' gu, don' ya'?"

Mr Davies and I went down the entry to his Ford Eight which was parked right outside the entry door, and I thought to myself "o wish some ov mi merts cud a sin this the "Gaffa" fetchin' mi inta werk in 'is car" but of course at this hour on a Sunday morning there wasn't a soul to be seen, on top of all that it was raining "cats and dogs", "fisherman's weather" I would call it.

I climbed into this narrow, but nice looking car quickly to avoid the torrential rain, and Mr Davies got behind the wheel. First he lit another cigarette off the one he had just finished, and threw the "nub" end out of the window, that naturally he had wound down (ha, bloody, ha) before hand. Mind you I have done that in later years, forgotten the window was still up, and thrown a cigarette end out of my car, but soon finding to my dismay that it will not go through glass.

29

He drew contentedly on his "fag" as if it was the first one of the day, but I've no doubt that it was anything but the first.He put the key into the ignition slot turned it on then pulled the starter, and the engine fired. Off we went turning right into the top part of Guest Street, and then turning right again at the junction with Hockley Hill, right by "The Wold" and "Hodgsons' " The Funeral Directors

The road in front of us was completely empty. Mr Davies just put his foot down and we flew up Soho Hill like a bat out of hell. I tried to look through the yellowing and cracked windscreen, but the rain was coming down so fast it looked as if I was swimming underwater at Monument Road Baths, so I gave up in the finish, and satisfied myself with glancing sideways out of the passenger window. I don't think Mr Davies could see too clearly either, for the little windscreen wiper he had was hardly sufficient for this heavy downpour. During the drive the conversation between us was limited, I mean what could I talk about to him, and equally important, what could he really talk about to me. Oh it satisfied me all right, because I was so interested in watching the scenery as we went on towards West Bromwich. I suppose in a way Mr Davies was also satisfied, because no conversation meant that he could continue to smoke his "fags" one after the other, and he did, which in turn intrigued me. Oh, I had seen Mr Warrener at Farm Street School doing exactly the same thing, but this was somehow different, this was my boss, and I "wuz a mon now" The rain eased a little as we passed "The Co-operative Laundry" on the corner of Holyhead Road and Park Lane, situated on the right, and then we went by "The Baggies Ground", although the rate we were going I didn't have the chance to see too much.

My Gaffer lit yet another cigarette as we went by "The Hawthorns" Public House, which lay back off the road, a striking building with trees and shrubs of all manner in the extensive front piece. Mr Davies threw the "nub" end out of the window, as he had done a few times during this journey, but this time due to the rain relaxing its intensity, he left the glass down, and I saw the "Yorkshire Imperial Metal Sports Ground", with its two large gates, and a high brick wall in between. "The Dartmouth Cricket Ground" was next, and then the "Sandwell Arch", which was at one time the lodge at the entrance to the Earl of Sandwell's residence. "The Arch" was beautiful in its structure, with huge wooden gates, stained and varnished, and the lodge itself situated at the side of this wonderful monument.

Over on the left hand side of the Birmingham Road was the different sporting recreation fields of a Girls High School, and running right through the middle of these various sports grounds was the narrow gauge rail track conveying coal, or other fuels from "Jubilee Colliery", or to give it its correct terminology "Sandwell Park Colliery" situated by "Wasson Pool", to its other part which was just off Roebuck Lane. Mind you most of this track lay underground, but you could see some of the track on the left hand side of the Birmingham Road going from Handsworth in the direction of West Bromwich.The little Ford Eight sped on passing Roebuck Street on the left, opposite its junction with Beeches Road with its long row of beautiful houses "o berrit's the posh part o Wes' Brom'ich" I thought to myself as we drove over these crossroads. There was further evidence of these "posh 'ouses" along the stretch between Roebuck Street and Roebuck Lane.

At the lane we veered slightly to the right and the character of the buildings started to change, not drastically at first, but they definitely changed. Oh they were nothing like New John Street West, or Guest Street, more like Douglas Road, Linwood Road, and Murdock Road in Handsworth, and as far as I could see through the yellowing rain splattered small windscreen, they continued to change, for the worse, as one went further on into West Bromwich. I naturally hadn't a clue where this Trinity Street was, so I settled back into the seat expecting to be riding in this lovely car for sometime, but I was to be disappointed.

We passed a couple of roads on the left, and three on the right, which I was to learn later were, Salisbury Road and Florence Road on the left, and Jesson Street, Bagnall Street, and Hope Street. Suddenly Mr Davies turned sharply to the left, pulling up in a screaming halt about three hundred yards down this road, which I now presumed was Trinity Street.

"Here you are Son, now you go up there" and he indicated with a long white index finger a dirt passage way between a long wall on the left, and a row of terraced houses on the right. "Ask for Mr Haynes, and tell him that Mr Davies has sent you, he will know what it's all about, and what to do, I have to go back to the dairy now I have an awful lot to do, so you'll be alright then Son?" "Yer-r-r o'll bi oright Sir, o'll gerroff now now an' gu an' si Mista 'ayes, tarrar then, an' thank ya'reva sa much fer bringin' me".

"That's alright Son, I think you'll find you'll like it here, cheerio then", and with that, after I had shut the passenger door, he did a smart three point turn and shot off back up the road again.

I watched as he made his way towards the main road. I saw the right hand indicator (or fish as we kids called them) slowly rise from the side of the car into an horizontal position, with its faint light flickering, a puff of smoke from the exhaust, and the Ford Eight vanished out of sight. I was to see, and ride in that little motor many times in the future, but not for a few months

I stood there on this damp and slightly depressing Sunday morning, not really knowing what to expect from this new venture. As I said, the rain had ceased in its intensity, and I looked upwards in the direction of Birmingham and through the dark clouds I saw a brief glimpse of the sun, although very watery, it was a good sign for the day to come. To confirm this I caught sight of a mist arising from some rooftops, and over to the left the beginning of a rainbow, which made me feel just that little bit better.

Looking up the entrance to West Bromwich depot, I thought how narrow the lane was between the house on the right, and the wall on the left, which was too high for me to see over the other side. The lane was straight for about a hundred yards, and then as far as I could see it turned sharply to the right, and I visualised the dairy being situated behind the houses which proved to be correct later on.

My immediate thoughts on the narrowness of this entrance was "Ow the bleedin' 'ell do they manige ta get the bloody milk up thaya?, they must carry it tup one crert at a time, I yope tha' rain't w'at they got me up 'ere fer, cuz o know w'at they can do wi' their bleedin' job if tha' the cerse?" I had a silent titter to myself at this thought. The right hand side of the lane was whitewashed half way up the side of the first of the row of terraced houses, and above that the top of the house was covered in what I thought was tar.well it looked like it any road up. On the left hand side, the side with the high wall, the bricks were red, blue, brown, and a few other nondescript colours. They were chipped, and cracked, in fact they looked as though they had been there for some time, and indeed looked ready to collapse at any minute. The floor of the lane however was a very different "kettle of fish", this consisted of small (about 4 x 4) blue cobbles, very much like the cobbles they used either side, and in the middle of the tramlines that up until March I939 ran through "Hockley Brook". Of course they were uneven, in fact in some places they were positively "pot holes", and with the rain this morning, and probably last night these holes were full with water, and reminded me of groups of miniature "Northwood Street Baths". This unevenness, and the holes I thought were caused by the constant traffic coming and going over the years.

Altogether the situation did not really please me, I would have sooner been at the dairy in Island Road. I thought "beggars cant bi bloody choosa's can they?"

I walked slowly up the lane. I could hear voices, and the clank of milk crates as I drew nearer the sharp turn to the right. After what seemed to be an eternity I reached this junction. I turned and the immediate picture in front of me was, a big man, quite sunburned, an old black trilby on his head at a jaunty angle, and a "fag" sticking out of the corner of his mouth, loading a flat cart parked in the middle of this small yard. In front of the cart was another man attending to the harness of the horse, a nice cob, in the shafts. It was this second man that saw me first.

"W'atchow want?" "God" I thought,"warra misrable lookin' bugga 'e is, an' 'e bloody sounds it an' nall". His face was thin, almost skeletal, beneath the tattered cloth cap he wore, his eyes were sad, brown in colour, but very sad, and there were lines and bags underneath them. The nose was long and hooked, and "snottie", it seemed as though he could not contain the continual running from the enlarged nostrils. He tried I was to find out later on, but he was never successful. He would wipe his nose with a grubby handkerchief, or if he could not get to this piece of rag, he would just wipe the fluid away with his forearm. His mouth was big, and narrow, and when he spoke it revealed a set of crooked, discoloured teeth. The body was thin, painfully thin, looking as though a good meal would not go amiss, and this wiry trunk was covered by a thick plaid shirt, with the sleeves rolled up to the elbows, revealing his spindle like forearms.

He wore a pair of old army jodhpurs, which funnily enough made him look a little better, not much, but, a little better. Over these jodhpurs below the knee he had a pair of leather leggings, and to finish off a pair of "'oss muck" covered boots. That was Frank the stableman I was to learn later, and may I add he was when I got to know him, a very nice, and pleasant chap.

"O said watcha want, wassamarra ya' bleedin' deaf or summat?" Nah-h-n o 'eard ja, o 'eard ja fust time", I replied feeling slightly indignant at the way he had spoken to me. "All o wanna know is, am yo' Mr 'ay'es, yo' don' look like a bleedin' depo' gaffa. but cho might be" I continued, beginning to feel my feet. This feeling was soon to be knocked out of me by this man's reply.

"O know w'atcha will get Son if yo' gu on in that way yo'll gerra bang up the bleedin' earole, tha's watchole get, an' 'is nerm ain' 'ay'es, it's 'aynes, an'yole fin' 'im in thaya" He nodded his head in the direction of what looked to me like a wooden roof over the top of a space between, what I thought was the stables, and the continuation of the wall I had seen on the left hand side of the narrow lane leading up to the "depot?"

The bloke loading the flat cart "bust owra laughin' at the end of this conversation between this "ol' misrable bloke" and me, and he shouted to the stable man, "yowed berra watch out Frank, 'e looks big enough, an' young enough ta ge yo' a bang up the earole, an' then yo' cun watch out can' ya'?", and he burst out laughing again. I liked this man straight away, mainly for what he said right then. There was something else I liked about him as well, but just then I couldn't put a finger on it.

"'E'd berra not try anythin' tha's all" Frank replied, and gave me a vicious look which I must admit frightened me momentarily. I wasn't quite sure if I could back up any kind of statement to this very miserable, and mean looking man.

I went across to this "roof kind of thing" and went in, no doors to open, nothing. As I entered I found on the right hand side a type of elongated pallet, and on top of this were several herden sacks filled with straw, which I found out later served as some type of seating arrangement, and bed of some sort, for the "fire watcher" whoever was on duty. On the left side were a couple of tressle like tables with books, papers, satchels, and other paraphernalia belonging to the business of milk delivery.

Above these tressles was a long narrow piece of wood with nails driven into it at various lengths, and attached to some of these nails were clip boards with different pieces of paper clipped on to them. On some of the other nails there were coats, and cowgowns of various colours and types hung on them. At the far end of this open shed, for that was the best description I could find for it, was a couple more tables, with a bench like thing, obviously home made, and a few rickety chairs. On the table were quite a number of tin mugs of various sizes, and types, and the largest tin tea pot I had seen to date, including the one that continually sat on "Our Mom's" table at home. The wooden roof was obviously continually leaking according to the marks on the whitewashed walls, and equally obvious no one had made any attempts at repairing them. All together this was a very poor show for an office, and whatever else it was supposed to be, it was positively "dickie pooh".

"Hello Son, what can we do for you?" This came from one of four men sat around the table at the far end of this mess, and I mean mess in every aspect. The speaker, although sat down, gave me the impression of being a big "fella". His hair was blonde, (not from a bottle either), and wavy, and it was very thick, he was fresh complexioned, and handsome to boot. Under his blonde eyelashes, were the most vivid blue twinkling eyes, which automatically conveyed to the recipient of them a wonderful feeling of confidence and happiness. His nose was long, like the miserable "bloke's" outside, but not crooked, it was big, but somehow it suited the rest of his handsome features. He smiled as he posed the question, and revealed beautiful white even teeth. He wore a white, spotlessly clean cowgown, and on each lapel was a circle of maroon cotton, or wool, and in this circle, in the same material were the letters "H.D.". A white shirt, again spotlessly clean, a starched collar, with a neatly tied thin red tie, completed the picture as far as I could see, for he had still made no attempt to get up from his seat.

"Mr Dervis 'as b'ought mi yup from owa 'rouse to 'ere, an' tol' mi ta arsk fer Mr 'aynes" I replied to the man's request, making sure that I had added the "n" as that bloke called "Frank" had told me. "Oh-h-h you must be the chap he phoned me about last Friday, well come on in Son and let's have a look at you, come over here and have a cup of tea" and he indicated a chair by one of the other three men.

I went across and sat down. One of the men poured a cup of steaming black tea out for me, saying "d'ya' wan some suga' an' milk Son?" "Ar-r-r thank ya', three spoonfuls please" I replied. This man kindly completed the task, and pushed the mug across the table in my direction. I took a pull at this hot tea, and sucked it through my lips, more than drank it, to avoid burning my mouth. Whilst I was drinking my tea, the man I had now assumed to be Mr Haynes, for he had not denied the fact, then again he had not confirmed it either, got up from the table and went out toward the small yard. When he reached the so called entrance, he shouted to someone "Ernie the new chap has arrived from Island Road will you take him with you for today, and probably all this week and see how he fairs, okay?" The reply was muffled, and I hadn't a clue what it was, but I assumed it was a positive one, for my Mr Haynes then said "That's lovely Ernie, he won't be long he's just finishing his tea, and he will be out."

Mr Haynes then came back into this "office?" and said to me "I've put you with Ernie Humphries for this week, and when I get things sorted out regarding the rounds, I'll get you fixed up with something a little more permanent. How will that suit you, e-r-r, o-o-o, I don't even know your name do I?" "Nah-h-h it's mar fault o neva told ja, an o shudda done, it's Ronnie Smith, an' o come from 'ockley Brook". "Not in 'The Brook' I hope" and he started to laugh, with me joining him, I understood the pun. "Nah-h norrin "The Brook" burr I mirras well 'ave bin with the way the rain come down this mornin' mighten I?"

"I Suppose you might just as well have, oh and by the way, although you'll have probably guessed by now I'm Harold Haynes, I'm the Manager of all this".He waved his arms around in a circular movement, indicating this load of old rubbish, and to confirm my thought's that it was an old load of rubbish he started to laugh again, having made another "funny".

I gulped the last of my tea down, and went out to the big man I had seen just a while ago. He was just putting the nose bags under the rear end of the cart when I went out.I went up to him and said " 'allo, mi nerms Ronnie Smith, an' Mr 'raynes tol' me that yo was Ernie, Ernie 'umphriss". He looked up at me from his crouched position, the "fag" smouldering in his mouth, slightly to the left hand side, and suddenly a great big smile came across his face. He was old, but I thought somehow he didn't seem it, he had sparkling brown eyes, with a devil may care look about them, a flattish type nose, and when he smiled he revealed teeth that were slightly apart, and although they were slightly brown, no doubt through this continual smoking, they seemed to fit in with his whole character. As I mentioned before he was quite sunburned, and this ruddy complexion reminded me of handsome film stars in far eastern areas of war. Ernie was handsome in a funny kind of way, well not so funny, as rugged I suppose, but I imagined that he was quite a "lad" for the ladies. He was of stocky build, and it would have been Ernie that I would have wished to have been on my side had I have gotten into a scrap of any kind. He was muscular, although not very quick in his movements, but there seemed to be that quiet strength, of both character, and body emitting from him.

"Ar-r-r rime Ernie, Ronnie, so yome comin' with me ferra w'ile am ya', well tharr'l bi nice, coz ov bin orff the ooks ferra bit now, an' o could do wi" a birrov 'elp, yo' look a strung enough lad, an' yo'll do mi the world a good until o cun gerron mi feet propa". At this he stood up, and I said "is there anythin' o cun do now Ernie, cuz it looks as if yove done it all". Nah-h-h yowa right nip, it's all done, an' Frank's seenta the 'oss fer me, so all o gorra do now is gu an' get mi book, an' things, an' we'll be yorff, mind yo' nip, we gorran easy un terday cuz the fact'ries am closed, so we ain' gorra gurra them, still yo"ll si berra tamarra warra mean, so yo' jus' jump up, an' I'll be with yarrina minnitt okay". "Ar-r-rokay Ernie, I'll do that".

I climbed up onto the left hand side of the long bench of the cart, and made myself comfortable, or as comfortable as I could on a hard wooden, wet seat, and waited for the arrival of my mate, Ernie Humphries.

He wasn't long collecting whatever he had to collect, and he to jumped up onto the bench seat and clicked the beautiful stocky horse into movement. Off we went down the narrow lane rocking over the uneven blue engineering bricks, moving very slowly to prevent any of the milk crates toppling off the vehicle before we reached the commencement of our round, wherever that may be.

At the end of the lane Ernie turned the horse to the left, and we headed down Trinity Street towards Burlington Road with "Trinity Church" dead ahead of us. At the junction with Burlington Road we had to turn right or left, because the church occupied all the area in front of us. We turned right, and then a sharp left, and then right taking us past a school on the left. Arriving at Trinity Road Ernie pulled on the left hand rein, and the horse obeyed. Over the railway bridge we went, and I looked down at the train lines below. We descended the hill and took the first right into Boulton Road.Off we went down there to the famous "SPON LANE", we crossed over this lane and headed off at a trot up Sam's Lane, into Lyttleton Street, and then on to Cambridge Street crossing Bromford Lane in the process.

During this journey outwards to the start of Ernie's round he informed me of the stableman "Frank's" character. He told me that although Frank looked a miserable old devil, he was really quite a "nice bloke". Momentarily I couldn't believe this, but Ernie assured me that I didn't have to believe him, for I would find out for myself eventually (which of course I did). He also told me of another man, who I had not seen that morning, due to the buses not running too early from where he lived, which was "Hockley". His name was Arthur Cheslyn. I must admit I felt a little happier by the news of this "Arthur Cheslyn" not being able to get to work as early as he did during the week due to the time of the buses. This would of course help me tremendously for that's what I had assumed, would happen, me having a prolonged stay here. Mr Haynes would fully accept the fact as truth when I turned up for work on a Sunday later than in the week, for this situation was already in force.

Ernie clicked our horse into a trot when we reached the junction with Oak Road, after turning left, taking us down a rather steep hill, passing the "infamous marle hole" on the right hand side.

He told me that normally in the week he delivered to Adams and Benson's, in Albion Road, Izon's Ironworks in West Bromwich Street, and one or two other factories in Oldbury Road, but today we started in West Bromwich Street at a few cottages, including "The Cut Cottage" I asked Ernie what the palace-like building was when we turned out of Cambridge Road into Oak Road,and he said "It worn' a palace, Ronnie, that wuz a museum, they keep all the ol' things, from times gone by in thaya. Mindyo' the gardin's am lov'ly, if yo' get time yo' wanna gu roun' thaya, it's eva so int'restin".

Ernie was a great bloke, although unlike Beth at Rowlands, and my lady at Island Road, he didn't give me any "munnee" or "brekfust" or anything like that. What he did do, which was most important to me, he treated me like a "mate", and it certainly helped me through a difficult period, the period when you are not a boy, but not quite a man, and this made me very happy indeed.

I stayed with Ernie for approximately two weeks and it certainly broadened my outlook on the geography of "The Black Country", although to all intents and purposes this wasn't the real "Black Country", I was to find this out in later years

His round as I have already mentioned started at "Adams and Bensons" in Albion Road, then it continued into Oldbury Road, West Bromwich Street, Roway Lane, Fountain Lane, serving "Cuxon and Gerrards" the pharmaceutical company, known throughout the world.

We then went into Oldbury itself, Freeth St, Tabernacle St, Talbot St, Union St, Church Street, New Meeting Street, Simpson Street, Flash Road, Cypruss Street, Broadwell Road, Century Road.

I got to know the round pretty well, mostly due to me liking Ernie quite alot. You knew where you were with him. "Ronnie watch 'er, she'll knock ya if she can, so mek sure she giz ya' the right munnee, an' don' stand any nonsensif one of 'er kid's comes ta the door, an' sez Mom ain' in, yo' jus' tell the kid, no bleedin' munnee, no bleedin' milk. Yo'll soon see 'er come ta the door, o know 'er rusband, an' 'e's a right un 'e is, if 'e fin's 'er knockin' anybody 'e'll knock eight bell's a shit ourov 'er e will, ar-r she wunt tek too much orf Bill, 'e likes 'is ale does Billy, 'e's an' 'ard werkin' chap 'e is, burr 'e wunt stand 'is missus owin' anybody 'e wunt" There were many more pieces of advice like this. He put them over to me, not as a man to a boy, but as man to man, knowing, I suppose that I was to soon be having a round of my own, and so passing on to me all the tricks of the trade. I was to realise this over the next few years. The customers, which naturally consisted of mostly ladies, were "a canny bunch" to say the least, and if they could "do you", then "do you" they would. Of course, I'm generalising in this matter, because for everyone that attempted to "do you" ninety-nine were smashing.

During my two weeks at the West Bromwich Depot I got to know the full team. They were quite an efficient happy team, first was the second in command, the Supervisor, and stand in, for all the rounds at the outpost, Charlie Cope. Mind you, Harold Haynes himself, although the depot Manager, would turn out and do a round, Harold did not sit on his behind and issue orders to everyone else, if the need warranted it.

Charlie Cope, he came from Stourbridge, and so rumour had it, was engaged to a local girl He had been engaged for some twenty-five years, I suppose that he wanted to be completely sure before taking the formidable plunge into matrimony. I thought "o bet the girl (?) worn't too bloody 'appy about it, still luv does funny things ta people but bloody twen'y five years, o worn evan tharrold was I?"

He was, naturally coming from the country, a fresh complexioned man, broad in the face, blue eyed, and I never saw this bloke without his cap on. He was a very slow, but efficient man, his writing was beautiful, and when he made the rounds book up, it was as clear as a bell, yes he was a very good number two.

Then there was "Arthur Cheslyn", I had a lot to do with Arthur during my stay at West Bromwich, although later on I lost contact with him. I finally found out exactly where he lived in Hockley, it was Ventnor Road just off Bridge Street West, only a spit from Joseph Lucas's Works in Great King Street. He lived on the left hand side of Ventnor Road, looking in the direction from Bridge Street, nearly opposite Jean and Betty Bishton's house, and just a little far"ther down than Horace Ward who was a "Captain" in The Boys Brigade at Friends Hall in Farm Street, and he also worked for "Tommy Shaw's Dairy" in Burbury Street.

Arthur, like, Charlie, was a fresh complexioned man, although unlike Charlie, he did not live in the country. He also wore a cap, and it was very rare to see him without it, but I did on some occasions, when he was indoors playing the piano He was a brilliant piano player, he didn't read music but he was brilliant, and it was through this talent that I got to know him as well as I did.

He had a very noticeable cast in his left eye, which caused the whole character of his face to indicate that he wasn't quite "the thing", "lame under the cap", "threepence short of a bob", "a bit loose round the brain box", but he wasn't. Admitted he was slow both in his movements, and his speech. I often wondered how he ever managed to finish his round, but he did, and quite efficiently too. He also had this "smoking habit" a lot of people attained during the "War Years". it seemed as though he was never without a cigarette in his mouth, and he didn't seem to smoke them, it was as though they just dangled there, and burnt themselves out. Occasionally he would blow outwards, with the "fag" still in his mouth, to remove the ash, and of course if you were anywhere in the vicinity of this action, you would have ash deposited all over you. Also, Arthur would have ash quite evidently down the front of his old "mac", which was another thing I don't think I saw him without, with the exception again, of him being indoors.

Despite all this he was a very nice bloke, he was short in build, and he shuffled he didn't walk. His feet, like my "Dad's" were always pointing east and west, when his body was facing north, and what feet! "God", I thought "'e'll neva bleedin' well fall ova with them plates o meat, they cova too much bloody ground, o wonda were re put's 'em w'en 'e's in bed, out the soddin' winda o suppose", and I tittered at this thought.

Then there was Mary, Mary Lewis. She lived on the Walsall Road on the right hand side in between Alexandra Crescent, and Sheldon Road. The only way I found this out was due to me serving her mother when I had my first round. She was a very nice lady, unlike Mary in looks, but kind and gentle, like Mary in her ways.

Mary was a tall very pretty girl, beautiful complexion, which required no make up, other than a little lipstick, and even that wasn't really necessary. She stood erect, and her figure was "jus' like a filum star's". She always wore a scarf, in turban fashion around her hair, and it was only when I saw her once or twice at home that I actually saw her hair, it was blonde (natural) wavy, and long. A jumper would cover the top half of this wonderful figure, and the pelvic area, and the legs were always clad in tight fitting smart jodhpurs, which looked most attractive, and probably very sexy, but I didn't think of things like that then. To finish off this vague description of a very lovely girl, she wore brown small, thick country shoes.

I think, by what Ernie had said, although he didn't divulge too much, that Mary absolutely adored him. They were seeing one another, although as Ernie said to me, not once, but often "o don' no w'at she siz in me Ronnie, om nearly fifty, an' she's on'y nineteen. She oughta bi guin' wi' somebody like yo', not with an' ol' mon like me. I keep on tryin' ta purer orff, but she wun' 'ave none on it, so ov jus' cum to gu alung wi' things, an' 'ope she don' get too serious cuz then I'll 'ave ta put mi bloody foot down. O can' 'ave 'er spoilin' 'er life ova w'at ris on'y an infatuation, cuz w'en the young blokes are around again, she'll 'ave 'er pick on 'em, still we'll wert an' see".

I thought deeply about what Ernie had said, I thought very deeply indeed, and even then at my tender age I could see the sense in what he was saying. I mean at that particular time most of the young men Mary's age were away in the Army, Navy, or Air Force, and only came home periodically if they happened to be stationed in Britain.Of course, the vast majority of these lads were overseas, and were likely to be for years.

Naturally I did not ask too many questions. For one thing it was completely beyond my intelligence, and for another it would not have been polite, and thirdly I was not versed in these matters at my age. I appreciated the fact that Ernie did treat me as an opposite, not as a "boy", although that is exactly what I was. Oh, I was practically as tall as I am now, and I had quite a good physique for a lad of fifteen like all lads of my age, psychologically I was not on the same plane, as a man,well, a normal man at the age of fifty or for that matter, a girl of nineteen. Personally I think that women generally mature physically, and psychologically, much sooner than lads. Still that's a personal opinion. The mere thought of me making an approach to Mary, whom I thought as "old" anyway, was monstrous, although again I did not mention this to Ernie, due entirely to the fact that we had become such good friends.

I should say to sum the whole issue up the partnership between Mary and Ernie was one that had arisen through very difficult times, I can't comment other than that because I was never to find out what happened in the end. All I do know is that in the short period that they entered my life, they were two very lovely people.

At the West Bromwich Depot there were two other people whom I worked with, but did not get too close to. The first was "Ollie", he did a big round,situated in close proximity to the depot itself He was also a great friend of Ernie's. Then there was "Sid" He was an old man, and he lived in Farcroft Avenue, Handsworth, just opposite "The Nick" and "Church Terrace". Ollie, or Oliver, to give him his full title, was a big built man, rather handsome in a rugged kind of way, not unlike Clark Gable, without the moustache His accent I could not pin down, although it wasn't "Brummie" or "Black Country", it was rather a rustic type of accent, that you would probably hear in Devon, or Cornwall.

He was a charming man, very gentle, although I should imagine if his dander were to be set up he could be quite an handful, but fortunately I was not to witness anything like that part of his nature.

"Sid" was old, through my young eyes, very old, I never saw what type or colour his hair was simply because I never saw him without his grey trilby hat. He had the largest hooked nose I'd ever seen, his eyes a beautiful blue, sunk deep into his head, as though they were trying to escape from everything altogether. This was true of his whole face, for it was covered with hollows, and wrinkles. The mouth was large, and again sunk into the lower cheekbones, and when he opened his mouth it revealed no upper teeth, and only two large stumps sticking upwards either side from his bottom gums. But this didn't prevent Sid from tackling meat, and other things like that, although it remained a mystery to all of us how he managed it, for one thing Sid liked was his "belly". Sid's body was thin, but wiry, and he had a slight hump on his back. Summer and Winter he would wear this long blue overcoat, and of course his permanent fixture, the trilby. He suffered unfortunately from asthma, and his breathing was very distressed at times, in fact many's the time he would have to lean against a wall, and fight for it. So consequently Sid had quite an amount of time away from work. Of course he shouldn't have been at work, but the Ministry of Works made it impossible for him to do otherwise. Naturally enough though being out in the fresh air gave him a look of well being, for, like most of these roundsmen, and women they became weather beaten through having to work in all kinds of climates one thing I do remember predominantly about this nice old man was the diamond ring he wore on his third finger left hand, it was the most beautiful thing I'd ever seen.

Well, there I was then at West Bromwich Depot, with a useful team, Depot Manager Harold Haynes, Supervisor, Charlie Cope, Stableman, Frank (?), and then the roundspeople, Mary Lewis, Ernie Humphries, Arthur Cheslyn, Oliver, Sid, and myself, it was in my opinion a very good team. I worked with Ernie for about two weeks, two valuable weeks, and he taught me a lot. He showed me how to do the books, and all the different forms, (Expectant mothers, people that claimed extra milk through illness, and forms that factories had to return to the milk roundsperson, for proof of the ration of milk that they were allowed for canteens for the workers, and for cooking etc, forms for the elderly, and for babies). The roundsperson had to collect these and return them to the office. I think the customers obtained these from the different "Labour Exchanges", where a counter was set up entirely for the use of the Ministry of Food Officer, but of course, this could vary from place to place. Ernie showed me how to process the receipts for goods out, and returns.

How to complete a "Statement for Debits" which the dairies system required. This was a list of all the customers that didn't pay on the Saturday, the usual day for customers to settle their bills. He let me reckon up the different bills for the customers, and put me right where I was going wrong. On a few occasions he let me go to the door, without any pre information, reckon the customer's bill up, collect the money, and where necessary give out change, naturally under his watchful eye. In fact, although it did not really fall to him to complete this part of my work, he taught me more in those two to three weeks, with his gentle approach to things, than probably someone else would have achieved in a couple of months, he was, to sum it up, "A GOOD FRIEND".

On the third or fourth Sunday when I turned up at the depot, along with Arthur Cheslyn, for we had got used to travelling together now, I found to my surprise no Ernie.

In fact there was no one in the depot save Harold, and a horse and float, which I recognised as "Mary's". We went into "The Shed" as was usual, and had a cup of tea, which again was usual, and sat down for a minute, when Harold came in and said "Could I have a word with you a minute nip?" I drained my cup and went to the entrance of the shed, and he said to me in muffled tones, although for the life of me I could not understand why, for there was only Arthur and I there, still he must have had his reasons. "Ernie has told me that you have been doing very well with him, and that you understand the workings of the books, and all the other aspects of doing a round, in fact he thinks very highly of you, so I wonder if I could ask you a personal favour, and if you say yes, it could be doing you a favour too eh?". I was to realise of course later on that this was a come on, which in turn was the reason that he did not wish Arthur Cheslyn to hear the conversation between us, because no doubt Arthur would have put his "two-pennuth" in, and in all probability stopped the plan Harold had thought out.

"Mary's mother has telephoned to say that Mary isn't feeling too well, so she won't be in for a few day's. I've phoned head office up but they can't help me. Charlie is out doing a round, and I have several things to do here. Although it's a bit sudden, and you haven't been supervised to taking a round on of your own, I wondered if you could manage to do Mary's round for the few day's she might be off. I wouldn't have asked you to do this if I hadn't have been really pushed, so what do you say young Smith then?"

On hearing this request I could hardly contain my excitement. All I could think of was telling "Our Mom and Dad, and the rest of the family" when I arrived back home, that I had been asked to do a round "on miyone". My answer of course was "who-o-o thank's Mista rayne's, thanks a lot, ar-r-r course I'll do it, o cun manige, Ernie's tol' mi yer'rythin' 'e 'as, o no o cun do it". Arthur by this time had started to load his own flat cart, and consequently had little idea of what was going on. Frank had got his horse from the stables, and was putting him into the shafts, so he was busy too, and anyway I don't think Frank would have taken much notice any road up. "Now Son the cart's already loaded, and I will explain where you start the round, but for the moment just come back into the office ? ? ?, and I will go over the round roughly with you".

Harold and I went back into the shed, and we sat down, with him pouring me another cup of tea. I drank this whilst he went over the rounds book with me, and he assured me that I was not to worry about the outstanding money the customers owed from the Saturday, but just to concentrate on getting the milk delivered, but never the less I thought "if om gunna do the bleedin' roun' om gunna do it bleedin' propa". but I didn't reveal these thoughts to Harold obviously.

The first customer on Mary's round was in Lower City Road, and Harold gave me rough directions to this road, and I said that I could find it easily, because to get to this Lower City Road I had to cover part of Ernie Humphries's round. Harold had mentioned Izon's, and Roway Lane, and I said excitely "Ar-r-r ro know w'ere tharris, tha's w'ere rernie serves innit?" Harold replied "that's it nip, that's exactly it, now if you go straight up Roway Lane to the main road as Ernie did, you'll have to turn right, and go along the main road for about a mile, well maybe not quite a mile, but anyway it's the first road on the left, now is that clear Son?" "Ar~r-r-r" I replied "O'll soon find dit, no trouble". He then showed me a rough plan of the rest of the round, which wasn't really that complicated, for it was a small round, and very compact.

After City Road, I crossed over the main Birmingham Road turning right again. I again took the first turn on the left into Trafalgar Road, where the bulk of the deliveries were to be made. It was an area that I was to become acquainted with in later years, delivering bread for Scribbans' then, Elm Terrace, Birch Cresent, Regent Road, Hill Road and so on.

When Harold was satisfied that I was aware of what I was to do he led me out to the waiting float and pony, and said "Don't worry about anything nip, I've loaded the float myself, so I know that's alright. I've put a pencil in the book ready for you, and if you do collect any money, and you're not quite sure of what to do, then leave it and we'll sort it out when you return okay?" Ar-r-rokay Mr rayne's, burr I'll be oright, 'onist o will", an' I thought to myself "He mus' think om a bleedin' idjet or summat 'e must".

I climbed onto the back of the float, where the reins were already threaded through the two brass loops situated on the front board, and clicked the horse into motion. Just as I moved off I heard Frank shout out to me "nah-h yo' bi careful wi' that mare young un, don yo gu rushin' a, she's a lovely girl she is, an' o'll know if yo' ain' looked arta ra, so yo' tek it steady now wun ya". "Ar-r-rokay Frank" I replied over my shoulder as I negotiated the sharp left hand bend which would take me to the exit from the depot "o wun 'urt ta 'onist o wunt".

Off I went full of excitement, just imagine I'd come to work this morning, and I was only a roundsman's mate, but now look at me, o wuz a roundsMAN, tha's worro wuz, a ROUNDSMAN.

I followed the route to Ernie's commencement of round, and wishing that I could see him to tell him I was doing Mary's round for a while, but I didn't see him, which I thought was rather unfortunate, for him, as well as me. I'd show them I thought, I'd show them that I was worthy of a round of my own. I did however see a couple of roundsmen from other dairy companies, that Ernie and I had spoken to whilst doing his round. One worked for Midland Counties Dairy, and their depot was in Bratt Street. The other one worked for Evesons Dairy and their only place was in Nelson Street. I shouted to them as I went by, hoping that they would notice that I was now on my own, completely in charge of the round, and getting a further thrill hoping that they had.

On I went up Roway Lane, onto the main Birmingham to Dudley road, and after a few moments spotted City Road. I turned the mare into this road, then had a quick look for the number of my first delivery. Having found this I pulled the horse up outside, checked the book again to ascertain what milk I had to deliver to this customer, and what a great thrill I had when I went up the path, and deposited the order onto the steps right by the empty bottles. As I was walking back up the path I heard a voice say "Doh yo' wan' any munnee this wick our kid, am they geein the milk away fer nuthin' then?" This was followed by a chuckle. I turned and saw a great big bloke filling the doorway, God he was big. A real tough looking face, with a huge moustache under what I can only describe as a "boxer's nose", and hanging out of his mouth was a long black pipe. I stood there for a few seconds, I really didn't know what to do "Well bring yer book Son, an' doh stand thaya, weem alwis gorra cuppa tea on fer Mary, so yo'll 'ave ter 'ave it wun' ya', so come on then, else it'll bi bloody cold" "Ar-r-rokay, on'y om nu on this roun'". I thought I'd better act as though I had been on previous rounds. I didn't want them to think that I was a novice did I? I went back to the float and placed the empties into the metal case, I picked the book up from in between the milk bottles, and again looked at the customers' entry, and sure enough there it was. The amount of money they owed from the previous week. To make sure that I did not make any further mistakes, I looked back at the other references appertaining to this house in City Road, and I found out that they always paid on a Sunday morning. I put my satchel on over my left shoulder, although there was no cash in it, I thought I'd better look as if I knew what I was doing. Anyway I thought, I was the roundsman, so I'd better do it properly. I checked the week's previous deliveries, and found that they had two sterilised, and a pasteurised on a Sunday, a "sterra and a pas" the rest of the week, so trying to impress myself, as well as everyone else I thought I'd better check Mary's figures and see if they were correct. "Big 'eaded sod" I thought of myself. Then on the other hand I thought what about if I did find out that Mary had made a mistake, it would have been a feather in my cap to find it out wouldn't it? I dismissed that thought immediately, thinking "w'at kinda s…tbag, are you to be 'avin' that kinda thought about Mary", so dismissed that altogether. I reckoned up eight sterra, at $4^3/_4$d a bottle was 3/2d, and seven pas at $4^1/_2$d a bottle was 2/$7^1/_2$d, the total being 5/$9^1/_2$ Then I looked at Mary's neat, and beautiful bookwork to find, not surprisingly, there in the amount carried forward, and the amount brought forward columns 5/$9^1/_2$d. I put the book into my satchel, and walked back down the path, and stood hesitantly at the front door, waiting for them to bring a cup of tea, and the money for me. I stood there for a minute, when suddenly a girl of about seventeen appeared from one of the doorways leading off the hall. She saw me and said "watcha wertin thaya fer, come on in, Mary aliss does, gu on in the back room tha's waya our Mom an' Dad'll be". I walked down this lovely neat, and tidy hallway, "God it wuz bloody posh", I thought, "o wish this lot could see 228", and then a further thought struck me. "o bet they ain' got the mob we've gorratt 228 though", but oh how wrong I was.

I knocked on the door that the girl had told me to go into, and a lady's voice bade me enter. It was a lovely room, looking out onto a big well kept garden. The bloke I had seen initially was sat in a big comfortable armchair reading the newspaper, smoking contentedly on his pipe. On the other side on a hard backed chair was a pretty, but buxom woman in the process of pouring tea out into a beautiful cup, and saucer, which she passed to me. said, "Sit yerslf down Son, there's ya' munnee on the terble thaya" and she indicated to a neat stack of silver and coppers. I picked it up and counted it. it was exactly right 5/$9^1/_2$d. I put the silver, a half crown, a florin, and a tanner, into one compartment of my satchel, and the coppers into another. I then picked up my cup to have a drink, when the lady spoke again. "We allis gerra birra chernge ready fer Mary cuz it 'elps 'er fer lerta ron, us bein the fust custama. An' don' ferget ta pick that tanna rup an' nall Son, we allis gi Mary a tanna, an' as she ain' 'ere yo' mirras well 'ave it. Gu on now an' pick it up, it wunt bite cha.O'll gu an' getcha summat ta eat, watcha wan a bercan san'witch, or w'at?" I didn't have time to answer. "A big mon like 'im want's mowa than a bercan san'witch Motha, ge 'im a good fry up, gu on thay's a good wench".

"It's soright I don' wanna putcha ta any trouble". I tried to intervene. "Trouble, trouble" the deep gruff voice went on "if ar' thought yo' wuz gunna bi any trouble od a kicked ya' rarse ourov 'ere afowa now, an' smart abourit as well" A deep bellied laugh followed. this comment. I started to feel a little embarrassed and the lady noticed this, and she started to laugh as well. "Doh tek any notice ov 'im my love, 'e's on'y jokin', look Abe yove med the lad blush. "'ell do mowa than blush Motha w'en them wenchis gerrold on 'im", Abe said from behind his newspaper, and there was another deep belly laugh. "Now gu on Motha an' get the lad's grub 'e mus' bi starvin' bi now". "Ar-r oright" said the lady, and off she went, apparently into the kitchen.

Abe never said a word after she had gone, so I just sat there not knowing quite what to do. Suddenly a girl came in, not the one I had seen earlier, but she was approximately the same age, maybe a year or two younger, but no more. "'allo", she started, "w'o am yo', an' w'ere's Mary?" "Mind yarrown bizniss, an' gu an' 'elp ya' Motha", the deep voice behind the newspaper said, quite sternly. "Ar-r-rokay Dad, o wuz on'y arskin' though tha's sall". "Ar-r-r well yo' gu an' arsk somw'ere relse then ma wench, an' leave the lad alone". Off she went, and we were returned to our silence again, but not for long.

The lady of~the house came back with a dinner plate of bacon, egg, pigs pudding, and some small kidney's, and told me to sit down and eat, whilst she cut me some bread and butter. I rose from where I sat, went to the table, and it was then that I saw this tribe of "wenches" follow the lady in, including the two I had already met.

They waited until I was at the table ready to eat, and then they more or less gathered around me. I gave a quick count, although it possibly wasn't a correct one, and this estimation revealed that there were about nine girls, and this time I did really blush. There was a rustling of newspaper and a voice (Abe's). "Now yo' wenches, w'atcha think yarra doin', gi the chap room ta eat 'is brekfust, come on now, come away, an' leave 'im alone, now come on now an' do as yome told" With that they withdrew although with some reluctance.

The lady of the house sat opposite me and told me that the reason they paid Mary on a Sunday was because she and her husband were out at work all the week including Saturday. They had got eleven children, the eldest was in the navy, and all "the bigguns" went to work. "The little un's" went to school in the week, stopping at school for the dinners, and going to their Aunt's afterwards, and all day Saturday. Abe would pick them up from the Aunt's at night time when he finished work. So really Sunday was the only day that they spent together, and consequently they made the most of it.

I in return told them about "Our Mom and Dad", where I lived, and how I came to be.working at Handsworth Dairies. They appeared to be quite interested, and they told me that I would be quite welcome there any time I was passing. I thanked them, but knowing heart of hearts this would never happen, it was such a distance from "Hockley Brook", but nevertheless I thought it was a nice gesture.

I finished my mammoth breakfast and thanked them. "I'll 'ave ta gerra move on else the otha people wunt 'ave their milk in time for dinner, lerralone brekfust", I joked, feeling a lot more at home with them now, and feeling a lot more confident about doing my first round on my own.

I walked slowly back up the path with the whole of the family on the doorstep wishing me goodbye, and I felt quite nice in my "belly" about this, although I was never to see them again.

Clicking the mare on to two or three doors up, I started the day in earnest delivering the milk at running pace, but making sure that if there was any money owing from last week I would knock the door and attempt to collect it.

The rest of the day went without incident, and I finished at the bottom of Hill Road at about one o'clock.I straightened my load up ready for the return journey to Trinity Street, taking the mare steady, as I didn't want to get into trouble with Frank.I entered Dudley Road West quite content with myself and the first day "with a roun' ov miyone."

I arrived back at the depot to find that everyone except Arthur Cheslyn, who was always last in, had finished and gone home, that is all the roundsmen. Frank was still there obviously, and in "the shed" I found, to my surprise, not Harold Haynes who was normally the last one at the depot, but Charlie Cope.

He looked at me and said "how have you got on young 'un?", I replied "Oh-h-h not too bad Mr Cope, o think ov done oright, I yope so any road up".

"Well we'll just have a look shall we, and repair any damage you might have done". He smiled, for he meant this statement in the nicest possible way, but nevertheless I was apprehensive.

I had unloaded the float, Frank had unharnessed the mare, and given her a drink before taking her to her stall for the night. God, Frank loved his horses, he handled them fondly, they were, I'm sure, his whole life.

I sat quietly whilst Charlie went through the book, checking the deliveries I had entered, and the cash that I had taken, reckoning this up on a sheet of paper as he went along. I tipped the cash out on to the wooden table and counted it out, putting it into piles, with the notes underneath, like I'd seen the roundsmen, and women do at Island Road.

Charlie completed his scrutiny of the book, and then totalled up the money I had taken then he counted out what I had collected, and on completion of this said "Yo' did alright young un, mind you it's a good job Harold had you to fall back on, for he should have done the round himself, with you helping him. He had to go somewhere urgent this morning (I found out later that he had promised his wife to take her somewhere), so he depended on you to complete the round in his absence. He will be so glad that you did as well as you have, but no doubt he will thank you himself in the morning. Anyway I shall have to get my skates on or else I'll miss the train from West Bromwich, and I'm late enough as it is. I've told Frank to lock up when he has finished, there's only Arthur to come in now, so tarrar nip, I'll see you tomorrow okay?".

"A-r-r-rokay Mr Cope, o'll see ya' tammarra, tarrar". With that he put an old raincoat over his arm, and with the takings for the day off all the rounds, except Arthur's of course, in a small leather brief case, and all the documents as well, he scurried off down the narrow lane.

Charlie had only just gone, and I was preparing to go into the stables to say "tarrar" to Frank when I heard the unmistakable rumble of steel rims on the cobbles coming up the lane. I decided to wait for Arthur, and take the return journey to "The Brook" with him. I wished that I hadn't afterwards, for he was so slow, unloading, even though I gave him a hand, for when we had finished, he started nattering to Frank, and they just went on and on. I don't think either of them "'ad gorra bloody um ta gu to. Finally Arthur came away, leaving Frank to lock up, until the firewatcher, whoever was on came on duty. We walked slowly up Trinity Street to the bus stop in High Street, between Thynne Street and Hope Street.

Our bus came after a long wait, it was a 74 West Bromwich Corporation Daimler. We boarded it and naturally went upstairs, for Arthur to continue with his "fags". After much, jumping and starting with this well kept vehicle, although old, we finally made it back home just after four o'clock by "Tippers" clock. I left Arthur on the "Brook" by "The Benyon" and ran up home to tell all and sundry about this absolutely marvellous day.

Dad was in bed with Mom, and the three little uns were in the garden playing, although they weren't such "little uns" now. Everyone else was out. I went into the back kitchen and looked inside the "black Birmingham Corporation stove", and found Mom had left my dinner in there, with my dish (it was the tin dish that she had cooked it in) of rice pudding alongside of it. I got a match from off the table and lit the twin row of gas holes running along either side of the bottom of the oven, adjusted the strength of outflow. I didn't want my dinner burnt to a cinder did I? I liked it baked as I've already told you, but I didn't want it burnt.

I then went back into the middle room and cut myself about six rounds of bread off the cottage loaf our Dad used to bake on the side at Bradfords. They did stop the making of fancy breads, etc during the War, but "Our Dad", still did us little treats, and I've no doubt he did a few for others too.

After I had cut the bread I spread a couple of them with butter and got them "down mi yodge" whilst waiting for my dinner to warm through. The kettle was on the fire, so I put some more tea into the tin pot on the table, and topped it up with boiling water, let it stand for a while and then poured my first "cuppa" out, put in about four teaspoonfuls of sugar, and a drop of milk into a cup, stirred it, and then sat back in "Our Mom's" chair, closed my eyes and drank deeply. God it was lovely, that first "cuppa" after such a while.

I took the dinner, and pudding out of the oven after a time, and put them on the middle room table. After scraping the dried gravy from around the sides of the plate and putting it into the middle, I commenced to devour this feast with zest.

I completed my first day doing a round "on mi yone" by going to the "pitchers". "The Palladidalum" of course. I had "bubble and squeak" on the evening, and then after a while of "chewin' the rag", I went off to bed, thinking who knows what's going to happen tomorrow, eh?

I did Mary's round all the week, and got quite used to the idea of being a roundsman, instead of a roundsman's mate. Naturally as the week went on I became more competent, and began to think of the round as being mine. I had serious thoughts about Mary not returning, not because of illness or anything like that. What I thought was that maybe she had got fed up with the job in general, and found other employment in an office, which I might add, seeing her, and talking to her, would in my opinion have been more suiting. These thoughts were constantly on my mind, and as Harold hadn't said anything different, I naturally thought "she ain comin' back".

On the Friday lunchtime when I returned to the depot it was a great shock to me when Harold said "I've called down to Mary's in Walsall .Road nip, and asked if she is coming in tomorrow. We are short of people, and it being a long day with customers paying their milk bills. She said that although she hasn't completely recovered from her illness, she thinks she can manage to come in tomorrow. I think that I'll put you back with Ernie for the day, and then I have something else for you, hopefully starting on Sunday, alright nip?

I was dreadfully disappointed of course, and it must have shown in my face, because before I could answer, Harold went on quickly "Look nip, I know I shouldn't be telling you this, but you really have been a good lad helping me out this week especially, so if I tell you, you must promise me you won't say anything to anyone will you?"

"Nah-h-h co's o wunt Mista raynes, o wunt letcha down, 'onist o wunt", and I started to get excited again wondering what he was going to tell me which was so secretive. I'd got an idea of course that he was going to put me on a round of my own, for I couldn't think of anything else for him to tell me, but, I still wasn't sure.

"Well nip, I've got to telephone head office today, because I think that the round that Mr Cope's doing at the moment will become vacant as from this Sunday, and I'm going to suggest to them that if they haven't got anyone else in mind that they give it to you I shall tell them how you have done Mary's round competently this week, and as far as I'm concerned you should be given first choice. Of course you understand that head office will have the last say on the matter, so don't build your hopes up too high, will you?"

"Nah-h-h o co's o wunt Mista raynes, an' thanks eva sa much ferrevrythin' yome doin' an' o wunt letcha down o wunt. I'm sure it will turn out alright Ronnie, but of course I don't want to promise you something, and then have to tell you that you can't have it at the last minute, but I should have something definite for you in the morning alright then?" "Ar-r-rallright then Mista Raynes, o'll wert till tammarra an' see then, an' thanks once again". With that I went and caught my bus home, filled with a mixture of apprehension, and excitement.

I arrived at work the next morning earlier than normal, for I couldn't wait to hear the result of Mr Haynes' conversation with head office. Mary was just loading her float up, and Frank was talking to her when I entered the yard, so naturally I went up to her to ask how she was feeling now. She said she was much better although, she wasn't quite right. Then she asked me how I had got on with her round, and was there any queries, to which I readily said "nah-h-h". I did remark about the first customer, and she smiled, and said to me, "you will never find a more loving, and generous family in the whole wide world, Ron, I feel more like one of the family than the milklady. Although they have such a big family, and they are mostly girls, they would still have me to live with them if I so desired, yes they are certainly a lovely family". I feel sure that she would have gone on talking, but then Ernie appeared on the scene from the narrow entrance. She made her excuses and went across to him, and they went to a quiet corner of the yard and started to converse in a secretive, and quiet manner. I immediately went into "the shed" expecting to find Harold Haynes there, but to my surprise the only person in there was "Olly". We exchanged "G'mornin's" and then he went out to load his wagon, whilst I poured myself a cup of tea.

I finished the tea quickly, and returned outside, where I found that Mary and Ernie were still in deep conversation, "Ollie" had nearly completed his loading, and no one 'else was in sight. I went and pulled Ernie's flat cart out, and having tied the shafts back up with the leather thong, I went back into the "shed" for Ernie's Goods Outward sheet, which I knew would be on the clip board on the table. I had found this out during my term as a roundsman that week.

I found the sheet I required and then I went out again and started loading for Ernie.This was of course to warrant my being there, for it wouldn't have looked good if I had just stood there, having done a round on my own last week, and not loaded the wagon up for my very good friend.

I had nearly completed this task when Ernie came to me and thanked me for doing it.

"Yome a good un Ronnie, yome a good lad, an' thanks, o think yome with mi terday, burr o know yo' a' "wi "mi tammarra, nor wi" anyone else, they got summat else fer ya' they yave". He gave me a broad smile, and a wink, blowing the ash off his cigarette whilst it was still in his mouth at the same time.

I didn't say anything, but it didn't stop my "belly" from tingling, and it didn't stop me wondering at the same time who had told Ernie about Sunday. It wasn't me for sure, so it must have been "Mista raynes" Was it possible that they all knew about me having a "'roun' ov miyone", and they were all keeping it a secret?

Still it didn't matter, not one jot, so I went on quietly finishing the loading. On completion of this I went back into "the shed" where Mary, Ernie, Olly, and Frank were sat quietly chatting to one another, waiting for the arrival of Mr Haynes or Mr Cope to check their loads out.

I went across to the table and poured another cup of tea, and before I could take a "swig" Mr Cope entered the "office" He wished everyone "Good morning", asked Mary how she was and they had a short chat. Then he said "Well I'd better check you out being as Harold isn't here. I think he had to go to Island Road this morning, before setting out for here. I'm not quite sure, but I think that's what he said yesterday, anyway let's get you lot on the road first". Then he turned to me and said, "Harold told me that you were to go with Ernie for today, and that he would see you when you came in alright Son". Ar-r-rokay Mista Cope, thank ya'" So, off I went with Ernie, feeling a little sad now that I had tasted the high-life, doing a round on my own, but being the "mon" I was I soon put this sadness behind me and got stuck into the working day.

We finished about five o'clock on that Saturday, and I went into "the shed" to collect my wages after unloading the wagon, which I did on my own, due to the fact that Ernie had got to pay in. Apparently Mary had waited for him to return, and they were again in deep conversation, so I didn't disturb them, but went straight over to Mista 'raynes. He was busy counting money from the rounds already in, and presumably, by the look of the leather satchel by him he was getting ready to deposit it in the bank's overnight safe, ready for the bank staff on Monday morning.

I didn't say anything but just sat there waiting until he had finished counting the particular amount he had in front of him, and then recorded it on a long white printed sheet.

On completion of this he looked up and said, "Here you are nip, here's your money", and he handed me the brown envelope which I knew contained the twenty-seven and sixpence.

I opened it and counted the cash, then put it in my trouser pocket, and sat there for a few seconds hoping that he would have some news for me, but he didn't say anything. He just returned to checking the money, and documents in front of him.

Eventually I got up and said "tarrar" to everyone, and went out of "the shed" to make my way home. I went across the yard, but couldn't go any further due to Mr Cope coming up the entrance on a small float, and pony, who was named "Nip", which I thought appropriate for him, for he was small. As he drew alongside me he said "has Harold told you about tomorrow Ronnie?" Nah-h-h, 'e ain' said anythin' burr 'e wuz busy Mista Cope", "Whoa" said Charlie to "Nip", and the horse stopped. He, Charlie that is, dropped off the float, put his arm round my shoulder and led me back into "the shed", and across to Mr Haynes.

Charlie said to Harold in a quiet voice "Well Harold what's happening tomorrow, is the lad doing it or what, don't forget we have Sid off tomorrow for a week, and if we have anyone go sick we'll be right in it?" Harold looked up from what he was doing, stared at me, and then put both his hands around his head, and shook it. Finally he lowered his hands and said to me "I'm sorry Nip, I forgot to tell you, and I did promise didn't I?" "It don' marra Mista raynes, we all ferget somtimes don' we? although for the life of me, I hadn't really got a clue what he was supposed to have forgotten, other than to see me when I came in, and he had done that ? "Tomorrow I want you to go with Mr Cope, and if he thinks that you are suitable, which he thinks you are already, then we are going to give you the round for yourself, alright, how's that do you eh?". That funny feeling in my "belly" came again. All I could do was to mumble "who-o-o-o tha's great, thanks eva sa much, thanks, om sure o'll be youright, who-o-o tha's great tharris" Then I suddenly stopped, and lowered my head, for both men were now smiling, and I thought they must think I'm a proper fool going on like this, so I said quietly, "Thank ya' eva sa much thank ya'" and I started to move away. They must have thought that they had embarrassed me in smiling, for Harold got up from his chair and came after me and said, "Now you won't let me down tomorrow Nip, will you, for I'm depending on you to do a good job, and who knows you might be the best roundsman I have eventually?" "I won't let you down Mista raynes, o promise yarr o wunt, butcha know o wunt bi yere as early-tamarra don "ya' cuz the buzzis don' run early so yo 'll know wun ya', burr I'll bi yearly ev'ry otha day arta that, cuz the buzzis run berra then".

"That's alright Son. Charlie can't get here very early on a Sunday anyway, because his train from Stourbridge runs a little later on a week end, so don't you worry on that score. Now off you go home, and be here as early as possible tomorrow, tarrar now". "Tarrar Mista raynes, an' thank yarr agen, thank ya'", and with that I scurried off towards my bus stop to return to "The Brook" a very happy "MON".

Mr Haynes had actually referred to Mr Cope, as Charlie to me, and more important, he had referred to me as being a "ROUNDSMAN", not a lad, or a boy, but a "ROUNDSMAN". This certainly was a wonderful day for me. As usual I informed all the family in turn about "'avin' a roun' ov miyone", but I might just as well have told the cat and dog for all the interest shown. The most important thing in my life then, was that it had made me happy, that not only was I going to have a round of my own, but I had really been accepted as a man. Of course over the next few years I was to learn in many different ways, that you have got to be seen to be a man, and also, which was most important, you had got to prove yourself to be a man.

I didn't need calling the next day. I was up as soon as I had woken, but still "Our Dad". had beaten me to it. "'ello Son, blimey yome up early ain'tcha, w'at's guin on special then?" "They've gid me ya roun on miyone Dad, an' o start on it terday, so o don' wanna bi lert ferrit the fust day do I?" "Nah-h-h, ya' don' wanna do that norron ya' fust day, mind yo' o rememba ya' Motha tellin' mi summat abourit in the "Turk" las' night, an' om really 'appy fer ya' Son, om really 'appy."

I pondered momentarily on what Dad had said "ya' Motha tellin' mi summat abourit in the "Turk" las' night". I had been wrong in my assumption that no one had taken any notice of what I had said when I got home from work yesterday, which made me think deeply about having thoughts on things, when you hadn't really got the full facts. I thought long and hard about this, and decided to be a little more careful in the future. Although I made many mistakes, even after that I did have the capability at that age onwards of realising that you must first weigh up what the other person has said, or done, before acting, or saying anything in what could only be described as a hypothetical situation, or deed.

"I'll getcha some brekfust afowa ya' gu Ronnie, cuz with ya' nu responsabilities an' ev'rythin' you'll need ta 'ave a full stomach, wuntcha, so yo' sit yaself down, an' pour yaself a cup a tea, ov jus' med it fresh, an' I'll 'ave ya' grub on the terble in no time". Ar-r-rokay Dad, an' thanks, g'want mi ta cut some bread as well Dad". "On'y fer yaself Son, cuz if yo' cut it fer the otha's as well it'll gu 'ard afowa they gerrup, an' wi don' wan' that do we?", and I heard a soft chuckle from the back kitchen. I cut about six slices of bread, and spread them with butter. (One thing about "Our Mom", although we were comparatively poor, she would not tolerate margarine under any circumstances.) By the time Dad had brought my breakfast in, I had eaten two of them, and was busy munching my way through a third. "Blimey Son 'ow many o them 'ave ya' stuffed?" "Three Dad, ya' don' mind d' ya', cuz if ya' do, o'll leave them otha's". Nah-h-h, o dain' mean anythin' like that Ronnie, yo' gerrit down yarr 'odge, it does mi good ta see ya' eat like that, burr I bet some people ud sooner keep ya' farr wick morran a fortnight, it's wuss than feedin' an 'oss. Still neva mind, as lung as we 'ave it, yo' cun eat it can 'ya"?

"Thanks Dad". "Well cun ya' manige any mowa then?" "Ar-r-ro could do wi' yanotha couple a pieces Dad please, om a bit 'ungry this mornin'" With that I got "stuck in" to the breakfast Dad had placed before me, with the sounds of his light hearted chuckling, and a gentle rubbing of my hair to accompany it making this most important day of my life, so much happier.

I got down on the "Brook" in plenty of time for my bus, and as usual Arthur was there. This had got to be a regular thing now, and we had got the bus's time down to a fine art.

"Warra bleedin' mis'rerble mornin'" was Arthur's first words to me, and I had to agree. It was one of those misty mornings, dull, and a fine but heavy continuous falling of rain, much like a mist that you get at the seaside, the one's that really soak you, and you're not even aware its doing so. The bus came more or less on time and Arthur and I went upstairs, for the sake of Arthur's "bronchial mixture", a packet of "Wild Woodbines". He lit up his umpteenth "fag" of the morning, and immediately choked on the first "drag". I think we'd nearly reached "The Regal" before he had got it partially under control. Arthur's cough was a continual thing, but it was better when he first lit up. It was a thing to be heard. He'd laugh away with his sad looking face and say to me "Bes' thing ta gerrit orff ya chest and he'd hold his Woodbine aloft. At the time I really did believe him, but not enough to emulate him, well, not for a while anyway.

We reached Trinity Street a little earlier than usual, perhaps the driver and conductor wanted an extra five minutes at the terminus at the bottom of Castle Hill, by the "Midland Red" bus garage.

On arrival at the depot we went into "the shed" where we found Harold, Charlie, and Frank. Everyone else had gone out.(Sid used to get a lift off someone with a car on a Sunday, the lucky bugger.) Charlie came across to me and said "Well are you ready for the day Ron, it's a bit of a nasty one, but never mind we'll be alright, we'll teach you the in's and out's, although by what I've been told you won't need much teaching"."Thank ya' Mr Cope", I replied. I didn't call him

Charlie because he had not said that I could yet, although as I said Mr Haynes had referred to him as "Charlie" but that didn't automatically give me permission to do so.

"Call me Charlie if we're going to work together Ron", he said, (so permission had been granted sooner than expected.) He went on, "I haven't loaded the float up, not because I didn't want to, but because I want to ascertain (o dain' know w'at the bloody 'ell that meant, burrit musta bin sommat good) how you get on. The more efficient I find you, the quicker you'll be going out on your own, alright?"

Ar-r-roright Mr...., sorry, Charlie, o wunt letcha down, o wunt bi lung pickin' things up, cuz o done Mary's roun', and tharrell bi berra fer mi wun' it" He smiled at me and said, Yes, by all accounts you did very well, and if things go alright today you might be on your own tomorrow. Anyway we'll see, now go and have a cup of tea and then when Frank has put "Nip" in the float you can go and load up, okay?"

"Ar-r-rokay Charlie". With that I went about doing what he had told me, whilst Harold Haynes and him stood chatting quietly in one corner of "the shed".

I finished the tea and went outside with the goods ticket. Frank had already put "Nip" into the shafts, and I went to stroke him. I did, and then when I went to walk away to load up, he took a bite at me. Frank burst out laughing, and said to me, He's a lovely little lad Ron, burr'e does like 'is birra fun, an' he'll nip yarr a little bit if 'e gets 'alf a chance. He wiped his ever running nose, still smiling at the incident, but I wasn't thinking of this at all. What I was thinking was that this was the first time that Frank had ever spoken to me, well in a nice hearted way, and I thought 'e ain't such a bad bloke arta rall". As if to answer my thoughts the sun broke through momentarily, which made me happier still.

I loaded the float and went back into "the shed" to inform Charlie of the situation. He said, "Well go and get the book, and your satchel, whilst I go out and check the load". I did this, and when I went outside Charlie had completed the checking, so we were ready for the road.

We turned right at the bottom of the entrance and went up to the High Street where we then turned left, but we only went along there for a short distance, when we then went right again into Thynne Street. Charlie who was driving "Nip" pulled up just inside this street, and said, "This is where we start Ronnie". I looked and found that we had stopped right outside "the Sela Cough place" (Wholesale Confectionery Shop), and my immediate thought on the matter was "I wuner if they gee yarreny free samples".

It was to this shop that we made our first delivery, so I imagined that someone lived over the shop. After that "my round" just went on in a natural course.

Beeches Road, Nicholls Street, Walter Street, Legge Street, Poplar Avenue, Lloyd Street, Woodward Street, Dagger Lane, then back up the lane to Slaithwaite Road. Then out into Hallam Street, Cotterell Street, Cranbourne Place, Kinith's Way. We turned around and went back to Hallam Street. Turning left and going back up to Clements Lane, Stoney Lane down to Lyndon by "Grant's Bakery", along Scott Street, although we didn't have any customers there. We turned right into Little Lane and went straight across to "Church Vale" We went down Church Vale nearly to the "Ring o' Bells" and "Old Church", but not quite. We turned again and came back up the Vale to Parsonage Street, into

All Saints Street, then we turned left into Stanway Road, served down there to Vicarage Road, turned right and went back up to Heath Lane.

During this first part of the round Charlie let me complete the bookwork, and collect any outstanding money, keeping a watchful eye on me, and correcting any mistakes I made, but I thought that he wasn't feeling too bad about the way that I was conducting myself.

I knew that the few days I had done on Mary's round had indeed helped me tremendously through this first day on "my round".

We turned left into Walsall Road, and I noticed another confectionery wholesaler, "Roberts", who occupied part of Heath Lane, Walsall Road, and Stanley Road with its premises. Charlie steered "Nip" into Stanley Road, but we didn't go straight up, we went into Bexley Grove, and in this Grove a little later on, a most amusing incident happened. Well, it wasn't amusing at the time, but when I looked back on it, it certainly was, but more about that later!

After Bexley Grove we re-entered Walsall Road. We travelled down there, cutting off on many occasions, weaving our way ever down towards "Stone Cross", taking in Hollyhedge Road, Penny Hill Lane, with its "Reformatory School", Sheldon Road, Alexandra Crescent, and then over the other side into, Caldwell Street (another story to tell there), part of Marsh Lane, and finally onto "The Whisty".

Charlie had introduced me to Mary Lewis's mother during the time before reaching "The Whisty", and she had invited us in for a cup of tea, which was very welcome, not having had one since we started out in Thynne Street. The weather was awful as well. That bit of sunshine we had when Frank had made his funny" was all the nice weather we had had so far, it had rained, and rained without letting up at all. It was still pouring when we entered Westminster Road from Hall Green Road, where we had made deliveries down there to within a few yards of "The Millfield".

We passed "The Red Lion" and went down the road and turned left into Lincoln Road and went up as far as "The Library", then doubled back down Glastonbury Road, turned right into Melrose Avenue, with me running down and serving a couple of houses to the left. We then went up one side and down the other in Beverley Road finishing up at its junction with Canterbury Road. We went up there delivering, including the side roads, Ripon Drive, and Wells Close, completing the round at the junction of Canterbury Road, and Beverley Road.

Charlie and I straightened the float up, at this junction, counting the empties, and returns. I completed the book, and quickly checked the cash, Which wasn't much due to hardly anyone being up, (I'd have to collect that tomorrow or in the week sometime I thought). We started our journey back to Trinity Street via Jervoise Lane, and Hollyhedge Road, picking up the stack of empties We had left on the side to relieve the weight on the float for "Nip" at the junction of Thursfield Road.

Up Hallam Street we went Charlie and I chatting away about this and that, but he never mentioned how he thought I had got on. Into Seagar Street, Reform Street, and then Overend Street to the junction of High Street, Nicholls Street, with "The Cop Shop" on the corner, and then the short run back to the depot.

51

We unloaded, and Frank put "Nip" away, then I paid in to Harold, and put the satchel and book on the table Without anyone saying a word, which made me a little disappointed.

Charlie and Harold chatted quietly to one another, and as I made a move to go home Harold said, "Hang on a minute Nip, I've got something to ask you". I went back to the table and sat down, wondering what was coming next. Didn't I come up to standard, didn't I do things right, with Charlie watching me, all these thoughts went through my troubled mind. Of course there was nothing that I could do about it until I had heard what they had got to say.

"Charlie doesn't think there's any need for him to come with you again. Oh, he might go with you on Saturday, but he thinks that you'll be alright, so do you think that you can manage? Naturally we would be grateful if you can, because Sid's away again, and if you can manage, then Charlie can do his round, leaving me free to attend to all the work here at the depot. What do you say then Son".

"No trouble Mista raynes, no trouble arall, o cun do it standin' on mi yed, an' od like ta 'elp ya', burrit tis my round innit, it is my round really?"

"Yes it's your round Son, but the checker usually goes with someone for a week, to see how they fare before we let them go out on their own (of course as I was to find out later this naturally was a load of old bull. They were short of staff.Never the less it filled me with pride at the time.) Then we check on them for about a couple of weeks after to make sure that they are alright, but Charlie has got every confidence in you, so we'll give it a try okay Nip?" "Ar-r-rokay Mista raynes, okay an' thank ya'".I looked at them both, sharing the thank you between them.

"Oh, and by the way Ronnie, I think it's about time you started calling me Harold from now on, now that you are a roundsman, alright?"

"Well, yer-r-r, tha's if yo' don mind tharris, 'arold. Of course I don't mind, I think it's only right, so off you go home now, and don't forget to be early in the morning".

I arrived home in double quick time, and gobbled my dinner down me, for I had got a certain job I wanted to do and it was most urgent. I had been thinking about it all the way home on the bus, and when I arrived home I was so glad that everyone was out, or in Mom and Dad's case, in bed.

I scrounged around the cupboards, the two on the right hand side of the fireplace, the one on top for food, and the one below for all kinds of junk, mostly working boots, and shoes, but no joy. I looked in the glass cabinet, but then thought well I can't get in there anyway' "cuz n you know who 'allis kep' it locked" Then I searched all through the huge sideboard situated on the other wall opposite the fireplace, still no luck. I sat back and gave the situation some serious thought, what I was looking for was a piece of stiff cardboard, roughly about 8 x 4, that's what I wanted for the job I had got in hand.

I wandered into the front parlour, and I searched through the other smaller sideboard in there, but still no luck. I knew that I hadn't got the item I wanted up in our bedroom, I'd got drawing paper, and other odd scraps of paper, but no cardboard.

Sitting on the battered, and torn, but never the less polished brown settee, I pondered my position, where could I, on a Sunday afternoon obtain a piece of cardboard 8 x 4?

Suddenly it hit me. "Our Mom's" Rinso packet in the kitchen (she had gone on to powder now, instead of "Lifebuoy Washing Soap", we were posh now that we had moved from 2/24 to 228), that's it, the Rinso packet. I bet there would be one that Mom had nearly finished "anyroad up" I thought, even if there ain't, o cud purr all the powda inta some news perpa, an' bost the box up, an' tek warr I wannid ourra that. Yes that's what I'd do, but I mustn't forget to tell "you know who" after I'd done it, because I still wasn't too sure that a "bost up the earole" wouldn't be amiss even though I "wuz a mon" now.

I hurried through to the kitchen and explored around, but again nothing. I felt absolutely dejected, because I had set my heart on completing this job I had in mind.

As a last resort I looked into the fire hole under the boiler where Mom put the rubbish ready to light the fire for the washing on a Monday morning. To my joy, and I nearly "widdled miself" over it, I found not a "Rinso" packet, but a much larger "Oxydol" packet, which would give me a lot more scope.

I removed the battered packet from the aperture under the boiler, which had got dried tea leaves (another thing Mom used to compensate the coal shortage), and several other pieces of unknown debris attached to it.

Placing my treasure onto the table I commenced to first clean all the debris off it.Once this was done, I got a knife from the table draw and cut along the edge of the bedraggled packet. It looked a sight, but I thought I won't have to tell Mom that I've emptied the powder out of her packet now, so that was one job less for me to do, and more important I couldn't possibly get into trouble either, or could I? You never knew with "Our Mom".

After the cutting I flattened the cardboard out on the wooden top, and decided which piece I wanted, and having done this, I then cut it carefully around with the knife. We didn't have the luxury of a pair of scissors, or if we did Mom didn't tell us lot where they were. Having completed this task to my satisfaction I then took the finished product back into the middle room, and placed it on the table.Then I went to the huge sideboard on the "entry wall" After "rooting" around for a while I found what I had been looking for, the bottle of "Stephens Blue Black Ink" and one of "Our Dad's" old pens. Then I got the bread saw which was on the table already, to use as a ruler.

First I pencilled roughly on the cardboard the exact lines I required for the job in hand. I went over these with the "Stephens Blue Black", and on completion of this I then entered into the top column across, NUMBER, STERA, PAS, T.T. In the first column below that I commenced, One, $4^3/_4$d, $4^1/_2$d, 5d, then in the column below that, Two, $9^1/_2$d, 9d, 10d. I went on this way right up to 24. I had indeed made myself a ready reckoner to save myself the trouble of trying to reckon up the customer's bill, mental arithmetic wasn't exactly to the forefront of my educational skills.

I smiled to myself on finishing this project. I thought I had done pretty well considering, it would certainly come in handy if Charlie couldn't come with me next Saturday. At least I wouldn't be floundering, for all I had got to do if someone had, had seven Stera's and seven Pas, was to run my finger down the numbers column, and the answer would be there, $2/9^1/_4$d for the Stera, and $2/7^1/_2$d for the Pas, bringing it to a total of $5/4^3/_4$d. It would be a doddle on Saturday I thought.

I held the cardboard in my hand and felt very pleased with myself, very pleased indeed. I would put it into the drawer of the table up in the bedroom, "our bedroom" until Saturday, for I thought I would surely know by then whether I would be doing the round on my own or not.

I arrived very early for work that Monday morning, full of pride, knowing that this round was mine, even if Charlie did have to come with me. But to my delight I found that he had already gone out on Sid's round. I went into "the shed", and Harold confirmed this, telling me that I would be on my own until at least Friday. Frank got "Nip" ready for me, and I loaded my float up feeling very happy indeed. Not about Sid being away of course, I felt a little sad about that, but that I was going to be on my own, on my own round for the full week, and hopefully prove my efficiency to Harold, and Charlie, which would lead to them letting me go out on my own on the Saturday. I did complete the round all the week, and when I came in on the Friday, Harold called me into the office, saying he would like a word with me. We were alone, and he faced me over the tressle table looking rather serious. Naturally, I was full of apprehension, so I stammered "Yus 'arold, w'at did ya' wan'mi fowa?"

"How do you feel about going out on your own tomorrow Ron?"

"O'll bi oright 'arold, o cun do it"

"Only Charlie has to go out on Sid's round unfortunately, and I have so much work to do here, I suppose I could leave it, but I don't want to really".

"Nah don' worry 'arol", I interrupted quickly, "O cun manige easy, 'onist o cun" "Alright then Ronnie, we'll give it a try, and see how you get on okay? "Ar-r-rokay 'arold, burr I wunt letcha down 'onist o wunt."

On arriving home that Friday night, I went straight upstairs and got my home made ready reckoner out of the drawer, sat down on the bed and went over it time and time again, trying to remember some of the figures.

Of course I did tell Mom, and the others. I couldn't tell "Our Dad" of course, for he was still in bed. Mom said "That'll bi good wunnit, d' ya' gerreny mowa munnee fer doin' it on yarrown?" "Nah o don' think so Mom". I thought to myself "Tha's all she bleedin'well thinks about, munnee, munnee, munnee".

Came the great morning and my stomach was churning as I travelled on the bus to West Bromwich, hoping of course that I wasn't going to make a mess of things.I started off in Thynne Street at the Sela Cough Shop, and knocked on the door, feeling very important, but still apprehensive. "'allo love" said the lady when she came to the door". "O doh remember seein' yo' befowa, am yo' anutha nu un then?

"Ar-r-rom on the roun' fer good now, o'll bi bringin' ya' milk frum now on".

"Blimey they'm gerrin younga, an' younga, 'ow much do I owe ya' then sweet'eart?"

"Three bob, 'sactly love", I said with confidence, for this was one of the easy ones. Eight bottles of Pasteurised at $4\frac{1}{2}$d a bottle. She gave me the exact money and I put it into my leather satchel, picked the empties up, and said "Tarrar love" and went back to the float. "A wert a minnit love", the lady's voice came over to me softly. I thought, "Warrav I done, o can 'ave med a misterk with the monnee, cuz that wuz easy enuff", so it was with great trepidation that I scurried back to the doorstep, and said "Warrizit love?"

"Yome in a big rush a' ya' young un, 'ereyar, 'ere's summat fer ya', yo' wuz a bit ta quick fer me, there ya' are now, tekit, I allis gi the milkmon, an' the breadmon summat fer thaya troubles, tarrar now". With that she put a "tanna" and a bag of "something" into my hands.

"Thanks, thank, ya' very much lady, it's very nice on ya, tarrar then".

"Tarrar Son, see ya' next wick then".

I ran back to the float again, and she went inside the house.I clicked "Nip". on to my second call feeling a whole lot better. Fancy a "tanner" and a bag of sweets, I'd had a quick look on the way back to the float, at my very first call.

"Blimey" I thought "If I gu on like this all day 'answuth Dairies wun' 'ave ta pay mi any bloody wergis at all".

So it was with confidence that I knocked on the door of my second customer. The rest of the day went without incident I'm glad to say, the more the day wore on the more confident I became, so naturally the more relaxed I became.

I stopped in Caldwell Street, and bought a packet of chips, which I ate with the corned beef sandwiches "Mom" had put me up that morning. This was swilled down with a bottle of Pasteurised milk.

I did very well indeed for tips that first day. When a customer gave me a tip I put it into my trouser pocket, just as I had done when I worked with Arthur Crump, and on completion of the round on "The Whisty" I counted the money up. It came to a grand total of 11/6d. I couldn't believe it.

I put this money into my pocket again, and then straightened the float up, ready for the return journey back home, via Thursfield Road that is to pick up the empties I had left there earlier to avoid "Nip" having to tote all that extra weight around.

I paid in, and Harold went through the book with me, and to my great joy everything was alright.

He looked at me and said, "Well Ronnie I don't think you need any more supervision, so the round is yours. You'll be on your own from now on. Oh Charlie might come with you occasionally, just to see if everything is alright, but I assure you this won't happen often." He gave me a great big smile, then handed my wages over to me, and wished me "Tarrar". Needless to say this was another very happy day in my life, and I went out to the "Palladium" on the night to celebrate. Naturally I didn't tell "you know who about the tips. I kept that to myself. I was indeed growing up. My stay at West Bromwich was rather short, which I thought was a pity, but during my stay I had plenty of things happen. I was fascinated at the way first George, and then Ron, who took over when George went into the paratroopers, drove "The Greenhouse" in reverse up the narrow alley way I would stop and watch every move when the greenhouse was there waiting to deliver the load from the head office. It was indeed a work of art to see them manoeuvre first this way, and then the other. No artificial aids to help them either. It was just sheer hard work on the part of the driver, and the steering on this 1934-5 Ford was nearly as hard as trying to push an elephant over I would have imagined.

Occasionally I would get a lift as far as Island Road if it was timed right, and I really enjoyed this. Riding in the cab of this "greenhouse" was just like riding in a huge wooden box.

The instruments consisted of a petrol gauge, an oil gauge, and a temperature gauge. The clutch, the foot brake, and the accelerator, the steering wheel, and the hand brake, and that was more or less the lot. Never the less, it was great fun.

George was wounded at Arnham, and I believe was invalided out of the Army, and as far as I know Ron went into the Army not long before I joined the Royal Navy.

They were two very nice lads, and what an introduction into driving they had. I bet they never forgot "The Greenhouse" like quite a few more drivers working at Handsworth Dairies in those War Years.

BEXLEY GROVE, I have quite a reason for remembering that Grove, quite "snappily".

I had been doing the round for some months when one day I went into the Grove. I jumped off the float to deliver to the second house on the right. Up the path I went whistling, placed the order on the step, picked the empties up, and was returning to my vehicle, when suddenly I heard a growl, and felt a sharp pain to my left lower leg. I turned and saw a black Highland Terrier, getting ready for another sample of "Smith Leg". I shouted at him, and threatened him with an empty bottle, which delayed him sufficiently from another attack on me, allowing me enough time to escape through the gate, which I closed securely behind me. Placing the empty bottles onto the pavement, I rolled my trousers up, which revealed quite a deep bite, and it was bleeding profusely. Whilst I was doing this the lady of the house came out, and in quite an haughty way, told me in no uncertain terms, that I should have made sure the dog wasn't about before coming down the path to deliver.

I couldn't believe it, here was me probably dying from this very acute wound, and all she could say was I should have been more careful. I just looked at her, and said nothing. The reason I said nothing was due to sheer ignorance, nothing else, I just didn't know how to handle a situation like this.

I hobbled back to the float, which made the bleeding worse, and I thought "Well o can' finish mi roun' like this, but w'at am o ta do?"

Suddenly one of my other customers in the Grove came across to me and asked what was the matter. I briefly explained. She had a look at the wound, and said the best thing for me to do was to go round to the Police Station in Hollyhedge Road, where I would at least get some First Aid treatment. The owner of the dog, had by now disappeared into the house, wanting nothing more to do with the situation I suppose.

I put "Nip's" nose bag on, and he took a sly bite at me, which I thought under the circumstances was to say the least, inappropriate. First the dog, and now my horse, not a very "nice day" up till now.

However I avoided "Nip's" attempt, and he gave me what I thought to be a vicious look then he set about chewing his feed.

I walked round to the Police Station with the blood from the wound now dribbling into my socks~ which was very uncomfortable indeed.

I entered the building through the ornately arched doorway, pushed open the inner door, and went to the desk with the police officer behind it.

"What cun ar do fer yo' then young un?" "Ov bin bit by ya dog Sir, an' o dain' know w'at ta do, an' a lady in the Grove tol' mi ta come 'ere an' let cho 'ave a look arrit"

"Oh she did did she, well come on roun' 'ere mi yold cock sparra an' le's 'ave a look arrit then". I did as I was told, the officer had a quick scan, and then he looked up at me and.said "Yo'll 'ave ta gu up the 'ospital with that young un, it's a bit too bad fer me ta do. 'ang onaminnit an' I'll get cha ra lift up ta 'allam, an' they'll see ta ya, okay". "Ar-r-rokay Sir", I replied, although I wasn't too happy about the hospital at all.

The officer called to someone in the back room, then had a conversation with him. This other officer came out and said "Come on Son, come and 'ave a ride with me in our posh car".

Outside we went into the back yard, where situated in the one corner was a beautiful. "Wolesley Sixteen", highly polished, its black paint gleaming. "Jump in Son, we'll soon "aveya" put right, an' don' worry, I'll wert fer ya'".

The only thing to mar the beauty of this wonderful machine was the white lines that were painted around the mudguards, and the hub caps, which of course was the War time regulations. The masks over the large headlights didn't look right somehow it looked as though they were going to a Halloween party. But other than these two items the "Wolesley" looked absolutely wonderful.

I climbed into the passenger seat as per the officer's instructions, and oh! the smell of leather, mixed with the lingering aroma of cigarette smoke, and other lovely aromas, which I couldn't put a name to right then. This was like a dream come true, I could have done without the pain in my leg, but then I wouldn't have had the chance to ride in this wonderful motor car, so I didn't worry too much about the dog bite.

We drove out of the yard, turned right into Hollyhedge Road, then went in a straight line up All Saints' Street, Church Vale, and finally into Hallam Street.

The driver steered us right into the main gates of the hospital, and then pulled up outside the casualty department. "'ang on thaya ra minnit Son" he said, and then disappeared inside the building. I looked around the inside of the car whilst the policeman was doing whatever he went in to do. The interior of the vehicle was as immaculate as the outside. The headlining was spotlessly white, the leather upholstery was polished squeaky bright, and the dashboard was so bright you could see your face in it. "God", I thought "O wunda if I'll eva 'ave a car like this?"

"Come on Son, ov fixed ev'rythin' up fer ya', yo' cun gu strert in, an' getcha leg done, an' then o cun tek ya' right back ta the stershun okay?" "Thankseva sa much Sir". and with that I climbed out of the car and followed him into the casualty. "So this is the young man that's been fighting the Scots", said the very stern looking lady, in the smart deep blue uniform. She looked pretty in a funny kind of way. It's rather hard to describe her. She wasn't Betty Grable, or Alice Faye, pretty, but there was definitely something. Perhaps it was the wonderful starched hat that was perched at a slight angle on top of beautiful brown hair, perhaps the whiteness of her even teeth, when she smiled after her obvious pun about "The Scots". The twinkle in her large brown eyes, or the way she spoke, which was definitely not "Brummagem" or "Black Country". There was a definite accent, but I couldn't put a name to it, but then why should I be able to? I mean

57

where had I travelled to, other than Barnt Green with the scouts on a Sunday school trip, and then that wonderful day I had had with "Jack Pittaway" at Atcham.

This lady had a perfect figure beneath the white starched apron she wore, and I was fascinated by the badges she wore on her left breast, and the silver chain with a watch at the end of it. I'm afraid this was just another lady I had fallen in love with and like always, this was indeed the real thing.

The policeman went outside. "Couldn't stan' the sight o' blood" I thought.

Mind you I wasn't feeling too happy about the situation myself, but I was a man now and I couldn't really show this fear could I?

"Over there you go my love, and sit in the chair". This was my lovely nurse again. I went over to the huge wooden chair, with different gadgets on it. It looked for all the world what I would have imagined an "electric chair" would have looked like. I did as I was told, and made myself comfortable, with both my hands in front of me, clasping them tightly, in anticipation of things to come?

Eventually she came across to me with a tray, and placed it on the trolley alongside the chair. The tray was covered with a spotless white towel so I could not see what lay beneath, but never the less, I imagined all kinds of instruments of torture, which this lovely looking lady would no doubt have pleasure in inflicting on me.

She first raised a flat piece of wood from the chair which stretched out like a thin cricket bat, and this she secured with some device. "Put your leg up here Son", she said. I did this, and then she rolled my trouser leg up, and commenced to clean the wound with something, which was cold, and it stung a little, well, that's what I thought anyway. It was "Cetramide" I found out much later. When she had completed this, the wound did not appear to be too serious after all. The nurse then applied something else and this time it was not imagination, it really did sting, and I jumped. "Alright my love, it will soon be over, and then we can wrap it up, and and you can go back to work". It wasn't over soon however, it seemed to go on for ever, and the stinging got worse, although to be fair after the initial feeling, it wasn't too bad. Finally she bandaged it up carefully, and said "That's it my love, you're all done. Now if you have any trouble, just come back to casualty, and bring this card with you, then we'll be able to see what was wrong with you immediately, saving time looking around for what you had done in the first place. Also trying to find out the treatment etc, so don't lose this card will you?" "Nah-h-h o wunt maam, o wunt lose it, 'onist an' thank ya' fer w'at chave done, tarrar now". "Bye bye love", she said "and take care won't you?". "O will maam thank ya'".

I went outside to find the policeman enjoying a "fag" with one of the hospital porters. He saw me and said O wunt be ya minnit Son, I'll jus' finish this, an' then we'll be yon owa way okay?" "Ar-r-rokay Sir".

He threw his "nub end" to the floor and stamped on it, finally said his goodbye to whomever he had been chatting to, and then came over to the car where I was standing.

"Yo' could a gorrin the car Son, o dain' mean ya' ta stand out 'ere, still neva mind it's a bit lert fer that now innit?" "It don' marra Sir", I replied, "o wuz quite 'appy standin' ourr'ere".

58

I got into the car, the officer got in the other side, started the motor, and in no time we were speeding back to Hollyhedge Road Police Station. I went back into the building with him, and then he handed me over to another officer who said he would have to take down what had happened.

We went through this routine, and on completion I signed the document. The officer said that I could go. Going out of the room, the officer who had driven me to the hospital was standing smoking another "fag". I thought there must be something in this smoking "lark", everybody seems to be enjoying doing it, I'll have to try it one of these times and find out for myself.

"Tarrar Son, an' mind 'ow ya'gu ferra bit, cuz it'll feel a bit funny ferra time, 'avin' 'ad ya' leg cauterised, okay?" "Ar-r-rokay Sir, an' tarra", I replied. I would have liked to have asked him what "cauterised" meant, but I didn't want to appear ignorant, so I just assumed it was something very special. What a tale I would be able to tell everyone when I got back to 228.

Back into Bexley Grove I went, and was just about to take "Nip's" nose bag off when I felt another sharp pain to my left lower leg. First of all I thought it was something to do with the "cauterisation" the officer had warned me about. When I looked down, and with "Nip" trying to take a lump out of my arm, for taking his grub away from him, I saw my friend "The Highland Terrier" at my feet again, trying his hardest to finish off my left leg, presumably before starting on my right!

I let out a wild yell, and put my boot up the dogs a..e, and he went off shrieking through the open gate, and back into his house.

I lifted my trouser leg cautiously, hoping against hope that he had not made it two in a row, but of course that was too much to hope for.

The second wound was larger than the first, and looked worse in all aspects, with blood starting to flow freely down my leg once more.

I thought to myself "W'atthebleedin 'ell am o gunna do now, o bet them coppas 'll think om a bloody right 'un, gerrin bit by the serm dog". I stood there not knowing quite what to do. I could ignore the whole thing, and carry on with my round, but dismissed this idea remembering what the policeman had said to me when I left the station earlier to look after the wound carefully.

Finally I decided that I had better go back to the police and let them sort it out. Although the lady's dog had bitten me twice I really didn't want to cause any trouble. So in order to evade making my brain work overtime, which I might add it wouldn't have withstood anyway, I decided finally to go back to the "cop shop".

I put Nip's nose bag on again, and then I retraced my steps to Hollyhedge Road once more.

"'allo Son, whats ya' trouble, ya' fergot summat then?" This was the officer I had seen on my first visit speaking. I just stood there not knowing quite how to explain my dilemma. "Come on Son, I ain't gorr all day ya' know, o gorra thousan' things ta do, so tell mi w'ats troublin' ya then?".

Suddenly I blurted out "That bleedin' dog's bit mi yagen, an' on the serm leg too".

"Do w'at?" the dumfounded policeman said. "That dog's gone an' bit mi yagen".

"Right, yo come with me Son, an' we'll get this lot sorted out, and smart too".

With that he took me back into the room where I had made my statement. I found the driver sat down having yet another "fag". I thought I really must try these things, for the second time that day.

"'allo Son, watcha fergot?" he said with the cigarette still in his mouth.

Before I could say anything however, the other officer interrupted "That bleedin' dogs bit tim agen, gu on Son an' show 'im" I rolled my trouser leg up revealing the second, and more acute wound. "Well one thing's fer sure Son, yo'll ave ta gu up the orspital agen, yo' can't gu on like this". He stood up, and moved around the table, saying to the first officer "Send someone round to the Grove, the numbers on the lad's statement, and see the owna of the dog, we'd berra get this lot sorted out." "I'll tek the lad back up ta the 'orspital, an' wi' them bein' so busy, o don' think they're gunna like this very much, okay Fred? "Ar-r-rokay Abe, I'll get somebody on that straigh'raway."

With that he went out of the room, and the other officer said "Come on Son, let's gu back up the 'orspital then."

" Well, well, well, I thought you liked me a bit Son, but to come and see me twice in one day, you must have it real bad. "The officer had taken me right into casualty this time, and stayed with me. I didn't reply to this joking statement the nurse put over to me, but the officer did.

"O'm so sorry about this Sister" he started in a very apologetic way " burr I yad ta bring the lad back ta ye', accordin' ta 'im the serm dog's bit 'im agen."

"Oh dear you are in the war's aren't you Son?", and she smiled when she said this to me in a very charming manner. Then she said to the officer "I hope something is going to be done about this, because I'm going to have to make out a report out on the matter, but never mind that at the moment, I'll be in touch with the station later."

"Yes Sister, I'll inform the duty sargent about tit, we'll o'll letcha gerron with watcha gorra do then", and then he turned to me "o'll bi in the serm plerce Son thatcha found mi earlier w'en yome ready, okay?" "Ar-r-rokay Sir."

"Come on then my love, I think you know what to do don't you?" I was a little cautious in my answer, due to the fact that I now knew that she was indeed a Sister, a most formidable high standing lady to "an' 'ockley ite" like me. Just Imagine I had been calling her "nurse", and here she was a "SISTER!"

I mumbled "Yus maam" and went across to the wooden chair for the second time in no more than an hour.

She repeated the treatment as before, but this time she put a huge bandage over the whole of the injuries.

I looked at her on completion of this treatment, and thanked her. She stared at me for a moment, with what I thought a curious look, as if momentarily she was in some type of trance. Suddenly she said "That's alright my love, it was a pleasure, well not a pleasure in the sense of happiness, but more that I liked making things better for you, although it should never have happened again. Does it feel comfortable then love?"

I looked up at her and saw sadness in her eyes, and to be quite honest I really didn't see why she should be sad. Of course I realised later that it could have been several things that had caused her to feel that way. The pity she felt for the way the dog had bitten me twice, or the fact that I probably looked old enough to be going into the services, or perhaps I reminded her of some loved one who was already in the services and had been away for some time. Of course I hadn't the sense, or know how to approach this very loving, caring, lady on the sadness which showed so evidently, that even a young lad like myself spotted a mile off.

"Yus Sista, it feels lov'ly, it's almost as if I yadn't gorreny thin' rung wi' me, thanks eva sa much, an' I yope o don' botha yarragen 'onist o do" "Off you go then love, and mind how you go, bye, bye." "T'rrar, Sista, an' thank ya'."

I went out into the area outside casualty, and saw the officer with another "fag" in his mouth. We went through the same motions as before, he finished his smoke, and then drove me back to Hollyhedge Road Police Station, where I made another statement out and signed it again.

On my return to Bexley Grove for the second time that day I found a police car outside the house where the dog lived. The gate was locked, and so was the front door.

"I went to "Nip", and removed his nose bag, which of course was empty by this time, so I filled it up again from the sack of feed on the float. He did have a quick bite at me, but again I was too quick for him, and gave him a light tap on his nose.

Having delivered the rest of my customers milk in the Grove, I went on my way to complete the round, realising I should have to get a move on to catch up with the time a little.

I never returned to the hospital, or the police station. "Our Mom" washed the bandages, and looked after the two bites, which healed quite quickly, although I did experience a lot of stiffness to the leg for a period after that, but fussiness wasn't in our way of life in those times.

The lady from Bexley Grove never paid me on a Saturday as was the usual thing for her to do, it was always her husband that came to the door. He was quite nice however, but the incident was never mentioned. I did hear the dog barking on a few occasions, but I never saw him, or her, loose in the street after that.

I reflected on the whole incident, when things had died down a little, and thought to myself that it was a twice <u>snappy</u> incident, which had a certain amount of <u>bite</u> to it's conclusion.

It was towards Christmas 1943 when I came home from work. I had long ago accepted the fact that I was a MAN in every respect, well to myself that is, what other people thought was their business. Well, I was doing a man's job wasn't I?. Oh! I wasn't getting a mans wages I grant you, but the "Whites" had made it quite clear to us young men that they couldn't, not wouldn't pay us anymore due to "The Government Orders" through "The Ministry of Works." That didn't stop them reprimanding us if our week end statements showed us to be 2/6d short though, and reminding us of our responsibilities. Although they didn't appear to want to say anything if we came 4/7d over on our weeks takings, that would sort itself out in the long run. I was very quick on the up take regarding this situation however, and I used to keep a very acute account of shorts and overs, so that if ever Harold called me in about a short I was able to show him my accounts over past weeks. So he used to smile, and say "Go on young Smudger, you'll do fine."

It was in fact a Sunday when I arrived home, and as usual everyone had had their dinner, and gone about their various activities for the afternoon. I went into 228, and was about to rush into the back to light the stove for my dinner, when I saw Dad sat in Mom's chair. This was an unusual thing, for he was normally in bed, after his session down at "The Turk", pending his nights work at Rowlands.

I stopped dead in my tracks, and thought what have I done, although I knew I hadn't been up to anything, must have been my devious mind. "W'arrow Dad, w'atchow doin' up like this then?" "Oh!!, it's soright Son, yer Mom's gone on up, burr I'd gorra see ya' ra about summat, so I 'ung on 'til ya' come 'um" " Shall o gu an' put mi dinna ron fust Dad, cuz om starvin'?" "Nah-h-h it wunt tek a minnit Ronnie o on'y wanna ask yarra ferva, an' if ya' say no, it wunt marra" "Ar-r-rokay Dad w'at cun o do fer ya'?" " Well it ain't w 'at yo' cun do fer me Son, it's warr I would like ya' ta do fer somebody else." He smiled at me, and reached into his "ganzi" pocket, and withdrew his Gold Flake, and I thought "Bleedin' 'ell 'e's gonna roffa me ya bloody fag 'e is", but I didn't say anything. He didn't however offer me a cigarette, he took one from the packet, replaced it back into his ganzi pocket, and then picked a box of Swan Vestas up from the table, selected a match, and struck it on the sandpaper. It burst into flame, and he lit his "fag". I watched as he sucked in the smoke from the "white stick", and drew it deep into his lungs. He seemed as though he had gone into a trance momentarily, he didn't say anything. His head dropped backwards, and he stared at the fly bedecked ceiling, it was as though he wasn't here, he was away somewhere on his own, with all his worries forgotten, he was very much at peace with the world. I again thought very seriously about taking this smoking up, it seemed to be very satisfying to everyone that did it

Suddenly his head came back to the normal position, and he took another deep "drag on 'is fag", but this time it caused a bit of coughing and spluttering. I still never said a word. When this spasm of coughing had finished, he got his handkerchief out and wiped his eyes, which had started to water more than usual. When he had dried them sufficiently, he looked at me and said "That's bleedin' berra Son, now o cun think strert." "Now w'at wuz o sayin' ter ya' Ronnie?" "Yo' wuz sayin' thatcha wan' mi ta do summat fer somebody, a friend ov yowas o think." "Ar-r-r tha's right Son, do yo' remember Bob the Supervisa down at Rowlan's, yo' know 'im as allis wears a trilby?" " Ar-r-rre allis 'mindid me yov 'umphrey Bogart 'e did" " Tha's 'im Son yo've gorrim, tha's the bloke, om glad yove 'membered 'im cuz it'll mek it easier warrime gunna ask ya' oright?" "Ar-r-rit's oright wi 'me Dad yo' know that", but I thought "Come on Dad an' gerrit out, om bleedin' 'ungry I yam, an' if we stay 'ere much lunga, it'll bi bloody suppa time, an' then o wunt need two bloody plates, cuz o cun 'ave mi dinna, an' mi bubble an' squeak all on the serm plert."

"Well Son as ya' know it's gerrin near ta Christmas, an' Bob an' me wuz talkin' down the booza the otha night, an' 'e wuz tellin' me tharrit wuz 'an' 'ells time ov gerrin' some toys ferris "gran'children, an' o could un'erstan' 'is concern ova the marra tryin' ta think ov a way o could 'elp 'im." "O thought abourrit w'ile we wuz 'avin' a drink or two", my immediate thoughts on that statement were, " Yo' mean ten or twelve Dad" "Then it suddenly come ta mi, o remembered them toys o yowan up in the attic, an' o thought o wonda if our Ronnie wants them anymowa." " Any road up o said ta Bob, o think owa Ronnie's gorra few things that might bi ov use ta ya' Bob, burr I'll atta arsk 'im fust." " o course Son 'e wuz ova joyed at warride told 'im, an' 'e's arst mi ta arsk yo' if yo'll sell 'em to 'im, so watcha think then?" " Ar-r-ro s'ppose 'e cun 'ave 'em Dad, cuz om too old now ta play we 'em, o mean om growed up now, so gu on an' tell Bob 'e cun buy 'em fer 'is Gran'kids."

"Ar-r-rokay Ronnie, o'll tell 'im in the mornin' w'en 'e comesta work, an' o'll tell ya' w'en 'e's comin' ta pick 'em up" "Ar-rokay Dad."

With that Dad went upstairs to bed, and I went through the usual routine of getting my dinner ready.

Dad left a message with "Our Mom" on the Tuesday telling me Bob was coming on the Wednesday night to pick the toys up. So off up the attic I went and looked around to see what I could sort out for the "young uns."

I arrived up in this sparse room in the early afternoon, looked at the whitewashed walls, well I say whitewashed, it looked to be a dull grey, so God knows when the last coat had been applied, and it certainly wasn't applied by any of "The Smith" family. The wooden floorboards were bare and dusty, and gave off an indescribable odour, not unpleasant, but still indescribable. I looked up through the dirty skylight and noted that night time was fast approaching, although it was only mid afternoon. The sky looked laden with snow, it was so dark and grey, which caused me to shudder momentarily as though this grey foreboding sky had penetrated into the room itself, and surrounded me with it's coldness. At that moment I thought "We ain' 'nalf gunna 'ave a bleedin' showa of snow soon" "Mind you I was still at the age when this thrilled me in all it;s aspects. It was just another thrill to me in a rather monotonous world.

Casting an eye over the toys I had collected over a few years, brought memories flooding back to me. I fondled my "Carter Patterson" metal truck, and thought about the money I had installed in the rear of it. I found myself opening the rear doors of the huge metal toy, just to check if there was any cash I had left in there. Of course there wasn't, which brought a smile to to my lips, thinking to myself " Ya' silly sod, yome much too bleedin' cute to 'ave left any munnee in thaya, arta the ten bob fiasco."

I thought about that incident momentarily, and although it didn't alter my original thoughts, I did have further ideas regarding "Our Mom's" motives for doing what could only be described by an outsider as a terrible thing. My ideas were that Mom must have been in a real pickle to have done such a thing, and she must have been beside herself with worry. I've no doubt that her original intention of paying me back was real, but it never materialised I suppose that the longer it went on, the further she put it to the back of her mind. Still the main thoughts on this matter were long gone, and in a funny way I now felt so sorry for Mom.

I picked up some of "The Minic" and "Dinky" cars, vans, lorries, and buses, and fondled them with the care of a cat looking after her young kittens. My thoughts went back to "Norton's" on the corner of Icknield Street and Key Hill where I had bought most of these vehicles with money I had saved from my various part time jobs. The time I had saved so hard to buy "The Minic Bus", which was indeed one of my most treasured toys. Week after week went by, with temptation running wild, to buy other things, and then when I had got the 7/11d necessary to purchase this love of my life, how I had gone up to Norton's, praying to God that they had got one left in stock.

The vast thrill when the lady dressed in her immaculate black dress, white blouse with the collar just peeping over the edge of the top of the dress, told me "Yes young fella, we have got one or two left." How I kept going up to the attic to see it, and sometimes play with it, after laying out all the "Dinky" cardboard pavements, traffic signals, street signs etc. Oh the thrill of it all, I was so happy alone with all these wonderful things.

I opened the large red box, the original box I had bought from "Woolworth's" on the "Flat". I took out the train, still immaculate from it's cradle of tissue paper, put the key onto the piece of metal protruding from the chassis of this lovely metal toy, and started to wind it up. On completion of this I moved the little lever just adjacent to the drivers cab, and the the motor whirred into life. Letting it run down I replaced it back into the box alongside the tender, carriage, signal, and metal lines.

All this for "a tanna" from the wonderful 3d to 6d stores.

What was I to give Bob then, which of the toys should I retain. God it was a hard decision to make. I had taken two paper carriers up with me, as well as a herden carrier, which had got a few holes in. I soon overcame this difficulty however all I did was, like Dad used to do for my boots when they had got holes in them, I "Bunged a birra perpa in it."

The paper carriers, one from "Blackwell's" in Hunters Road, and the other from "Cockram's" next door to "Izons" on "The Brook", I thought I would put the smaller toys into, and the larger ones I would put into the herden bag, which had the name of "Spencers" on it. They were fruit and veg merchants "On The Flat."

I stared hard at all the toys on the large shelf, I couldn't make my mind up. I again looked up through the sky light, hoping some kind of inspiration would descend from up there, but all I saw was the grey sky getting darker, and the first of the snow flakes falling gently. I thought hard about the kids that were going to open their eyes on "Christmas Morning" and see all the presents "Father Christmas" had brought them. The cars' vans, lorries, buses, trams, the train set, all the pavements, signals, and figures of people going with them. The huge metal "Carter Patterson" lorry which had brought me such a lot of happiness. I gave a deep sigh, I had at last come to a decision " I WOULD GIVE THEM EVERYTHING." Well I wouldn't exactly give them everything, for I intended to ask Bob for a pound. I mean I didn't know what value to put on these toys, I don't really think I could put a value on them. They had brought me a great deal of happiness, and now they could bring some "otha kids" a further amount of happiness.

So I started to put the toys into their respective bags. Most of these were still in their original cardboard cartons, so no problem there.

By the time I had loaded them up ready for me to take downstairs for Bob to pick up the following night, it was nearly dark. A last look to the sky light revealed to me that it was now snowing really hard, for the glass was now covered in a white blanket.

I gathered the three bags up' but I had to leave the big metal lorry, for it would have been too much to carry, and off I went carefully back down the stairs to the middle room.

"Our Mom" was out back, and the three "little uns, Ginge, Dot, an' the Babby" were playing in front of the roaring fire. As usual the cat and dog were in their normal position, nearly up the fire.

"Watcha gorrin the bags", a question from "Dot", "Mindyarrow bleedin' bizniss" a no nonsense answer from me. "I'll tell our mom yome swearin' an' she'll geyarra belt up the earole, so there" " Yo' cun tell w'atcha want, an' om too big ta 'ave a bang up the earole any road up, so shut ya' gob then." "Gu on our Ron tell us w'atcha gorrin the bags then please-e-e." I thought about the "bang up the earole" and the prospect of it happening wasn't that remote, for "Our Mom" could still move a bit sharpish. I've no doubt she could still hit as hard, so I decided that I would tell "Doss" what she wanted to know. She would probably have found out any way, because it was my intention to put these bags into the cupboard below the "food cupboard", and of course all she had got to do was wait until I was out and she could have a "nose" for herself.

I took the bags over to them in front of the fire, and took out the contents, which all three of them viewed. After a while they lost interest in my prize collection, saying "Warra lorra bloody rubbish", and then returned to the game that they had been playing. Of course I was most indignant at this remark, but I didn't say anything, I thought "Bloody kids, wadda they know."

I opened the bottom cupboard, and started to pull out all kinds of old boots and shoes, most of them long passed repair, old tins with all kinds of things in them. This of course renewed the three girls interest, and in no time at all they were helping?

What a mess we made of things, and who should arrive on the scene right at that very moment?, you're right "Our Mom."

"W'at the bleedin' 'ell's guin' on 'ere yo' lot, get that bleedin' lot back in the cu'board, an' bi quick abourit, else there'll be ya bleedin' whalin' fer rall on ya', now come an' bi quick abourit." "O wuz on'y..." "Yo' cun shurrit ferra start orff, o berrit wuz yo' that purrem up to it." A quick answer to me, and one which I didn't have the courage to retaliate to. The three "little uns" started tittering at this, remembering what "Doss" had said earlier about Mom being able to give me "a bang up the earole." An' yo' lot cun pack tharrin, else there'll bi a few tanned arses guin' round, come on an. purrall these things away." Mom interrupted pointing to the various things that girls had been playing with when I had entered the room originally.

" Mom "I ventured cautiously "is it toright if o put these things fer Dad's mate in the cu'board, jus' fer tonight, till 'e picks 'em up tamarra?" "Ar-r-r yo' cun purr 'em in thaya, cuz ov already 'ad a word with ya' Dad, an' 'e's tol' mi yor'll aboaritt, but mind ya' purr ev'rythin' back tidy wuntcha?" "Ar-r-ro course o will Mom, w'en I purrit all back it'll bi tidier than it wuz befowa o emptied it." "An' less o ya' bleedin' cheek an' all, yo' still ain' ta big ta 'ave yarr arse tanned now ya' know" More giggling from the three "little uns", and a swift reprimand from Mom caused it to cease.

I went back up the stairs to the attic, it was now of course pitch black, so I had to feel my way up, and then when I arrived I had to feel my way around for the big metal lorry. I finally found it, and I was glad to return to the light and warmth of the middle room. I stowed everything away and closed the cupboard doors, and felt completely satisfied with the whole operation.

On the Wednesday night I was sat doing a cartoon in colour when Dad arrived back from "Rowlands" with Bob. I had taken up painting again, after a long period of time, had lapsed, mainly due to the fact that I couldn't get any water colours. As luck would have it however, someone in the street had brought a tin of "Reeves Watercolours" over to "Our Mom" and told her to give them to me, because they were no longer needed by whoever had been using them. The paints themselves had hardly been used, and I was very happy about that, but I'm afraid my enthusiasm for painting right then wasn't exactly at a premium.

Anyway when I had got settled into my new job with "Handsworth Dairies" and had got used to the idea of being a fully fledged roundsman, I now found that I did have a bit of time on my hands, so I took up painting. It was cartoons I was into at the moment, especially cartoons with shapely "topless" girls (naughty Ronnie.)

"'ello Son, ya' know Bob don' ya'?" I stood up and went over to Bob, and shook hands (well all men do this don't they?). "'ello Sir" I said, not forgetting my manners, "'ello young Ronnie, blimey yo've grown a bit since o last sin ya yo'll soon bi big enough to gu in the army, 'ow old am ya' now Son?" "Om Fifteen, burr I'll bi Sixteen in January." "Ar-r-r well they wun' 'ave ya' fer ra w'ile yet will they, but blimey yo' look big enough, an' old enough." "Would ya' like a cuppa tea love?" our Mom joined in, and by the look of her face she didn't like the conversation much.

"Ar-r-r thanks Mrs Smith, o could do wi' one, it's brass monkees out thay, an' it's jus' started to snow again, we slipped in the van once or twice comin' from the bak'ry din" we Artha?" "Ar-r-r it wuz a birr 'ard guin' I'll grant ya' Bob."

Mom poured Bob a cup of tea out, I went across to the cupboard, and got all the bags out. Having done this I returned to the opposite side of the table, and took some of the items out to show Bob. He looked these items over, in between drinking his tea, and according to the look on his face he was highly delighted. I took a few more toys out of the bags, and Bob said "These am just great Ronnie, God the kids'll bi yappy with these I'm sure." Then I went and got the "Carter Patterson" lorry out, and said "This guz with 'em as well Bob, an' the train set," "Well Son" he went on "Ov gorra ask ya' afowa ya' gu on any mowa, 'ow much d' ya' want fer rall this lot?"

I really hadn't anticipated talking of money in front of Mom and Dad, but then what option had I? With my head lowered, and embarrassment rising, which of course made me start to sweat, I couldn't find the words to say, when "Our Dad" interrupted the silence. "Well o thought yowed come to a decision larst night our Ronnie, dain' yo' tell mi a quid fer the lot?" All of a sudden my mind had been made up for me, for I must admit I had started to weaken, and thought that a pound might be too much. "Well if that's alright with Bob, it's sall right wi' me, a quid then, fer the lot mindja."

"Blimey Ronnie, that's a bloomin' bargin, an' no doubt's abourrit, the gran kids'll bi yova the moon wi' this lot I cun tell ya', thanks eve sa much, yome a good lad Son, an' yove med mar gran kids 'appy this Christmas tha's fer sure."

Bob reached into his inside pocket and drew out his wallet. From this he took a pound note, which he handed to me, and then he thanked me again.

He finished his tea, and then turned to Dad and said "come on then Artha, I'll drive ya' back ta the berkry, an' then I'll tek these round 'um', an' w'en ov parked the van up in the yard' I'll come down to the (and he mentioned the pub, situated on the corner of New John Street and Aston Road) an' 'ave a couple of pint's with ya' okay?"

" Ar-r-rokay Bob, o cun leave mi fust 'and fer ra w'ile, so tharr'll bi fine."

They departed into the snow outside, which by this time was falling heavily, I followed them outside, heard Bob start the "Morris Commercial" one ton box van up, turn it round, and then off they went into the heavy falling snow back to Rowlands a couple of miles further up from 228.

"Our Mom " didn't say anything about the pound I had received off Bob, but she did give me some queer looks, and then made references about how short she was, and didn't know how she was going to make ends meet this week. I'm afraid it all fell on deaf ears, for I had made up my mind what I was going to do with the money I'd had off Bob. I was going to "Hockley Post Office" up Hockley Hill tomorrow when I came home from work, to buy my first "National Savings Certificate" for 15/-, and the other five bob I was going to spend on myself. I thought "Yo' cun gu on all ya' like our Mom, but yo' ain't 'avin' any o this, not on ya' bloody Nellie yo' ain't. That is exactly what I did with the pound that Bob had given me for the whole "caboodle" of toys with Mom having no temptation put in her way for a repeat of the " 10/- incident."

Not long after the Christmas of 1943, about the end of January, beginning of February, I pulled "Nip" up in Caldwell Street to deliver, when a lady with a baby in her arms approached me. It wasn't one of my customers, so I was naturally a little on my guard. "Excuse me love" she started "o wunda if yo' would 'elp me?" "Ar-r-rif o can lady " "Well o live at the back o the fish an' chip shop, an' ov gonnan lef' mi key in the 'ouse, o wonda if yo' could come an' 'ave a look, an' seef yo' cun open it some 'o please? " "Ar-r-rokay love "I replied" om sure I'll bi yable ta do summat fer ya' "

Well I was sixteen now, and some of my mates had told me I could pass for nineteen easily, well they must have been right, because I didn't have any trouble getting into the picture houses when there was an "A" film, and in some cases when there was an "X" film on. So with the confidence of being a MAN I strode down the entry in between the fish and chip shop, and the greengrocers to open this lady's door for her, I intended to prove to this lady that she was indeed dealing with a MAN and not a boy, in case she had got any ideas on that subject.

On reaching the bottom of the entry she turned to the right, and entered through the dilapidated wooden gate. Right in front of us was a low building, much like the "brewhouse" we had in the yard at 2/24 Guest Street. This of course was the kitchen to the main building. It had a metal framed small windowed casement, and the glass didn't look as though it had been cleaned in "onks", still that was nothing to do with me. Alongside this window casement was a small wooden door, with a "Yale" lock in it. The lady turned to me and said "This is the one love, d' ya' think ya' cun do anythin' with it?" I went round her to the door and although I hadn't a clue about these things I tried to look most professional. I poked and prodded, and pulled and shoved. I looked first up at it, and then down at it, and I hadn't got a bloody clue what I was looking at, or what for. Finally when I had run out of "whoos" and "ahs", I turned round to the lady and said, "Nah om sorry love, o can' do anythin with it, yo'll 'ave ta get someone with some idea rabout these things, sorry love."

" O-o-o-o don' leave mi love, ov gorra gerrin, mi bleedin' 'usband 'll kill me if 'e comes um' an' fin's of locked mi bloody self out, can' ya' push it open or summat please love, please?" I was to find out later that it wasn't her husband at all, for he was away in one of the services, but that's "tittle tattle" from the local "gasbags", and I wasn't particularly interested anyway.

"Well as long as you don' mind love" I said, flexing my muscles for the oncoming battle with this wooden door. "Nah anythin's berra than bein' out 'ere in the bleedin' cold" she replied. There was a complete change in her attitude now, to when she first approached me about this situation, and although my years were tender, my brain certainly wasn't. She had been rather servile when she first saw me, but now she was almost bordering on arrogance. First I pushed the door in a series of short blows.

It gave way a little but not enough. I tried a little harder, nothing. Then I walked back a short way, and tried a run at the door, but still nothing. I looked at the lady and apologised once again, and her reply…, "W'at a big strappin' lad like yo' can' even open a bleedin' thin little dowa like this. Bloody 'ell w'at d' they mek men owra now, titty bottle slops. Gu on ge it a good bash, an' get the bleedin' thing open fer me, an' mi babby, 'e's bleedin' freezin' ta death 'ere. Gu on ge it a good un." "Okay love" I answered, thinking to myself," she ain't much of a lady this one" "as lung as yo' don' mind o don' mind gein' it a bash, so yo' stand clear."

With this I strode back as far as I could, and braced myself for this onslaught on the door. I tensed myself up, and faced my right shoulder forwards, and commenced my run up. I hit the door and there was an horrendous cracking sound. The door gave way, and I went careering on into the interior of the building. Finally I hit a cabinet of some sort on the opposite wall, which had bottles, crocks, and jars of all sorts on it. I fell to the side of this cabinet after hitting it with a tremendous amount of force, and landed on my "arse." I lay there for a couple of seconds, and watched in fascination, as this huge cabinet swayed slowly, very slowly away from me. I watched in awe, but couldn't bring my reflexes into action quick enough to prevent what was in the process of happening, so I just burst out into a fit of laughter.

The cabinet continued it's course of falling, but like a film that had been slowed down, so was the rate of it's progress The lady was trying to get into the room through the split I had made, without too much success, and I couldn't move off the floor for laughing.

Finally the cabinet hit the deck with a deafening thump, and the two drawers it held spilt out all over the floor, with their contents doing the same.

"Ya' bloody fool why dain'tcha bleedin' well do somethin' ta stop it, look at all the bleedin' mess yove caused me." "O donno warrime gunna say w'en miyusband comes 'um'." "Don' jus' lie thaya, gerrup an' gimme a bleedin' 'and ta lift this thing up." I stopped laughing due to this outburst, and got to my feet. I went over to the cabinet, and lifted it back into position, and cleared up most of the mess. Then I turned to the lady and said " Well love ov done all o cun for ya', so I'll gerrorif now, an' gu an' finish mi roun'."

She didn't say a word, she just glared at me, and I thought to myself " Om gunna gerrourra 'ere afowa she does summat she might regret, or ri might regret." If looks could have killed I would certainly not be writing this now, and that's for sure.

Mind you I burst out of laughing again on my way back to the float, for on leaving the kitchen I automatically opened the door by the yale lock, and pushed what was left of the door open, to allow my exit. I mean can you imagine it. All that was left of the door was the square frame, and a bit of plywood attached protruding about six to eight inches from it all the way round. Naturally I didn't think of this until I was half way up the entry, I could have walked straight through the split I had made with my "bull like" charge.

That lady never said a word, and I never saw her again, thank God, but I did have another laugh when I reached the top of the entry. The bloke from the Fish and Chip Shop said to me "W'at's 'app'nin' Son, it's funny burr I could a swore someone was breakin' in at the back on us, did yo' see anythin'?" I couldn't believe what he had said, but further more I couldn't believe my answer it was like a shot out of a gun. It was one of those answers you normally think of about two days after the event, and you say to yourself "I wished I'd have thought of that at the time." My reply to this shop owner was " YO' COULD BI RIGHT MATE, I THINK SOMEONE 'AS JUS' BROKE IN." I burst out laughing again when this man went tearing down the entry I suppose to the aid of this not very pleasant lady.

Just after this "break in", I went down Clements Lane and stopped outside a small factory that I served from Monday to Saturday. As usual I went inside with their order in a metal crate, a thing I had done on several occasions before. I used to go just inside the gate to the works. Then on the left hand side was a little office, come reception area, and it was into this place that I delivered the daily milk.

On this occasion however I witnessed a crowd of women, just a little further inside the factory itself. They were in a circle, and seemed to be doing something to an object on the floor. What was really funny however, was they seemed to be having the time of their lives. They were laughing, and I could hear some of the shouting going on from where I stood. "Gu on Alice ge 'im so mowa" 'e ain't gorreny unda that bit thaya" " Don' ferget ta ge 'is bum a load as well Cornice" "Yo' come an' 'ave a gu, yo' ain' 'ad ya' bloody turn yet" "Come an' 'ave a look young un it might bi small now, burrit wunt allis bi small, an' it's w'en it's gruesome thats w'en ya' gorra watch out, cuz w'en it's gruesome, tha' s w'en ya' trouble starts", a burst of laughter at this comment.

I went to move closer to the scene to investigate what was going on, but the gentleman that I usually had the money off on a Saturday, came out of the office and stopped me from going over. "Doh yo' gu ova thaya Son, else them wenches 'll 'ave yo' down as well the way they'm feelin' terday, yo' jus' come in 'ere, an' wert till they've finish't, come on now." I didn't argue, I went inside the office with the milk and the man turned to one of the three ladies in the office, and said "Gu an' mek the milkmon a cuppa tea Clara, we don' wann 'im guin' out thaya with that mad lotta buggas on the loose do we?" The one whom he had called Clara, said "I don't know how they can be so disgusting to such a young lad, they're animals, that's what they are, what would they do if it was one of their Sons Albert?" "Love, ya' can' stop this kinda thing 'appenin' in a factry, it's all part and parcel of servin' yarra 'prenticeship, they doh mean any 'arm, well, not really they doh, now gu on there's a good wench, an' mek that cuppa tea."

Clara did as she was told, and went off into another room, and the gentleman bade me to sit down.

The tea was brought, with a couple of home made cakes as well. "Gu on get them down yarr 'odge Son, big chap like yo' should be erble ta manage them." I did as I was told. Whilst munching the first of the cakes I asked the gentleman what was going on outside, and why didn't anybody try to intervene. " It's very difficult fer mi ta' tell ya' Son, but w'arrit 'mount's ta, is w'at's called tradichon, it's allis bin done, an' it'll probably allis be done." "W'en a young kid start's orff 'is life in a fact'ry, like thisun, 'e 'as ta gu through this thing thay'm doin' to 'im." "They don' mean any 'arm ta the lad, burrit's summat like w'en a young redskin

69

is gunna be ya brerv, 'e 'as ta gu through certain rigmaroles..." At this point the gentleman looked up in the air trying to sort out the right words to give me an answer.

"Yo' mean 'e's gorra gu an' kill a bear or summat, an' bring back 'is skin, ta show 'is fertha 'e's done it, that kind a thing ya' mean Sir?", I interrupted.

"Yo've gorrit Son, tha's the kind a thing o mean, an' tha's w'at them wenchis is doin' ta that young un out thaya, but tek a werd of warnin' Son, doh yo' gerr intaferrin cuz they'll 'ave yowa trousis orff in two minnits flat they will, an' yo' bein' the big lad yo' am, they'll bi mowa than curious ta know w'at yo' got inside them trousis." With this he burst into laughter, although for the life of me I couldn't really see anything to laugh at.

Never the less I had already decided to take his advice and steer clear of the inside of the factory altogether, for it was a worrying thought to know that WOMEN could behave like that. I mean, to me women were the fair, and weaker sex.

I came out of the office after finishing my tea, looked cautiously to the left making sure there were no women in sight, and fortunately there weren't. The lad they had, in my mind anyway, so brutally abused still lay there in a pile of old oily rags his trousers still around his ankles, and he was crying bitterly. What made me very angry though was the mess his lower abdomen, groin, and "private parts" were in. Every where in that region, and as far as I could see, around the rear of his back, and "bum "was thick black and brown grease. He looked as though he had been dropped into a barrel of the stuff. I felt so sorry for him I thought I've got to go and try to help him, and indeed moved off in that direction, when I felt a hand grip my right shoulder. The voice of the gentleman whispered urgently into my ear "Ov tol' ya' Son leave well alone, yo' jus' gu on ya' way, an' deliva ya' milk, don' try ta 'elp. We'ed all like ta do that, an' most of all me, but don' cuz if ya' do, the poor little bugga r'll 'ave ta gu through it all agen. W'at's mowa, if they cop the one 'elpin' 'im, 'e, or she will gu through the serm thing, so gu on now, an' do yaself a ferva, there's a good lad." With this, he turned me around with very strong hands and guided me to the gateway leading back into Clements Lane. I jumped aboard the float and clicked "Nip" into motion, and mentally thanked God for a narrow escape.

When I delivered the milk to the factory after that I was always in and out like a flash, and on pay day I never lingered at the office door, I just went straight in, and once I received the payment, and my weekly tip, of a "tanna", I always had a look round cautiously to make sure none of those women were about. I even used to alternate the time of delivering, just to make doubly sure.

I did see some of the women on occasions, separately of course, and there would be that "smile", that oh so knowing "smile", and sometimes there would be a comment "'ow ya' guin' mi yold beauty 'e" Aintcha comin' in ferra cup a tea we us then?"

"Come on mi love we wunt 'urt a big chap like yo'", and so many more comments similar to that, but I wasn't having any, 'norra birrove it." I did see the lad quite often as well. As time went on he did become a little "cocky", and gave me a bit of cheek at times, so I thought in the finish, "Well it served ya' right, ya' cheeky little bleeda, they orta rave put some o the bleedin' grease in ya' gob as well." I didn't say anything to him of course, I mean he might have been in league with the women now that he had been initiated into the business. If that was so, he might equally have been trying to tempt me into the factory, for them to commit the same type of treatment that they had dealt out to him, which I've no doubt would have given him a great deal of pleasure, and satisfaction. The only thing I wanted anybody to grease was my palm with silver preferably.

It was round about this time, January, February, or March, 1944, just prior to my re call to "The Head Office, Island Road," due to some vast re zoning of deliveries ordered by "The Ministry of Works" or "The Ministry of Food" or both, that I met up with the new man on "The Midland Counties Dairy", who delivered round the "Whisty" as well as myself and "The Walsall Cooperative" bloke.

The young chap whom I used to see every day suddenly disappeared off the scene, and this new (old) bloke took over his round. I don't know why the young chap went, whether he was called up, went onto another round, or what, but he went.

We exchanged greetings every day, just like roundsmen do. I did ask where the other chap had gone, but he was a little evasive "'ow the bleedin' 'ell should are know, me yold pal, all o know is tharrime bleedin' well stuck with it. W'arra load a bleedin' knockers this lot am, I yave mowa trouble gerrin the money in orff one soddin' street on this round than I yad gerrin the bleedin lorr orff the 'ole of of mi custamers on me yutha round, o'm pissin' well browned orff with the lorronnit. "

I didn't think I could have had a more explicit, down to earth answer than that, although it still didn't tell me what had happened to the other bloke, and what's more after that first outburst, I wasn't too bothered either, so I kept well clear of the subject during further conversations with this angry, disagreeable old bloke.

You can imagine the surprise I received when he came to me in Canterbury Road one day and said "A, Nip der yo' get perd on ya' returns." "Returns? "I answered, quite bewildered, "O don' getcha, watcha mean?" "God Son, yo' bleedin' thick or summat. o thought I'd med niself clear renough, d' ya' get perd fer the em' ty bleedin' bottles yo' tek back ter ya' depot?" "Oh-h-h o see w'atcha mea, w'y dain' ya' bleedin' well say so in the fust plerce, an' then od a soddin' understand ya'."

I was begining to feel my feet a bit, due to the inference of me being thick. "Oh-h don' gerrall stroppy wi' mi, om on'y gunna try an' 'elp yarra bit tha's all, try an' put summat yowa way, tha's all, burr if yo' don' wanna know, then it's alright bi me." He started to walk back to his electric float after this comment, but I shouted after him "Look mert, I ain' bothered one way or the otha, w'atcha got guin', burrif there's summat innit fer me, then there's bound ta bi summat innit fer yo' in tha?"

"If yo' cun afford ta throw tharraway then it's up ter yo' innit?"

He stopped dead in his tracks, turned around and came back to me. At first I thought "Christ I yope 'e ain' gunna belt mi one, fer mi bein' cheeky, cuz o dunno if o could 'andle 'im or not, 'e might bi yold, but Christ look at 'is build."

Still there was nothing I could do about it now, it had already been said, so I just braced myself for whatever was coming. "Yome right Nip" he started "O'm sorry, o shouldna bin too bleedin' 'asty wi' mi shoutin' mi mouth orff, burrit's this bloody round gerrin' mi down, still neva mind about that now."

At this comment I relaxed, and started to get mentally more assured of myself, thinking that I had got the better of this man, but I didn't intend to show it, I thought that caution was the better of two arguments. "Nah-h-h, o don' get perd on the return of empties, w'y do ya' arsk?" "Well our gaffa's started a nu system, an' in it we get perd so much fer rour rempties, so if yo' don' get perd fer yowas…"

At this point, I'd fully grasped the gist of his intentions so I spoke out, determined to refute his earlier statement about me being thick, "…Yo' w'an' mi ta letcha rave somma my empties, an' so mek up yowa rempties, an' then yo' get mowa munnee, tha's great tharris, but w'adda I get?" "O tell ya' w'at, I'll ge ya' five bob fer ev'ry three cersis o' empties yo'll let miyave, 'ow about that then?" "Ar-r-rit suit's mi fine, well d'ya' wan' some terday?" I was a bit short of cash on that particular day, so I thought "I mirras well strike w'ile the iron's 'ot." "Well yo' ain' anythin' short ov a nine bob note am ya' Son?" I thought "Yo' cun gu on old un, om enjoyin' this I yam, yo' apparently ain' met some of us 'ockley ites up till now." "No o ain' mert" I replied "So is it on then, da ya' wan' some empties terday, or don' ya'?"

He tilted his leather satchel and sorted around in it until he found whatever coins he was looking for. He lowered the satchel to it's original position, and then handed me two half crowns." "'ere ya' are" he said "'ere's a dolla, now tell mi w'ere ta pick the empties up from." I told him that I left the first load of empties in Hollyhedge Road by the junction with Thursfield Road, and to take the three cases from there. "Okay Nip" he said, and then went back to his float, and continued on his round. I fondled the two half crowns in my hand, and thought that I was now financially okay until pay day, and it had been so easy really. I finished my round, and then as usual straightened my load up by "The Library" in Beverley Road, before returning to the depot.

I clicked "Nip" on, starting the journey home, and en route pick the other stack of empties up, minus the three crates of course, from Hollyhedge Road. On arrival at the junction with Thursfield Road, I looked at the stack of empty bottles, and thought, "It don' look as though tharrold mon 'as took 'is three crerts. " So the first thing I did was to check them thoroughly, to confirm my thoughts on the matter. No, all the empties were there.

What was I to do?, I could hardly wait until this bloke had finished his round, for I wanted to get home now that I'd finished. I could hardly leave three crates there could I? I mean what if he didn't pick them up, because he could have forgotten that he had to, couldn't he?

I thought about this situation for all of two minutes, and then I mumbled to myself "Sod the silly ol' bugga, I'll purrall the bloody empties onto my cart, an' if he sez anything tommarra, I'll tell 'im tharr I jus' loaded mi cart, an' dain' botha ta count anythin'." So with this thought in mind, I loaded the cart and went merrily on my way.

I didn't see the "Midland Counties" bloke for sometime after that, and when I did catch sight of him in Westminster Road, I went over to him and said " Worrow,'ow ya guin'?" " Ar-r-r not ta bad Son, an' yo'?" I thought to myself "'e don' 'memba anythin' abourrit, 'e's bloody well fergorrall abourrit, 'e 'as, so o'll keep mi gob shut." "O fair ta diddlin, yo' know." We chatted like this for a few minutes, then we said our respective " Tarrarr's ", and he went up Westminster Road, and I went down. The incident, well that remained as empty as the bottles themselves.

I only went to Stone Cross on one personal occasion during my time at Trinity Street depot, and that's when I attended the "Stone Cross Cinema" at the invitation of a new man who had started at Handsworth Dairies on one of the new rounds installed through this re zoning. He lived on the estate at the rear of the cinema. His wife I remember gave me a slap up meal, and after that we went to see "Roger Livesey and Deborah Kerr" in "The Life and Times of Colonel Blimp."

The new re zoning, how did it affect me? It didn't, it was "Handsworth Dairies" that re zoned me. Handsworth Dairies re zoned Ron Smith back to Island Road, because of diminishing manpower. Poor old Charlie Cope was put back onto my round, for the time being they told him??, and Harold Haynes, well he continued to work like he had always done, twenty four hours per day, for eight hours pay. Two very nice men with misguided ideals, and theories.

My return to "Head Office" however was not without it's happiness. First of all I could resume to travel to work on my trusty steed "The Kingsway", and secondly I could renew my friendship with "Horace Willetts." Of course I would have to start to harness my own horse again, but that wasn't too much of a problem. To sum it all up, I wasn't too upset by the transfer back from Trinity Street to Head Office I thought I would get over it, although in all fairness it was a very nice period in my life.

I was to have a great surprise though, about six months later, for they moved the whole depot back to Head Office, and then I had everything, all the friends I had at Island Road plus a bonus, all the friends from Trinity Street. Sadly there was one exception though, and that was Mary Lewis. Ernie told me that she didn't want to travel all the way to Island Road and had consequently gone through the "Ministry of Works" channels, and secured herself a job of vital importance in some official capacity, which proved what I had!said earlier, she looked too good to be a "MILKMAID."

I started back on a Sunday about April 1944, and went to Vic first to see what I'd got to do. He ruffled through some papers until he found a note that Mr Davies had left for him. He told me the round I was designated to do, and then sorted the appropriate book out and handed it to me, "Yo'll find the satchel, an' all the otha stuff 'angin' with the 'arniss in the tack room Ron." he told me. "W'ose comin' wi' me?" I enquired. "Yo' must bi jokin' Ron, we'em that bloody short 'ere ev'ryone o' the checkers are out on roun's, an' there's on'y mi 'ere ta cope wi' this lot, so off ya' gu, yo'll 'ave ta do the best ya' cun okay?"

There wasn't a lot I could say to Vic that would have made any difference, so I just nodded my head and made my way to the stables, leaving him still ruffling through another pile of papers, and not looking too pleased about. things either.

"'iya Ronnie mi yold pal" this was Horace's greeting on seeing me enter Mrs Thomas's tack room. He was in the process of making another cup of tea for her and him. "G wanna cuppa, afowa ya' gu out then?" It was as though I had never left Island Road, this warm hearted greeting from him. It was so natural you would have thought he had just come to work with me that morning, instead of being apart for God knows how many months.

"Ar-r-rocace, thank ya'" and off he went to attend to the tea making "'ello Mrs Thomas, 'ow ya' bin keepin' then?" "Oh not too bad Ronnie, it's nice to see you again after all this time, are you back for good now?" "O don' know, o don' think they do eitha. "I replied, nodding my head towards the opening to the stables indicating the management out there.

"What round are you going to do then?" "O don' know about tha' reitha, all Vic tol' mi wuz ta cum in 'ere, an' od find the satchel, an' every thin' "

"Oh this is what he must have meant then when he came in this morning and told me that a chap was coming in this morning to do a round, and to give him these "and she indicated to all the necessities in a corner of the tack room bench.

"O course Vic wouldn' know w'o it wuz cumin' would 'e, well any road up we know now don' we?"

I went across to where the tackle was, and sorted it out ready to put onto my cart when I found out which one it was.

Whilst waiting for Horace to return with the tea I opened the round book up in an attempt to find out just where about the round they had given~to me was situated.

Inside the front cover I found a piece of paper with all the directions, and necessary comments appertaining to this new round. There was a rough,map to guide me out to the start, and then onwards about the round itself. The comments were very helpful, one example was "Don't serve Cox and Danks and… Foundry today, they are both closed" and another was "All the milk that you have left, don't return it to dairy leave it at Mrs Lees shop, your first customer on the corner of Wood Road and Oldbury Road, and pick it up the next day." There were lots of comments like these, potential "knockers", which customers liked their milk delivered round the back', and which customers to give that extra special treatment to. In fact the whole paper was indeed a mine of information, and I mentally thanked whoever had put it together.

The start of the round didn't bother me too much, because I did have a rough idea of the locality. The map indicated that I should, go past " The Baggies Ground" up to the lights at Beeches Road. Turn left down Roebuck Street down there to the junction with Roebuck Lane. then left again and go the whole length of "The Lane" to it's junction with Oldbury Road.

Turn right and just follow my nose, until I saw "Moyle and Adams" food place on the left, and Wood Street was just a little way past there.

I was quite confident of my bearings when Horace returned with the tea, so I settled down with him and Mrs Thomas to enjoy a quiet drink before starting out on my new venture.

It must have been ten minutes later, just when I was going to "make a start", when this young lady entered the tack room. She had the most beautiful, smiling, friendly face. Hazel eyes, twinkling mischievously, a small dainty nose, full lips, soft, with just a hint of lipstick on them. Brown hair, wavy and hanging just a short way down her back. Her figure was hard to describe but she was not obese, or painfully thin, for she had a heavy coat on. The one thing I did notice was her hat. It was a beaut.

It was red in colour, but it appeared to be an enlarged version of a man's trilby, with the rim at the front dipping well over this girl's gorgeous face.

"Hello Gabrielle?", Mrs Thomas spoke first, and then Horace turned round and said "Worrow Gabe, 'ow ya' guin' then mar lovely?" "Hello Mrs Thomas, Good morning Horace, I hope that you've brushed (and she mentioned her horses name) down well for me?" " Ar-r-r-r yo' know od do anythin' fer yo' don' ya'?" and I noticed a smile appear on his face. This angel of a girl just looked at him, and said "Chance would be a fine thing my love, wouldn't it?" "Ya' know ya' love mi really don' ya', yome jus' too shy ta say it ourrin the open, tha's all innit?" "I'd sooner go out with my horse" she said in reply, but she had a lovely smile on her face as she uttered these words, so at last it sunk in to me that this probably was their usual banter. It was a normal bit of fun that they ensued in each time they met.

"Who is this handsome shy stranger we have with us then Horace, I haven't seen this one before?" "Sorry Gabe, 'is nerms Ronnie, Ronnie Smith, an' 'e comes from 'ockley 'e does." "'e worked 'ere afowa, last year, but they sent 'im orff up ta Wes' Brom'ich they did, burr 'e's back now fereva we 'ope don' we Ron?" "A-r-r-ri yope so 'orice, o don' wanna gu up thaya ragen" I replied, naturally lying in my face.

I didn't want this good looking girl to think that I didn't want to come back to the head office, I mean she might have taken it the wrong way mighten't she, and the last thing I wanted to do was to upset the apple cart before I'd even got to know her did I?

What she did next was a shock to my nervous system for she strolled across the room and put her arms around me and planted a lingering kiss on my right cheek. She then turned and went back towards the rows of hooks, presumably to select her horses' harness. Whilst doing this she half turned with the most beautiful smile on her face, which revealed wonderful white teeth, with one of the front two slightly crossing over the other, which definitely enhanced her beauty, and said "I hope to see a lot more of you handsome, a lot more." Then she burst out into another fit of tinkling laughter, before she disappeared out of view.

"Look she's made him blush" said Mrs Thomas, and she too started to smile. Then she added "Don't take any notice of Gabrielle Ronnie, she's a right flirt she is, although don't get me wrong, she's just full of fun, isn't she Horace?" "O-h, ar-r-r, owe Gabe a smashin' girl, allis ready ta ge a joke, as well as tek one, she's a real smasher is owa Gabe. "

I picked up my things from the table, and went to get the harness for my horse. Horace intervened and said "Yo' stop an' 'ave anutha cuppa tea Ronnie, I'll get Dolly fer ya', an' 'arniss 'er rup fer ya'." "Yome good ta me lerrin' mi borra ya' bike an' ev'rythin', so I'll do yo' a ferva, oright?" " A-r-r, rokay 'orice, an' thank ya', an' don' ferget now tharr rime back yo' cun borra mi bike like yo' did befowa, okay ? " " Ar-r-rokay Ron, an' I'll ge it a good clean fer ya' raswell, okay then?" " That'll bi great 'orice great." With that he went down the same aisle that Gabrielle had, to collect my horse's harness.

I had another cup of tea, and by the time I had drunk it Horace was there with Dolly. I went out into the main building and we walked up the rows of floats and carts until he stopped at one of the floats and said " This is yowas Ron, now watch 'er" pointing at Dolly "she's a bugger on four legs this one. She'll 'ave a kick atcha, an' she wunt bi to fussy abourra bite or two neither, ge 'er a bleedin' dab up the earole, an' lerr 'er know w'ose boss, not too much ya' un'astand, just enough ta purr 'er in 'er plerce oright?" "Ar-r-rokay 'orice, an' thanks fer tellin' me cuz o don' fancy a bleedin' bite, or cracked shin bone. "We both had a laugh, and then put Dolly into the float without too much hassle, although I must admit she did try, but Horace just dabbed her snout lightly, and she stopped.

Horace went about his work, and we agreed to see each other when I came in, and I joined the queue of vehicles leading to the loading bay.

I found that I was next in line to Gabrielle, but she didn't talk to me, she was talking to another very pretty girl driving a flat cart, and she was situated in front of her.

This other girl as I have said was pretty but not like Gabrielle, she had a thin face, very pale. Her hair was darkish brown, and was swept to the back away from her forehead. Her eyes were deep brown, and her eyebrows were pencilled over, but never the less quite attractively done. The nose was roman in style, although not that prominent, the skin was like alabaster, and the mouth was thin, with a very dark lipstick applied.On most girls it would have looked terrible but with this girl it was indeed very attractive, just like the eyebrows. Just one thing that I didn't like about the whole set up however, was that she appeared to be smoking most of the time she and Gabrielle were talking, and I thought she was too beautiful to spoil the whole vision by this habit. Different to Gabrielle however, she had got a light coat on and she did reveal a very lovely slim figure. My conclusion on the two girls was that they were as different as chalk and cheese really, but they both had beautiful lines, and ways that made them both equal, and if I had had to choose between them I couldn't honestly say which girl I would have picked.

When we reached the loading deck at last, this girl in front of Gabrielle had nearly completed loading, so consequently when we were half way through loading, she had made her way down towards the road.

Gabrielle finished her loading, but before she went out she came up to me and said I've told Joan all about you, I hope you don't mind?" "Nah-h w'y should I mind, om gunna bi werkin' with ya' rin I?" I replied, not knowing quite how to deal with the situation, not really having had anything to do with grown up girls to date.

"Alright Ronnie, don't get shirty, I only thought you might like to know who she is." I realised I had made some kind of mistake but it wasn't meant to be intentional so I had to make amends, and quickly, because I didn't want to fall out with this lovely girl before I'd even got the chance to know her better.

"Om sorry Gabrielle, o dain' mean ta bi nasty or anythin', onist o dain't"

"It's alright Ronnie, maybe I took it the wrong way. Anyway I shall have to move or I'll have the rest of them at the back of the queue on to me. Before I go however, her name is Joan, Joany Boulton, and she comes from Icknield Port Road.I live just across the way there." She pointed in the direction of Sandwell Road "in Cranbrook Road, anyway tarrar love I'll probably see you tomorrow okay?" "Yer that'll bi great Gabrielle. I'll see ya' termorra then"

With that she clicked her horse on down the drive, and I finished loading my float.

Driving along Birmingham Road at a very fast pace, Dolly was so different to "Nip" in many ways, and one of them was speed, she was indeed a very fast girl. We passed "Ted Sanford's" Coffee House. I noticed that he wasn't open, so I supposed that he only opened Monday morning to Saturday lunchtime. On to "The Baggies Ground" which brought memories of the ride in Cyril Davies's little Ford Eight, although it was only really a short time ago. At my age though it seemed a lifetime ago.

I didn't really have to drive Dolly she seemed to know exactly where she was going, which was very pleasant in a way. It allowed me room for my favourite pass time, "day dreaming" which I did with great enthusiasm. I thought about Gabrielle and Joan. Oh I'd thought about girls before, as I've so often mentioned, but this was different somehow. I couldn't put my finger on it at all, but I was so excited within and this was strange also. The girls I'd had dealings with before were girls the same age, or younger than myself, so I came to the conclusion that this was part, if not all the cause of these strange feelings I was experiencing. I couldn't be sure but I thought that it might be these two girls, although older than me had taken a shine to me, which I assure you was not an unpleasant experience. But what was I to do?, that was the real question. There was no way I could fathom that out at the moment, I had got too much on my plate trying to fathom out this new round, the second round of "miyone." So I dismissed the thought of the girls, but only for the time being, for I intended to return to that when I had got the round sorted out. Never the less these thoughts put me into a wonderful frame of mind for the task ahead.

I turned into Roebuck Street, and then into Roebuck Lane as per instructions. First I passed over "Summit Bridge" with the lines of the " G.W.R." railway, and canal below, and then over the famous "Galton Bridge" with the lines of the "L.M.S." railway, and Birmingham canal below, moving on until I reached Oldbury Road, where I turned right. As I drove along this road I noticed another cafe. It was an old pub turned into a cafe situated right on the corner of Feeder Street. I made a mental note that I would pay it a visit one of the times when it was open.

On I went to the junction of Mallen Street with Spon Lane, passing "The Spon Croft" on the right, and the "Baths" just in Mallen Street on the left. Dolly jogged on and we passed the old "Tram Sheds ", and "Moyle and Adams" Wholesale Grocers before finally arriving at my first customer on my new round "Mrs Lees."

I put the order for her shop up, one dozen sterra, and half a dozen pas into one metal crate and carried it to the door. After putting the crate onto the floor in order to open the door to the shop, I found to my surprise the door was locked, so I gave a knock, and waited. Moments later a door in the rear of the shop opened, and a lady came out. She came the few steps leading to the shop itself, lifted the counter, and unlocked a small gate beneath it, before coming across to the door leading into the road.

She smiled at me through the glass of the door, whilst undoing the various locks and bolts attached to it. I assumed this to be Mrs Lees, she was a very small, but full figured lady. Grey hair brushed back into a bun, her skin was almost yellow.

Large blue eyes, which seeped to be laughing, causing little creases either side, which in a funny way made her seem a little younger than I guess she really was. A small squat nose, but not unattractive, and thin lips which somehow didn't really fit into the general construction of her face. Behind those lips spotless white dentures.

Over the dress she wore was a beautiful clean apron, as was her complete general appearance.

At last the bolts were undone, and the door opened, she gave me a most beautiful smile and said in a very soft and gentle voice "Om eve sa sorry mar love, tharr I worn open, but the chap as us'ally deliva's doh come at this time, 'e's normally lerta than this." " Oh-h, tha's soright love" I replied, full of an inner feeling that I was going to like this lady, which proved so right later. "Am yo' gunna bi bringin' the milk from now on then Son?" " Ar-r-ri expect so love, all o know is they took mi orff anutha roun' tharr I did in Wes' Brom'ich, an' put mi on this un. Burr I don' know w'etha it's perminent or not yet." "Now love, w'ere d' ya' wan' mi ta put the milk fer ya'?" "Oh jus' purrit ova thaya Son, jus' w'ere the em'tis am, oright?" "Ar-r-rokay." I placed the full crate where she had indicated after removing the empties.

Picking the empties up again after placing the order down, I moved towards the door to the road, when she said "'ang on a minnit love.

The otha chap allis 'ad a cuppa tea we us on a Sundee mornin', cuz all the coffee 'ouses is shut, so would yo' like one, or a' ya' bothered?" "Ar-r-ri could do wi' a cuppa love, an' thanks eva sa much, w'ile yome doin' that I'll gu an' put Dollies nose bag on, okay?" "Arr-r-rokay love, yo' do that an' I'll getcha tea fer ya'.""

Dolly had a quick go at me, and I dabbed her one, she had another go, so I dabbed her another one, and then she packed it up, and looked at me with what I thought very suspicious, and crafty eyes. I gave her one of my best "'ockley ite" looks and told her in no uncertain terms, that if she carried on this way we weren't going to be friends. I don't think she took a blind bit of notice, so I just laughed and let it go at that. I put her nose bag on, and she quickly occupied herself in "chuffing" the corn down her "'odge."

Going back into the shop I found not only a cup of tea on the counter, but a "Spam sandwich" in a piece of grease proof paper waiting for me. I thanked Mrs Lees for her kindness, and she informed me that this was the normal thing on a Sunday, and if I desired it would carry on this way. We also discussed the leaving of the milk when I had completed the round. She called into the back of the shop to her daughter. When she arrived she asked her to show me where to collect the milk the previous roundsman had left yesterday, and that she said was where I was to leave my overs at the end of each day. There was one proviso however (I thought there might be). If she (Mrs Lees) required any extra milk for her customers (nod, nod, wink, wink.) during the time of leaving the milk, and picking it up, she would be allowed to do so, and I could put it on her order the next day. Well, what could I do, I didn't know all the circumstances of the round as yet, but I was quick enough on the uptake to know that something was on hand, and that it would be for my benefit, as well as others. So I agreed to all the rules, which brought a smile to Mrs Lees face, and I in return put on a smile for her, but I reserved judgement for later.

I left Mrs Lees shop and clicked Dolly into motion moving further on down the road. I found the number of my second customer, which was a house just before Beresford Road. My deliveries took me along the one side of Oldbury Road until I got to the Junction with Popes Lane, and Frazer Street. I went further along the dual carriageway until an opening in the slabs in the middle of the road allowed me to turn Dolly around. I then started serving along the opposite side of Oldbury Road until I reached the end of this dual carriageway, which was right opposite, well practically right opposite Beresford Road.

Whilst turning Dolly at the first opening in the carriageway, which was opposite Blakely Hall Road, I met to my surprise "Ernie Humphries". I pulled up and had a chat with him. I stated "W'atcha doin' down 'ere Ern, yo' dain' usta serve 'ere w'en ar come with ya' did Ya'?" "Nah Ronnie" he replied "it's all ta do wi' this bleedin' reshufflin', they've gid part of my roun' ova ta the Midland Counties bloke, an' arve got this part of 'is pitch. It's all a bleedin' mystery ter me." "Ov also 'eard that wee'em all comin' down ta Island Road soon. Bloody 'arold's doin' 'is nut cuz there wunt bi any gaffa's job ferrim thaya, so 'e'll 'ave ta gu back ta bein' a supervisa ragen, 'e wun" like that, cuz yo' know w'at supervisa's is, they'm on'y bleedin' glorified relief blokes nowadays, so 'e'll bi guin' back on the roun's agen wun 'e?" I must admit this took me back a little, so I pursued the conversation in this vain. Although at the end of it I didn't get to know much more, other than Mary probably wouldn't be coming to Island Road, because of the distance. Most of this talk that Ernie and I had turned out to be the truth, and although I didn't see Harold Haynes much after that I do believe that the dairy did give him, and his brother, who was a supervisor inside the dairy, a very rough deal indeed.

I clicked Dolly across the main road into Beresford Road and commenced to deliver both sides of the road. Turning round at the top I then went left into Fisher Road, where I delivered up one side and down the other bringing me back into Beresford Road once again, I moved on back towards the main road then turned left again into Seymour Road, this time I delivered both sides until I reached Rood End Road.

On reaching this point I began to realise how different this was to the first round I'd been on. All the calls were compact. Consequently I hardly ever got on the float. All I did was click Dolly on, take the milk from the float, and deliver it to the door of the customers. l didn't always have to click Doll on either she knew the round backwards, so as I delivered she moved on. My first round was spread over a very large area, but not this one according to the rough map drawn for me. In fact it looked a "doddle."

I moved into Rood End Road, and turned right which brought me into Birmingham Road. Retracing my steps, I came to the opening at the opposite end of BlakenHall Road. This was practically opposite Pope Lane I had got to turn left into. According to the map I'd got to go the length of this lane to Tat Bank Road, where I turned left again. I travelled up Popes Lane passing "Nixons" the haulage firm and carried on to the end as instructed where I turned left and found myself faced with a very steep climb. this took me over the "Titford Canal" which led to the "Titford Feeder."

I got off to take the weight off the float for Dolly, and walked on the pavement alongside her. Over the first bridge we went, with the railway sidings on the right, and factories which lay back off the road on the left. I made a mental note of "Cox and Dank's", one of the customers I would have to serve tomorrow, and moved on towards the next bridge. The hill wasn't as steep now, but still steep never the less, so I stayed where I was on the pavement with Dolly moving on pulling the laden float. Eventually we passed over this second bridge, which had "Western Road" running off to the right just before it. I presumed that the "Western" in Western Road had something to do with it running alongside the track of the "Great Western Railway" the track which ran from "Snow Hill" through Hockley, Winson Green, Smethwick, Langley, and so on into "The Black Country."

Just over this second bridge I noticed the foundry I'd got to serve on Monday, and I made a note of that. Dolly and I passed Wellesley Road, and my deliveries commenced again. Up Tat Bank Road I went serving either side as per the piece of paper, then turning around at the top, and trotting back down to Wellesley Road, with me doing exactly the same down there until we reached the end by Vernon Road, when we had to turn right. On the left hand side for a little way up this road was the frontage to some firm, and it was at the end of this frontage that I started to deliver once more. After Vernon Road, I came back into Wellesley Road and then went into Shirley Road serving both sides up there, and back down yet again. Finally into the last road off Wellesley Road, which was Gresham Road.

After Gresham Road I entered Rood End Road which was the last road of my round. I turned right, and delivered up one side to the junction with Tat Bank Road and Warley Road opposite, then turned around and came back and delivered the other side to Gresham Road.

"The School" occupied the left hand side between Gresham Road and Shirley Road, so no deliveries there, but on I went until I reached "The Bell Inn", which is famous in the Oldbury area. Rood End Road turned left then, and my last four calls were on the righthand side, just before you got to "Plucropt" the place that made some type of fertiliser (phew what a pong??), and "The Albion Bottle Company."

"The Bell Inn" as I've already said was quite famous. The reason for this fame was, that it was the oldest pub in the area, and what a beautiful building it was, well still is as far as I know. It was originally built by a gentleman named "Mark Barker" in 1859, and had The Grand Victoria Pleasure Gardens, an orchestra, stables, a marble alley, and pavilions. To commemorate this gentleman's building the local borough even named a thoroughfare after him, "BARKER STREET" which runs along the back of the pub.

Mind you this immediate area around where my second round for Handsworth Dairies finished was abound with history.

"IT'S A LONG WAY TO TIPPERARY", a song that was sung by the troops of both the 1914-18 War and the 1939-45 War, and what an inspiration it must have been to the lads. It was, and still is a legend . This song ranked with all the other big songs, and in some cases outstripped them, songs like "White Cliffs of Dover" "Lily of Laguna" "We'll Meet Again" " Pack up your troubles in your old kit bag" "Nellie Dean" "Just like the Ivy on the Old Garden Wall" "Harbour Lights" "Roll out the Barrel" "Sweet Adeline", and oh so many more that I could tell you about, but that would be a story in itself. This song gave courage and help at times when spirits were low, and must have given the lads that little bit of home when they were so far away, it was a most memorable composition.

The composer of "IT'S A LONG WAY TO TIPPERARY" is buried not a couple of minutes away from where I delivered my last bottle of milk that day. His name? JACK JUDGE, THAT WAS THE NAME OF THE COMPOSER.

Going back to the turn of the century, in Oldbury lived a Fishmonger named Jack Judge. He was indeed a very likable man, and had friends in the local area in abundance. He was of Irish and Black Country descent, who at one time was a good amateur singer, and song writer. This amateur status didn't remain with him for very long however, and finally he gave up his "day job", and turned professional travelling around the "Old Music Halls."

It was whilst he was performing in Stalybridge, near Manchester on the 31st of January 1912 that he wrote the immortal song. Now everyone, including myself must have thought initially that the "Tipperary" he referred to in the song was the one in Ireland. Not a bit of it, it was a reference to his home in Oldbury "Tipperary Gardens."

Jack wrote the song when he was 39, and during the First World War became a million copy seller, and so the saying goes, it was probably the most famous song of that War.

Back home in Oldbury however, he apparently owed a friendly favour to "Harry Williams" who kept a pub in Low Town Oldbury "The Malt Shovel", and the agreement between the two men apparently was, that due to this favour owed, Jack allowed "Harry's name to be to be seen on the song sheets as a co-author.

After a while "Harry" along with his brother Ben moved out of Oldbury into a country pub near Kenilworth. This pub was originally called "The Plough", but they changed it to "The Tipperary House", but is now called "Tipperary Inn" and is situated near FEN END.

Harry Williams died in 1924, and was for sometime thought to be the main author of the song, although in complete fairness to "Harry" he personally never made any such claim himself.

Jack died in 1938 on the 25th July, and was buried in the churchyard in St Pauls Road the continuation of Cemetery Road, "Smethwick Cemetery"

To commemorate this man there has been a "Tipperary Gardens" and a "Judge Close" named after him.

At the "Tipperary Inn" is an old framed photograph of "Harry and Jack "as co-authors, with "Bert Feldman" the publisher of "It's a long way to Tipperary." Also there is a framed memento which says… "In remembrance of Harry Williams of Tipperary fame, world famous song, which helped save old England."

What a great deal of history for such a small area, but of course I didn't realise all this as I straightened my load up in Rood End Road, for my return to the dairy via MRS LEES SHOP in Oldbury Road.

Horace was waiting for me when I arrived back at the dairy, well I say waiting for me, he was just finishing what he had to do before going home for his Sunday lunch. Again I walked with him as far as his road, but of course this time I had my bike with me, and after a short chat on the corner of Murdoch Road I mounted the cycle and made a fast return to "The Brook."

As I went over the crossing by Icknield Street I saw our "Dad" talking to a couple of his mates and I recognised one of them as Mr Atkins. I shouted over to them as I went by, and dad told me to tell "Mom" that he would only be a couple of minutes and would be up for his dinner.

I told Mom, and she said "Ar-r-rile bleedin' well believe that w'en 'e comes through the bleedin' dowa." She was right, for it must have been a good three quarters of an hour before Dad "sho'd his face" through the door of 228.

Things were more or less the same, the routine didn't alter, and I went to bed that night reflecting on the first day on my new round. I wondered about "tips", would I get as many as I got on my first round, and this worried me a little, because I had by this time got used to the fifteen or sixteen shillings extra that I received from my customers. I had got used to some of the dodges, like an extra bottle here and there, which brought me a "tanner" or "thrupence" from the recipients. Still I thought I would have to weigh things up on this new round, but the situation at Mrs Lees brought a little confidence to me, there must be more in that than met the eye, but I would have to wait and see.

During that first week on the round I kept a rather low profile, but nevertheless I kept my eyes "skinned." Cox and Danks were my first surprise, and then the foundry by "Western Road." I called on the Friday as usual, and naturally they had to pay me then, because although the workmen came in on Saturday, the Office Staff didn't.

I delivered the order in the crate, and asked where, and who I had to go to for the money. After being told, I went over to a very pleasant looking lady, who said "Oh you're new my love, what's happened to the old milkman?" "O' don' know, ma-am, o really don' know, all o do know is that they told mi, that I'd gorra do the roun', so 'ere ri yam." She laughed, I don't know whether it was my accent or what I had said, but she laughed, it was a lovely gentle laugh though, and whatever it meant, I liked it a lot. She went over to a big desk, and from one of the drawers she took a large black tin box, and opened it. "How much do we owe you love?" she asked, and I told her. The lady removed the amount from this tin (The petty cash box) and paid me the amount owing. I marked it paid in my round book, and put it into my satchel.

I was about to move off out of the office, and pick the empties up from outside, when the lady said "Hang on a minute love, here you are this is for you" and she handed me a small brown envelope. "We always give the delivery men some thing at the end of each week" she went on. "Oh-h-h thank ya' ma-am, thanks eve sa much" which brought another session of laughing. This time I must have blushed and showed my embarrassment to the lady because she then said "Oh I'm awfully sorry if I've embarrassed you my love, but I always like the Birmingham accent. It's so different from ours (although for the life of me I couldn't find anything wrong with her accent, it was so "posh."), but for some silly reason it always makes me laugh. I hope you'll forgive me for this silly phobia." I did forgive her, but I hadn't got a clue what I was forgiving her for. I left it at that though, I thought silence in this case was better than questioning.

"Oh love whilst we are on the subject I wonder if I could ask you a favour please?" "Yere, cause yo' cun, if o cun do anythin' fer ya' yove on'y gorra ask." "Well the previous milkman, would on occasion leave us an extra bottle of milk or two when we require it. Although I don't want to get you into any type of trouble, I wonder if you could see your way clear to doing the same for us? " "No problem at all ma-am, if ov gorrit yo' cun 'ave it any time, okay?" "At this reply, not only did she burst out laughing, but some of the other staff, men as well did the same. I thought I'd said "a funny" so I joined in as well, but as usual I hadn't got a clue what I was laughing at.

I went outside to the float, put the empties away, and then opened the brown envelope, and inside was a "half a dollar." I thought if I go on at this rate Handsworth Dairies can keep their 27/6d a week, I'll be picking more up in tips than they pay me. I put the two and sixpence into my trouser pocket, and clicked Dolly on up the hill to my next call, the foundry.

On arrival I went into the small, grubby, and dusty place, they called "The Office" and put the milk down by the side of the old desk just inside on the right.

The big fat gentleman sat behind this desk removed the smelly pipe he was smoking from his mouth and said "'ow do our kid, yome a nu un ain' ya'?" I thought to myself I won't have any problems here with my accent, none whatsoever.

"Ar-r-rom nu Sir, burrit ain't the fust time o done a round of miyone, I 'ad anutha one afowa this un." He looked at me, staring intently through pebble glasses, drawing on the foul smelling pipe as he did so. After a few seconds, he said "O don' s'ppose yo 'll bi with us lung will ya'?" "Wunt bi with ya' lung Sir, o don' know watcha mean, ov on'y jus' come onto the roun' this wick" "Well warr I mean Son, is it wunt bi lung afowa they 'ave yo' in the Army will it?" "Nah-h-h, o see w'atcha mean now Sir, nah-h-h they can't tek me yin the Army, although w'en o do gu o wanna gu in the Nervy, tha's warr I want. Nah-h-h they can' 'ave mi yet, cuz om too young, om on'y sixteen yet." A look of surprise came over his face, and it was quite clear that I had shaken him somewhat. Although I was only sixteen, I was really a big chap for my age. I was nearly 5ft.10. and had quite a build, I reckon it was something to do with all that loading of bread at Rowlands, and the work I'd done for nearly all my childhood, from about the age of eight or nine.

" Neva, yome neva on'y sixteen Son, o can' believe it, God blimey w'at's ya' Motha fed yarron, bloody dynamite or summat?" I must admit I felt rather proud at this outburst, it was quite nice, and it boosted my ego quite a bit. "Ar-r-ri yam, o wuz sixteen las' January" "We could do wi' yo' in thaya," and he pointed towards an open door right opposite the one leading into this office.

I looked in the direction he had pointed, and saw nothing really, because through that door there was nothing but thick brown dust, and the smell was terrible. " Yo'wed earn mowa in thaya in two days, than yo' earn on ya' milk roun' in bloody seven Son" " Nah-h-h o wudden wanna werk in thaya, o like bein' ourrin the open o do, it's berra fer ya'" " Well if eva ya' chernge ya' mind, yo' come an' 'ave a word wi' me Son, an' I'll fin' yarra job in no time, okay ?" "Nah-h-h-h, thanks Sir, burr I think I'll stop w'ere ri yam, but thanks any road up."

I told him what the bill was, and he went through the same motions that the lady had at " Cox and Danks", asking me for extra milk. This time however it was for a very good reason. Although the workers in the foundry had a good ration due to the terrible dusty, and lung clogging job they did they could always do with more. Consequently I told this gentle man that I would definitely drop him some extra, when I had it on board. He thanked me very much, paid me the amount I'd asked for, and then he said "'ere ya' rar Son, 'e's sommat fer ya', an' thanks fer bein' so un'erstandin'" and he put a "Florin" in my hand. I thanked him, collected the empties and went back out to Dolly. I thought to myself as I continued my deliveries "Blimey four an' a tanna already, an' there's all tommara ta gu yet." I had visions of money pouring down on me from everywhere, lucky old me.

"The Nash Brothers" in Vernon Road extended my capital gains for that first Friday by a shilling, which brought my total to five and sixpence in all, not much now, but a fortune then. These tips were given every Friday during the whole time I was on this round. Unfortunately I wasn't to find out how I would have faired at Christmas Time, because I was transferred yet again.

On the Saturday, the normal day for accounts to be settled, I was in for another big surprise, much better than even I had anticipated.

Starting at Mrs Lees, who after paying the bill, gave me a shilling, I was given the odd "tanna" " thre'pence", and the amount of people who told me "doh marra about the chernge milkmon" was never ending. When I reached the end of my round that first Saturday, I straightened my load up,: and then I counted all my tips for the day, which I had put into my trouser pocket, keeping it separate from "The Gaffa's" money.

On completion of counting I just couldn't believe it, so I went through the count again, and no, it wasn't a mistake, I had been given, by these kind people in "The Black Country" the sum of nearly "TWO POUNDS," I think the exact sum was £1. 19. 4d, but adding to this the 5/6 d from yesterday brought me a grand total of £2. 4. 10d. I stood on the back of the float, whilst "Dolly" finished the last of her feed, and gave a mental thanks to God for these wonderful people. I know it was a material form that I thanked God, but it was the only way I knew at that period of my life, and I'm sure that he forgave me for the one thing I couldn't be guilty of, IGNORANCE. In a funny way however I really didn't see it that way at all, I was thanking God for the way these people must have thought about me, in their generosity. Perhaps I was all mixed up about the whole thing, but one thing that was prevalent, and this was fact, a God's honest fact, at that moment of time I was so happy with the people, and I reckoned they were happy with me, ignorant, or not.

I clicked "Dolly" on from Rood End Road, down to Mrs Lees, left the milk I had over in the wooden shed at the rear of her shop, and then went on along Oldbury Road home.

I passed "The Baggies Ground" and knew they were playing at home a good while before I reached the ground itself, for as I was passing "Dartmouth Cricket Ground" I could see the white flag fluttering from it's pole indicating that a first division match was in progress, well I say first division match, I think they renamed the title during the war, but never the less it indicated that a first team match was in progress anyway.

As I passed by the ground itself, all the buses, both Birmingham Corporation and West Bromwich Corporation were lined up ready to convey the spectators to their homes on completion of the match. There was a sudden roar from within the ground, which made Dolly jump. I steadied her down, telling her it was alright, and she regained her composure. Smiling to myself I wondered who had scored, or nearly scored "The Baggies" or the other side. Of course it was nearly the end of the season then, I wasn't quite sure, I didn't take too much notice of football then after the fiasco at Farm Street Junior School. I didn't hold out too much hope of signing on for the "Brummigam Backward Team" let alone "The Baggies" "The Villa" "The Blues" "The Wolves" or even "The Saddlers" so I left football alone altogether.

I unloaded, Horace put Dolly away, then I made my statement out in Mrs Thomas's tack room, although she wasn't there, she had gone home a long time ago. Off to the office I went and paid in, collected my wages, and went back down to the stables to see how long Horace would be, and also to collect my bike.

Horace said that he was going to be some time yet, and for me not to wait for him, so I pushed my "Kingsway" out into the drive ready to ride home back to "The Brook."

Since reckoning up the amount of tips I had received that afternoon I had been thinking what I should do with all this new found wealth. All the way back from Rood End Road to the dairy, it had been niggling at me.

I passed the "New Inns", and looked at it for the "umpteenth" time. It never ceased to bring out my greatest admiration for the builders who had built this place, it really was wonderful in all it's architecture. It was, and deserved to be a landmark of Handsworth, a landmark of some distinction.

The big black and white clock overhanging Holyhead Road, just before the entrance to the most famous "Princes Suite" indicated that it was twenty past four. I thought to myself 'Yo' ain' done sa bad fo the fust day, fust pay day, on a new round "and I knew that I could improve on that eventually.

It was whilst I was passing "Handsworth Market" that I came to a decision with what to do with all this lovely money I had received off these wonderful "Black Country People." As I passed by this busy thoroughfare with its usual throng of people pushing their way in and out, not only into the market, but "Hawkins" "Fosters" and other notable stores surrounding it. Soho Road was a very busy thoroughfare indeed in those days, even with the war on. It was indeed the cream of shopping centres. All the business men, and their wives would be there no doubt mixing business with pleasure during this shopping event. It really was a pleasure those days to see nice people, with nice manners; so sedate, and gentle, but with business intentions in mind. It has changed over the years, changed considerably, but one can't ever forget, and who wants to, what it was like then?

It was "The Post Office" that lay back off the road, with it's area of well laid slabs, and edging stones, looking more like a patio, than a front entrance to a civic building that gave me the final decision as to what to do with the money I had received from the people on my new round. I would put it where I had put most of the money I had received from "Bob", when he bought my toys for his grandchildren. I would buy another couple of saving certificates, and I would still have plenty of money over to spend on myself.

I did think about giving "Our Mom" a little extra, but dismissed that thought after a while, because if I did that she would naturally become suspicious, wondering where this extra cash had come from. It was a great pity that I couldn't give her a little more money, because I really did want to do this, but I was always completely aware of the possible consequences if I did so. I did solve this particular problem later however, and believe me it really was what I wanted to do for Mom.

What I did was I told Mom that I was getting a little more than the 4/-d she was giving me, out of the 27/6d wages each week, in tips. Not much more, I lied, but a little more, so I told her in future you can keep all my wages, I didn't want any pocket money at all. Oh she looked at me suspiciously, and questioned me about it, but this time I was on top of the situation, and I lied my way out of it quite successfully. Well it wasn't hard was it? I mean after all I was giving something away by the lies I was telling, not taking something off Mom, as would be the usual case for one wanting to tell lies.

No, on the whole I thought I did pretty well with these lies, Mom was benefiting from it, without me divulging how much money I was getting from the good people of Oldbury each week, which I might add, improved with the weeks going by on the round.

Mind you it was a bit of a trying time when I was again moved off this round to be put onto another one, for the benefit of the dairy, as you will see. I could hardly put a stop to Mom's extra money could I? But as everything turned out for me, it got better, and better as my time went on at Handsworth Dairies.

I rode down Soho Road that first Saturday of my new round, speeding down Soho Hill at an alarming rate. I could move when I wanted to on that "Kingsway". Fortunately for me "the coppa" on point duty at "The Brook" was calling the traffic on from the West Bromwich, and Birmingham "Fanny Brown" directions. I was just past "The Wold" on the corner of Guest Street before I started to peddle again to take me up to "The Post Office" at the top of Hockley Hill, just before "The Gulley" which led to Key Hill, and "Harry Smith's" the Ironmongers.

I bought my two certificates from the lady behind the counter, and thought to myself, "o bet she thinks om a rich bloke, buyin' two stiffic'ts", which made me stick my chest out with pride as I left the ornate building, which was to play a very big part in my life later.

The "Crown Offices" those day's, even before the war, and for quite some time afterwards, were always open until six o'clock on a Saturday, which of course was a great benefit to the public, who were now working more hours, and very difficult shifts in this oppressive time. I mean a lot of people were putting their money into "National Savings" because there was no doubt about it at that time they were offering the best interest rates, and people were earning a great deal more money than they had been doing. Most important however, they were earning this money, but had very little to spend it on, consequently a lot of them were saving for when the war would be over.

I arrived home after I'd put the money away, and went upstairs to our bedroom, to put my saving certificate books away safely, I thought, in the drawer of the table. I was mistaken about this safety precaution however, because "you know who" was still every bit "12 pennies in the bob upstairs" she was a very cute lady was my Mom. Having said that however, I think that she was a little more wary of me than she had been, with the "Ten Bob Note incident" because she didn't say a word, although, I did find out in a round about way that she had indeed been checking up on me, and further more, knew practically every move that I'd made, like I've just said, she was cute very cute.

"'allo Ronnie, ya' dinna's in the oven, I'll gu an' gerrit fer ya' o wunt be ya' minnit, yo' sit down an' powa yaself a cuppa tea, ov cut some bread an' butta fer ya', so yo' cun start chobblin' that down yarr 'odge" "Ar-r-roright Mom" I replied. She was always extra nice to me on pay day's, same as she was with the "big wenches, an' owa kid" on a Friday night, and "Our Dad" on a Saturday morning. I can see her now with her bits of paper she kept in her well worn brown purse, reckoning up what she owed to others, and more important what they owed her, although in fairness to the others, it was nearly always the former reckoning, she did most of all.

Mom returned from the back kitchen in no time at all, and placed my well baked dinner in front of me. I had then, by the time she had gone into the kitchen to get the dinner, and arrived back in the middle room with it, demolished four rounds of the six rounds of bread and butter she had put out for me. Like I said

I could always eat, and I'm the same today. "Bleedin' 'ell Ronnie, 'ave yo' e't them already, yo' must 'ave a bleedin' lung stummick, 'ang on an' I'll cutcha some mowa, ya' do want some mowa don' ya'?" "Ar-r-ro could do wi' a few mowa pieces Mom" I answered. "Ask a bleedin' foolish question, o mirrass well 'ave ast ya' ta gu ta the bloody moon, as yo' sayin' ya' dain wan' any mowa grub, still it wun' 'urt ya' reatin' like ya' do, so gu on an' gerrit down ya'" and she gave me a most beautiful smile, a thing Mom didn't do very often.

It was that very smile however that made me change my plans slightly. I finished my dinner, and I could see that she was anticipating the handing over of my weekly earnings. She was sitting in "Her Chair" with her back to the window which looked out onto the back garden. I could sense more than tell, that she would be getting anxious about the handing over of the money, because when she had her face towards you in a direct line, as she had with me then, the light, whatever the weather would stream in through the back window, throwing its beam onto you. .Consequently it kept her features in darkness, so it was more that I sensed her anticipation than saw it.

After that lovely smile I began to think, well it wouldn't hurt to give Mom just a little extra, and I devised a reason for giving her that little extra, without giving away the whole truth of my extra income from the good people of Oldbury. I decided to tell Mom, that I'd had a few tips off the customers, and if she was short (and when wasn't she short, don't make me laugh) then she need only give me 2/- instead of the usual 4/- if it would help her?

I finished my dinner, and drank my "umpteenth" cup of tea, and then sat back in my chair for a quiet contented few minutes. "Od berra gu an' wash these few pots up" said Mom suddenly rising from her chair, which of course was another way of saying "Come on Ronnie warrabout mi wergis, o ain' gorr all night". Added to that she had got to get everything ready for Dad to go down to "The Turk", then get herself ready to follow him some time after. Yes, you didn't have to use words in our house to know what was wanted, either wanted to be done' or wanted to be given.

I reached into my trouser pocket and handed my brown envelope over to Mom, unopened as always, and said "'ere ya' are Mom, 'ere ya' are yo' tek It, an' yo' cun keep it all." I had changed my mind again, that's me I'm afraid, spontaneous. Sometimes I'm wrong, well most times I'm wrong with this spontaneity but I always meant it to be for the best. One thing it did for me though, it always made me feel happy, so there can't be anything wrong about that can there?

"Watcha mean Son, o cun keep it all, warram yo' gunna do fer monnee if I yave it all, yove gorra 'ave summat ain'tcha?" "Nah-h-h it's soright Mom, on this new round they gid me, ov 'ad a few extra tips, about four an' a tanna (another lie) so o thought, well om gerrin mi pockit monnee, an' a tanna ova so I'll ge owa Mom some extra." She looked at me rather suspiciously, I think it was a natural talent she'd got for this. After a few minutes she said "Yo' ain' doin' anythin' rung am ya' owa Ronnie?" "Nah-h course I ain't Mom, 'ow could I do anythin' rung, like o tol' ya' it's tips, burrif ya' don' wannit then I'll 'ave mi fowa bob pockit monnee as well, an' tharrell gi mi eight an' a tanna ta spend, so ya' can please yaself (I really was pushing my luck with those last few words.)

However it didn't affect Mom's reply. Either she heard it and decided not to say anything about it, due to this gift of "four bob" I was giving her, or she didn't hear what I had said. Anyway the answer didn't come as any surprise to me. "Nah-h-h it's soright Ronnie, o don' know w'at med mi say that, o don' know w'at come ova me, an' thanks fer the monnee, it wun' 'alf come in 'andy, yome a good lad Ronnie, thank ya'." With that she bustled off into the kitchen with the dirty plates, and cups to wash them, but not before I caught a quick glance at a few tears running from those brown eyes of hers.

I went back upstairs to "our bedroom" thinking about those few tears, it wasn't like "Our Mom" to cry, unless "Our Dad" had been "balling" at her or something. I sat on the side of the bed, and thought about what I was going to do that night. Pictures, no, I didn't fancy the pictures, but what else could I do?, there wasn't much on offer. I sat there pondering for a while, and then I suddenly remembered somebody, I couldn't think who it was, but they had told me about the Y.W.C.A. club up Soho Hill. I tried to think who it was had told me, for then I could have gone round and asked them if they were going, and I could have gone with them. Anyway whoever it was said they had a "smashin' time" there, table tennis, blow football, and all kinds of "donnuck", and that there were lot's of girls as well. So I thought well I'll walk up there and see what's what, that's what I'll do.

Of course 1 couldn't go yet I thought (but I found out later that I could for their hours were very elastic), and it would give me time to "tart" myself up, well you never know do you?

I heard "Our Dad" moving in the other bedroom, and knew that it must be about six o'clock, or getting on that way, it was remarkable how our Dad woke up from his sleep at this time. Of course he always said to Mom before he went to bed after a session at the "Turk" on Saturday dinner "Don" ferget ta geus a shout Lil abou' ralf five six a'clock, o don' want the bleedin' vica' tellin' mi yorf agen fer bein' lert fer the service". He would laugh in that gruff, mucus coagulated sound of his, as he trod his weary way upstairs for a well earned rest. Have no doubt about it my Dad, as nearly all other Dad's in Hockley, worked bloody hard, really hard all week, and deserved their few pints, and bit of fun at the week end. My Dad in particular went to work, when he worked at "Bradfords" at about five at night, and he didn't return home until about half eight to nine o'clock next morning, and he did that six nights a week. The hours were even more when he went to "Rowlands" and as I've said before he got one week a year holiday, and he didn't always take that. His other holidays, oh yes he had Christmas Eve off, because he had to go in most Christmas Nights to bake for the next day. Oh, very occasionally he would have an extra day if Christmas day fell on a Saturday, but this wasn't very often. Then there was "Bank Holiday Monday", but he still had to go in on the night time, and so it was with the other holidays, one day holidays, Easter, and Whitsun.

I sat and listened to Dad, and knew exactly what was coming next, <u>AND IT DID!!</u> I heard the "Swan Vestas " scratch on the side of the box, lighting yet another "Gold Flake", and then the inevitable coughing, and retching. This continued for a while, and then I heard him say to himself, "Tha's berra, o cun breath now," although for the life of me I couldn't see how. I had tried to smoke recently, but I must admit that I hadn't quite got used to the idea yet. But make my breathing better, I really couldn't make that out at all.

Having a rough idea of the time now, I thought I'd better not get up to the club too early, not on a Saturday night, because I should imagine that people wouldn't be turning up until late, due to the fact that they hadn' t got to get up the next morning. With me it was different, I'd got to get up, but that thought didn't bother me in the least. Pondering this idea, I came to the conclusion that if I got there for about eight or half eight, that would be plenty of time.

I figured out that it would only take me a few minutes to throw some water over my face, put some brilliantine (it was lavender brilliant cream in an oval tin with a lovely picture of lavender, which I had bought from Mrs Davies's) on my hair, change my shirt, and put my Sunday best suit, and shoes on, and I would be ready, so what was I to do in the mean time?

First I thought I might do a little drawing, and went into the drawer to search for some paper and pencil, but then I changed my mind. As I opened the drawer I saw my old cigarette card albums, some of a few things I didn't let Bob have when I sold all my toys to him for his grandchildren.

Removing them from the drawer with loving care, I casually looked through them. The first was "Association Football" and then "Famous Cricketers " "Flags of the Nations", all in silk from Kensitas, the first two from "Wills" After that came "Air Raid Precautions" by "Players", and finally "Safety First on the Road" again issued by " Wills", and "Boxing Champions" by "Players."

Everything went out of my mind momentarily, the Y.W.C.A. Handsworth Dairies, all the tips I had had, my saving certificates, my whole concentration was in these "fag albums." I put them on the bed beside me, and picked them up one by one to go through them carefully. First of all "Association Football", the names of the famous players of the day "Stanley Mathews of Stoke City" "Tom Finney of Preston North End" "Dixie Dean of Everton." "Raich Carter of Derby County" "Frank Swift of Manchester City" "Jackie (wo-o-o Jackie) Milburn of Newcastle United." " Viv Woodward of Aberdeen." "George Swindon" "Eddie Hapgood" "The Compton Brothers Les and Dennis (also cricketers when the football season ended)" "Ted Drake (the bloke that scored seven against the "Villa at Villa Park"), all of Arsenal fame. Then closer to home "P. Astley" "Fred Biddlestone" "Bob Iveson" "George Cummings (the only full back Stan Mathews didn't like playing against)" "Frankie Broome" "Ronnie Starling" signed from one of the Sheffield teams for a big fee all playing for Aston Villa. "Harry Hibbs" who later transferred to Walsall, of Birmingham City. "Walter Boyes" " Ted Sanford" both of West Bromwich Albion. I think that Bryn Jones came later, but it is worth mentioning that he was the first player to break through the £10,000 barrier, he came to Wolverhampton Wanderers for £14,000.

Then I looked casually through "Famous Cricketers", and noted "Don Bradman and "Len Hutton". After that the greats of boxing "The Brown Bomber, Joe Louis" "Len Harvey" "Tommy Farr" "Flags of the Nations" only held a slight thrill for me, due to all the different colours, and of course the main fact, that they were silk and not card. "Air Raid Precautions" with it's pictures of stirrup pumps, and how to use them, gas masks, how and when to use those. More interesting to me in this album was the paintings of the different vehicles being used, fire engines, ambulances etc. So it's not surprising that the last one I looked at with longing care, it even had the edge over the football album, and that was "Safety First on the Road"

It wasn't the safety first aspect that I was interested in, it was the beautiful paintings the artist had done depicting the safety instructions. "Don't throw rubbish out of a moving vehicle." "Always look in your mirror before moving off." "Don't ride in between the tram lines on your cycle." Always observe in your rear mirror before turning to the right." Never reverse out onto a main road", all these and many more instructions on good sensible safety first. But oh, the trams, buses, lorries, charabancs, motor bikes, horse and carts, and all the other many vehicles, especially the different types of motor cars painted in such detail that you could tell what make they were without any written instruction, so wonderfully illustrated. "Singer Bantam." "Austin Seven." "Morris Cowley (Bull Nose and Square.") "Alvis Coupe, and Sports." "Ford Eight" (like the one Mr Davies drove). "The Wolesley Hornet, and Saloon" "The Morgan Three Wheeler." "The Trojan chain driven van, which was very popular with "The Brooke Bond Tea Company." It was used by other firms, but this was the most predominant user. "The Austin Cambridge." "The M.G", and oh so many more. I did have an album on motor cars, and also railways of the world, but I kept them separate to these albums, due to the fact that I hadn't managed to "get" the complete set of "fifty" which was the amount required.

Looking through these lovely albums I lost all track of time, when suddenly "Ronnie am yo' up thaya", it was "Our Mom". Bloody 'ell what time was it, I hope that I wasn't going to be too late for the club.

"Yer Mom, om up 'ere, watcha want" I replied, making out as though I knew exactly what I was about, but not wishing to let Mom know I had been drifting back in time through the "ciggy albums."

"soright Son, om on'y lerrin ya' know om orff down "The Turk" ta ya' Dad, an' o dain' know w'etha ya' wuz guin' out or not, tha's sall." "Wo-o-o thanks Mom "I pretended to be so grateful. Well I was in a way, but I'd have been more grateful if she had done it earlier, because I knew that it would be near to eight o'clock now, that was the normal time for her to go down to Dad. "Om comin' down now, thanks eve sa much." "Arr-rokay Ron, well tarrar then om orff now." "Tarrar then Mom."

I've never moved so quick in my life. I threw the albums back into the drawer, and then put my best "togs" on, raced down the stairs, and straight into the back kitchen, threw some water over my face and dried it on the towel (???), after that I applied my "Lavender Brilliantine", and combed the "gooey mess" into a look alike of my Dad's hair style through the small cracked mirror resting on the brick shelf just above the concrete flat sink.

Everything alright, I dashed back through the middle room, and said "Tarrar" to "Our Lil" who was looking after the "Young Wenches" while Mom went down "The Turk". In saying "Tarrar" to Lily, I noticed the time on the big "Smith's Alarm (which didn't work) Clock (I meant the alarm not the clock itself) situated perilously near to the edge of the mantlepiece over the fireplace, and saw that it was only just after "'alf seven"

I thought to myself "Bloody 'ell all that rushin', and there wuz no need ferrit arrall." I slowed down, and walked down New John Street West to the "Brook" saying "'tallo" to Mr Belcher, who was still dressed in his "werkin' togs." His "off white decorators apron" hanging below his more than average abdomen. "Warra belly" I thought. Then I saw Mrs Nash, and her youngest daughter Violet standing on the doorstep. I looked at Violet and wished I was older, she really was a beautiful girl.

She said "Hello Ronnie", and I replied, rather shyly and I also said "'ello" to her Mom.

Over "The Brook" I went thinking what I would do when I reached the Y.W.C.A., I mean I couldn't just go "bowling" in there and say "Ov come ta join Missus" could I? I passed "The Palladium" and was just going by Elvins, and unfortunately no nearer to a conclusion of what I was going to do when I arrived at the club, situated in what used to be a church. I heard a shout from across Soho Hill "Warrow Ron, ow ya' guin', lung time no see." I looked across the road, but couldn't recognise anyone I knew, but then a chap came running across waving his hand at me. Finally he reached me, and I still had difficulty in recognising him, until he reminded me that he went to "Icknield Street School". This still didn't ring a bell, but I thought I'd better pretend that I knew him, save any hassle. It was evidently obvious that he knew me, and if I had said "Om sorry mert, burr I don' know ya'", it wouldn't have been very pleasing for him, and I could tell that he wanted to be friendly, so I told a little lie.

He introduced himself as "Billy", I can't remember his surname now, but he was a real nice bloke. We were pals for a short while after this initial meeting. "W'ere ya' guin' too? "he asked me. "Oh o thought o gi this club 'ere ra try" and I pointed to the direction of "The Roebuck" public house. "Oh ya' mean The Young Women's Christian Association" he replied and then started to laugh. "Oh bloody 'ell, ya' mean there's on'y girls 'llowed in thaya, od 'eard as blokes wen' as well" I replied. After he finished laughing he said "Nah yome oright Ron, it's a joke among us blokes, it is The Young Woman's Christian Association really, but cuz' the war's on they've med it that both wenchis an' blokes cun gu." "Thank God fer that" I said. " Iwuz gunna gu ta "The Villa Cross", burr I don' really fancy' the picha tha's son, o dain' know w'at ta do really, burr I'm in this club, an' I'll come with ya' if ya' like, okay?" "Oh tharr'd bi great Bill, o wuz wondrin' 'ow o wuz gunna gerrin any road up, but yove answered mi question now, an' thanks."

So we went to the club, and up the steps entering this old church. Inside where I suppose the main body of the church used to be were table tennis tables, with some of them occupied by both girls and chaps, and around the perimeter of these tables others just stood, drinking tea, or some other liquid from cups, and nattering away to one another. As we walked by, one or two wished Billy "Warrow," or "'ello", but one girl said "Am ya' guin' up the dance ternght Billy?" "Ar-r-r rin a minnit, arta ov got mi mate inta the club (Blimey they'd make something of that statement nowadays wouldn't they?), 'ave ya' sin Miss..." (I've forgotten her name now.) "O think she's up thaya with the blokes w'o are gunna play ternight, am yo' gunna 'ave a gu on the drums ternight Billy?" "A-r-ri might, if the bloke in the band'll let me". "Don' worry Billy, 'e'll letcha, cuz yome a berra drumma then 'e is, I'll se ya lerta then." "Ar-r-okay then love" was Billies curt reply and we went right to the top of the room to a passage on the right hand side.

Through the passage we went, turned right, and then left which led us to a steep flight of wooden stairs. On the way up these stairs we heard, the scale being played on saxophone, and then a blast from trumpet, the tuning of piano, and in the background of all this, the muted sound of snare, base, and tom toms being tested for sound by the drummer, with the occasional clash of symbols. This excited me somewhat, but I assumed by the girl who had asked Billy if he was going to have "a go" on the drums, that my new found friend had experienced all this before.

Reaching the top of the stairs, we turned left sharply, coming back on ourselves, which led to a narrow passage running alongside a small stage. At the end of this passage was another hall similar to the one below. We came to a stop whilst Billy looked around for the lady he wanted.

This hall was already filling with "wenches and chaps", they were sat around the hall on benches, and a few chairs. In the far corner was a couple of tables set up, with sandwiches, cakes, pop, glasses, and cups, so I assumed that they served tea as well. Behind this table were a couple of "old women" (they must have been every day of thirty or so?), and they were serving. Well one of them was, but the other one was talking to a big woman, and I mean big.

"Ar-r-r there she is, come on Ron, le's gu an' 'ave a word with Miss…, tha's 'er ova thaya, by the wimmin tha's servin' the grub an' ev'rythin'."

Over we went across this fairly large hall. We waited until she had finished talking to the lady behind the bar, then Billy said "'scuse mi Miss o know it ain' propa burr I brought mi mate along wi' me, an' o won'ered if 'e could stay fer the dance ternight please?

I looked at this lady and straight away she reminded me of my "Cousin Edna", Edna Woods. She lived in Moilliett Street with "Our Uncle Bill and Aunty Lil." This lady was like her in most respects. Her hair was deep brown, and wavy, but shortish, her face large, big brown eyes behind very strong lensed glasses, broad nose, almost negroid, and full thick lips, which were soft.

When she smiled, which she did when she turned to see what Billy wanted, she revealed big white "tombstone" teeth, again just like "Edna's." Her figure, well what can I say? It was big, with all the big things attached to it, including her clothes, and again just like "Our Edna" she was jolly, always most pleasant. Mind you throughout my life I have found this most predominant, that fat people generally are very jolly, and have a naturally happy nature. Edna was not always "big" though, I remember her very well, before she met her husband to be, she was as slim as a reed, and a very attractive girl to boot. I did find out later in life however that it was through a medical condition that she attained the proportions she did, and not through gluttony.

She said in reply to his request "Of course he can stay Billy", then she turned to me and said "I hope that you will attend on Monday night, then we can enroll you into the club properly. We could do with a few more men in the club, no sooner they come in, and join, they are off again to join the Army or something." "What is your name by the way, I presume Billy has told you mine?" "Mo nerms Ronnie Smith, an' yes I'll come on Mondee, I'll bi lookin' forward ta that o will, an' thanks fer lerrin mi stay ternight, it's nice on ya." "Well bye bye for now Ronnie, and I'll see you on Monday then?" "Ar-r-rokay Miss, I'll bi yere."

"D' ya' wanna drink w'ile wim 'ere Ron?" Billy said after this lady had gone. "Ar-r-rile gerrem though, yove done enough fer me orlready, watcha want?" "O'll 'ave a cuppa tea, an' a san'wich" he replied smiling. There was a pause, and then he said "O betcha thought o meantcha ta pay fer the san'wich as well din ya'?", he was still smiling. "Well as a marra a fact o wuz gunna buy it fer ya' rany road up, so it would'en a come as a s'prise ta me", and with that I made my way to the two tables that served as the counter, leaving Billy standing where he was. I orderd "two teas", and then I turned to Billy, and said "W'at kinda san'wich yer want then?" " Nah-h-h, o dain" mean ya' ter pay fer mi san'wich as well Ron, od a paid fer that miself, 'onist", no smiling now though. "Soright Bill, I'll gerrit, yo' cun get the next one okay?" "Ar-r-rokay Ron, I'll 'ave Spam then, cuz the cheese allis giz mi the bleedin' gut's ache, an' thanks."

I collected the order, and then Bill and myself found a bench alongside some girls he knew, and sat down waiting for the band to commence to play.

After a while the band started up, the band leader announcing a "quick step". The song they played was "In the Mood", which I suppose was to get everyone going hoping to make a pleasant evening. I listened for a while. they were good, very good, so I settled down to enjoy the music for the evening. I really had learnt to appreciate this type of music, although "Our Dad" said "Warra bleedin' noise, taint like the old tunes, it's all bleedin' American tripe, tha's warrit is."

Billy got up and had a few dances, he was a very good dancer, and he could jitterbug really well, so he was very much in demand. Me, well I couldn't dance at all, and I must admit that I thought it all a bit "cissiefied", so I naturally hadn't bothered to learn. Never the less I was enjoying the evening, and I really did want to join this club. It was something different, and to me it looked as if it was going to be exciting as well. I mean all these girls, I thought, great, this is going to be great.

"The next dance Ladies and Gentlemen will be a Ladies invitation, thank you "it was the band leader again. The band struck up with a waltz "I'm in Love with two Sweethearts". As all the other tunes they had played that night so far it was excellent.

I sat there quietly. Billy had been "waltzed off" by the girl that had asked him if he was going to play the drums later. The lights had been dimmed slightly, and I contentedly watched the couples dancing by. This I thought was a whole new experience, and I was really enjoying it. I decided there and then that I would definitely join this club on Monday next.

"Excuse me, but would you like to dance?" I had been so entranced with the dancers, the music, and the general atmosphere of everything, that I hadn't noticed anyone approaching me. When I turned to see who had uttered these words, it had given me a bit of a start.

She stood there, a really nice girl. Dark wavy hair, a fresh complexion, as though she had lived in the countryside all her life. Big brown eyes, twinkling in the half light, her nose slightly broad, but attractive never the less, thickish lips red and soft, but no lipstick, in fact no make up at all. Her figure was a bit thick set, but not fat, and it was good. I liked this girl as soon as I had looked at her. She looked good, appeared good, and I found out later she was good in every sense of the word.

She smiled revealing lovely white teeth, a little uneven but nice. "Excuse me, but would you like to dance?" she repeated. I had been so busy looking at her, that I had forgotten the request, well not forgotten it, but become "flumaxed". I mean I had never been asked to dance by a girl before. I had a little laugh to myself at this thought. Then I pulled myself together, and thought this nice girl will think I'm terribly rude taking all this time to answer a simple request. I blurted out "Om sorry Miss, burr I can' dance, od love ta 'ave a dance, burr I'll on'y bi treadin' on ya' toes, cuz ov neva danced befowa. Om eve sa sorry yove bin troubled, an' thank ya' ferr raskin' me, thank ya'."

She just stood there and didn't answer for a while, then she smiled again. It was a most wonderful smile, and she then said "Look I hope that you won't take offence at me for what I'm about to say, but would you like me to teach you to dance. You don't have to say yes, if you'd rather not. I know some men aren't bothered about dancing but if you would like me to teach you, I would only be too happy to do so?"

"Well o don' know, o feel a birrov a fool really Miss, burr I would like ta learn. Ov bin watchin' a bit, an' o think od like it, burr I don' know w'etha od bi yenny good or not, watcha think then?" The ball was firmly back in her court.

"Yes come on then, or else the waltz will be over, before we've even started." I stood up and went onto the floor with her, and she told me what I'd got to do. Off we went around the floor, of course mistakes were made, by me but to my surprise, and the girl's not too many. "You seem to have a good sense of rhythm and it's helping a great deal "this girl informed me, as we skirted around the outside of the floor. Mentally my chest swelled with pride at this statement, and equally swelled was my head, for with that statement being uttered I suddenly thought I was "Fred Astaire", and with dire consequences. I thought I could do without guidance and proceeded in my own way. Result, I went a… over tip, and landed on the floor, much to the amusement of the girls and chaps in the vicinity where it happened.

The girl smiled down at me, and offered to help me up, but I refused and got back up myself. She said, still with that lovely smile "I think you have a way to go yet before you reach ballroom standards, but you are very good." I mumbled my apologies, and we went on dancing to the cheers of the same people who had been laughing a moment ago, which did my ego a power of good.

The three songs for this particular waltz finished, and naturally escorted this girl back to her seat. "Thank you very much" I said when she sat down amongst her girl friends. She looked up at me, stared for a moment and then replied "I wish they had more ladies invitations, and then I could teach you to dance a little more, that's if you'd like to?" "Well couldn' I come across anyway, an; ask ya' ferra dance an' nobody'd know if o could dance or not would they?" Another smile "Of course you could, how silly of me not to have thought of that, well I'll be seeing you then?"

There was a pause. She seemed to be searching for something else to say, and the only thing I could think of at that moment was, that she didn't know my name, so…" Oh by the way mi nerms Ron, Ron Smith, an' ove jus' come ta the dance ternight, burr I'm gunna join the club on Monday. O mean if om gunna 'ave a dance with ya' we'ed berra know one anutha's nerms, 'adn' we?" "Oh hello Ron." She offered her hand to me, and we shook. "My name's Peggy, Peggy Seal, and this is…." and she introduced me to her friends, and their names I have forgotten, but Peggy Seal never. I told them that I had come with Billy, and they all knew him. In fact I thought that everyone in this club knew one another quite well, and with each minute I spent here I was begining to like it more. It was in fact a completely new experience for me.

I continued to dance with Peggy, not only that but when I went back to Billy after the first dance, he suggested that we join the girls, which made it easier for me to ask Peggy to dance.

The band leader announced that there would be a short break whilst the lads had some refreshment, after the next waltz. It was during this dance that Billy went over to him, and I could see them having a quiet conversation.

This break for the band came, and they went off down the stairs "Ta gu up ta "The Roebuck", Billy informed me. When they had gone, Billy went across to the area set aside for the band, and another lad came from across the room and went to him.

Billy got behind the drum set. The other lad placed himself onto the piano stool. I waited excitedly. My mate, although I'd only met him again that night was actually going to play drums. The pianist started off with one of Glen Millers' numbers "Moonlight Serenade", with Billy coming in quietly, but competently. They sounded terrific. They played "A" Train" "String of Pearls", and then after a request by some of the girls the two exploded with "Drummin' Man" one of Gene Krupa's favourites. When they started up with this number, the whole crowd surrounded the band area, including Peggy, her friends, and me. Billy really excelled himself, he really was a good drummer, and the pianist was great as well. I found myself wishing that I could play drums like that. I did think of asking Billy if he would teach me, but I never did.

All too soon this most lovely evening came to an end, and we all made our way to the exit in Soho Hill. I had had a wonderful evening. I met some of my old school friends, and informed them I was joining the club on Monday. Amongst these friends was Dolly Coates, but of course I only knew her as Dolly. She was a little older than me, but I knew that she lived in Bridge Street West somewhere by Renee Barnes, and "Nunky Collins." I had said "'ello, 'ow are ya'" and she smiled and returned the compliment, but she was with a group of people so I didn't see her again that evening. I was to see her quite often, and I did meet her husband to be "Ron Blundell" at a later date.

We all stood outside this church cum youth club, and chatted away until the girls decided that they had better get off home if they didn't wish to get on the wrong side of their parents. We all said our goodnights, some promising to meet on Sunday night, and others on various nights. I told Peggy that I would be at the club definitely on Monday. She said that she would be there too, so we shook hands again and said "Good night" to one another. She went off with her friends up Soho Hill, and I went across to Billy who was talking to some more of his mates. We eventually broke away, and went back down Soho Hill towards "The Brook". I asked him if he would like to come up to Ma Davies's for a last hot fruit drink. He declined the offer, and left me at the junction with Claremont Road, right opposite "The Palladium", promising to see me again up the club sometime.

We said our "Goodnights he crossed over to Claremont Road and I carried on to "The Brook" itself. As I passed by "The Gulley" one of Scribban's horse and carts rumbled by me, a faint light showing through the black painted glass of the candle lamps either side of the cart. I immediately thought that it might be Racker Price, for he was usually the late bloke at Scribbans'. The reason for this late bloke tag of course was, that these type of men could not resist having their beer no matter what. Of course with Saturday being the day that people settled up with the breadman, or the milkman, meant that they would be much longer on the road. Consequently it did not allow them enough time to get back to their locals, so they used the different pubs on their round. How they managed to reckon up people's bills, and deliver the bread I'll never know, but they did.

95

What's more in my experience they did it quite well, in fact most of these types of blokes were better than average rounds men. Not only did they complete their rounds efficiently, but they seemed to gain new customers like nobody's business. In every bakery that I knew of anyway there was always one, or sometimes even two blokes that arrived back very late on a Saturday night. Although there was much grumbling by all the staff that had to wait for their return, such as stablemen, cashiers, and supervisors etc, they were always accepted with great tolerance. In fact in most cases it was deemed a great character honour for them somehow, although I never personally saw it that way. I always liked to get finished as quickly as possible and return home. Still it takes all kinds, doesn't it?

I watched the horse and cart as it rumbled its way over the cobblestones into Whitmore Street, which was the last evidence of the trams running down there, from "Tippers Corner". I thought momentarily of "Billy Short" at Rowlands, and another man, I've forgotten his name now who worked at Bradfords. All of the same mold as Racker Price they certainly were characters, wonderful characters. I little realised that I in this decade would be working for the same firm Scribbans', and "Racker" would still be coming in last from his round situated in the Kingstanding area.

Eventually the horse and cart disappeared around the bend by Soho Pool Wharf, and I walked across by The Benyon making my way up to Ma Davies's for a chat and a nice hot fruit drink.

"Warrow Ronnie" it was Jackie Walford who greeted me when I finally arrived in the shop just past New John Street West "'ow ya' diddlin' then?" "Warrow Jack, ov jus' bin up that club up So'o 'ill, an' ov 'ad a smashin' time. 'Ello Mrs Davies could I yavan' 'ot drink please, one o them blackcurrant one's o think, d' yo' wanna nutha one Jack?" "Ar-r-rokay Ronnie, thank ya'."

We sat there quietly, just Mrs Davies, who enjoyed a chat with us, Jack and myself, talking about this and that. All of a sudden Billy Gisbourne came in, wearing his Home Guard uniform. Very smart he looked, though rumour had it that he wore it but he wasn't really in the Home Guard. I must admit I had never had it authenticated, so I ignored the whole issue. Just a few minutes after Billy came in, Billy Farrington from out of the terrace by 'Bertie Harpers' shop in Icknield Street arrived. He was referred to as the local spiv, but again how true that was we'll never know. What I do know, and what I saw with my own eyes, was both of these men were quiet, and spoke well of everyone. Also they were both, always impeccable in their dress. They were always smart and neatly turned out, one in civilian clothes, the other mostly in uniform. I've no doubt that people more closely associated to these two men could give another version of them, but that's how I saw them, and that's how I remember them. They were two grand lads as far as I was concerned.

We all started chatting, and having a few laughs. Some other lads who I didn't know came in, some in uniform, and some civvies. In next to no time we were all as one big happy family. All of us were from Hockley, which of course we found out in our conversation. We talked about everything, from the trams being taken off the Hockley routes, the buses being installed, and the benefits for and against. We went on about the war, naturally. Suddenly we heard the quiet voice of Mrs Davies say "I'm sorry lads, but I must close now, it is getting late, but if anyone wants one last quick drink then I'll get it for you, but you must drink it up quickly, for I am a little tired."

" Nah-h-h, it's soright Mrs Davies," we all replied, almost in unison. We never imposed on this good lady's wishes. "We'll all gerrorff now, but we'll mek sure that yowa door's locked afowa we gu um, gu'night then."

"Goodnight boys, I'll see you all tomorrow no doubt?"

"Ar-r-ri 'spect yo' will Mrs Davies, I 'spect yo' will." With that we all piled out of the shop, and waited outside until we heard the bolts locked, and the keys turned. We all went our different ways, and I finally said "Gu'night" to Jack at the top of Frankie Anderton's openin, and wended my way happily the few yards up to 228.

It was well past midnight as I pushed my way into the house through the entrance in the entry. Everywhere was in darkness, complete darkness, so I thought I'd better not light the gas lamp, knowing me I'd probably break the mantle in the process, so I shut the door after me, and went straight upstairs to bed.

Our Kid was fast asleep, I could hear his breathing, quiet and even, so I undressed quietly laying my Sundee Best on the table. Then I searched under the bed for my working things, found them, and sorted the shirt out from amongst them, and put it on. Climbing into bed as gently as I could, so as not to wake Arthur, I then stretched out and lay there thinking about the evening's events.

No doubt about it, it was a completely new experience for me, and I really enjoyed it. I mentally made a note to ask Peggy on Monday night when the next dance would be, and more important, whether she would be there to give me further instructions. I really had taken to this dancing business. It was as though something new had entered into me, something not only new, but exciting. I found that the music was nice, and certainly the company at the club was nice. It really fulfilled everything I wanted, and more. The feeling that I was going to burst with all this new found excitement overwhelmed me somewhat, and I found that although I was lying perfectly still in bed I was sweating profusely. My thoughts then went on to dancing with Peggy. This of course I really did enjoy; to hold a girl in my arms for a period as long as the three dances to every type of dance played was nice. The feeling was quite wonderful, but it wasn't like the feeling I thought I might experience if I had been dancing with Ginger Rogers, Alice Faye, Betty Grable, Lana Turner, or anyone like that, but it certainly was new, and I was looking forward to this dancing thing again.

I then gave some thought to Peggy. She was, as I've already said, a very nice and a very attractive girl, but my thoughts on her were, I must admit, more like a sister and brother relationship. Well, that was my initial thought, anyway, I think it was.

I was indeed in a turmoil about things altogether. I couldn't seem to find an answer to it, although on the other hand I didn't make it a definite issue. Never the less I still wondered, although not too intently, on what the possible outcome would be.

Eventually I must have dropped off into a dreamless sleep. The next thing I knew, 'Our Dad' was shaking me gently, reminding me it was time to get up, and go to work. I got up straight away, gave thought to last night momentarily, smiled to myself and thought "Well warreva's gunna 'appen will 'appen any road up, so I'll jus' gerron an' enjoy it."

I got through Sunday okay. I went to 'The Grand Picture House' at night. There was a film I wanted to see which was, of course, the reason I didn't go to the club.

I woke up excitedly on the Monday morning, and rushed off to work. Unfortunately, everything didn't go to plan. I approached 'The Cross Guns' in Soho Road I spotted my friend Horace waiting by the bus stop. I pulled up and said "Worrow mate, yome a bit lert intcha, w'a' s 'appened, lert night las' night?" He smiled at me and said that he had been out late. It was one of those knowing smiles. I pretended I knew all about it, but really I hadn't got a bloody clue as to what it meant. Never the less I went along with it. "Well, o wuz a bloody mon arta rall worn't I?"

" 'ow ja like ta do us a ferva Ron?," was his next question.

" Are rany thin' 'orice, jus' nerm it."Lend us ya' bike, an' then o cun gerr inta werk on time, an' then yo cun cop the buzz, cuz it wunt marra about yo' bein' a bit lert will it?"

Of course, I was rather reluctant to do this really. I wanted the day to get on so that tonight would come a little quicker I knew it was silly, but that's how I felt. On the other hand Horace was my friend, and I didn't want to see him in the soup with the head stable bloke, who was also the blacksmith 'Sid.'

"Ar-r-ro course 'orice, 'ere yo' 'ave mi bike, an' I'll see yarra bit lerta, in Mrs Thomas's shed, okay?"

"Thanks a lot Ron, yove served mi life, O wunt fergerrit."

So with that he took my 'Kingsway' and rode off up the road, and I took his place in the queue to wait for the bus.

When I arrived at the dairy I found that Horace had already harnessed Dolly up for me, and put her in the float as well, so I hadn't lost any time at all.

I passed 'Teddy Sanford's' place, because it looked a little crowded with a long line of horse and carts, and petrol vans, and carried on to the coffee house on the corner of Feeder Street, which fortunately wasn't so crowded. I had gotten into the habit of sharing these two places for my morning breakfast, and cup of tea, whichever took my fancy, or - and this was more to the point - all according to how hungry I was that particular day. Of course cash was not a problem any longer for me, due to the gradual increase in tips from the people on the round, now that they had got used to me, and I had gotten used to the things they wanted from me.

I pulled Dolly into Feeder Street itself. I didn't like to leave her on the main Oldbury Road, with the amount of traffic. This included the Midland Red's going to either Oldbury or Dudley one way, and Birmingham the other, conveying workers to their different places of employment at this time in the morning.

I put her nose bag on, and she took a friendly nip at me, which I quickly avoided, then I gave her a gentle tap on her nose. This had indeed become somewhat of a routine with her and I. I think she was telling me in a way that she really loved me - well, I took it that way.

I went into this old boozer turned coffee house and went up to the 'Ann Shelton' look alike, ordered a large mug of tea, and three spam sandwiches. What was it about this ladies sandwiches, perhaps it was the meat itself. Never the less, she certainly made a lovely sandwich. It didn't matter where I went to, no one could ever match her's.

Finishing the round I went home and messed around for a while, not really doing anything in particular. It seemed ages before seven o'clock came. When it did I went upstairs and put mi Sundee Best on. I came down to be greeted with "Oh-h-h, an' w'ere ram yo' guin' ternight then, gorra wench ta see then a?" "Bloody 'ell 'e looks posh dunn 'e?" "Yo' mind watcha doin' with them wenches Ronnie." I tried to ignore all this 'Mickey' taking. I did blush however, which of course incited them into further comments, mostly from our wenches. Ruby Coney was there as well and she was giggling away, and making a few comments of her own. This made me a little bit careful of what I said, because I could have possibly got away with it from our wenches, but another wench, well, I wasn't too sure.

In the finish I left the middle room, and went out in sheer exasperation at these giggling bloody wenches. Off onto 'The Brook' I went. it was too early to go up to the club, so I mooched around for a while, looking in the different shops, to pass the time away. In the finish I got really browned off and made my way up Soho Hill to the big ornate ex church.

When I arrived I found to my surprise that I wasn't the only one that was slightly early, for there on the steps leading to the entrance was a gang of about eight chaps roughly about my age, though some were just a little bit older, sitting on cold concrete slabs.

"Worrow mate, o see yome a birr early aintcha?", said the biggest of the crowd.

"Ar-r-ri thought od come a little bit in front of time cuz it's the first time ov come in the wick, ov come ta join up. O wuz 'ere on Sat'dee night w'en they yad the dance, an' it wuz great, burr I dain" see yo' lot thaya?"

"Nah-h-h mate we cudden come on Sat'dee, we 'ad otha things ta do, dain' we?" He turned to the other blokes for confirmation of this statement, as though he thought that I didn't believe him or something. At this question to these other blokes they all burst out laughing, and repeated in unison "Yere we 'ad berra things ta do."

I thought to myself "Funny bleeders these lot, od berra watch miself" so went on "Well it must 'ave bin bleedin' funny ta mek yarrall laugh like that, o wish odda bin thayfi misllf, an' then o' coulda sin the bleedin' joke." With that I went to turn away, thinking I don't like the look of them, but I'll play it safe there's too many of them for me on my own. I further thought, at least if I'm in a position to run, I'll have a head start on them.

Unfortunately when I went to move down Soho Hill, I found my road was blocked by a crowd of people coming up the hill, presumably coming to the club. I turned and made my way up the hill, but who should be facing me but Peggy, with a few of her mates. I had to stop and say hello to them, and further more I had to go back up the steps with them into the club. One of the girls in the crowd coming down Soho Hill was the lady that looked like my Cousin Edna, and it was her that I had come to see.

The lady opened the doors, and we all went in. Once inside and the black out curtains were drawn she put a light on in the very ornate porch. Then she opened the inside doors, whilst we stood where we were. By this time of course I had more or less teamed up with Peggy, for she was the only person I really knew. The lady went into the main building and put these lights on in preparation for the night's activities.

I suddenly heard a right chowrow behind me, and turned to see what is was. "Oh take no notice of them Ron, they are all mouth and trousers. That Billy and his gang from Handsworth, they think they are funny, but no one takes any notice of them really. Now you come on over here and see Miss... , and she will sign you in properly."

"Ar-r-rokay Peggy." With that I went over to a small desk situated in the far left hand corner of this lower hall.

I did all that was necessary, paid my weekly fee, which was one and sixpence, and that was it. I was a fully fledged member of the Y.W.C.A. I had already decided not to mention this Y.W.C.A. to anyone, for they might have gotten the wrong idea about things.

On completion of my initiation into the club I went across to Peggy again and to my surprise I found her to be talking to this big fellow, whom I had presumed to be the leader of this 'Handsworth Gang.'

" 'ello Peggy," I started off. I was of course nervous, well, a little nervous of Peggy. Immediately I'd said " 'ello." I realised it was wrong, for we had already met that evening. Naturally, I was more than a little nervous of this big guy. "Well, ov signed in, an' om now a memba of the club," but it was the guy that answered, not Peggy.

"Worrow pal, mo nerms Billy, Billy Dipple, an' all them chaps that yo' saw on the steps, are mi merts. It's nice ta see anutha ferce in 'ere," and with this he stuck out a huge hand for me to shake.

Billy Dipple moved away after this initial welcome. Of course, I had had other ideas about this bloke, and none of them good, so I was more than happy that he wanted to be friendly, which he did, for during this initial conversation this was his indication.

I asked Peggy if she would like a cup of tea, or something, and she said yes she would. So I went over to the make-do canteen and got some tea and cakes, then returned to where she was seated.

She explained the general running of the club, and what kind of activities there were. Debates on all kinds of subjects were held and apparently were very popular. Then they did plays, which they put on themselves then invited the general public in - at a fee, of course - which was given to a good charity. All kinds of pastimes were mentioned. The one I was interested in at that moment she never mentioned, so in the end I had to say "Warra bout dancin, Peggy, don'tcha do any dancin' in the wick?"

"Well-l-l, no, not really, but I tell you what, they do hold a tea dance here on a Wednesday afternoon. It isn't run by the club, someone else runs it. Anyone can attend, so if you're interested?"

"Well, as ya' know, o can' dance yet, well not very well any road up, an' o wuz thinkin' that yode bi thaya. It's no good mi guin' on mi yone, so I'll lave ta wert till Sat'dee night. Do they 'old dances ev'ry Sat'dee night Peggy?" I had gabbled my conversation to Peggy, trying to hide my disappointment. "That was really the main reason I had joined the club, to learn to dance, or at least be able to go round the floor in some type of efficient way."

She stared at me for a moment, and then that smile came onto her face again. Not a condescending smile, but a very understanding one. Then she said "Well Ron, I do have some Wednesday afternoons off, and I know that you do, so what do you think? If I come we could dance together, and then no one would know only me that you can't dance properly yet will they? Who knows, in a couple, or three weeks, you will have gained enough confidence to go to dances on your own then." This was one of the better moments of my life. I couldn't have wished for a better proposition, I had really gotten into this dancing lark, and Peggy was the answer to my prayers. I really couldn't thank her enough, and on top of all this she had got that Wednesday afternoon off, so it was 'all systems go.'

Peggy had to go off somewhere just after this, so she left me on my own. I sat there for a while, then I thought I'd better make an effort to do something, I just couldn't sit here all night. I had noticed that most of the people had gone up to the other hall above, so I decided that I'd go up there and see what was going on.

When I arrived in the upstairs hall I saw that Bill was having some 'donnuck' with his mates. They were chatting to some of the girls and it was my intention to go over to them, but I suddenly heard a voice, in a very Welsh accent say "Hello there, I haven't seen you before, have you just joined our happy band?"

Turning around I saw a very big, attractive girl. "O ov on'y jus' joined Miss, jus this minnit, downstairs. O did come tathe dance on Sat'dee night, burr I dain see yo'."

"No, I didn't come, I was going to, but I had a last minute change of plans, which made it impossible."

She really was very attractive, her hair was thick, and lustrous. It was pushed upwards, and then finished off in a plaid down the nape of her neck, and the colour was chestnut. Her big brown eyes twinkled, but gave off a certain defiance, with the eyelashes long and thick. Her skin was like alabaster, the nose very Roman. On anyone else it would have looked awful, but on this girl it certainly was an added attraction. Her lips were extremely thin, but perfectly shaped, and teeth matched everything else; they too were perfect. Like I said, she was a big girl, but her shape was well proportioned despite this. Her legs were beautiful, which really didn't go with the size of her body, but never the less this was something that would be overlooked with all her other attributes.

" My name's (she did tell me but like so many other things, I've forgotten) and I'm what you might call a general factotum in the club, I'm more or less part of the furniture. I introduce students when they come here from other parts of the country Sometimes I meet them off the trains, get them fixed up with lodgings, and all that kind of thing." She smiled after this lengthy introduction, and I wondered if she had realised that I hadn't got a bloody clue what she was on about. I did however appreciate that smile, it did wonders for my ego.

We chatted on for a while, and most of her chat I didn't understand, but put on a knowing face, anyway. I was, to put it in a nutshell, out of my class with this most attractive, and well educated girl. Never the less it didn't stop me admiring her greatly, wishing that I could have her charm, and intelligence. I was to see a great deal of this girl, but alas only fleetingly, just to say "Hello" etc.

This Monday night didn't come up to my expectations. I thought that it would be like Saturday night again, but it wasn't to be. Consequently after about an hour I began to get a little 'cheesed off.' Of course it wasn't the club's fault, it was mine. I didn't want to play any of the games provided, and Peggy had gone off somewhere, with her mates. Well, she wasn't my keeper was she?

In the end I decided to leave. I found Peg, and reminded her about Wednesday afternoon, and she confirmed that it commenced at two o'clock. Of course, I didn't tell her the real reason for me leaving early I told her that I'd got to meet someone, and she accepted this. I thought at the time that her lovely eyes denoted a slight disappointment.

I went downstairs not knowing quite what I was going to do, when Bill Dipple arrived on the scene. "W'ere ya' guin' mert, 'ave yarrad enough already?"

"Nah-h-h, o thought od gu an' get mi some chips or somethin', om bleedin' starvin', an' theyve on'y got cerks up thaya."

"Yo' wanna gu up Kelly's then mert, up on the main So'o Road, it's great up thaya, an' yo'll l getcha belly full o' grub if yome 'ungry." We allis tek Albert 'ere, up ta Kelly's, fer a good blow out, don' we Al?"

This Albert he questioned about the 'blow out', looked a bit on the soft side to me. Bill must have cottoned on by the look on my face, because he went on, "Oh, don' worry about 'im mert, it's a bloody sherm it is, jus' cuz 'e ain't quite twelve pennies to the shillin', nobody wants ta know 'im. Now me an' mi merts think a bit different to others, an' we tek 'im nearly ev'ryw'ere with us, cuz 'e ain' a bad lad am yarr Albert?" The lad looked at Bill, and gave a big grin, and made some type of gurgling sound, which I assumed was a positive answer to Bill's question.

Albert would be about seventeen or eighteen when I met him at the Y.W.C.A for the first time, although due to his condition, he didn't appear to be anywhere near that age. He looked about twelve to fourteen. He wasn't a bad looking lad really, slightly stooped and slow in movement. One thing I do know about him though, he absolutely worshiped Bill and his friends This friendship was to go on for many years, for although I wasn't part of the set up, I used to see them periodically throughout the years that followed, and Albert always appeared to be with Bill and his mates.

This meeting of course changed my whole point of view about Bill Dipple. Outwardly he looked a very tough bloke, and he was very tough, but he took care of Albert with the fondness, and care, a Mother would have for her child. Right from the word go, after this meeting I assumed the greatest respect, for Bill Dipple and the Handsworth gang, and this respect remains with me to this day.

I have seen Albert on his own in later years, mostly in Black Patch Park, Winson Green, and have greeted him with the usual " 'allo", and that same grin has appeared on his face, with a gurgling sound, that I assumed meant "Thanks mate for bothering to associate with me." This in turn gave me a wonderful sense of being; this was what real life was all about, I thought.

I came out of the club on that Monday night, and found that it was raining slightly. Instead of walking to Soho Road as had been my intention, I went across to the bus stop just past Claremont Road, opposite 'The Roebuck' to ride to my new eating place. What was it called? Kelly's, that was it, Kelly's Cafe. Bill had told me exactly where it was, just on the left-hand side of Soho Road, past Boulton Road. When the conductor arrived to collect my fare I told him, "One ta the 'Cross Guns' please."

Alighting at the stop, I went over Boulton Road passing the ironmongers on the one corner and the wool shop on the other. In between the tobacconist's, and 'The Little Red Shop' I found 'Kelly's Cafe.'

Oh what a gorgeous smell there was coming from within. The windows were steamed up with all the cooking going on inside, and the blackout shades also made it difficult for me to see what the layout was. In the end I opened the door, and went in. It was absolutely packed, mostly with blokes, but there were a few girls about too. This one room was heavy with the smell of different meats being cooked, of tea, coffee, cigarette smoke, girls' perfume, blokes' brilliantine, and God knows how many other distinctive aromas, but it was all pleasant enough. I made my way to the counter on the far side of this single-roomed shop, and joined the large queue waiting to be served.

Behind the counter, in a spotless white shirt and apron was - I learned later - one of the Kelly brothers. He was an attractive man, short in stature. Dark wavy hair, blue eyes, thin pointed nose, and thin lips, but putting it altogether, and probably with a much better description than I have given, 'a good looking guy.' One predominantly, unfortunate feature about him, however, was a very pronounced limp, due to a shortening of one leg, which was compensated by him wearing a very high soled and heeled boot.

At last it was my turn to be served. I had scanned the board with its chalked menu. I gave the spam, powdered egg, and cheese sandwiches a miss, finally settling for a couple of sausage sandwiches. Behind the counter was a girl, as well as Bill Kelly, serving another girl, much younger than the one behind the counter, collecting the dirty crocks from the tables and taking them out back somewhere. It was evident that a good deal of the cooking was completed out front, behind the counter, I imagine that the main cooking was done out back.

It was Bill who served me. "Watcha want cocka?, he asked with a slight cockney accent. Whether he was a cockney or not I never did find out, not that I was bothered anyway.

"Two sausage san'wichis, an' a cuppa tea please," I replied. He went to the big pan on the cooker, and commenced to prepare my order, which he served very quickly. I paid the 1/6d for the meal, 8d each for the sandwiches, and 2d for the large mug of tea. I then, turned from the counter to find out where I was going to sit to enjoy these most fragrant smelling, and appetising looking sandwiches.

I scanned the one and only room, peering through a smoky haze, but couldn't see any vacant seats "Oi, mate, oi, yo', ova rere." I turned slightly from where I had been looking. After a couple of seconds I saw this bloke waving his arms at me, evidently trying to attract my attention. When he saw that I had at last spotted him, he then pointed downwards, and following his direction I noticed the empty stool right by him.

I moved over to this bloke, and put my plate and mug on the table. "Thanks mate for gein mi the nod," I said, and sat down.

"Yome nu around 'ere aintcha?"

"Ar-r-rov bin past 'undreds o times, burr I've neva bin in befowa, burr it's nice innit?"

"Ar-r-r we use it ta lot, me an' mimates 'ere, thas w'en we come on ta the 'Monkee Run' lookin' fer some tarts, don' we Pat?"

This last question was directed at a very mournful looking bloke, God he looked as miserable as sin. I thought when I looked at him a little closer that he was going to burst into tears any moment. That was my first impression, but oh, how wrong I was.

A smile broke out on this bloke's face. Well, it wasn't a complete smile, it was as if he had eaten something, and was now in the process of regurgitating it. "Oh are, we always come lookin' fer tarts, mostly in the wick though, cuz there's otha things we do ov a wick end." This grimace of his seemed to widen. I took this as him having told a joke or something, but I didn't pry. Whatever it was, was their business and not mine.

I got stuck into my sausage sandwiches, and liked them so much that I didn't really want to talk to anyone. There were three blokes around this table, but at the time I didn't know whether they were with one another or not. As I've already said, "I dain' wanna stick my nose in."

I finished my meal at last, and supped my mug of tea. "Blimey mate, yove enjoyed tharr ain'tcha." This was from the bloke, who had directed me to the table. He was a very thin lad, his hair was blond, really blond, and curly. I envied this about him; he reminded me of Danny Kaye. The face was very narrow, and he sported a thin nose, which matched the face. Eyes blue, and very lively, the lashes were long, just like girls. His narrow lips, when he smiled, revealed big white teeth. Smartly dressed, well as much as I could see of him. Yes, I thought, "Yo' could pass as Danny Kaye yo' could. The guy he had called Pat had brownish hair, very smart, and wavy. His complexion, unlike 'Danny Kaye's' whose was very pale, was the exact opposite, a very blotchy red. Eyes that seemed half asleep, slinky in a way, were a kind of brownish blue, and underneath the left eye was a reddish spot, which I assumed was a birth- mark. The nose was flattish, but not as evident as a boxer's flat nose, and beneath were lips that seemed to have a permanent snarl on them. When he parted them, which wasn't too often, they showed very good teeth. Pat was also smartly dressed. The descriptive character I have given did not match his real character, however, for he was a very nice bloke.

The third lad hadn't said anything so far; he was busy smoking, and looking around at the tarts in the coffee house. His hair was of a nondescript colour, due to the amount of grease he had on it, but never the less it was smartly plastered. This lad's face was red, and I mean red it was like 'A Turkey Cock's A.' Big blue eyes which were watering all the time, and a big nose to match. His mouth was large, and this guy laughed, he laughed a lot and revealed a mouthful of rotten decaying teeth, but he didn't seem to mind about that, so I thought "O berr 'e thinks, bum ta ev'ryone." Unlike the other two he didn't sport a collar and tie, he had an open neck shirt, under an old sports coat. In the short time I had been with this character I'd learnt that he really was a fun bloke. It appeared to be a 'disease' with him, this general happiness.

"D any on ya' wanna nutha cuppa tea?", I asked, ignoring the statement from 'Danny Kaye.' I thought they seem to be friendly enough, I was always one for getting to know someone new, and I enjoyed it. 'Bad Teeth' said, "Ar-r-rile 'ave a cup mate." 'Solemn Features' just said "Nah," but 'Danny Kaye' said, "Nah it's soright mate, I'll gu an' gerrem." I refused this offer, and said "Look mate, yo' got mi a seat, so o think o owe yo' summat, so let mi getcha a cuppa tea it's the least o cun do."

104

"Ar-r-rorlright then, we'll all a one," was the final reply from this lookalike 'Film Star.'

I went across to the counter, and ordered four mugs of tea. This time it was the lady who served me. I took the mugs of tea back to my new found friends, placed them in front of them, and they thanked me. Settling back onto my stool I fished around in my jacket pocket, and finally withdrew a packet of 'Senior Service.' I had obtained these from Mrs Lees that morning. I had started smoking, just a little then. I really bought these 'Senior Service' though, to show off on my appearance at the Y.W.C.A. this evening for the first time, but, of course, things didn't materialise as I thought they would. Consequently no reason for producing this posh packet of fags was there? I offered the fags around, and 'Bad Teeth' took one, 'Solemn Features' did the same, but 'Danny Kaye' refused, telling me he didn't use them.

After lighting our 'ciggies' we sat comfortably, supping tea, and drawing deeply on our 'Senior Service.' 'Danny Kaye' was the first one to talk. "Well o' suppose we'd berra get ta know each otha 'adn' we? We can' sit 'ere all bleedin' night, addressing one anutha with ah, an' um, an' w'atsit."

He turned to me and said, "Mo nerms Artha Jones, but all mi frien's call mi 'Danny Kaye,' and with this statement he brushed his hair back with the palm of his hand. I supposed that what he was telling me was "Don' yo' think o look like 'im?"

"I thought, that's w'o yo' looked like, w'en yo' called me yover, yo' do look 'actly like 'im." With that I stuck my hand out and we shook. Arthur, or should I say 'Danny' then introduced the other two guys. First 'Solemn Features,' "This is Pat Gallagagh, an' 'e lives in Brewery Street, an' laughin' boy ova thaya (he pointed to 'Bad Teeth') 'is nerms Joe… (again I've forgotten his name, but never the lad, he really was a good pal) an' 'e lives up Church Terrice, just afowa ya' get ta the 'cop shop' on 'oly'ead Road. I live at the back of the shoeshop just afowa ya' get ta Brewery Street, do ya' know w'ere o mean?"

"Ar-r-ro think o do, there's some shops jus' lay back orff the road, jus' arta yo' pas' Milestone Lane, is that the plerce?"

"Ar-r-r yove gorrit, it's an openin, an' it leads ta some 'ousis up the back, burr owa rouse, is on the left 'and side, an' it is the old livin' part of the shoeshop, burr it's sealed orff now." They all then looked at me.

"O don' come frum roun' 'ere rat all. O come frum 'ockley, ' 'ockley Brook.' "

"O' we don' get down thaya much," said Joe. "We like ta stick roun' owa'rr rown end don' we?" and he looked at the other two for confirmation of his statement.

"Ar-r-r we don' move frum roun' 'ere much, we gerrall the donnuck we wan' roun' an'swuth. Any road up w'at brings yo' up 'ere all the way frum 'ockley then?"

I explained briefly about the club, and then getting browned off, when I realised there was to be no dancing, I went on and told them about the Tea Dance on Wednesday afternoon, and Peggy. When I told them this I think that they assumed that Peggy was my girl friend, by the looks they gave me. I of course did not deny this. What the hell, I thought.

On completion of the rather lengthy up-date of my reason for being up in 'an'swoth, Joe (of the bad teeth) said, "D ya' wanna come wi' us up the monkee run ferra bit then? Er-r-r, oh we don' even know yowa nerm w'arris it?"

"Oh om sorry, mo nerms Ron, Ron Smith."

"Well, would ya' like ta come wi' us up the monkee run then?"

"Ar-r-ro course o would, anythin' ferra chernge."

"We all left the cafe, and went in the direction of 'The Regal' to look for 'tarts.' During the course of this search for girls, we chatted and got to know one another better. Danny, and Pat, didn't mention where they worked, but Joe did. He worked for a butcher just past 'Bannister and Thatchers' situated on the corner of Holyhead Road and Crocketts Road, opposite 'The Albion' cinema. I told them that I worked for Handsworth Dairies Joe interrupted this flow of conversation, telling me, "There's a bloke up owa terrice nerm Bob Jones who werks thaya, d ya' know 'im?"

"Nah o don' know 'im, burr I 'spect o will soon. Mind yo' I ain' bin thaya, at Island Road lung, cuz ov bin up Wes' Brom'ich. Wa's 'e like any way, jus' in cerse o bump inta 'im, an' o cun tell 'im o know yo' ".

"O-o-o-o 'es a big lanky bloke, eva sa bleedin' thin, but tall with it, 'e looks like a stick a bleedin' r'ubob on legs, tha's warr 'e looks like."

With this last comment he burst out laughing, and Pat and Danny joined in, so I presumed that they knew this Bob Jones as well.

We walked up as far as Joe's work place, the butchers, and he told me that he earned good money, and Danny said "Ar-r-r 'e's a good un is Joe. 'e allis shares 'is dough we us w'en we'em broke. O don' know w'ere 'e get's it all frum."

They told me, all of them in turn, although different aspects, of the normal outing they had on a Sunday. Apparently they caught 'The Fisherman's Express' from Handsworth and Smethwick Station at the bottom of Booth Street at 8.15, which took them to Bewdley. They alighted at Bewdley, but the train went on through Arley, Highley, and finally finished at Bridgenorth. They spent the day there then returned at about seven o'clock in the evening. The rest of Sunday they spent up the 'Monkey Run' and in 'Kelly's.'

Of course, you have already realised why it was called 'The Fisherman's Express.' This was the train, normally a steam engine, but sometimes the new 'Mono Rail Car,' which was a single vehicle, much like a single deck tram, which ran from Snow Hill Station to Bridgenorth. Most Brummagem fishermen used this for fishing the Severn. I have been back in time quite often on this self same line, bringing back memories in their entirety during the 'eighties, and 'nineties through the courtesy of those dedicated people who run The Severn Valley Railway. It never fails to take me back in time, for they have achieved what a lot of other people strive for 'absolute genuine re-creation' of the way this line was run. Stations, staff, and the full working of a truly great age, 'The Steam Era.'

Danny, Pat, Joe, and myself crossed over the Holyhead Road, and looked at the cabinet containing the stills for the next week's showing. Then we went across the road to 'The New Inns' and on back down passing 'The Princes Suite,' and Farcroft Avenue. When we went by Handsworth Social Club we heard music being played. We stopped and listened for a while, and assumed that there was a dance in progress. This naturally renewed my interest in this 'dancing lark' again.

The rest of that evening was spent in much the same vein. Chatting away. getting to know one another, and in between that shouting across the road to some 'tarts' that happened to be passing. We did stop and talk to one bunch of girls, but nothing arose from this, so we went on our way.

All three of them invited me on the trip to Bewdley, but of course I had to decline due to my work. Joe said, "W'y don' ya' knock one orff, an' come with us Ron, it wun' 'urt, they wun' miss ya'."

"Nah-h-h od berra not, that Davies bloke ud 'ave mi guts fer gartas, 'e's a bleeda 'e is, 'e'd 'ave the Ministry ov Werks bloke up ta me, 'e would. The larst thing o want is that bloke arta me, cuz yome in real trouble if 'e get's 'old on ya'. Thanks any road up it's nice on ya' ta arsk mi, burr it'll bi to troublesome."

Finally, we said our "Goodnights" and promised to meet again on Friday. Danny told me to call for him, and then we would take it from there. I caught the bus at the stop just opposite 'The Regal' and made my way back to 'The Brook' and 'Ma Davies's' for my usual nightcap.

These three lads were to play a prominent part in my life, during the latter part of the War, right up until the time I joined The Royal Navy . After that, like so many other friendships with all kinds of people, they seemed to fade without any apparent reason. It was Danny that I had more to do with than Joe, or Pat, but just like the buses that ran up and down Holyhead Road, we passed one another frequently.

I rushed home from work on Wednesday, had my dinner, but during the meal I kept looking at the clock on the mantlepiece. "W'a's sa marra wi' yo' our Ronnie, yo' gorra date or summat. Yo' ain' gorra wench ta see 'ave ya'? If yo' 'ave yo' mind 'ow ya' gu we 'er, don' yo' come bringin' ya' troubles um wi' ya', we gorr enough troubles as it is."

"Nah-h-h Mom, I ain' gorra wench ta see, well I yave gorra wench ta see, burrit ain' like that. This wench is learnin' mi ta dance, but don' tell the wenches will ya'? 'er nerms Peggy, Peggy Seal, an' o met 'er up at the club, up So'o 'ill, las' Satadee, tha's sall Mom,'onist itis."

'Our Mom' wasn't completely satisfied with this answer, but what option had she? "Well yo' jus' watch w'at yome doin' tha's sall?" I hadn't got a bloody clue what she was on about. Watch what I was doing ? I was only going to dance with Peggy, I wasn't going to kiss her or anything like that. I mean it wasn't like that between Peggy and I, all it was was dancing. Anyway I didn't want to start kissing yet, and least of all Peggy, for like I told you earlier she was just like another sister to me. I mean if I did go out with a girl that I was in love with, whatever that meant, I would have to watch what I was doing then wouldn't I? If I started kissing her too much, she could have a baby couldn't she? The last thing I wanted was to have to go home and tell 'you know who' I had given a girl a baby. God she was bad enough normally. If I went home and told I had been kissing a girl too much, and now she was having a baby she would really blow her top.

Eventually, I went upstairs and for the second time that week I donned my Sundee Best.

I arrived at the club just gone two fifteen. Entering the lower hall I found that it was completely empty, which straight away brought on a panic attack. I thought, what if Peggy had been having me on, and there wasn't any tea dance? Then I reasoned with myself, she wouldn't do that she was too nice. All kinds of things ran through my mind. I just stood there, not quite sure what to do. Finally I made up my mind, I'd go back home, Peggy had told me a lie, there wasn't a tea dance, or any other kind of dance for that matter.

I turned and was approaching the exit, when I heard Peggy's voice behind me. "Ron, come on this way, the dance is upstairs. I bet you thought it was down here and no one had turned up didn't you?"

"Nah-h-h Peggy, I just thought, I ain' gorreny fags, an' o wuz guin' tasee if they'd gorreny at that shop nearly on the corner Naden Road." I had, had to lie, and that one was the first that came into my mind. It seemed to go down with Peggy, for she went on, "Well hurry up then Ron, or else you'll miss the first waltz."

"Nah-h-h I'll ferget the fags, om smokin' too much any road up, I'll ge 'em a miss." I went back to Peggy, and we went upstairs together. Half way up we heard the band strike up with "When I grow too old to dream", so we hurried, and when we reached the top hall, we went straight onto the floor. It was wonderful, it's what I had been waiting for since last Saturday.

We spent that first Wednesday afternoon in a world of our own, just Peggy and me. All the other people there didn't know us, and we didn't know them, so we just had the afternoon to ourselves, and we danced, and danced, and danced.

All too soon, however, it came to an end. It's marvellous isn't it, when you are really enjoying yourself how quickly the time goes by. I said "Tarrar" to Peggy at the foot of the steps, and said that I would see her tonight. Off she went to her house in Villa Road, number seventeen. (I had found out this earlier.) I went in the opposite direction to 'The Brook.' I was on top of the world; I was on 'cloud eleven.' It really had been a wonderful afternoon. Dancing was the thing during this period in my life, and I was looking forward to Saturday night.

My life had taken on a new shape. Of course, I didn't know this was happening, but does anyone? I was going through a further stage, one for which I should have received special guidance. Who was to give this assistance that would put me on the right road? The answer was simple, of course, no one. As I've said so many times, the war had caused so much upset in everyone's lives. Not all tragic, though I'm glad to say. Many a success story came from out of the final ashes of this 'War of Wars' against Germany, Italy, and Japan.

Dolly, my mare, gave me three upsets during our short but loving period together, the first two both happening in Gresham Road. During the war apples were only seasonal; you'd either got too many, or practically none at all. It was roughly about August or the begining of September that the first incident occurred, when apples were just really coming onto the market from the orchards around Evesham, and that area.

We turned into Gresham Road as usual to serve the customers either side up to Rood End Road, but today just up on the left-hand side was a horse-drawn flat wagon with an home made canopy over it. I hadn't seen this vehicle before, but I didn't attach too much importance to that. Several things appeared, and happened that I hadn't seen, or heard of, so it wasn't a great surprise to me to see this strange vehicle in the road.

The wagon was laden with vegetables and fruit, mostly apples, so I imagined, although I was never sure, that this bloke was one of the many fly-by-nights who were predominant at this time, when everything was in short supply, These spivs could, and would, get you anything - for a price that is.

I pulled Dolly up, and went down the first entry to deliver round the back. Oh God, when I returned, I just couldn't believe my eyes. At first glance I thought that she had just moved up the road a little, which was a thing she did on occasions. I wasn't too concerned as I wended my way back up the entry, and couldn't see the float where I had left it. On arrival at the top of this passageway however I looked and all I could see at first was the back end of the float alongside this dilapidated flat cart. I ran up to the carts as quickly as I could, and when I arrived at the scene, I realised that it hadn't made a scrap of difference me hurrying. The bloke's cart was absolutely devastated, Dolly had had a whale of a time! Apples, cabbages, carrots, and everything else on his cart had been chewed on, well most of them any road up. It was a bloody mess, and I had to think quickly. I thought if ever this bloke comes back to his cart and catches Dolly and me now, God knows what would happen. The thought of physical violence against my finely tuned features didn't appeal to me one bit. I hadn't seen this bloke, so I didn't know what I might have been up against. I did the only thing any decent 'ockleyite would have done: I 'pissed off', ourove it in double quick time!"

I turned Dolly around clicked her on speedily back down the short stretch of Gresham Road, back into Wellesley Road, turned right going quickly to the end went back up Vernon Road to the top, where I turned left. I passed the other boozer, nearly opposite 'The Bell,' Inn and turned left again to the location of my last customers.

I served these last few customers first, and then turned Dolly around, and commenced doing this last part of my round backwards, for obvious reasons, which I've no need to spell out for you.

By the time I re-entered Gresham Road to serve the customers I had left because of the incident, I could see no sign of the flat wagon. I sighed with relief, but just like me, it brought on a fit of the titters.

I never said a word to anyone about this most unfortunate incident, and no one ever referred to it. I never saw that cart in the road, or in any of the roads I served for that matter, so I thought that I had correctly assumed that he was indeed one of these fly-by-nights, and was happy, thinking that I had chalked one up against the 'enemy.'

The second incident in Gresham Road wasn't quite as bad. One of the customers, again on the left hand side of the road, was in the custom of giving Dolly a carrot or two when I'd delivered the milk. If she was out she would leave the carrot by the empties, and I would give Dolly the little present.

One day when I went the lady was out and this time no carrot. I left the milk, picked the empties up, and didn't give the matter any further thought. I delivered the milk up the next entry, and when I returned I found Dolly still outside the first entry. Normally she moved up the road with me as I went. This time however she had not moved. I had to go back finally and fetch her, and she was most reluctant to move. She took a nip at me, and I dabbed her one. She was most adamant, she could not be moved. In desperation I said "Well yo' cun bloody well stop thaya then ya' stubbo'n little sod." I started to deliver the milk from the float to customers, without the mare moving. (That was my intention anyway.) After a couple of deliveries I returned to the float only to find the rear end of it protruding from the first entry. I nearly died.

When I got to the site I found that she had managed somehow to get part the way down the entry, but in the process she had wedged the shafts firmly between the two low walls separating the little front gardens of these houses. I couldn't get to her, although I pulled on the reins she wouldn't come out. In the end I had to go and knock on the front door of one of my other customers in the same block of houses and request permission to go through the house, and then go up the entry from the bottom.

One of the ladies allowed me to go through, and I made my way up the entry, and after much shoving, and threatening, and swearing I may add, she moved slightly backwards, and I thought I'd won. You must be joking. Let a man get the best of her? forget it! I moved her backwards about three feet, and suddenly she charged forward again, and wedged the float even more firmly. I just didn't know what to do. She was so stubborn was Dolly. I stood there for some time trying to persuade this bloody minded, brown fur coated 'woman,' on four legs to go in reverse, but nothing, nothing at all.

"Co-o-o-e-e-e, co-o-o-e-e-e, Mr Milkman. Mr Milkman, are yo' thaya?" I thought "Norra nutha bleedin' woman come ta plague mi bleedin' life o wonda w'o this can be." I looked back down the entry, nothing. I went right to the bottom looked left, and then right, still nothing. I walked back up the entry, and thought perhaps the lady who had shouted was shouting some other milkman in the street. I just stood there trying to figure out what I was going to do, when all of a sudden, "Mr Milkman, can yo' move yarr 'orse on'y o ca'n' get down mi entry.

I looked around the float, and Dolly the bloody vicious, and could just see the lady who I now realised was talking to me. It was indeed the lady who normally gave this rogue on four legs her carrot. Suddenly it struck me what had happened, and I thought what a bloody fool I had been not to realise it. Dolly had not been given her carrot that morning, and consequently had gone down the entry after it, thinking the lady had forgotten her, which of course was true.

"Ar-r-r-r love I'll move mi yoss, w'en yo' bring 'er carrot out ferr 'er, cuz tha's w'y she's in this bloody mess, she's come arta rer treat, tha's w'at she's done."

I was so grateful really, and at the same time I was mad. Grateful that the lady had turned up, which would undoubtedly solve the problem; mad because I hadn't thought of the situation earlier, so preventing all this happening in the first place.

Eventually the lady returned with Dolly's treat, which she handed to me. First, I had to show Dolly the carrot, to make her understand that her treat had arrived at last. Then with this vegetable close to her nose I gently backed her out of the entry. I didn't know whether it would work, but to my great relief it did.

When we had at last extricated the float, and the 'naughty Dolly,' I examined the vehicle for damage. There was some, but to my relief it was minimal. Just a bit of paint scratched off the shafts, which I didn't think even worth mentioning when I arrived back at the dairy.

The third incident was very frightening for me, as well as Dolly, and it could have ended tragically.

I was returning to depot from my round when it happened. Dolly had been very queer during the morning. She was having a go at me more often than usual. Every time I returned to the float after a delivery, even if I didn't have to go anywhere near to her, she would turn her head and make a snap at the air. Not only that, but she was kicking back at the front of the float, and that was unusual, for she was hurting herself more than the wood. Naturally I just thought that she had "got one on 'er," so I took no notice.

I turned into Roebuck Lane with Dolly really straining at the bit. All of a sudden she increased her rate of pace to an incredible speed, and I realised very quickly that I was losing control. I had to lean backwards pulling hard on the reins until I was nearly flat out, but it made no difference, she still raced on at a tremendous speed. I really was scared now. People were shouting at me as I went by, thinking I was driving the mare too fast, not realising, of course, that it was the exact opposite, the horse was running away with me!

We passed over 'Galton Bridge' at a great speed, with the float swaying from side to side precariously. By now I was terrified. I pulled on the reins, first right, then left in a sawing motion to Dolly's bit in an attempt to stop her flight, but to no avail, she kept going like a thing possessed.

By now we were fast approaching 'Summit Bridge' with its sharp left-hand bend. As we got nearer, and nearer, I could sense that my runaway mare was not going to stop, and furthermore she wasn't going to negotiate the bend, she was indeed heading straight for the bridge structure on the right-hand side.

I completely froze, I just couldn't do anything. The thoughts running through my mind in those few seconds were stupid. I wondered what Handsworth Dairies would say if Dolly were hurt, and the anger from the stable staff, including my dear friend Horace. I loved this horse and I didn't want anything to happen to her, although she was a 'bugga.' I also thought the way the load of empties were swaying that they would certainly all smash at anytime now, and that would be another rollicking from the gaffers.

Dolly did exactly as I had thought she would, she went in a straight line across Roebuck Lane towards the iron structure. Fortunately there was no traffic coming in the direction of Smethwick, and silly though it was, I was very grateful for that. However there were people on the pavement heading in both directions, and I shouted to them to get out of the way. On hearing me those who heard me warned the others in the vicinity, and they all crowded together out of the path that Dolly was taking.

Tears were forming in my eyes, for it was the only expressive thing that I could think of at that very moment, for I really didn't know what was going to happen next.

We reached the edge of the pavement, only about four foot from the bridge. I had given up all hope when suddenly Dolly stumbled and tripped over the gutter, which caused her to fall, and she continued the rest of the length of the pavement on her front knees. This brought the whole float to an abrupt halt, throwing the crates of empties all over the road. Me?, well at that moment I just didn't care about anything. I was so grateful to God for this preventive action. Only He knew what might have happened if my lovely Dolly hadn't tripped over that pavement.

I looked up to the sky, and I thanked Him mentally, as I have done on several occasions during my lifetime.

"Ya' silly young bleeda, w'at d' ya' think yarr playin' at, yo' could a killed us bleedin' lot, an' ya'self alung with us. Yo' 'adden oughta be allowed ta drive an' 'oss, ya' mad bugga. "Look w'at yo've done ta the poor bleedin' 'orse, ya' ought be yashermed ov yaself ya' 'ad. W'at wuz ya' drivin' sa fast fer son?"

This and many more caustic remarks were made, but I couldn't move I couldn't even answer at that moment. I was so relieved that the accident hadn't been more tragic. I can't, even now put into words the relief I felt. It was as though I had been re born. That is the best expression I can put into words, to explain my feelings right at that moment.

Quite a crowd had gathered around the float. Some of the blokes had got Dolly to her feet, and were looking at her injuries, and others were surrounding me giving out verbal abuse. Not one word of sympathy, which is what I was crying out for. In the finish frustration got the better of me, and I turned on these people, and I shouted to them, all of them, in a loud voice. I was crying quite openly at the same time.

"You Bastards!" This wasn't me at all, I've never made a habit of using this type of language, and at that time I'd never used any language like that at all. I'd never had the urge, or the motivation up until this moment of time. Of course, I had heard it used by others on several occasions, but to use it myself, never.

"You bastards, w'y don' ya' gi me a chance ta tell ya' what 'appened? Why don' ya' lis'en ta me, instead o mekin yarrown bleedin' stories up?" At this outburst everything went deathly silent. You could have heard a pin drop. One or two of the blokes, big blokes, looked at me menacingly, and a couple started to come towards me. I still stood on the back of the float - defiantly.

"Oright son, don' getcha self all upset then, jus' tell us warrappened." This was a lady of about forty, I thought, but she might have been younger. At that age I really couldn't differentiate. I mean a woman, or man for that matter, was old at twenty five, to me.

I turned to this lady, and I was so grateful for those few words. I was still crying, and I couldn't get the words out immediately. She held her hand out for me, and I took it and alighted from the float. Then she guided me to the wall by the side of the bridge, and offered me a fag which I took, thanking her. I lit the cigarette and drew the acrid smoke down into my lungs deeply, and it seemed to calm me down somewhat. After a few more drags, I began to feel more myself. I had stopped crying, and hated myself for doing so in front of all these people, which was another sign that I was now regaining my composure.

A small crowd had now gathered round to hear my version of what really happened. Others were still attending to Dolly. I looked at the lady who had been so kind and directed my words to her. "O don' know w'arrappened really, but w'en o turned inta Roebuck Lern frum Ol'bury Road, Dolly suddenly wen' mad, an' raced away wi' me. There worn't anythin' o cud do, she jus' wen' mad. O love mo 'orse, o do, o wudden 'urt ta, od soona 'urt miself o would. She jus' wen' mad, an' started ta gu orff as though the devil wuz arta rer."

I could feel the tears welling up in my eyes again, and this kind lady must have suspected it, for she intervened and said "Oright son, yo've 'ad enough fer one day, and o think all these people 'ere believe warras 'appened now. Don' upset yaself anymowa, are yo' 'urt attall?"

"Nah-h-h om oright, an' thanks love, thanks a lot, burrows mi yoss, is she oright?" One of the blokes spoke up then, "Ar-r-r, she's oright nip. 'er front legs am scerged a bit, but nothin' serious, jus' tell ya' sterble blokes w'en yo' get back ta ya' dairy, an' they'll fix 'er up."

I still went round to have a look for myself, though, in spite of this reassurance.

Dolly had certainly calmed down quite a bit now, in fact she was more placid than I'd ever known her to be. I stroked her nose, and held her head close to me, and she in return gave a big sloppy kiss up the right side of my face. I thanked God again, I was so glad that no harm had come to her, I really was so grateful.

When the truth was known to everyone, they couldn't do enough for me. Someone gave me another fag which I lit up, and the blokes collected all the crates up from the road, putting them back onto the float. Two of the men had stationed themselves either side of the accident, and were guiding the traffic around.

Once everything was back to normal, I thanked everyone profusely for all they had done. Some of them apologised for thinking the worst initially, and I told them "Well yo' worn't supposed ta know, wuz ya' ?"

" Ar-r-r but wi shoulda gid ya' time ta tell us son, instead a guin' orff 'alf cock, afowa we gid ya' time ta 'splain. "

One of the blokes even offered to ride back to the dairy with me to make sure all was well, and to explain to the dairy what had happened. I refused gracefully, and thanked them all once again.

Dolly's injuries were only superficial, and I was really surprised at that for she had taken a terrible tumble. I clicked her on, and she moved off at quite a slow pace, for her anyway. I thought to myself "P'raps yove 'ad enough as well my ol' lover." I let her go her own pace all the way back to the dairy.

On arrival there I unloaded then went into the stables. It was Frank who came out to me. Horace had gone home for his 'dinna.' Due to the accident I was later than usual, so I didn't see him as I normally did.

Frank had been one of the last to leave West Bromwich depot, for obvious reasons. He had to clear everything up after all the other staff had gone. He didn't like Island Road, he would have preferred to stay in West Bromwich, his home town, but in these times one couldn't pick where, or when one went. The Ministry of Works told you where to go and what to do.

" 'allo, warrave yo' bin up to then young Ronnie? "His eyes still watering as usual, and his nose still running. Now that I had got to know him a lot better though, he was a little more happy with me, than he had been.

I related the story to him, and stated that if need be one of the witnesses would come to the dairy and confirm this. One of the men had even given me his address to contact him if need be.

Frank looked the mare over carefully. He then turned to me and said, "Nah-h-h Ronnie, there wun bi any need fer that, that mare should nevea rave gone out like she was."

"Oh" I replied, not knowing what to think about this situation now. Before I could say anymore however, although I wasn't quite sure what I could have said. Frank carried on with his conversation, even ignoring my "Oh."

"She's in season, no wonder she wuz feelin' a bit frisky, an' kicked over the traces."

This completely flummoxed me, I just hadn't got a clue what he was on about, but as usual I didn't say anything, for silence in my opinion, was golden in this situation'

"Leave it ta me Ronnie, I'll 'ave a wor wi' Sid (the blacksmith, and head stableman, who had a house rented to him by the 'White's' right next to the dairy in Island Road). We'll sort this bloody lot out, so don' worry it's nuthin' ta do wi' yo', oright son?"

"Ar-r-roright Frank, an' thank ya', thanks eva sa much."

We unharnessed Dolly, and I put the float away, whilst Frank took Dolly for a drink, and then led her back to her stall. I followed just to make sure she was alright. Frank told me that in all probability I would be having another horse for a few day's at least, just to give Dolly a rest. When he said this, a smile came on his face, as usual I didn't understand, but I smiled with him anyway.

"I'll si to 'er wounds, an' they'll bi oright in a day or two, an' then yo' cun 'ave 'er back agen, okay Ronnie?"

"Ar-r-r tharr'll bi great Frank an' thanks once agen."

With that I went up to the office, did what I had to do, and then returned to the stables, picked up my 'Kingsway' from where Horace had left it and went back home to 'The Brook.'

One thing I haven't mentioned, however, and I thought it most important at the time, was that out of this terrible accident, and what could have been very tragic circumstances. Not one empty, or full, bottle of milk got broken! Every bottle was intact, when the men at the scene of the incident re-loaded the float.

As Frank had predicted I was given another horse the next day, a little chestnut cob, she was a lovely little thing. I had her for over a week, before Dolly was put back on the round. The day I had her back, what was the first thing she did? You're right, she had a quick nip at me, and I gave her a quick dab of the nose. Our relationship had not been altered by this most awful incident. In next to no time the whole episode had been forgotten by her, and me.

Summer 1944 was the summer the farmers had a most wonderful yield of milk from their herds. Milk was abundant for a few short days. I made the most of it, as did many of my mates at the dairy.

A note was put up in the Supervisors shed telling all roundspeople that they could increase their daily orders for more or less what they wanted.

What I did straight away was to double my normal 'rationed order' and arranged for a meet load, to accommodate this extraordinary event. I arranged for Ron, the new driver of 'The Greenhouse' (George had joined the paratroopers by then) to meet me at the bridge in Tat Bank Road, at its junction with Popes Lane, and Engine Street. This bridge ran over the Titford Canal. What a birthday we all had for a few days. I was leaving everyone double their rations If they wanted anymore I gave them that as well. At that week end, and the week end afterwards the tips I received was nobodies business I can tell you.

To give you some idea as to the extent of the amount of money given to me, as a 'thank you,' although really it wasn't anything to do with me. If anyone should have been rewarded it should have been the cows. Anyway as I was saying to give you an idea of the money I got, Hockley Post Office on those Saturday nights benefited by three quid each time for Saving Certificates. What's more I had more than enough left to really have a good time with my new found friends, Danny, Pat, and Joe.

Then there was 'The Great Furniture Polish Scam.' What a caper was pulled then!

It all started when I went down Wellesley Road one Saturday. Normally I used to deliver the milk to most of these customers on the front doorstep, but on a Saturday it was the custom for most of these people to want me to go round the back to collect my money. The reason was simple really. Most of the women in the households went to work, which of course was compulsory for most during the war. Consequently all the housework, washing and the many other things the lady of the house attends to, would have to be done at the week end.

On this particular Saturday I went round the back to my first customer in Wellesley, Road knocked on the door, and whilst waiting for the lady of the house to come I noticed a jam jar on the window sill of the kitchen, the exterior sill that is. More important than the jam jar itself however, was its contents. About an inch up from the bottom was a brown liquid. Dark brown at its base, and then it lightened in its colour as it progressed to the top.

The lady paid me, and I didn't comment on the jar, naturally. It could have been anything, and the lady would have been within her rights to tell me "ta mind miyone bleedin' business." I continued my journey down the road, and each house I went to, there it was, on the exterior window sill, the jam jar with this brown liquid in it.

Curiosity got the better of me in the end, so at about the fifth call I said to the lady, full of confidence, because I had seen the same jam jars on the other people's window sills, "W'a's all this love, these jars wi' the brown stuff in 'em?"

"Oh that," she replied, "it's a real bargin, tharris. We've 'ad a bloke call roun', an' 'e's gorra great big tin ov the stuff, an' a bag a jam jars as well. 'as ya' know yo' can' get fernitcha polish fer love ner money now, an' this bloke 'as gid us the arnsa."

"Oh" I said, 'ow's 'e done that ?"

"Well," she continued, " 'e's poured a drop o' this stuff inta the bottom ov the jam jar, an' added the serm amount o' watta to it, an' 'e's tol' us ta leave it out doors fer one night an' w'en it solidifies in the mornin', then we cun scoop it out, an' polish anythin' wi' it. I wanned ta 'ave two jars, burr 'e said 'e couldn' do that, cuz it wuz sa scarce. Mind yo' om 'appy ter 'ave this bit, at least o cun gi' mi ferntcha a good guin' ova now."

I went away from this lady's house, not very convinced with the whole story, then I reasoned with myself, well it might be true. I mean if the bloke had worked at a place that made furniture polish, and then invented a formula for continuing making it, with other ingredients, well good luck to him. It would certainly do the housewives a favour, because you couldn't get 'Mansion,' 'Cherry Blossom,' 'Kiwi' or any of the other brand-name polishes for all the tea in China then.

Never the less I was very dubious about the whole affair, and if the guy had come to me with a jam jar with an inch of what looked like dark urine to me, I know what I'd have told him to do with it.

How right I was. I went round the same houses, in Wellesley Road, Vernon Road, Shirley Road, Gresham Road, and even Rood End Road, and God knows where this bloke had sold this piss on the Sunday morning, and there were the jars, still there and nothing had happened. I even picked one up and shook it, it was just the same, it hadn't solidified as the bloke had said it would. Of course this made me even more suspicious, but, it wasn't anything to do with me, so I said nothing.

It was about four weeks later that a bloke in Tat Bank Road told me that the police, had caught a bloke somewhere in 'Brum' who had been selling bogus furniture polish to housewives around the Birmingham and Black Country areas. He showed me the local paper The Oldbury Observer (I think that was it's title, anyway it was The Oldbury something or other) and they had done quite a spread on this 'Furniture Polish' deception. including comments by some of the local people who been done. Wellesley Road was mentioned, but fortunately not the other roads. Years later I was to meet a very good friend of mine who worked on this newspaper, situated in Birmingham Street. His name was Peter Swingler. He was a reporter for them, then he went onto The Birmingham Mail, where he did a cartoon report called 'Down your way.' What he did was to go to a street, pick out a few of the residents, portray them in cartoon fashion, and then give comical captions about them He made a very good job of this, and I would follow them avidly, because at that particular time I was into 'cartooning,' also football. Pete was definitely into football as well. He helped to run, and played for, as I did with 'Hockley Sports,' 'George Street Villa,' a team from Stourbridge.

None of the ladies mentioned this 'Furniture Polish' scam to me after that, I think that they felt ashamed that they had been done, not particularly for the money alone, that was important enough at 1/6d a jar, but that they had been taken in by such an obvious con trick.

It was in Shirley Road that I had a very abusive fracas with an old gentleman. I was delivering up there one day when this old gentleman came down the opposite side. As usual I was whistling and singing, and yodelling 'Milko' as I went down the different entries to deliver my daily pintas. This old bloke passed me by, and then he turned and said something to me which I didn't honestly hear, so I shouted, "Yo' ll 'ave ta speak up mate, o' can' 'ear w'at yome sayin' " He spoke again, and I still couldn't hear. Thinking it might have been something important I went towards him.

When he saw me doing this he lifted his very heavy stick in the air and waved it threateningly at me. This completely threw me. I had never seen this bloke in my life before, and here he was threatening me with this heavy stick. The first thing I did, obviously, was to stop dead in my tracks. The last thing I really wanted at that moment in time was a belt around the head, or any other part of me for that matter.

So from a safe distance I shouted to him, "W'a's a marra wi' ya ya' silly old bleeda, I ain't neva sin ya' befowa, tell mi, warram o supposed to 'ave done?"

He almost screamed at me when I made this comment. "Yo' basta'd yo', w'y aintcha in the bleedin' army like mi son? Guin' roun' 'ere singin' an' mekkin' a soddin' noise like that, while mi son's out there?" and he pointed angrily in the direction of Rood End Road with this nasty looking piece of wood. "We ain' 'eard frum 'im fer months now, an' 'ere yo' are walkin' about all nice ant comfortable. W'y don' ya' gu an' join up like all the otha blokes as done, big strung bloke like y'o.

He was going to carry on, but I felt at this point I had better explain, so I interrupted his flow of abuse, and I had to shout to make him hear. Consequently in no time at all, we had an audience, (Isn't that always the case?) "Ya' silly old sod, o can' gu in the army, or any thin' else fer that marra, om on'y sixteen, o ain' seventeen till nex' January, an' then o wanna gu in the nervy, so don' keep guin' on at me."

"Ya' bleedin' liar," he bawled back at me "Yome tellin' bleedin' lies in front o th' wimmin, cuz yome a bleedin' conshensus 'jecta, tha's w'at yo' am, yarra bleedin' parasite, a scrounga, gu an' bloody well gerrourra mi sight afowa I belt ya' one wi' this stick. If I wuz a bit younga od knock eight bell's a shit ourra ya' tha's warr I'd do." With that he turned and stomped off down the road away from me, still shouting abuse, although he wasn't now facing me, so I assumed he was relieving his pent up feelings about his son.

I shouted after him telling him that if he came down here tomorrow I would bring my National Registration Identity Card which gave my Class Code and other information bearing out my true identity address and age in it, to prove that I wasn't what he believed me to be. This old bloke went off down Shirley Road, turned left into Wellesley Road, and disappeared. I was never to see him again.

I must admit I was very angry at first, I mean, no one want's to be termed what he called me. I wanted to go down the street after him and make him understand that I really was only sixteen, and then express how sorry I was about his son being so far away, and not being able to contact them. I wanted to do all these things, I wanted to help this old man in his moments of deep sorrow, but I just stood there, because I wasn't equipped educationally to talk to him like that. I just didn't know how to approach him with this type of expressive conversation which hopefully would make him understand.

One of the ladies who had been listening to all this conversation came across to me and put her arm around my shoulder and said "Ne'er mind love, don' tek any notice o' the silly ol' bugga, 'e don know w'arr 'e's sayin'."

"Burr I wanned ta 'splain to 'im, tharrit worn' like tharr a tall, I yam on'y sixteen; o wish o could gu in the nervy, o will as soon as om old enough, w'y wudden 'e believe me?"

"O don' know son, it's a funny world wi' live in at the moment, w'o knows w'at's runnin' through tharr ol' bloke's mind, w'arreva rit is, it's tragic, tha's warrit is, so yo' jus' leave it be an' fergerit." "Now come on son yo' come wi' me an' I'll mek yarra nice cuppa tea, okay?"

I went with this kind lady, when I'd put Dolly's nose bag on, and had a couple of cups of tea, and I did feel better after that. I thanked the lady on leaving, and she said, "Now don' yo' gu worryin' ya' self abourrit now, yo' fergerit 'avin' 'appened, oright?"

"Ar-r-rokay love, an' thanks fer revrythin'."

As I said I never saw this old man again, but I did have thoughts on the matter, which no matter how hard I tried, would not leave me Of course, they did in time, but it was a very long time before I could completely dismiss them from my mind entirely.

It did teach me one thing however, the realisation that I was, well outwardly to all others, growing up very fast. I was fast becoming a man, although I didn't have the mental attitude of a man, I certainly had the physical looks of a man.

My romantic episodes during the time I was working for Handsworth Dairies were good but, bear in mind, things weren't quite the same as romantic episodes are today. The reason for this is quite obvious, we were scared of the most natural thing that happens between Woman and Man - 'Babies!'

This was not applicable to me personally, because as you read about my bit of courting, there was about as much chance of the girls I went out with conceiving, as them attaining the throne of England. Don't kick it, however, Sex is not the end of the world. Yes, it is essential, but those early romances may not have come up to the expectations of my partners, but it was very nice all the same. It was romantic in all its aspects. I don't care what anyone says, they were, for me anyway, really good times, although I was ignorant of the whole aspect of this love thing, due to my poor but strict, almost Victorian, upbringing.

Nothing was ever mentioned at 2/24 Guest Street, or 228 New John Street West, about this subject. In fact the whole subject was 'dirty.' I think that I can speak for nearly all the people in Hockley at that time, that the subject of anything remotely to do with the physical union between Woman and Man was never discussed; it was always referred to as 'dirty talk.'

My first outing with a member of the opposite sex, was with Joan Boulton. (I've already mentioned this very attractive lady, so I won't go over that again.)

I came in after finishing, which was by then a complete wholesale round which took me to nearly all the shops of Handsworth. I started in Wattville Road, and finished in Grove Lane, right by Dudley's, the furniture people. This was the round the dairy had put me on after the Oldbury area.

I finished unloading my flat cart, took 'Dick', the big dray horse, out of the shafts, and was putting my cart in to the line of other carts when Joan came by having completed the same task. "Hallo," she said, "how are you getting on, it's been ages since I've seen you."

"Oh smashin' thank ya'; mind yo' they keep on muckin' me ya roun', first this round, an' then that un. Still o don' mind really, o suppose o like a birrov a chernge sometimes." At this comment Joan started to laugh. Her whole face lit up. Then she said, "I bet you say that to all the girls."

"Oh no, o dain' mean anythin' like tharr I dain't, o meant, werk an' ev'rythin' like tharr I did." At this point I had become terribly flummaxed, and I looked down at the floor trying to think of the next thing to say to this lovely girl.

"Oh, you are a shy one aren't you, I was going to ask you when you were going to take me out, but if you're that embarrassed, perhaps I'd better not." With this statement she started to laugh again.

I was in a real turmoil, I had never had a proposal like this before, I just didn't know what to say. Still looking at the ground, I didn't hear Horace approach.

"Worrow yo' two love birds, wassa marra yo' 'ad a row or summat?" I looked up, and boy, was I glad to see my great mate. With him on the scene courage came bounding back to me. "Nah, 'orice, we ain' hadda row, she's jus' pullin' mi leg, about tekkin' 'er rout, an' o dain' know w'at ta say ferra minnit, tha's all."

"Who said anything about pulling your leg Ron, I was deadly serious." This remark completely floored me. It was the very first time in my life that this had been said to me, and I was so ignorant, I really didn't know how to answer this delightful girl.

"Come on Ronnie, don' let the bleedin' school down mate, the wench 'as arst ya' ta gu out wi' ya', gu on mek a dert, an' don' 'ang about or I'll bi guin' out wi' ya. I'll see yarrin a minnit, ov jus' gorra gu an' finish in thaya." With this comment Horace nodded, and winked at the same time, indicating the stalls.

When Horace had gone I turned to Joan who was still in the same position as she had been at the beginning of this conversation. I said nervously, "Would ya' like ta come out wi' me then Joan, we cun gu ta the pitchers or summat?"

"Yes I would Ron, I would like that very much. I can't come with you tonight, or tomorrow, I'm sorry, but I've made other arrangements, but how about the day after that?"

"Ar-r-r tharr'll do me fine Joan."

"Do you know where Icknield Port Road is Ronnie?"

"Ar-r-r, it's jus' up past Dudley Road 'orspital innit, on the left 'and side, jus' ova the way frum that big boozer on the corner ov 'eath Street, an' Dudley Road."

"Yes, you've got it, I'll meet you there then, at say six o'clock?"

"Ar-r-r tharr'll do mi fine, an' thanks Joan, I'll bi thaya ron time, Thursdee at six o'clock then?"

"Yes, lovely Ron, see you then?"

I watched her as she made her way out of the stables, to go up to the office. I thought she was wonderful. As she went out of the main door, she turned and flashed me another one of those mystical smiles, which sent me into another tizz wazz. I waved, and then I went into the other section of the stables, to seek out my friend Horace.

"Yove gorra bi firm wi' wimmin Ron, yove gorra show 'em w'o's boss." This was indeed the voice of authority. He had been around, no doubt about that. I had found Horace cleaning out one of the stalls, and he stopped his work when I arrived, giving me first this vital piece of information about the opposite sex.

"Ar-r-r," I answered. I hadn't got a bloody clue what he was on about, as usual. "Oh-h-h, they'll tell ya' they don' wannit, but they do, they allis do. So yove gorra gu abourrit in the right kinda way."

" 'ave ya' rorice, o dain' know about that."

He looked at me, and a smug attitude came across his face. He was completely 'in charge' of the situation; he was the complete authoritarian, and he was enjoying every moment of it.

"Yove gorra gerr' 'em guin' Ronnie, thas w'at ya' gorra do, an' if yo' don' do it right, yo' ll neva get no w'ere, an' tha's a fact tharris. Now w'en yo' tek Joannie out, yo' tek a ta the pitchers, cuz it'll bi the best plerce this cold weather." It was

119

about October/November time of the year, so that made a great deal of sense to me.

"Gerra some sweets, or choclits, if yo' cun, an' gerrem down 'a, w'en yome snuggled up in the back row o the pitchers. Don' do anythin' then though, yo' lerra eat them fust, an' then w'en she's finisht 'em, then start."

Start? What's he mean by start? So far I had followed him, and it all made sense. I wanted to go to the pictures, and I knew where I could get hold of some chocolates, and sweets, so there was no problem there, but I was going to do this anyhow. I couldn't figure out this business of 'starting' though. What had I got to start?

Horace must have seen the look of perplexity on my face. Added to that I hadn't said anything in this conversation up till now, well of any real contribution anyway. He said "Come on Ron, le's gu an' sit down ferra minnit, an' wi cun 'ave a good ol' natta, eh?"

I must admit at this point I was absolutely intrigued at the conversation we were having and even more intrigued as to where it was going to lead.

We walked up to the end stall where the bags of oats, chaff, and other feed for the horses were stored, and we sat down on some of the bags. Horace took out a packet of 'Park Drive' and offered one to me After lighting our fags he took a long drag on his, and looked momentarily up towards the roof of the stables. I supposed that he was looking for inspiration on how to give me the necessary advice regarding this 'start' thing he had been on about.

Finally after a few seconds of silence, which seemed a lifetime to me, he smiled at me and said, "Ron, o wantcha ta tell mi the truth, cuz otha wise o ain' gunna be erble ta 'elp ya'."

"Ar-r-rocourse o will 'orice, ya' know o wunt lie ta yo' yo' know that mate."

"Ar-r-r know ya' wudden lie ta mi Ron, but warr I mean is, warr I'm gunna arsk ya', is kinda personal, an' as yome mi mert, o wudden wanna offend yarrin any sherp or form, d' ya' unastan' mi Ron?"

"Ar-r-ro think o do 'orice, yo' gu on an' arsk mi yenythin' o don' mind cuz we'em mert's in we?"

"Ar-r-rokay then Ron," he continued, "burr if o get a bit to near the bleedin' knuckle, yo' tell mi, an I'll stop okay?"

"Ar-r-rokay 'orice, okay." I was getting a little impatient with him now, what was all the fuss about? I mean, what was more simple than taking a girl out. You met them where they arranged, and you went to the pictures, or wherever, and then you took them home, or wherever they wanted you to take them, and you said "Goodnight." That was it, and it was pleasant, and uncomplicated. I couldn't for the life of me see what all this was leading to. Perhaps he was going to tell me how many kisses I was to give the girl because I'd heard that if you gave them too many kisses, or you kissed them too hard or something they had a baby, didn't they? I didn't say anything along these lines, however, I thought Horace might have thought that I was attempting to teach him something, and I didn't want to give that impression at all, especially to one of 'mi bestist merts. So, I kep' mi big gob shut.

" 'ave yo' eva bin out wi' a girl befowa Ron?"

"Ar-r-rocause I yave 'orice, o bin out wi a lorrove 'em." (Lie number one. Well, I couldn't tell him I hadn't could I? I would have looked a real 'nana'.)

"Nah-h-h, Ron, o don' mean walkin' up the monkee run, an' 'avin' a birra donnuck, wi' ya' merts, an' a bunch a wenchis. O mean 'ave ya' reva bin out wi' a wench on yarrown, jus' yo' an' 'er, an' stayed out lert wi' 'em?"

I looked down at the floor of the stalls, and mumbled, "Ar-r-r, cause I yave.?" (Lie number two. I was still looking at the floor when Horace spoke again.) "Well, w'at didja do with 'er then Ron?"

I looked up, and stared at him for a moment, and then I said " We w'en ta the pitchers, an' o put mi yarm roun' 'er, an' we 'ad a kiss, an' ev'rythin', an' it wuz smashin'." (All lies.)

"Dain' ya' do anythin' else, Ron, dain' ya' ge 'er ra French kiss, or bite 'er ears, or anythin' like that?"

I looked at him in amazement. I didn't need to say anything, my face told him all he wanted to know.

"O think we'd berra start agen Ronnie, don' yo?" I started to sweat profusely, and I certainly couldn't speak. It was like being in front of Mr Locker, or Mr Margerrisson, the headmasters of Burbury Street, and Farm Street schools respectively, again.

"It's oright Ron, o ain' gunna bloody eatcha, om on'y gunna bring some good 'elp fer ya' tha's all mert."

"Yome right 'orice, I ain' really bin out wi' a girl, well, not like yo' said any road up. Joannie will bi the fust one."

"Right ho," he continued, sounding his 'haitch' in a very authoritative way. Like I said, I think he was enjoying this new role of tutor, on this most delicate matter. "Now we cun gerron wi' worr I wuzgunna tella yarr about, now o know w'at's w'at. Now w'en yo' tek Joannie out on Thursdee, yo' tek a ta the pitchers like o said. W'en yove gorra settled in nicely, then ge 'er some o the stuff ya' got an' lerra chobble on that. W'en she's 'ad 'er fill, an' settled down ta watch the film, then's ya' chance, cuz she'll be in a nice mood then, 'ave ya' gorrit Ron?"

"Ar-rr," I replied, but I'm afraid he'd lost me after giving Joan the chocolate, or whatever I managed to get from my favourite supplier, a general stores situated just inside Station Road on the left-hand side coming in from Holyhead Road. Either Horace wasn't explaining the situation very well, or - and I favour this theory - I was 'to bloody thick' to understand the gist of what he meant. I could have intervened, but I thought I'd only make it worse. Horace would think he'd really got a thick 'un on his hands. That was the last thing I wanted him to think, so I opted for the pretence of knowing what he was on about, and then I would do what I wanted to on the date with Joan.

"Ge it a birra time, an' then putcha rarm aroun' 'er, an' gradu'lly pull 'er towards ya', pull 'er closa. W'en she's cuddled up nice an' tight, then yo' start."

"Oh ar-r-r, om with ya' 'orice, then I start." Then I start, but what do I start? I thought to myself, I wish I knew what all this start meant, I mean if I've got my arm around the girl, I've already started haven't I?

I sat there wondering what was coming next. I fumbled around in my cowgown, and extracted a packet of 'Gold Flake' (Our Dad's favourite). I had reached the stage in smoking where I was in the process of trying all kinds of cigarettes, in an attempt to find which one I liked best, and which suited me. I'd tried 'Capstan Double Strength', they didn't seem double the strength to me. They dain' even seem as strong as 'Willie Woodbines'. By God, they reached the bottom of ya' bloody socks, w'en yo' took a deep drag. 'Park Drive', 'De Restze Minors', 'Senior Service', 'Churchman's No.1', 'Players', 'Pasha', and God knows how many more, but in the finish I settled for 'Woodbines'.

Pushing the packet towards Horace I said " 'ere ya' are 'orice, le's 'ave anutha fag, befowa we gu on talkin'." He took one from the pack, and then accepted the light I offered from my 'Englands Glory.' Taking a deep drag at the 'Gold Flake' he continued his lecture on women.

Looking up at the roof again, I thought he must be looking to God for inspiration this time, because there can't be a lot more that he can tell me about this romance thing. I mean, I'd seen all the John Wayne, and John Payne, Errol Flynn, Maureen O'Hara, Alice Faye, Betty Grable, and Lorretta Young films, and it all seemed happy enough to me when the film ended with them kissing one another, what more could there be ? Never the less I decided to sit back and listen to the 'Professor'.

"Now where wuz I?", Horace said, still looking up at the roof with the expression of a very worried man. I thought, "Blimey, o' mus' bi gein' im an'nard time, I 'ope 'e don' mind." I then thought I'd better show a bit of enthusiasm, so I blurted out "Ov jus' pulled Joan closa to me 'orice, an' she's real close now, in fact o cun 'ardly breathe, she's that close."

He stared at me for a moment, with a very puzzled look on his face, then a cynical smile came on his lips. "Yo' ain' tekkin' the piss ourra me are ya' Ronnie?"

"Tekkin the piss ourra ya' 'orice, w'at meks ya' say that? I ain' tekkin' the piss ourra ya."

"Well it wuz jus' the bleedin' way yo' 'minded me yov' w'ere o wuz, tha's sall. Burr if yo' say yo' worn't then o s'ppose o gorra believe ya' ain' I?"

" 'onist 'orice o worn tekkin the piss, 'onist o warn't'

"Oright o believe ya' but bleedin' thousan's wudden't." With this last comment of me taking the rise out of him, he burst out laughing - and I joined in!

"Now w'atcha gorra do next, yo' gorra bi crafty about, cuz ya' don' wanna mek a misterk. Watcha gorra do is werk yarr 'and under 'er armpit, d' ya' get me?"

I dain't, but I'd come to the conclusion that if I kept asking questions I wasn't going to get back to 'The Brook' till bloody midnight, so I just said "Ar-r-r."

"Now at this point if she starts actin' funny don' gu any fertha. Ya know, if she starts wrigglin' about, an movin' 'er rarm, or pushin' yarr 'and away, then pack it in ferra bit, cuz yo' could upset the w'ole apple cart, but don' give up, cuz they like a birra messin' about at fust. D' ya folla me Ronnie?"

He'd completely lost me. I might just as well be being instructed on the intricacies of the workings of a number 74 tram. I just said "Ar-r-r" again and decided to let him get on with whatever he wanted to say, and pretend to listen. I just hadn't got a clue what he was on about.

"Now arta a while, if yo' don' do anythin', she'll wonder w'y. She'll begin to think ya' don' like a, or summat. So it'll be yer w'o starts to mek up ta yo'. She'll say summat like 'Wassa marra, wor 'ave odun to ya? Ya still like mi, don' ya' ? Come on love, putcha rand back w'ere it wuz, o dain' mean anythin' 'onist o dain't.' When she does that, or summat like it, yo' know yove gorrit med, an' then yo' tek it frum thaya, oright Ron?"

"Oh-h-h, are 'orice, om wi' ya'."

"Yo' don' seem ta be, I hope I ain' wastin' mi time tellin' yarr all this lot."

"Nah course yo' ain't 'orice, ov bin lis'nin', 'onist o yave." (Another bloody lie, he'd lost me ages ago, and furthermore I wasn't remotely interested in what he was saying.) I wanted to remain with my beliefs on love and romance as I had always done; I didn't want another version of it. To me, love and romance was just as I had seen it on the films, and in the books. It was something to be revered, it was something beautiful.

Not all this physical stuff, it spoiled it somehow, feeling around a girl, which in all probability she didn't like, or enjoy for that matter (?) At that moment all I really wanted to do was to have a kiss, which would have been the end to a wonderful time with a girl.

On the other hand, however, I didn't want to upset Horace, because after all he was one of mi bestist merts, worn't 'e? Also I took into account the fact that he was a very tough hombre, very tough indeed. The last thing I wanted off Horace was a bang up the bloody ear'ole. So, weighing all the facts up very quickly, I decided to at least show interest in what he was saying, and keep on the right side of him.

"Gu on 'orice, gu on, I'm all ears, gu on w'arrappens arta ov put mi yand back w'ere it wuz, afowa she'd shoved it away, come on tell us."

"Tha's berra Ronnie, o know yome tekkin' int'rest in warrime sayin' now. Well once yove gotcha rand back w'ere it should be, then yo' cun start in really then."

I couldn't wait to hear what was coming next. I wished he'd hurry up and then I could get off home to 'The Brook' instead of listening to all this bloody twaddle.

"Yo' start by pushin' yarr 'and further, an' further round until yove gorrit on 'er tit, oright?"

"Ar-r-r tha's great 'orice, gu on."

I'd got no intention of doing any of this; it was 'dirty,' that's what it was, 'dirty'. No girl in her right mind would like any bloke doing this to her, would she ?

"Now she can' say anythin' can she? Cuz she's already told ya' ta putcha rand back thaya, an' she don' wan' any mowa trouble, with yo' guin' all moody agen an' sayin' nuthin', does she?"

"Nah-h-h, cors she wunt 'orice."

"So, then yo' start playin' with 'er tit, yo' know, like w'en yove gorran oringe in yarr 'and, yo' jus' keep on, rollin' it, an' squashin' it, but gentle like, cuz ya' don' wanna 'urt ta do ya'?"

"Nah-h-h 'orice." This really was boring me now, I mean no girl would want you to mess around like that.

"Arta ra w'ile she'll start moanin', an' groanin', but don' tek any notice o that, cuz that means she's really enjoyin' w'at yome doing."

I thought this is getting worse this is, now I've got to make the girl moan and groan, it just didn't make any sense whatsoever, but I had to go on listening, wishing it had never started in the first place, but what could I do?

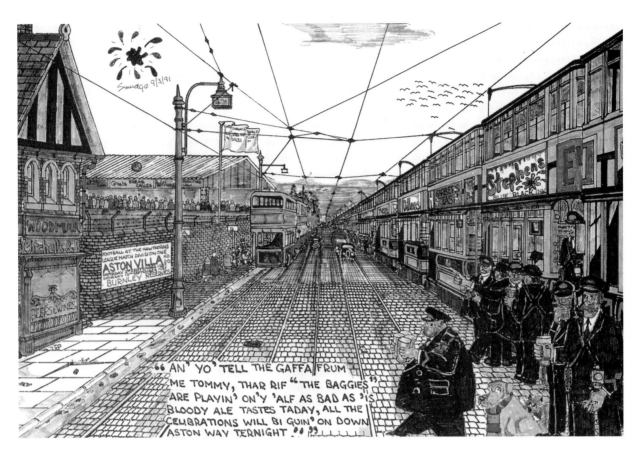

"Dartmouth Square" West Bromwich, Staffordshire, in the twenties.

"The Sandwell Arch" Birmingham Road, West Bromwich, Staffordshire, about 1938.

"The Stone Cross Inn" The junction of Walsall Road and Hall Green Road, Stone Cross, West Bromwich, Staffordshire, about 1920

"The Limerick and Market Place" Gt Bridge, Staffordshire in the thirties.

"Saturday Evening" Birmingham Street, looking towards Dudley, Oldbury, Worcestershire. *1938*

"The Annual Sunday School Trip" Paradise Street Railway Station, West Bromwich, Staffordshire in the thirties.

"High Street" Stourbridge, Worcestershire about 1910

"The Market Place" Dudley, Worcestershire. Christmas 1911

"Farley's Tower" Carters Green, West Bromwich, Staffordshire. 1938

"Then w'en she looks as if she's guin' ta faint or summat," Horace continued, "tha's the time, ta try an' getcha rand into 'er frock, an' then play wi' 'er tits in the raw, an' she'll . . ."

" 'orice, 'orice, w'ere the bleedin' 'ell are ya?"

This was Sid the head stableman calling, and was I glad to hear him; I'd really had enough, more than enough of this dirty talk.

"Soright Sid, om 'ere wi' mi mert, om jus' 'avin' a fag tha's all." With that Horace stood up and said to me in a quiet voice, "We'll finish this talk some otha time Ron, okay, od berra gu now, orrile 'ave Sid on mi back. Oright Sid, om on mi way."

"It's about bleedin' time an' nall, we've gorra stack ta do an' norra lorra time ta do it in, so come on an' le's get crackin'.""

I didn't see Horace, or Joan on the Wednesday, or Thursday. I must admit I kept out of Horace's way on purpose, for I didn't want another ear bending from that direction. I was really looking forward to my first real date with Joan.

I had been to the tea dance at the Y.W.C.A. with Peggy on the Wednesday afternoon, and I had told her all about Joan. Peggy said she was glad for me, and hoped I'd have a lovely time. After that she appeared to go quiet. I couldn't understand this, but still never mind I thought, she might be upset over something.

We spent the whole afternoon dancing, and I was getting better by the lesson now. Still not quite Fred Astaire, but definitely better, and Peggy had indeed commented on this improvement, so it must have been right.

On the Wednesday lunchtime I asked 'Our Lil' if she would lend me the silk scarf that Jack had bought her. It was R.A.F. blue, and it had the insignia of the Royal Air Force on it. I wanted to borrow it, more or less to show off, although of course I didn't admit to that. The 'Battle of Britain' pilots were much to the fore, with their daring dog-fights, and devil may care attitudes towards the Luftwaffe. The pilots, and their pranks in the mess rooms at all aerodromes, all portrayed in such films as "The First of the Few.' I wanted to bathe in their glory I suppose. I wanted to pretend that I was one of them, one of the 'Few'. Of course I realised that I couldn't kid anyone that I was even in the Royal Air Force, but I think somehow I wanted to fantasise to myself that I was a 'Battle of Britain' pilot, and think that everyone else thought that way too.

"Yes of course yo' cun borra it Ronnie," Lil answered. Lil was a very quiet, giving, lovable girl. She had always been very kind to me, and she wasn't going to prove me wrong in this instance either.

"Yo' will bi careful wi' it though, wuntcha? Jack bought mi that, an' it's very precious to mi, so don' lose it or anythin' will ya'?"

"Nah-h-h Lily, o'll guard it wi' mi life o will, an' thanks a lot."

"Soright Ron, o don' mind."

With that she went off upstairs to get the scarf for me. On her return she handed it to me with another warning to be careful, and then she went off to work at 'The Palladium.' I took the scarf back upstairs to our bedroom, and once up there I looked at this precious possession of 'Our Lil's.' No doubt about it, it was a lovely thing, and the insignia on the bottom of it stood proud. It had been sewn on with a lot of care in silks. I felt a lump come to my throat when I looked at it, remembering all the young pilots who had given their lives, or were maimed, fighting for this very same insignia. The words of Winston Churchill came to my mind: "Never in the field of human conflict was so much owed by so many to so few." I placed this treasure of Lil's into the drawer carefully, ready for this evening, an evening that I hoped would be every bit as wonderful as I had planned it to be.

I just messed around the house during the afternoon, not really wanting to do anything. At last we had our tea, and then the others started to come home from work. It was of course dark by then, and getting close to Christmas 1944. I went upstairs to my room, and lit a candle that was stuck in a fancy looking candle holder. It looked like an oyster shell, with a tube sticking upwards, where the candle was placed. Then an ornate handle to complete the holder I had lit the candle after pulling the curtains, of course, although the A.R.P. wardens weren't as strict as they had been owing to the fact that the Allies were now well and truly on the offensive in Europe. The likelihood of the 'Luftwaffe' flying over Birmingham now, was very remote indeed. Never the less London, and the South Coast were having a very rough time of it with the introduction of the 'Doodle Bugs'.

I removed my working clothes, and put them under the bed by the po as usual, ready to be on hand when I went to work the next day, although at that moment tomorrow was the last thing on my mind.

Donning my 'Sundee Best' I picked up the candle and went into Mom's and Dad's room, situated at the front of the house facing the blacksmith's shop, and held the flickering light in front of the cracked mirror of the old dressing table. I adjusted my tie, and made sure my collar was straight. I went back into our room and got my 'herring-bone' overcoat, from off the chair (a recent acquisition) by the back window and, finally, withdrew the precious scarf from the drawer of the table. Again I looked at it, it was beautiful. I went back into the front bedroom again, and first put the scarf around my neck, tying it carefully, so that the insignia was showing for all to see, and then I donned the 'herring-bone' coat.

What a picture I thought I looked. I reminded myself of William Powell without the moustache in his films with Myrna Loy. God, I thought I looked the cat's whiskers; what a bloody big head. Still we all went through it, didn't we?

After a few last minute adjustments, I went back into our room, blew the candle out and placed it back onto the table, and then wended my way back downstairs.

It's funny I know, but the Smith family, all of us, had got used to feeling our way about in the dark, due to the fact that the only light we had was the gas light in the kitchen, the middle room, and the front room, and that was it. Not another light in the whole house. So when you went to bed, it was either candle, or dark - tek ya' choice!

W'ere the bleedin' 'ell yo' guin', all toffed up ta the bloody nines. I thought, here we go again, the same old rigmarole. Mom wasn't in the middle room so I took a chance with my reply. "I'm orff ta see if a sieve 'll stop a fart droppin' in ta the bloody flowa."

"Oh-h-h, bin in the knife cu'board 'ave we, I yope Mom ain' 'eard ya'."

"I yope Mom ain' 'eard w'at?" This was 'you know who' coming in from the back kitchen, just when she shouldn't have.

"Well speak up," she continued "warris it that Mom shouldn'"ave 'eard then?" 'Our Kid' stared back at Mom, for it was him that I'd directed the smart alec reply too.

"Ar-r-r it wuz nuthin' Mom," 'Our Kid' replied, "it was on'y me yan owa kid 'avin a birra donnuck. It wuz nuthin,' Mom, nuthin'."

"Silly pair ra sods" was Mom's curt reply, and she went on with her business.

I looked at 'Our Kid' and thanked him with quiet words, and he just smiled.

Our Arthur had had a rough old time during the War. (I might have one or two of the facts wrong, but basically the story is right.)

When the War commenced he had just started work at 'Southall and Smith's' in Villa Street, just opposite 'Buttons.' He first joined the Home Guard when he became of eligible age, and it was his intention to join the army eventually.

However, this was not to be. At that time Ernest Bevan was the man in charge of deployment of labour, and out of all the men eligible for military service, he retained so many to serve down the coal mines. Appropriately they were called 'Bevan Boys'.

'Our Kid' was one of these 'Bevan Boys.' He kicked up a row about it, and went up to the Army Recruitment Centre in James Watt Street, but to no avail. God, he was so disappointed, for he desperately wanted to go into the army. Even to the people concerned it didn't make sense. Here was a man who had served in the Home Guard more or less since its initiation from being called 'The Local Defence Volunteers'. He had been trained in weapons, discipline, and routines of the army. He was in fact a very prime candidate for going straight into the army, but no.

The 'powers-that-be' decided he had got to go down the coal mines. Arthur never took to it right from the word go. He never showed any interest in the initial training, and didn't relish the idea of going underground. So it was a non-starter from the beginning.

When he came home on his week-end leaves, which of course was not every week-end. The system was more or less as per the armed services, but naturally they weren't so far away from home. Many's the Sunday night, when he should have returned to the town where the coal mine was situated, he would not return. Of this situation I am not quite clear.

Eventually our Arthur was taken ill with nerve problems. Don't matter what they (The Authorities) threatened him with, he would not budge. I remember his hair falling out through this nerve problem, and finally he would not venture outside the house.

Presumably a medical board was arranged, and at long last he was released from this work he hated so much. He was however disappointed again, because for some reason or other they still wouldn't have him in the army.

After a time, when he started to recover from his illness, he went back to his job at 'Southall and Smith's', resuming his trade as a toolmaker.

It was indeed a very traumatic period for 'Our Kid'. One which should never have happened in the first place. Arthur was never up to all this rough and tumble in life. He was a quiet, kind, and gentle man. He was my brother, and a man could not wish to have such a lovely lad so closely related, and further more so closely loved. Of course like so many other situations in life, I didn't realise this love between us until much later in life. It made me sad to realise how much

I'd missed by being so blind, about this closeness between us, but as they say, with the old adage: 'That's life, isn't it?'"

I winked at 'Our Kid' as I made my way to the door, smiled, said "Tarrar" to 'Our Mom,' went out into the entry, to make my way down to 'The Brook' and the bus stop by 'The Turk' in Icknield Street. There I would catch the Number 8 Inner Circle bus which would convey me on the first part of my journey to my date with Joan.

As I stepped out of the entry into New John Street, I felt rather than saw, that it was drizzling; not actually raining, but a fine drizzle, which in my opinion soaked you far more than rain itself. It was very cold now, much colder than it had been during the day. I pulled the collar of my herring-bone up around my neck. I smiled to myself thinking how I didn't really need a hat, due to Ma Davies's lavender brilliantine. It sure was water repellent. When you applied that to your hair, nothing would be able to penetrate it. Snow, rain, sunshine, anything. It was just like cart grease with a nice smell. Well I thought it was a nice smell. (I can't account for other folks' tastes.)

As I walked down the street I thought how much the conditions, and the area reminded me of the start of one of those horror films. Due to the black-out regulations all the lights that one could see were dimmed so much, that they made little difference at all. In fact it made the dirty, murky, darkness all the more sinister.

Of course, having lights blazing as we did before the war started, had now, in 1944, lost all significance. Everyone was saying "It wun 'alf bi nice w'en we cun 'ave the bleedin' lights guin' agen, an' ev'rythin's back ta normal." But I think that it had now gone on too long, and everyone's memory of what the lights were, had largely been forgotten.

The traffic passing up and down the main road seemed like ghosts floating past one another, the noise somehow muted by this dense, dark, murky, dirty atmosphere added to the spiritual effect on not only the traffic, but the people as well. Their voices seemed so soft, when they spoke to one another, or greeted someone in the street. I came to the conclusion that it must have been the density of this atrocious weather that made things as I've described.

I walked down the street to 'The Brook,' and on reaching Hockley Hill I had to be careful crossing over due to this strange quietness. Finally, I arrived at the bus stop in Icknield Street, and found to my disappointment a long queue. The clock on the mantlepiece at 228 had told me that it was a quarter after five when I'd left, so I contemplated whether I should walk or not. I didn't want to be late on this my first date with a woman. Joan was about nineteen at the time, so to me she was definitely, a woman, and not a girl.

I didn't have long to contemplate, however, and also luck was on my side. I stood there for a few seconds, trying to make my mind up, when suddenly a bloke in the queue said "Bloody 'ell, at lung larst, a bleedin' bus." I turned and looked in the direction of 'The Benyon,' and through the dense mist I could just make out the shape of a bus pulling out from Farm Street. I sighed with a breath of relief, and thought "Thank God fer that."

The bus however was sometime before it came across 'The Brook' into Icknield Street due to the copper on point duty holding it up in favour of the Birmingham and West Bromwich flow of traffic. I was not on my own either when I was urging the bus to come over 'The Brook.' I could hear the comments from the other people standing there: "Come om mert, getcha finger rout"; "Bloody 'ell if 'e don' 'urry up, I'll miss mi bloody buzz at Spring 'ill." "I'll bi bloody lert fer fire watchin', an' 'ave that silly ol' bleeda on mi back if o don' 'urry up." I thought to myself, "None on ya' rave gorra more 'portant date than I've got, so w'y don' shurrup?" Good job I'd only thought about it, and hadn't let it flow from 'mi gob.'

At last the bus made its way slowly over 'The Brook' and pulled up at the stop."Two on top, an' fowa inside, tha's sall." said the conductor. This comment brought a fresh depression over me, I thought, "Om neva gunna mek it, an' on gunna look a right nana tamarra."

Needless worries, I needn't have even thought about them. As the first bus, an old A.E.C. pulled away, the rest of the queue, and myself saw that another bus was following in its wake. This second bus was a Daimler, and more important, it was only half full, so there was no fear now, of any of us being left behind. I went upstairs when the conductor allowed us on, I was dying for a fag. Once I'd reached the top, I found myself doing the same thing that I'd done when I was a nipper. I made my way to the front of the bus, hoping that a seat would be available above the driver, and that I could pretend that I was driving. However the seat on the right-hand side was occupied, so I had to settle for the left.

I lit a 'Senior Service' and drew the acrid smoke down inside me, giving me the illusion of complete serenity, and peace with the world. Good thing this nicotine I thought. It made you relaxed under any kind of pressure, work, worry, or anything else for that matter. It was a wonderful invention I was now well into. I hoped that Joan liked this brand of cigarettes. I had managed to get hold of a couple of packets from the same shop that I'd obtained three packets of chocolate crisp, which were safely tucked up in my 'herringbone.'

The bus moved off with a few violent jerks, and then settled down to a smooth run along Icknield Street. It was always the same with these new-fangled pre-selector gear boxes. I suppose they were alright really, but I preferred the old type gear box; at least if you made a mess of changing, it was only you who you could blame, but with this new fangled idea, well (?), it was doubtful whose fault it was.

I looked out of the left-hand window, but due to the lights inside the bus being shaded with their celluloid collars, much akin to the collars I wore when I was in the choir at St Saviours, the windows being dirty through the weather outside I couldn't really see much, but I tried anyway.

We passed the small yard where a man kept his taxis, and knew that right opposite this establishment was the school I went to for a brief spell, Icknield Senior Boy's. On we went passing 'Bertie Harpers' parents shop, and 'Bill Lewis's' main scrap yard over the way.

I felt the bus stop, and knew we were not at the stop outside 'The Bull', it was too soon, so I guessed that it would be the old 'Albion' coach, picking the workers up from the factory which lay back off the road, just before the row of cottages, and 'Nortons.' When our bus finally re started he veered first right, and then left, and as he did so I looked intently below. I was right, it was the old coach that came from Brades Village, near Oldbury. Having seen this dilapidated bus on several occasions when it was light, I was surprised that it was still going. It belonged to someone named 'Lloyd's Coaches', and I was to find out at a later date that the home for this old lady was on the left-hand side of East Dudley Road, nearly opposite Junction Street.

Soon we were stopping at the stage by 'The Bull', with 'The Centric Cycle' shop over the way. Off we went again under the bridge by Hockley Railway Passenger Station, on past 'The Mint' until we reached the junction with Hingestion Street. This stage was situated right outside the Ladies and Gents on the triangle by Warstone Lane, and Carver Street.

This triangular island consisted of toilets, a horse trough, and several trees. I supposed the thought behind the trees when the gentlemen planned it was, well we've provided amenities for the Ladies and Gents, so we might as well give the dogs their own watering hole, also. I smiled at this singular thought and deemed it funny. Then my mind wondered back to the 'George Street West' capers. I looked through the window to see if I could see the water trough, but it was impossible from this angle. I giggled to myself when I envisaged the scene of me washing all that horse muck off me, after dumping it over the bully's head. Further thoughts, made me wonder what he was doing now. As I said, he was older than me, so he'd be in the forces now (?). I wonder if he ever thought about that day, hoping that he would meet me to seek revenge; or would he be laughing about it now that it was past history. I would never know. Our bus made the final climb, for me anyway, up Icknield Street past 'The New Hudson' on the corner of Pope Street, and then on to Spring Hill Library. The lights were for us so we crossed over Spring Hill and Summer Hill straight away to stop outside the bank in Monument Road.

Alighting from the bus, I went round the back and ran across Monument Road, dodging a couple of cars coming from the Edgbaston direction. I passed the Atkinson's house "The Turf" on the corner of Monument Road, and Spring Hill, which was in complete darkness. Down Spring Hill I went to the bus stop just a couple of yards along, and found only a couple of people waiting there. I stood behind the last of these two, and looked across at the Library. In the misty atmosphere, with all its wonderful architecture, it reminded me of the castle where 'Count Dracula' lived. I knew that just around the corner from there was the 'pawnshop' where on occasions I used to visit for 'you know who' on a Monday morning, before going to school. I smiled to myself, as further thoughts invaded my mind. How 'Our Mom' would change pawnbrokers, when she got into any problems with the current one that she was dealing with. "Happy Day's" was my last thought on the matter, because a Bearwood bus from town arrived on the scene.

I went upstairs again on the bus. This time both seats at the front were occupied, so I just sat on the nearest available seat on the left-hand side. I lit another 'Senior Service' and returned to my day dreams. We passed Ingelby Street, and I thought about 'The Palaise de Dance' at the top, and wondered if I would ever do my 'Fred Astaire' routine in there. Then there was the pub on the right-hand side about half way up which my cousin, Bertha Woods, kept with her husband, Chris, later.

We then moved on up Spring Hill from George Street West, passing in turn Spring Hill Passage, Steward Street, Eyre Street on the left, and College Street on the right. As we moved on my mind became filled with all things appertaining to this part of Hockley. People generally used to term this 'neck of the woods' as Ladywood, but it wasn't - well, not postal wise it wasn't, it was Hockley.

I thought of the tale someone had told me of the licensee of the pub on the corner of College Street and Spring Hill, who used to play for Aston Villa in goal. One Saturday night a mob of blokes threw bricks through his windows, swearing that he had been paid to give the game away on that day, a Cup match. How true this tale was was never authenticated. I mean, it could have been a gang that just did it because 'The Gaffer' had refused to let them stay after time, or given them a bad pint. It could have been because he had dotted one of them for some reason or other. Tales do get out of hand when they have been told over and over again. People tend to add just that little bit extra to a tale, don't they? After about ten times of re-telling it's nothing like the original tale.

I thought about 'Verrachcias' and the old man with his gaily coloured cart, and the dozy looking donkey pulling it down Guest Street on a Sunday afternoon.

We entered Dudley Road at the rise of the hill, with the bridge going over the 'Birmingham Canal.' Past 'Barker & Allens', 'Earl & Bournes' in Heath Street South, and on the other side 'Horseley Engineering' with their offices in Western Road, opposite " Summerfield Hospital, and 'Brookfield House.'

Our bus stopped right opposite the old entrance to Dudley Road Hospital and according to the length of time we were stationary a good many people alighted.

We moved off eventually passing Aberdeen Street, then Heath Street, with 'The Lee Bridge Tavern' on the corner, Northbrook Street, Barford Street, Icknield Port Road, and finally Winson Green Road, that housed 'His Majesty's Prison,' before arriving at the stop for me, right outside Summerfield Park.

I got off the bus, and walked back to Icknield Port Road filled with excitement. In this short walk I passed the Police Station, right by the main entrance to the park, thinking I don't want anything to do with that lot in there. Funny isn't it how we get these different phobias? Like passing a police station, fire station, hospitals, dark mysterious houses; places that have had a crime committed in them, high bridges, tunnels, and God knows how many more.

Finally, bursting with excitement, apprehension, and butterflies in my stomach, I reached the corner where I was to meet Joan. Again, on the corner was situated an 'Atkinsons' public house. (How many corners didn't have a 'pub' there?)

No Joan, but then I didn't know the exact time, so I might have been early. (No watches in those days, they were only for the rich people.)

I waited, and waited. It seemed an eternity to me. On the opposite corner to the 'Atkinsons' public house was yet another pawnbrokers. I thought, "That'll be right handy on a Friday night when the clothes are redeemed. Get the ol' mon with a few ales down him, and then tap him up for the money to redeem his best clothes ready for Saturday.

"Hallo love, have you been waiting long?" I was off in one of my daydreams about the bloke being pressurised into giving his wife some money to redeem his pawned clothes, so these words came as a shock to me.

I turned quickly to find Joan right by my side.

"E-r-r, no, love, ov on'y jus' gorrere miself. I ain' too lert am I?" I stammered. As soon as I'd uttered this answer I realised how futile it was. I laughed in a silly boyish manner, and went on in an inane way. "Well, worr I me'nt ta say wuz, if yo' wuz early, an' I wuz lert I would 'ave........", and suddenly I realised that I didn't know what the hell I was talking about.

She started to laugh, a soft tinkling sound. Realising that I was all at sea with what I wanted to say she then said "Well never mind love you're here, and so am I, so it doesn't really matter does it?"

"Nah-h-h o don' serpose it does, does it."

At this I started to laugh; she had made me feel so at ease, and this laugh of hers was so infectious.

"Well, w'ere d' ya' wanna gu Joan?" I asked. "There's a good film on at 'The Grove', it's one I've wanted to see for a while now. Le's gu an' catch the buzz then, eh?"

"No Ron, let's walk it, and then we'll be in time for the last programme. It'll save getting in the cinema half way through the main feature, won't it?"

"Oh, I 'adn' thought o' that, burrit's a good idea any road up." So off we went walking side by side along Dudley Road, talking about this and that, but mostly talking about work. It was the only subject I could think about momentarily. As we went past 'The Yorkshire Grey' at the corner of Moilliet Street, I told Joan that I had got an Aunt and Uncle who lived there. I then carried on telling her something about Auntie Lil and Uncle Bill, Uncle Bill being 'Our Mom's' brother.

I could sense that Joan really wasn't interested in all of this, so whilst in the middle of this conversation, I tried desperately hard to figure out something else to say. Finally I came up with the idea of telling her of my intention to join the Royal Navy. So I went babbling on, without much idea of what I was on about, but I was enjoying it anyway, although Joan wasn't saying much at all.

Suddenly when we were just about to cross over Dugdale Street, she pushed her right arm through my left, and snuggled up very close to me. I looked at her for a moment, and she looked up at me, and said "You really don't have to try to impress me Ronnie, you're a very nice man, and I am enjoying being with you alright, so just relax, and let's enjoy the evening together."

"Er-r-r, yes Joan, yes, anythin' yo' say, cuz o' know om enjoyin' bein' wi' yo'. it's really great it is, om glad yo' come out wi' me, o really yam."

I really didn't know the routine of going out with a girl at all, as you've probably guessed by now. Joan putting her right arm through my left was enough. I didn't even realise that a woman should walk on the inside, and a man the outside. Still Joan didn't comment on that, I think she was too kind. She must have realised by now how naive I was with this particular activity, and thought she would make it easy for me. Probably she had got more common sense in her little finger than I had got in the whole of my body at that time. At last we arrived at 'The Grove'. There was a queue for the front and rear stalls, so I took Joan straight in and ordered two for the balcony - big deal !

Entering the dark musty atmosphere, we stood by the usherette who took the tickets, waiting for the other usherette to guide us to our seats. After a short while our eyes got used to the darkness, quicker than the return of the second girl, so we wended our way down the aisle, and finally found a couple of seats about three rows down. We settled into our seats, and I asked Joan if she wanted an ice cream or anything but she refused politely. Then I said that I had brought some chocolate crisp, and she changed her mind, and accepted the packet when I offered it to her.

The advertisements were on when we sat down, so we knew that the films would not be divided; we would see the whole show without interruption. Most of the advertisements concerned the local shops. 'Sleeman's Motors' although they hadn't any cars to sell momentarily assured customers that when the war was over, they would be giving their customers the very best service. The 'B.C.S.' was well to the fore. Local home-made bread and cake shops, and cafes were there in force, but, of course, as everything was rationed, there was very little for them to sell. The reason for this continued advertising was to assure people in the thought that they had not been forgotten. A good seller though for when everything returned to normal.

The second feature started at last, and Joan and I settled further back into our seats to enjoy it. We munched on the chocolate crisp, and then lit our fags when we had finished the confectionery. Whilst the film was in progress I thought about what Horace had told me in the stables. I turned and looked at Joan, not distracting her attention from the film. I thought she looked so peaceful, and content with the world. Drawing on the 'Senior Service', the smoke filtering down her nose, and mouth. No doubt about it she was a very beautiful woman indeed, and I thought how lucky I was to be here with her. Not in my wildest imagination could I think that she would enjoy me trying to pull her closer to me, and fondle her body. Fancy trying to nibble her ears? What an absolutely stupid thing to do. No, I was determined that I wouldn't insult her by doing anything like this. I finally put Horace's lectures on 'Men and Women' out of my mind completely. I settled down and enjoyed both films with Joan, with only one interruption.

Just after the main feature had started Joan moved a little closer to me, and then whispered "Why don't you put your arm around me Ron, I'm sure we'd be more comfortable like that" I thought what a nice gesture, this was better than I thought it would be. Imagine, on our first date I was going to hold her in my arms? It was a lovely feeling being close to Joan. The scent from her perfume, and lipstick was absolutely wonderful. I was nervous, very nervous. I hoped that she wasn't going to suggest that we have a kiss, or anything. Not with all these people around. She didn't however, and we just sat there with my arm around her until the end of the programme. The National Anthem was played, we stood up, and made our way out of 'The Grove.'

When we emerged from the cinema we found that the mist had gone. All the damp atmosphere had vanished. It was a cold, clear, moonlight night. I took Joan's arm and put it under mine, and then asked, "Do you want to get the bus home?" She replied, No, let's walk Ron, it's too nice a night to catch buses." So we started our walk back to Icknield Port Road. Passing a fish-and-chip shop which was fortunately open, I said "D'ya' fancy any chips Joan."

"No thank you Ron, I'm not really hungry, but you get some if you like."

"Nah-h-h o don' think o'll botha, o berr owa Mom's got summat fer me fer w'en o gerrin." She laughed quietly at this last statement of mine. I didn't understand why, but I didn't say anything. I didn't think it necessary to bother her. We chatted away about this and that on our way back up Dudley Road, A laugh at something or other, and silence when it was serious. I was enjoying myself to the full, and I assumed that Joan was too.

We crossed over by Heath Green Road, and City Road junction, naturally, to be on the right side for her to go home up her road. It was my intention to ask if I could see her right up to her house wherever in Icknield Port Road that may be, what happened next proved that to be unnecessary.

We arrived at the first entrance to Summerfield Park. It hadn't got a gate, or railings for that matter, they had been taken away a long time ago for the 'War effort.'

"Let's go into the park for a minute or two Ron, I'm really enjoying tonight, and would like it to go on for a little longer please."

The world exploded for me!, I couldn't believe my luck. She must like me, she must. I was going to take her straight home, and I would have been more than happy with that. Now we were going to elongate our evening in this most romantic atmosphere. We went into the park, and chose a bench adjacent to Dudley Road. We sat, and I drank in the whole scene. It was like daylight, the moon was shining that brightly The grass in front of us was covered in a thick frost. During the day snow had threatened throughout, so this could be the beginning of that arriving at last. I resumed the position we'd had in the cinema. I put my arm around Joan, and she cuddled closer to me. The fragrance from her was even better than it had been in 'The Grove'. It was mixed with the stark coldness of the evening, and it appeared so nice, and comfortable to my nostril's. God, I was in my seventh heaven. I was such a lucky bloke. God was so kind to me, giving me this wonderful life.

"Would ja like a cigarette Joan?" I offered. "No, not right now Ron, just hold me, and let's enjoy this moment", she replied. It was just like the 'pitchers'. I knew that I'd got to do something other than just sit there holding her like this, so I came to a decision. I would kiss her, and risk the consequences; that's what I'd do.

I turned slightly to the right, and put my other arm around her, and she didn't resist. I pulled her closer to me, and she let her head loll back a bit. Then I placed my lips on hers, and pressed. I could taste the sweet smelling perfume now, and it drowned my mind in it's fragrance. I was in another world, it was wonderful, it really was.

At last we parted, slightly breathless from this first kiss, and I said "God, that was luv'ly, Joan. Ov neva rad a kiss like that befowa." She never said a word, but she undid her heavy coat, and then she said "Come on Ron, put your hands inside, it'll be a little warmer for you." I thought, I'm alright as I am, what have I got to put my hands inside the coat for, but, on the other hand I didn't want to annoy Joan, not at this stage. I must admit I was a little bit frightened, but I thought there must be something nice about it, for Joan was a very nice girl. So with great reluctance, I put my arms around her, inside the coat.

She was right, it certainly was much better. It was warmer, and I could get much closer to her. Oh this was heaven indeed. I could feel her soft body, I could almost hear her heart beating. Oh God, I didn't know what to do with myself. We kissed yet again, and was beginning to get lost in this wonderful atmosphere. I was in another world; everything around me seemed to be non-existent. Joan was clinging to me and was, I thought, having the same wonderful experience that I was.

Suddenly she started moaning softly. Not the kind of moaning 'Our Mom' did when one of us were playing up, or when 'Our Dad' was up to his 'anks again, when he came back from the 'boozer.' This moaning was so soft, and dreamy She looked as if she were going to pass out any minute. Oh my God, I thought to myself, this is jus' warr rorice 'ad bin on about, jus' afowa Sid came an interrupted us, I'd gorra startid. I pulled away in alarm. I didn't want anything to happen to Joan. I wouldn't have had anything rotten happening to a nice girl like her.

"Oh don't Ron, don't go" she murmured softly, and attempted to pull me back into our former position, but I wasn't having any of that. I must be strong in a moment like this. "I don't really want to go Joan", I whispered to her "but I must get you back home or else your family might wonder where you are."

The magic of the moment had gone. Not for me however, I was still on top of the world, this had been the most wonderful evening of my life. Joan, however, I thought had changed. She stood up and said "Alright Ron let's get off home then shall we?" I was too happy to see this change, although naturally I knew in later years "what was really what."

Joan had taken notice of me before we did kiss too often, and she got pregnant. I had been strong, and stopped this awful thing happening. I bet Joan felt proud of me as well (?).

I walked her up Icknield Port Road, to one of the entry's on the right-hand side. Only about four to six houses past the garage which lay back off the road. We stood there for a while, and I put my arms round her again. We kissed once or twice, and then she said that she would really have to go. We never mentioned meeting again. I couldn't think straight, the 'tiswas' I was in, but later I thought well, I'll see her often enough when at work, and we can arrange something then. Off she went up the long, dark entry. I was wishing that I could have gone with her. I desperately didn't want to leave her really, I wanted this to go on for ever and ever. The fragrant aroma of her hung heavily in my nostril's. It was as though she had left a trail of it as she walked slowly up her entry to her home.

Eventually I tore myself away from that dark entry in Icknield Port Road to make my way, sadly, home to 'The Brook.' I crossed over the road into the bright moonlight; it was so bright it was almost like daylight. Good job the 'Germans worn't comin', cuz they'd 'ave 'ad a bloody birthday in this light, I thought. Off I went down Dudley Road, crossing over once again out of the dark side of the road into the one lit by moonlight. I was so happy . God couldn't have given me anything better. This was something new in my life, something exciting and adventurous. I thought to myself, I'm in the same league as John Wayne, Victor Mature, Tyrone Power, Errol Flynn, Clark Gable, and the many more romantic, and tough film stars. God, I was so happy, I wanted to shout out to the world how exciting it had been tonight with Joan, my sweetheart. I wanted to dance down Dudley Road, and all the way home to 'The Brook.'

I passed 'The Lee Bridge Tavern', crossed over the LMS line, and 'The Cut', then Dudley Road Hospital, with its only entrance just before Western Road. This entrance was so ornate, having a low brick wall, with iron railings sprouting from it. These hadn't been removed yet, for some reason or other. The wide brick path and pavements running in between leading to an ornate kind of bridge. I think that it was a kind of Gothic architecture, this bridge, it was indeed most beautiful. On the right-hand side was the reception room. A small window by the large wooden door was the place one would knock on to obtain a casualty card, or inform the receptionist of your appointment for whatever department you had to attend. It also housed all the files for the whole of the hospital. On the left-hand side was another door but I'm not certain as to what function it played in the hospital's routine.

I eventually turned into Western Road. Only one bus had passed me on my journey home so far. I thought, I'm glad that I'd decided to walk. Me being so happy I didn't really want to talk to anyone at that moment. I passed by Summerfield Hospital, a dark, imposing place. The black-out regulations making it even more eerie. It was so quiet that night walking down Western Road, I could have been out in the most remote part of the countryside. I imagined that this is how it would be.

I could take in the full view of 'The Workhouse' due to the fact that I'd crossed over once again when I entered Western Road, for it was there that most of the moonlight fell. I passed by 'R.White's' the 'Pop plerce' on the right, and over the way was 'Brookfields House.' A plerce fer rold blokes w'en they couldn' gerra night's kip. Well, that's how it was described then, the same as the old image of 'Summerfield Hospital' being the 'Workhouse.' It had been a workhouse at one time and for people living in any age, old habits die hard.

Many a time when I worked on the ambulance service, years later, we would go to pick up a patient destined for the hospital. They would naturally ask which hospital we were taking them to. When told they would kick up an awful row, saying. "Yo' ain' tekkin' me ta no bloody werk'ouse, od soona stop 'ere, od sooner die than gu thaya. Me finishin' mi days in the bleedin' werk'ouse? God no, anythin' bar that!"

It would be very hard indeed to try to convince some of these people that it wasn't the workhouse now. It was a Geriatric Hospital, and it wasn't the same as it had been years ago. I'm glad to say however that we did have a big percentage of success convincing these patient's that the hospital's only sin, if that's the right word, was that it was an hospital for old people. Much like The Children's Hospital in Ladywood Road, is a hospital for children, and The Birmingham Accident Hospital, in Bath Row, was a hospital for accident victims.

One story regarding this situation I must repeat, though it was so funny, and yet so humane I think that it's worth the effort:

George Murphy, an ambulance man stationed at Henrietta Street, went out to a call from a doctor's surgery (a Bed Bureau was the terminology for this call-out for an ambulance), with his partner. They arrived at the house somewhere in the Kingstanding area, fairly early in the morning, to convey an old lady to the hospital. When they arrived at the door they were met by the lady's relatives, who, right away, told George and his partner in no uncertain terms, that she wasn't going to go to no 'werk'ouse' and nothing nor no-one would make her change her mind. Now any ambulance man worth his salt would have appreciated this information prior to seeing the patient themselves, and George was no exception.

On the way up the stairs to determine what equipment would be required to remove the patient from her bed into the ambulance, it gave him the time he required to consider what action, if any, would be needed to convince this good lady how urgent it was that she should go to hospital. He came to a conclusion to what he was going to do, and what a wonderful thing it was that he put into action. I learned this not from George himself (he was a very modest man), but from his colleagues of that time, and also a couple of the officers.

George entered the bedroom where the lady was, without his partner. He had told him to wait downstairs, but he did take two of the patient's female relatives with him.

"Hello my love," he started, but that was as far as he got. "I ain't guin' an tha's bloody final, I ain' guin' ta no bleedin' werk'ouse, so yo' cun clear rorff, an tek ya' ram'blunce wi' ya'."

"Now are you sure that you don't want to go?" George answered quietly to the lady. She turned towards him, and said "Ov tol' ya' once an' om tellin' yarragen, I ain' guin' an' tha's that."

"Okay then love, if you're not coming there's nothing else for it."

"W'atcha mean, there's nuthin' else fer rit, w'atcha gunna do. I ain' guin' ov tol' ya', I ain' guin', so yo' cun bleedin' well clear rorff, gu on gerrourra mi youse."

First George removed his uniform cap, and placed it on the dressing table, and then he took his jacket off, and placed that on the back of a chair. When he did this he turned, and winked at the two female relatives, more or less indicating them to go along with what he was doing. They confirmed that they understood, with a smile.

He then undid his tie, and placed that tidily over the same chair that he had placed his jacket. Then he started to unbutton his shirt, by this time the lady's curiosity got the better of her. "A-a-a, watcho bleedin' doin', w'atcha tekkin' ya things orff fer, come on tell me?"

George ignored this question, and carried on unbuttoning his shirt, and he was about to remove it when the old lady almost squealed "A-a-a, w'atcha bleedin' doin', w'atcha tekkin' ya' clo'es orff fer, w'atcha doin' a owa (and she mentioned one of the female relatives) tell 'im ta pack it tup, tekkin' 'is clo'es orff in ma bedroom it ain' right it ain'." No answer was forthcoming from this relative however. I suppose she'd had enough of the old lady's tantrums by then.

"Please Mista, w'atcha doin', tell me?"

"I'll tell you what I'm doing love." George said at last, with a lovely smile on his face. "Don't you worry none my love, I won't take you to the hospital if you don't want to go, of course I won't. I wouldn't do anything a lovely lady like you didn't want me to. It would be like going against my own mother, and I wouldn't do anything like that not for all the tea in China," he continued in his soft gentle Irish brogue "but it's like this my love, I've got up out of my bed very early, a lot earlier than I normally would have done, at your doctor's request, to come out in this terrible weather, to take you to see another doctor, who will examine you, and furthermore, make you well again. What do I get? Nothing but abuse from you telling me that you're not going. Although it will be better for your family, and for yourself if you would, but you don't want to go, so there's nothing anyone can do about that. One thing I can do though," he went on. The old lady at this point was very interested in this story, and was by now listening intently, "Ar-r-ran w'at's that bleedin' cleva dick?"

George stared intently at this lady for a few seconds, and then he gave her the biggest smile, and again continued with his answer. "I'll tell you the same as I've told my mate downstairs, when your family first informed me that you wouldn't go to hospital. I said to him, 'if that lady still refuses to go to hospital when I get up them stairs, then I'm going to get into bed with her, and have that hour I lost this morning coming out for her.' So move over my love because as soon as I get the rest of my things off I'm going to cuddle up to you, and have that hour I promised myself, alright?" With that he started tugging at his shirt to pull it out from his trousers. A burst of laughter came forth from the old lady. She laughed until the tears rolled down her cheeks. When at last she contained herself she looked at George and said "Ya' cheeky young bleeda, o betcha would 'ave, ya' would 'ave gorrinta bed wi' me, wouldn'tcha?"

"What do you mean my love, would have, I am!" and with that he pulled his shirt completely off. This caused another outburst of laughter from the lady. Everybody stood still until this second outburst subsided. "Putcha bleedin' clo" es back on ya' cheeky young bleeda, it's bin a lung time since I yad a laugh like that, burrit wuz werth it, I'll gu ta bleedin' orspital like ya wanned mi to, burrif o don' like it, yo'ed berra come an get mi yout agen oright?"

"You have my promise on that princess, if the ambulance service won't let me, then I'll come in my own car and fetch you, okay?"

"Oright, now off ya' gu now, cuz o wanna 'ave a piddle afowa o gu, an' o don' wan yo' roun' mi w'en om doin' that, so gu on down, an' 'ave a cup ov tea, an' I'll tell one o' the wenchis w'en om ready, an' then yo' cun tek me." She looked up at George and gave him a big smile, and George reciprocated this by going across to her, and giving her a lovely smacker on her lips. This story was so insignificant, yet was so full of love, and more important, humane, that it was well worth repeating, and I hope it will be repeated again, and, again, for it's worth the merit.

As I approached Brookfield Road, after crossing over yet again, to stay in the moonlight by New Spring Street, I felt what I first thought to be rain on my face. I looked skywards seeing the deep almost blue colour of the heavens to try to ascertain my thoughts. Nothing, I could see nothing, it was rain. I passed Prescott Street, and thought to myself " 'ow lung agu wuz it, tharr I wuz bringin' perpers roun' 'ere, fer Mista Phelps?" The dripping cakes from 'Blackhams Bakery' on the left, and the 'Bluebirds Chocolate Caramels' from the little sweet shop. The first shop past the terrace that ran up the side of the home-made bakery. I was completely lost in these thoughts as I walked down the hill towards Hockley Railway Yard in All Saint's Street. In fact I could smell the scent of the big shire horses which were stabled at the rear of these houses that I was passing now, on the left-hand side. What a lovely combination, this cold frosty night, and the aroma of horses. One conjured up thoughts of these stables, so nice and warm, whilst we on the outside cold and damp. It was a very comforting thought, that man looked after his most valuable friend like this.

As I took the turn into All Saints Street from Crabtree Road, I looked up the long ascending concrete path leading to these stables, stopping and giving it some deep thought. As I looked up towards the stables, someone opened a door somewhere up there throwing a shaft of light outwards. In this momentary shaft of light I saw white flakes descending. It wasn't rain then, as I had first thought, it was snow.

I stood there a while longer, and after a few minutes the density of the snowflakes increased. So much so, did they increase, that I witnessed the start of the path being covered with a white layer. It had now started snowing in force. I was really enjoying this, as only a sixteen year old lad could. I wanted to stop out all night in it. The falling snow, now that it was thickening, and falling so heavily, made the moonlight look darker, but the whole effect was more like daylight now, than daylight really was. It was indeed a beautiful night for me. I moved off after a while, and crossed the long bridge taking me over the shunting yards below. I could hear the hiss of the little tankers, and then the sudden outburst of steam. The muffled tones of the many railwaymen, carrying out their various duties. The clanging when the wagons were coupled up, and the shout to the engine driver that everything was clear. I thought of all these things I had listened to whilst I lay in bed on winter nights at 2/24 and 228 later. This time, I thought, I'm here on the spot. So instead of going down Lodge Road to 'The Flat' as had been my intention, I turned right into All Saints Road, intending to have a look into the yard over the big barred gate, which I had done with 'Our Arthur' when I was a kid.

The smell of bread being baked at 'Scribbans' Bakery' on the corner of Lodge Road, and Goode Street reminded me of how hungry I was. This mixture of bread being baked, the smell of oil, steam, and the horses gave me the sort of memories I wished for. I wanted to put all this night into a secret compartment and hold it forever, so that on occasions I could go, and open the compartment, and re live it truly. Of course, this was only a dream, but I've never forgotten the thrill of it all, silly though some people may find it. To me it was everything, to me it was life.

I went down All Saints Road, and stopped at the barred gate. I could only see shadows with my eyes., but my memory gave me another picture entirely. It gave me men, horses, engines, wagons. The little tankers pushing and pulling various wagons from here to there, and then back again, until they had got the right wagons on the right line which made up the particular train. It gave me 'Our Kid' and all the other friends I used to see on these excursions on a Saturday morning. Time stood still for me, as still as I was, standing by that gate. I thought again, God is so good to me, I wonder if I'm worth it all?

At last I came back to reality, for I'd got to get up in the morning, that's if it wasn't morning already. I'd lost all track of time, though that of course didn't bother me greatly now. Mom didn't give me any hassle, about what time I came in. I think she was wary about all the wenches though, but with us blokes, what harm could we come to? I walked down the rest of All Saints Road until I came to Piddock Street where I turned left, which would bring me to the commencement of 'The Flat.' I looked down this very small street, for a while. The small terraced houses on the left in complete darkness, and on the corner with Lodge Road were the business premises of 'Twist's,' caught in the semi-darkness caused by the direction of the moon's light. It all looked very eerie indeed. Complete silence reigned, just the snow falling quite heavily now. On the right were more terraced houses, but of different architecture. In fact they were completely different, but they were bathed in the complete light from the moon, which gave it a ghostly look. The reflection from the moon shining directly into the windows of these houses on the right, gave an impression that the people had all their lights on. I reached the corner and stood outside the chemist's shop on the corner of Piddock Street, and Little Park Road. I knew that I should be on my way home, but looking at the sight before me, I couldn't resist drinking in the whole atmosphere. I thought it was such a wonderful scene, I wanted to hold it for ever, and show it to other people, who could not through all kinds of different circumstances see this sight as it was.

I looked first at the Atkinson's public house 'The Abbey Vaults', with the little post office situated next door. I remembered its colour from other times. It was the colour that buildings were more or less restricted to in the thirties, green, or brown. If you were really rich, or you were the owner of a lot of public houses or shops, etc, then you could really let your imagination run wild, and have your premises 'grained' just like 'The Abbey Vaults.' It was a very nice building. All the woodwork was grained in a very professional style, and varnished until it literally gleamed. The 'Atkinsons' sign was displayed over the top of the lower windows. Gold wood lettering on a vivid red background. It was a beautiful advertisement for the brewery, situated in Aston Hall Road, by Aston Hall, Witton Church, and not forgetting 'Villa Park'.

'Ansells Brewery' and 'Frederick Smith's Brewery' could be found in the same location also. 'Ansells' at the junction of Park Road, and Lichfield Road, and " Smith's " down on the right hand side of Lichfield Road, somewhere between Church Road and Thimble Mill Lane.

All the brickwork of 'The Abbey Vaults' was plastered over, and painted cream. The name of the pub was signwritten over the main entrance on the corner of Park Road, and Lodge Road in Old English. On the opposite corner was 'Fred's Cafe', one side of it in Ford Street. Over the way from that was 'The Wine Shop' (Douro's I think). The last corner before getting back to where I stood, was occupied by 'Yarnolds', the curtain people.

The whole area was now bathed in moonlight, and blanketed in a very deep layer of snow. It was so peaceful, and quiet. One or two people were wending their different way's, presumably to their homes. They left little imprints in the snow, they appeared to be prints just like the birds made when they were feeding on some breadcrumbs that kind people had left out for them.

It's difficult for anyone to describe fully any type of scene for no-one thinks alike do they? That night however for me was the epitome of happiness, the night I lived my first date. I was so full of happiness I thought that I would burst, and I wouldn't have minded right there and then, because it would have described to everyone how I really felt.

I have mentioned 'Abbey' and 'Ford' quite often, and there is something quite significant in those words appertaining to Hockley itself, which I think the reader should be aware of, if they aren't already.

First of all 'Abbey.' This was a 'Folly' built in 1780 somewhere between Whitmore Street, and Soho Hill. 'HOCKLEY ABBEY' was built single handed by a gentleman named 'RICHARD FORD', hence Ford Street was named after him, and 'The Abbey' was remembered by 'The Abbey Vaults'. To go a step further 'The Abbey Vaults' in Lodge Road was commonly known in the local area, as the 'Big Abbey.' If you went up Key Hill you would find another pub, a small flat-fronted house on the left-hand side going towards Hockley Hill, and this was known locally as 'The Little Abbey.' 'John Rabone', who had large premises that occupied the whole area of Whitmore Street from Heaton Street to Ford Street, was named 'The Abbey Works', and another firm, 'Collins' in Hockley Hill, right opposite Guest Street was named 'Abbey House.' So 'HOCKLEY' was famous, in a modest kind of way through history; 'great innit?'

It was with great reluctance that I left this wonderful 'live dream', but reality had to prevail. I had got to get up early. I trudged, and I mean trudged, because the snow had fallen so heavily, so quickly that it was now quite deep everywhere, along 'The Flat', passing 'H. V. Smith's', 'Spencers', 'The Birmingham Co-operative Society', 'F. W. Woolworths', 'A. D. Wimbush's', 'The Brown Jug' just by the bakery. The church which lay back off the road, and finally made my way into Icknield Street for the last leg back to 'The Brook.' I remembered yet again my eight an' a tanna football from 'Norton's', and looked across at their premises, and smiled to myself. Down the steep incline I went just past the terrace with about eight houses, and a great many trees contained there. Down I went below the road level, passing Selleys the florist-cum-greengrocers, and then several small cottages, before coming up the other side bringing me back on a level with the road again. The railings alongside the road, which were put there to stop any vehicles crashing down into this man-made depression were now covered in a kind of pattern of snow. It looked quite pretty standing out against the blue black of the sky. It reminded me of a needlework pattern, made by some very clever lady. Then, as an after thought, I thought to myself "fat bloody chance them railin's ud 'ave, if a numba eight fell ova rem, guin' down thaya." In my mind I'd spoilt the whole effect of my first thoughts.

I glanced over at the row of cottages set back slightly in between the modern factory, and 'Norton's', and imagined it being a Christmas card, and wondered why someone had not painted them in this light at sometime or other.

I looked down the last part of Icknield Street leading to Hockley Brook. It was now inches deep in snow, virgin snow. There wasn't a mark on this lovely blanket provided by Mother Nature. The bright moonlight, the snow falling heavily, the blue-black of the sky, and the pure whiteness of the blanket of snow. This was certainly a picture that would be very difficult for any artist to reproduce. God, I wished again with all my heart that I could hold this moment, for all eternity.

I made my way reluctantly towards 'The Brook' trying to hold every step I took. I kept looking backwards to witness my single track, the only marks in this pure blanket of snow, but which would be covered again in no time at all due to the heavy fall. Eventually I trudged up New John Street West, and into our dark, dim, entry. Opening the door as quietly as I could, I then moved into the middle room. On entering the room I witnessed a wonderful scene, almost as wonderful as the scene I had witnessed outside on my journey home from my date with Joannie Boulton. The fire was still burning in the grate, the kettle, as always, perched crazily on the burning coals, and whistling in a soft gentle sound. The crackling of the fire, and the flickering light it threw across the room, gave it a richness I'd never seen before.

It had been so bitterly cold outside, and now, suddenly everything was warm and still. It was akin to climbing into bed, and after a couple of minutes feeling that warmth suddenly coursing through your whole body, until at last it completed its journey, and you were nice, and content with the world.

As usual the cat and the dog were evident, snuggled up together, but this time they were not on their own. Somewhere along the way, we had gained a couple more kittens, and a small brood of chicks. I think the latter was one of 'Our Dad's' ideas. It all looked so cosy to me. My first intention was to light the gas mantle, but I quickly changed my mind, for there was enough light from the fire, and to put the gas on would have been a sin really. Its light would have proved rather garish when it finally popped, and flickered into light. It would have broken up this most comfortable, warm, and lovely atmosphere, and that's the last thing I wanted.

I removed my 'herringbone' and threw it on the couch, by the back yard window. Then I went round by the fire. The little chicks started to cheep, and the kittens, cat, and dog, just gave me a quick glance, and returned to their slumbers. Mom had left me about half a dozen cheese 'doorsteps', so I didn't have to bother about cutting myself some 'bread-an'-screrp.' I got hold of the 'Birmingham Mail' and used it as a glove to remove the kettle from the fire, and put some of the water into the big metal teapot on the table, and then returned it to its original position. I then added another three or four teaspoons of tea to the pot, which undoubtedly still held some remains from previous users. I know it wasn't strictly to the rules for making tea, but then in the 'Smith household' our teapot was never empty. All we did was keep filling the pot up when it became empty. So, no problem.

I sat down in 'Our Mom's' chair (a sin normally) and pulled a cup towards me, putting milk, and about four spoonfuls of sugar in. Then I commenced to eat the sandwiches, whilst the tea brewed, or should I say 'stewed.' That woke all the animal family up, when I started in on the sandwiches. All of them suddenly, as if some hidden finger had prodded them, jumped up and gathered around my feet. I put some crumbs down for them, making sure that one didn't have more than the other, and we all settled down to chobbling. I drank about four cups of tea after the sandwiches, and then lit a 'Senior Service,' sitting back contentedly to enjoy a smoke before going up the 'wooden hill to Bedfordshire.'

I sat there enjoying the fag and thinking about the evening. It had been wonderful, no doubt about that. I was really content with my thoughts, and my 'ciggies.' I lit another cigarette. This moment was too good to miss.

I finished my second fag since arriving home, and threw it into the still blazing fire. It was nice, sitting here in 'Our Mom's' chair. I snuggled down into the cushions, and closed my eyes. I thought to myself I'll just lie here for a few minutes, and then I'll make my way upstairs. The 'animal family' had returned to their normal positions, having had, all they could scrounge and were well into slumberland before I'd even closed my eyes. God, I felt cold; it was as though I'd suddenly been immersed in a barrel of cold water. What was causing all this discomfort? The mist of sleep started to go away, and reality was coming back to me. I'd dropped off to sleep after having my supper, that's what had happened. The fire was now only red embers. The 'animal family' were snuggled closer together, to keep the warmth with one another. I got up from Mom's chair, stretched myself, to straighten out any stiffness through lying awkwardly, and then I looked at the clock on the mantlepiece. I was pleasantly surprised, it was only just after one o'clock. I picked my 'herringbone' up off the couch, and went upstairs to bed quietly. 'Our Kid' was snoring away contentedly when I entered the bedroom. So I placed the overcoat softly onto the chair by the window, and then undressed placing 'mi Sundee best' on the table. After getting stripped, I searched under the bed, feeling first the 'piddle bucket', then my working clothes. Finally, I found what I'd been looking for: 'mi wick day shert.' I hastily donned the shirt, and jumped into bed. I snuggled up to him. He gave a few grunts, snuffles, and groans, and then went back to his snoring, and even breathing. In next to no time I was warm, and I fell into a deep dreamless sleep.

I didn't see Joan for quite some time after this most pleasant night out with her, but somehow this didn't make a great deal of difference, or for that matter worry me a great deal. Oh, I thought about it, I thought about it a lot, but in those days, like a good many more at my age we were so happy with life as a whole that when we did have a real share of happiness for only a short while, we appreciated that particular moment, and then stored it away in the more pleasant chambers of our minds. I suppose really, to put it in a nutshell, it was like that extra present one would receive for a birthday, or Christmas. One which you weren't expecting.

I talked about Joan a great deal. I talked about her with reverence, for this had been my first real date. It was something to be talked about. I told Danny, Joe, Pat, and Peggy, right from the start to the finish. In fact I talked about it so much, I must have bored people in the end. Like other events though it gradually faded. Not in my mind, it stayed there as fresh as ever, but the re-telling of that night faded.

I was enjoying my work at Handsworth Dairies more, now that I had been put onto a wholesale round, for this meant that I didn't work on a Sunday. Mind you, I certainly made up for it in the week, because instead of finishing early, as I had done on my previous two rounds for the firm, I was now finishing much later. However, Mr Davies brought to an end these Sundays off. After the first week or two on this new wholesale round, he would be in the habit of calling down at 228 on a Sunday morning, getting me out of bed to go and do a round due to someone not turning in. I soon got wise to this, and decided that something had got to be done. First, I approached 'Our Mom' and asked her to say I wasn't in, when Mr Davies called, but she wouldn't agree to do this. So what I did then, was to stop out on a Saturday night, either at Joe's in Church Terrace, or one of my other mates, then when Mr Davies called, Mom would go up for me, and… no Ronnie! So she had to tell the Gaffa " 'es norr 'eya."

Eventually Mr Davies had me in the office, and told me that the company expected me to be available on a Sunday to fill in if necessary. I wasn't having any of that bunkum. I told him, "Well Mr Davi's, o can' stop in on a Sat 'di night, can I cuz yo' might bi callin' fer me early Sundee mornin', an' worr about if o mek 'rrangements ta gu out on a Sundee, or summat. O mean it wuz yo' that put mi on the 'olesale roun' in the fust plerce worn it?" He finished up telling me I'd got to do as I was told or he would have to take further action, and he gave me one of his menacing looks.

I had the good fortune to mention what Mr Davies had told me to 'Our Mom.' Now although she was a good straightforward person, well, in many respects that is, one thing she couldn't abide, and that was people threatening anyone she was connected with, and especially her own brood.

"Oh 'e bleedin' well did, did 'e," she replied when I had finished my story " we'll 'ave ta bleedin' well see about that wunt we?"

I remembered the Johnnie Kingham episode, when I punched his nose in a fair fight, down Frankie Anderton's openin'. Blimey, 'Our Mom' soon put paid to that little lot, and quick about it. So I didn't fancy Mr Davies's chances when he came knocking on the door next time. Besides the conversation with the Gaffer, which Mom didn't like she also didn't like the idea of me staying out at night anyway, as she had told me so often.

For me of course it was a godsend. Having Mom on my side was like having a couple or three blokes. Inevitably it happened, he came, and I was awake. I knew it had got to be him this early on a Sunday morning, so I went out onto the landing to listen.

"Watcha want?" A muffled tone which naturally I couldn't hear.

"D' ya' pay the lad fer comin' in w'en yo' wannim, fer ran extra day?" Muffled reply.

"Well don' come 'ere ragen, cuz 'e ain' comin', an' tha's that, 'ave ya' gorrit? an' anutha thing w'ile we'em arrit, don' yo' gu threat'nin' mar lad agen, cuz if ya' do, yo'l 'ave me ta reckon, wi', an' yo' wun like tharrat tall, now bleedin' well clear rorff, an' o don' wanna see yarrere agen right?"

Bang ! I think the whole of New John Street West heard it. I nipped back into bed, and 'Our Kid' said "W'at wuz tharrall about owa Ronnie?" I related the whole story, and we lay there giggling like a couple o' wenchis.

*   *   *

My second romance came in the wake of the first. Now whether they had discussed that Thursday with one another I don't know, and they weren't about to divulge that, were they?

"Hello-o-o, big boy!" This was Gabrielle, when we were in the queue for loading one morning. "How's your love life then?"

Now having had that romance with Joan, I was feeling a little more forward about women. I wasn't a boy any longer. I knew what it was like to go out with a girl. There wasn't much anyone could tell me now, so the answer I gave Gabrielle that morning wasn't so surprising.

"Oh, my love, life's great 'ow's yowas Gabe?" She came to me and gave me such a wonderful smile, put her arms around me and gave me a kiss, full on the lips, just as she had done when I first arrived at the dairy. Of course this added to my ego regarding women. I put my arms round her, and held her tightly, and then, returned the kiss, which in all honesty I thought would have surprised her, but it didn't. She snuggled up closer, and we stood there kissing one another for a while. Eventually she broke away, to move her horse forward, and also because all the other roundspeople at the back of us were cheering us on. On completion of moving her horse, she came back to me and said "Well, you've ruined my reputation now, so when are you going to take me out?" 'ow about ternight, love?" I replied, "Great!" she said, "Do you know where I live?"

"Norexactly, o know it's ova thaya" and I nodded in the Island Road direction.

"I live down Cranbrook Road, number (she told me, but I've since forgotten) just on the left-hand side before you get to Bush Grove. So what time can I expect you then?"

" I'll be at yowa rouse at about 'alf six then Gabe, if that's soright wi" yo'?"

"Yes, that'll do fine, see you tonight then?"

"Ar-r-rokay love."

I'd made it, I'd got a date with another woman older than myself. I thought "they mus' like yo' Ronnie, there mus' bi summat about yo' they like." It never

143

entered my mind that they might be having a bit of fun at my expense. Never the less I'm glad it was like that. I personally wouldn't have had it any other way. I did have thoughts about this later, of course, but right then my ego had been boosted and I was indeed enjoying the whole situation - and let me tell you here and now, I wasn't on my own either. This was all part of the plan, by women.

I met Gabrielle, as arranged and we went to 'The Albion.' I followed the same procedure as I had done with Joan, with the exception of 'Our Lil's lovely scarf. Chocolate crisps, arms around her. We did however have a few kisses in the cinema, which we didn't with Joan, and Gabrielle didn't smoke, so I gave it a rest for the evening to fall in with her plans.

We returned to Cranbrook Road after the date, and we stood in her porch for sometime afterwards, and we had more kisses, with me forgetting that she might become pregnant, I was enjoying it so much. Eventually she had to go in, and I made my way home to 'The Brook,' and again a very happy lad.

Like with Joan, I didn't see Gabrielle again for some time, but it didn't bother me. I liked life, and I was living it in the only way I knew how - happily. Don't get me wrong, however, I did see both the girls on a good many occasions due to us working together. In fact Joan confided to me that she had become engaged to a bloke who was a supervisor at Hawleys Bakeries on Moseley Road, and I wished her all the very best. Life to a great extent was like that those days. No animosity at all.

I have mentioned Arthur Cheslyn and his piano playing, and it was through this particular ability of his that I met my third girl, and what a formidable girl she was. Arthur moved to Island Road from Trinity Street, not long after I did. Unlike me, however, he was kept on the same round. We met one day as we were unloading at Island Road, and he mentioned that he was going over to 'Bromi'ch' on that Saturday night to play at Mrs Knights house in Boulton Square. It was someone's celebration or other, and he asked me if I'd like to go along. He added that it would be a bit of company for him on the journey over there, and back again, with us living so close to one another. I agreed happily. I was getting in to a kind of rut dancing every Saturday night at the club. This was most welcome really, it would give me further experience. I mean going over the border into West Bromwich on a Saturday night. This was something reserved for older people. Birmingham folk used to flock to 'The Black Country' on a Saturday night for the music in the pubs. In Birmingham the Watch Committee wouldn't allow pubs to have a licence for music then, so on a Saturday night there would be a mass exodus on the 74, 75 or 73 buses to West Bromwich mainly, but further afield if they thought necessary, to get the type of entertainment they required.

Arthur and I met on 'The Brook' by 'Tippers.' This was of course the best place for us to meet, him coming from Ventnor Road, and me from New John Street West We got off the bus at the stop in between Florence Road and Trinity Street, and then went down the street where the depot had been sited, As far as we could make out now, it was a taxi firm's yard.

Both of us went on talking and smoking, as we wended our way to Mr and Mrs Knights. I was really looking forward to this. It was all new to me. Our Mom and Dad had had parties of course, but then I was too young to stop up. Consequently the only part we took in the proceedings, was on the Sunday morning when we met our new 'aunties' and 'uncles.' This time I was actually going to a party, I was

144

going to be one of those 'uncles'. Well that's if they invited me to stop overnight, and furthermore if they had got kids, which I doubted due to their age.

At last we arrived, and were they pleased to see Arthur. Well they made out that this wonderful welcome was for both of us, but you didn't need to be Einstein to fathom out exactly who they were really pleased to see. Anyway we settled in, and a glass of beer was brought for both Arthur and myself although I hadn't drunk any alcohol before. I thought about refusing, and asking for a drink of pop, or something else, but then I reminded myself that I'd been invited to an adult party, so I must drink what adults drank, so I received the beer, and thanked Mr Knight who had poured it for us.

I had tasted beer before. This was when Dad sent me down to Hardy's on 'The Brook' to fill his bottles for him. I've mentioned before how I used to lift the paper label Mr Hardy placed over the top of the cork, or screw cap, when I got outside the outdoor. I did this in the dark entry which ran between 'C.V.Bull's' butchers shop and 'Bendall's' the bread and cake shop. I'd pull the label half off, and take a measured swig, and then replace the tag. This I would repeat until all the bottles were at the same level, and then I would return home. Dad on occasions would say " 'im down thaya ain' gein' us a very good measure lately, I'll 'ave ta 'ave a word wi' 'im I will," and he'd look at me with that old fashioned look. He knew, he knew very well why the measure had gone down. One thing I'd forgotten in my innocence, was my breath. Funny how Dad always bent down to me to thank me for fetching the ale wasn't it?

I drank beer, and smoked, and we played games. Arthur played the piano, and we sang. It was the games, however, that I enjoyed the most. Especially when it required the girls at the party to sit on the bloke's laps. This was a feeling I'd never experienced before. It was very nice; it did something to me which I couldn't rightly explain, to myself that is. The more beer I drank, and the more we played this type of game the more interested I became in these sensations I was experiencing. It was thrilling, and caused a funny feeling to come over me, but I still couldn't figure it out. I was 'thick.'

In the early hours of Sunday morning, about one o'clock, the Knights decided to call it a 'day' (Rubbish my jokes aren't they?) Arthur and I, with 'no offers' to stay, didn't fancy the walk back to 'The Brook', but what option had we? We couldn't very well ask Mr and Mrs Knight to put us up, like my Mom and Dad would have. We remarked on this as we made our way down Boulton Square into Boulton Road. One thing in our favour, however, was that we'd had enough booze to put us in a better frame of mind for the journey, and we were both glad of that. Also for me there were two further advantages. The first was that I, unlike Arthur, hadn't got to get up later to go to work. The other? During the course of the evening Mary, one of Mr and Mrs Knight's daughters, and I had made a date for the following Tuesday evening. It was Mary who had sat on my lap for most of the evening when we had been playing games, and also for sometime when we hadn't, and I liked it.

We had kissed during 'Postman's Knock,' and one or two other games which required a kiss or two. Also we had gone out into the back yard, and had a few extra kisses as well. Mary had kissed quite differently to Joan or Gabrielle. I can't explain it, but it was certainly different. So much so, that I was looking forward to Tuesday with great gusto. Little did I know what that evening had got in store for me, and how it was going to turn out vastly different to what I expected. The walk back to 'The Brook' from West Bromwich turned out to be much more pleasant than I anticipated. We smoked, and chatted as we wended our way surely, but slowly, due to Arthur's condition, whatever it was, and in next to no time we were saying "Goodnight," although as we reminded ourselves with a laugh, it should have been "Good Morning."

During that walk I did mention to Arthur about my intended date with Mary. I told him that I intended to take her to 'The Imperial' at the top of Spon Lane, close to Dartmouth Square. He chuckled in his own inimitable way, and turned to me, and said "Yo' bi careful young Ronnie, don' yo' gu purrin 'er rin the bleedin' puddin' club will ya'?" I had never heard this terminology before, and I hadn't got a clue what he meant, so I thought I'd better answer in the same line as the question he'd asked me. So I just said "Nah-h-h w'atcha tek me fer, cause o' wunt purra in the puddin' club." Never the less this reference to 'pudding clubs' intrigued me. I'd heard of 'Provident clubs,' 'Christmas clubs,' 'Holiday clubs,' but never this one. I did remind myself at the time to pursue this 'pudding club' thing, but I never did. Of course it was disclosed at a later date, like everything else in life, but I didn't pursue it myself.

During the time between that Saturday night, and the Tuesday that I'd got the date with Mary I did a lot of thinking. I thought about the sensations I'd felt when she, and the other girls sat on my lap. Then I thought about Horace's talk with me in the stables. I was thinking that the two might probably be connected somehow. The more I thought about it the more convinced I became. Perhaps Mary wanted me to be right close to her, just like Horace had explained to me? I couldn't go to Horace for advice on this very serious matter now due to the fact he had gone into the Royal Navy. So it was up to me now, I'd got to decide for myself, and I knew exactly what I was going to do.

I went to Mary's house in Boulton Square on the Tuesday night full of hope for a pleasant and fruitful evening. I had managed to get some chocolates, as well as the chocolate crisp. I'd also managed to get some 'Capstan Double Strength' although I wasn't quite sure why I'd done this. Perhaps I somehow thought it would give me the necessary strength for that evening, whatever was to come of it.

We walked up Spon Lane, I had my arm around her, and she didn't object, so I thought well that's a good start anyway. I took her upstairs, I didn't want her to think I was a skinflint, and we settled down about four rows from the back, which of course was full. We finished the chocolates, and we smoked, and then I put my arms around her again, and pulled her closer to me, still she didn't say anything. I kissed her, as everyone else around us were doing, so I thought well I'm doing nothing amiss.

I thought about what Horace had told me; now what was it I had to do next? Oh, I remember, I'd got to work my hand underneath her armpit. That's it, that's what I'd got to do, brilliant! I dropped my hand casually, and worked it between the back of the seat, and her back. Mary shuffled a little, and I took this to be a sign of acceptance, I never imagined that she might have been uncomfortable with what I was doing, and was too polite to tell me. I left my hand there for a while, but in the end I'd got to move it, it was going numb. So I pushed it further round, and finally I got it under her right armpit.

Still she said nothing, so I was getting rather excited by this. Horace was right after all, it was the right thing to do.

Again, I left my hand where it was, but again I felt that numb sensation start. This was it, if I could get my hand further round it wouldn't have so much pressure on it. So off I went into the journey of the unknown. My hand finally arrived on Mary's right bust, and I started to move it clumsily. This time however she did object, not verbally, but she pushed my hand away with the inside of her arm.

What was it Horace had said, I thought to myself? Yes, that's it, don't go on if they make any objection. Leave them alone, and they will think you don't like them or something. Give it a bit of time and then give it another try. That's exactly what I did, and I kept on doing it. She'd shove my hand away, and I'd put it back. In the finish I made one last determined effort, and she must have thought to herself "If 'e duz tharr agen?" The result was tragic.

I pushed my hand quite firmly under her armpit, and clutched wildly at her right bust. She grabbed my hand with her left hand, and shoved it away, equally as firmly, and at the same time she said "If yo' doh pack up tryin' ta feel mat tits om gunna bang yo' one up the bleedin' earole." That statement couldn't have come at a more opportune moment. It arrived just as the couple on the screen went into a fond, silent embrace. There was a deathly silence around us for a few seconds, and then suddenly everyone burst out laughing. It was a madhouse. The couple on the screen were still clinging to one another in a passionate silent embrace, which didn't warrant laughter from the audience. In fact what it should have brought out from them at this particular part of the film, was tears, and yet here they were just by Mary and I, rolling about in laughter. If anything, it should have been me in tears, and believe me I nearly was.

Eventually everything calmed down, and the people returned to the film. I moved slightly away from Mary, sulking. I just didn't know what to do, I was so embarrassed. First I went hot, and then cold. I didn't know what to do or say. So I just sat there and pretended to watch the film. After a while I felt an arm sneak through mine. I turned, and Mary whispered "Om sorry love, o dain' mean it ta turn out like this, but cheer rup, an' enjoy the pitcher." She snuggled closer, and it made me feel a little easier.

We walked back to her house, and she said she was sorry again, and let's forget all about it. We even had a bit of a snog outside her house, before we went in for a cup of cocoa, prior to me returning to 'The Brook.

Nothing was mentioned about another date, as I left the Knights' home, and I was glad really. My ego had really taken a battering that night, and I don't think I could have stood another bashing like that. In fact girls were definitely the bottom of my list. I gave it quite some thought as I made my way home that night. However my spirits were raised somewhat when I finally reached 'The Brook'. I found that 'Ma Davies's' was open, so I went in to find most of the usual crowd still drinking and chatting. It was certainly this last part of the evening that perked me up, and made the whole thing seem funny in this light. I did go to four or five more parties with Arthur Cheslyn at the Knights, and I did see Mary quite a lot, but no more dates. I never referred to that Tuesday, and neither did she.

We had a lot of fun however at these parties, which both of us joined in. We didn't allow my ignorance - for that's what it was - on that Tuesday night, to spoil our friendship. The last time I saw Mary, and the Knights for that matter, was at one of their anniversaries. Mary by this time was courting a sailor, and I was well on the way to joining the navy myself. It was a short period in my life, but a very happy one. The Knights were one very nice family; very nice indeed.

After I had got over the disappointment of Mary, I left girls alone for a while, and I started to go out with my mates, Danny, Pat, and Joe in earnest. Fate has a funny way of doing things, however, for it was due to this very action I took, going out with my mates, that I met girl number four during this romantic period of my life.

Danny, Pat, Joe, and myself met on the Saturday night, and Joe informed us that his Mom and Dad were spending the night at friends. So if we wanted to, we could stay overnight at his house in Church Terrace. Well, we couldn't refuse an offer like that, so we agreed to a man, that's what we would do. Joe also told us, that he had bought us all a set of fishing rods, so we could do a spot of angling when we went to Bewdley the next day.

Danny, Pat, and myself thought Christmas had come early, we just didn't know what to say to Joe. What we really wanted to say was "W'ere the bleedin' 'ell 'ave yo' got the monnee from, ta buy us these rods?" but of course we didn't, we just thanked Joe over and over again. Never the less we did discuss this situation about were the money came from, when we were alone.

Naturally we came to no satisfactory conclusion, so we agreed as a man "Sod it, if e's geein, we'em tekkin', an' taters to were the monnee come from." So that concluded that question and answer. It was never mentioned again.

The four of us had a great time on that Saturday night. Up and down the 'monkey run' we went, shouting across the road to our other mates, and to girls that we might have fancied. We called into 'Kelly's Cafe' for some nosh or a drink, on several occasions. When you're that age food never seems to fill you. It was on one of these occasions when we had been into 'Kelly's', that I met this girl.

All of us came out together, and we were deciding which way we should go. Up towards 'The Regal' or down as far as 'Sandwell's Coaches' just in Ninevah Road.

" 'allo Danny, 'ow are ya'?" This nice feminine voice interrupted our deep discussion, and we all turned to see who was the speaker. It was one of about five girls just passing, that had addressed Danny, five very pretty girls'.

"Oh I ain' doin' sa bad, 'ow am yo' Sylv'?"

"Oh, I'm oright, it's bin a lung time since we went ta the 'Grand' innit?"

"Ar-r-r, w'y d' ya' wanna gu wi' me agen?"

"Ar-r-ro don' mind. "W'ere ya' guin' now, this bright Sat'dee night then?"

"Oh, me yan mi merts am jus' 'avin' a birra donnuck, tha's sall. W'ere ram yo' lot guin' then, a-a-a?"

"Well if yo' can think ov anyw'ere forrus ta gu, we'em willin'," and she turned to her companions at this statement, 'ain' we girls?"

At this they all started to laugh. Danny waited until the laughter had died down, and then said "Warrabout comin' up Wasson Pool we us blokes then Sylv'?"

"O' watch we don't " she replied sharply.

"O know w'at guz on up thaya . .", but before she could carry on with this comment Danny interrupted her. "Well if yo' know Slyv' then we'em oright then, in we, cuz o wun afta teacha ranythin' will o?"

"Ya' dirty mindid sod" Sylv' replied, all indignant. This time it was Danny, Pat, Joe, and myself who burst out laughing. I don't know whether the other three knew what they were laughing at, but I certainly didn't. Oh, I knew the fundamentals of what they were saying. It was dirty talk, but what Sylv' and Danny were on about was another thing altogether.

"Well ain' ya' gunna buy us girls a cuppa tea then, it's bloody cold stood out 'ere?"

It was Joe who answered. "Are come on le's gu back in agen, o could do wi' anotha cuppa anyway." So with that we all trooped back into 'Kelly's.' After 'Kelly's' we again stood outside to discuss where the nine of us were going. Joe had certainly done us all proud. Sandwiches all round, and cups of tea, and when we tried to share the payment, Joe wouldn't hear of it. Finally, after a short huddle we all decided to go to 'ansa,' for although it was getting slightly late, the park during the war was never closed. (Well, how could they close it?, There worn't any pailin's wuz tha, they nicked 'em fer the Army, an' that.)

Off we went in a noisy fashion down Soho Road. We turned into Linwood Road, and then into Dawson Road, we took the second on the left down Dawson Road into Woodstock Road, passing Arthur Road, and took Chantry Road into Grove Lane. Going along the lane until we reached the entrance just opposite Douglas Road, and into Handsworth Park (or to give it its correct name, Victoria Park) we went, still kickin' up a bloody rackit. As we passed by Douglas Road, I gave some thought about our Auntie Bertha and Uncle Alf. They had been moved temporarily into a house in Rookery Road due to a bomb damaging their house. Not a direct hit, naturally. It was blast damage from a bomb dropping close by. I wondered if they had moved back into number 73 yet, or if they were still in Rookery Road. I giggled to myself momentarily as my thoughts went on. What would "Our Aunt' think of her nephew if she knew he was galavantin', with 'wenchis' as well, in her 'posh' park? Then I made a mental note, to call at 73 one of the days, to see if she had indeed returned, and then I could tell Mom.

I don't think that she had informed 'Our Mom,' so I thought better to be safe than sorry. In actual fact I did call on the Monday, and ascertained that Aunt Berth', was safely restored in her own house once more, but more to the point she had been back sometime. I thought I'd better not tell 'you know who' the last part of this news, there might have been eruptions knowing our Mom.

The nine of us went to one of the many shelters in the park. This one was situated right by the tennis courts. Being so many in number the bench on the one side of this Victorian built shelter wasn't sufficient for all nine of us, so we had to split up, five one side, and four the other. Fortunately I sat by the girl I'd taken a fancy to on our first meeting, so I was in luck. We talked, canoodled a bit, but nothing serious, and we smoked. Well I say we smoked, the girl I sat by didn't smoke, which I thought at that time rather childish. I tried my hardest to get her to have one of my 'Senior Service' but she was adamant. We kissed, in between talking to the other couple, Danny and Sylv', and made stupid remarks to one another. I wished that this girl and I had been alone at first, but then I thought of Mary Knight, and was glad that my best friend was here.

Eventually the girls said that they had better get going or they'd have their Moms and Dads out looking for them. So we wended our way out of the park into Holly Road. We stood where the gates used to be, and I thought we were all going back along Holly Road to Soho Road again, but I was wrong. The girl I'd sat by lived in Belgrave Terrace, just before 'The Ivy House' on the corner of Ivy Road. The other four girls lived in the opposite direction, round the Booth Street, Crockett's Road area. Well, as I'd been sat by the girl I supposed that it had fell to me to see her home, and I asked if she would like me to do this. "Yes I'd like that very much" she replied. I had to make hasty arrangements with Danny, Pat, and Joe, to meet them later, due to the fact we were staying at Joe's house.

Finally, it was agreed that we would all meet at the bottom of Church Terrace, at whatever time we had finished saying "Goodnight" to our girl friends. Naturally none of us had got watches, so we just had to hope for the best that we wouldn't be too far apart with our 'goodnight' manoeuvres. So off we went down Thornhill Road, and the rest of the gang went rowdily along Holly Road. I put my arm around the girl, and she didn't object, so I pulled her closer to me, and she seemed to like that as well. So my thoughts again turned to Horace's lecture. This time, however, I didn't intend to try on the first night.

I decided to give it a couple of times, and then go ahead with my plan.

We arrived at last at the bottom of her terrace, situated just before Handsworth Railway Station. Going just inside the terrace, into the shadows, we stood up against the shop wall. Being close to her was very nice, very nice indeed. We started kissing, and I rather gathered that she was enjoying this as much as I was. This made me very pleased indeed. The feelings I was experiencing were, to say the least, lovely. I couldn't understand what they were all about, but that didn't stop me enjoying them all the same.

"Ron, o shall 'ave ta gu in soon, cuz mi Mom 'll bi lookin' for me. Om sorry o can't stop lunga, cuz om really enjoyin' miself wi' ya', burr I don' wanna gerrinta trouble wi' mi Mom, an' spoil it for anutha time."

To say I was enjoying myself at that particular moment would have been the understatement of the year. Something was happening, and I felt that that wasn't going to be all, so of course I was disappointed when she said this. Bearing in mind I'd got all night. Well, I'd got until eight o'clock in the morning any road up. I'd got to go with my mates then to catch 'The Fisherman's Express' to Bewdley. "Does that mean yo' wanna see mi yagen then love?"

"O course o do, o like ya', o like yarra lot o do."

"Well we'em guin' ta Bewdley termorra, if yo' wanna come, butchole 'ave ta be yup early, cuz the trern guz at quarta rarta reight frum the sterchun down Booth Street, so mek ya' mind dup then."

"Nah-h-h, o don' think o wanna come ta Bewdley, cuz it's a birr early fer me, but warr about w'en yo' come back 'um, yo' wunt bi lert comin' back will ya'?"

I thought about this for a moment or two. We usually got back about sevenish, and then we normally had some donnuck together up and down the 'monkey run'. I suppose Danny, Pat, and Jo wouldn't mind if I went off for one night. Then I thought, well it doesn't matter, I can arrange to see her, and then if my mates don't agree, then I can just let her down, and not turn up. Yes that's what I'd do.

"Ar-r-rokay, o tell ya' w'at, I'll meetcharat 'Kelly's' say about quarta rarta seven, but don' get mad wi' me, if om a bit lert will ya', cuz o don' know w'etha the trerns am gunna bi lert do I?"

"Nah-h-h, I'll 'ang on for ya' Ron, I'll un'erstand. Well I'll 'ave ta gerrorff now, orrile be in trouble. One thing Ron I ain' told ja, the reason o can' come ta

Bewdley wi' ya', it ain' becuz it's too early, well not really it ain't. I yave ta 'elp our Mom wi' the 'ousewerk, an' ev'rythin' on na Sundee, it's the on'y day, tharr I can, I yope yo' unastand?"

"Ar-r-ro course o do, the wenchis in owa rouse 'ave ta 'elp Mom, an' that alwis falls on a Sundee, don' worry abourrit, o un'astand."

With that we clung together, and had a few more 'goodnight' kisses, and then she went off up Belgrave Terrace and home, I went back along Soho Road full of excitement. I thought again about these feelings I'd had. Which I still had actually. I liked them, and was looking forward to tomorrow night. Who knows, maybe I would find out what it was all about? Just think of it. I wasn't going home tonight. Tomorrow me and my mates were going for some donnuck out at Bewdley, and then I'd got this girl to come back to in the evening. God, how lucky I was. It was wonderful, this life of mine was so wonderful. I wanted to tell everybody how lucky I was as I wended my way to meet my mates, my great mates, to whom I would naturally tell everything, and we'd have a good old natter. I was looking forward to seeing how they had got on too.

To complete my happiness for that evening I met Horace on my way up Soho Road to Church Terrace. I was just passing 'The Pump Tavern,' nearly opposite 'The Grand Cinema' when I saw a bunch of blokes in front of me. One of these men wore sailors uniform, and another one was in army gear. They were walking slow, and having a laugh and joke, smoking and generally having a good time. I wanted to get up to Church Terrace as quick as I could, to be with my mates, so in next to no time I was overtaking this bunch of blokes. "A, a, Ronnie, it is Ronnie innit?" This familiar voice called to me when I'd passed the group. I stopped, and turned slowly, and then I remembered the voice, it was Horace.

"Well-l-l, long time no see mate, 'ow ya' guin', God, yo' look well."

"O-o-o I ain' sa bad, o can't grumble, ain' it about time yo' come inta the Andrew then Ron?" This floored me. 'Andrew' what the hell was 'The Andrew'?

Horace laughed. Of course he was emphasising his new found 'sailors' talk' on me. "W'arr I meant Ron, wuz ain' nit about time yo' joined the navy?"

"Nah-h-h, I ain't seventeen 'til nex' January, burr I'll bi joinin' then, if they'll bleedin' well 'ave me tharr is."

We nattered on for a while in this fashion, but it was perfectly clear, even to me, that him and his mates had got somewhere in mind to go, and they wanted to get there pretty soon. Where they could be going at this time of night I'd no idea, and I wasn't about to ask them either. I was getting wiser by the day about this naiveness of mine. I knew that I should know a great deal more than I did, but who could I go to for information? Nobody, that's who. I would be too embarrassed to ask in the first place, and I would probably be even further embarrassed by some of the answers, and probable ridicule I would have to suffer, which in turn would make me more embarrassed. So I decided that silence would be definitely golden in these circumstances.

Eventually we said our respective 'goodnights,' and they went off, much quicker than when I first saw them. So whatever it was, or wherever they were going, they certainly didn't want any more delays.

That Saturday night very near to Christmas 1944, was the very last time I saw my dear friend Horace. I have had the picture of him with me ever since. He looked so smart, as he always did, but in his naval uniform he looked the tops.

151

They disappeared out of view, and I crossed the road by 'The Red Lion' and made my way swiftly up to my mates up by Holyhead Road Police Station. When I arrived at Church Terrace, I found to my disappointment only Joe waiting by the bottom of the terrace.

"Worrow Joe, w'ere ram the othas then?"

"Om buggered if o' know, Ron."

"They w'en orff up towards 'The Baggies' ground ages agu, an' o ain' sin 'air nor ride on 'em since. Mind yo' od gid yo' up an' all, yo've bin sa lung."

Nere mind, come on le's gu up the 'ouse, an' 'ave a cuppa tea, the otha two know w'ere we'll be, okay?"

"Ar-r-rr rokay Joe."

After we'd had a cup of tea, we decided to have a smoke outside, it was such a beautiful moonlight night.

Joe and I stood there for a few moments, well, we'd only got half way through our cigarettes when two things happened simultaneously. The first thing to happen was the two wanderers reappeared, talking together quite excitedly as they approached us, and, as they were coming up the drive the sirens started to wail.

The air raids had become quite rare nowadays, and when the sirens did go, it was rarer still for anything to happen. So we ignored the signal, and all four of us just stood there smoking and talking.

Apparently Danny, and Pat, had made arrangements with the other two girls for a date on Monday night. My first reaction was, oh God, I've gone and made arrangements to meet this girl for tomorrow (or was it today?, for I think it was well past midnight now, although not quite sure, due to the lack of watches) on our return from Bewdley. Obviously I had got to tell them, 'cuz we wuz merts worn't we?'

"Look, yo' lot, ov med a dert fer tammorra night, w'en we get back frum Bewdley, I yope yo' ain' gunna play yer bleedin' ferces wi' mi, cuz it's done now, an o can' change it." I thought attack would be better than defence on this particular occasion, which visibly proved right. I don't know what their thoughts - their real thoughts - on the matter were, but having kicked that one around in my mind I came up with the answer rather quickly, which was "Sod 'em, thay ain' my keepers." Actually what I was doing was reassuring myself that I had adopted the right attitude toward the situation.

"Nah Ron, tha's soright" said Danny, with a big grin on his face. "If yove gorr 'er guin' on ya', an' ya' getcha roats tommorra, well why not, we'em all forrit int we Pat, an' yo' Joe?" Are course we yam, it'll bi grert fer ya' Ron. It don' mean wi gorra come back early though does it?" This was Joe putting his two pennuth in.

"Nah, ov tol' da, if om lert, shi cun wert, an' if she don' wanna wert then shi cun do w'at the bleedin' 'ell shi likes, cuz o wun' lose any sleep ova ra." With this we all laughed, and my chest swelled out with pride, I had proved to these lot that I was the 'gaffa' with this girl, and she did what I wanted, or we did nothing at all. Of course, none of it was true. Had I said anything remotely like this to the girl she would certainly have told me what to do, and in no uncertain terms either. Never the less it made me feel great in front of my mates at that particular time.

We all stood in the terrace talking quietly, and smoking, until Joe suggested that we go indoors, and he would make some tea, and sandwiches, which we all readily agreed on. After the meal we tried to get some sleep but of course this proved impossible, we were too excited, so for most of the night we nattered about this and that until we saw the first streaks of light break into the darkness of-night. During one of the times when I managed to drop off into an uneasy sleep I had vague dreams of a number of happenings, some quite recent. Horace Kwi was the one most prominent. He worked at Handsworth Dairies at one time. With a name like Kwi, he was obviously Chinese, but the nearest he had been to China was the cups he drank out of. His one uncle however lived on the left-hand side of Richmond Road walking from the Soho Hill direction. This was the house we were all frightened of when we were younger, thinking all kinds of things about these very gentle people, kidnapping being the top of the list. Horace was a very good friend, only for a short time, but never the less a good pal. He lived in Station Road with his Mom, Dad and family. Eventually he left the Dairy, and I wondered how he had managed to do this with The Ministry of Works being so strict on people moving about. One day Horace was there, and the next he had gone, so I didn't attach too much importance to it. Then one day, as I was serving in Holyhead Road, a 'Bywaters' van pulled up outside 'Mallens' the cooked meat shop, just past Pococks, the chemist's on the corner of Crockets Road.

"Hiya Ronnie, 'ow am ya' guin'?" I had got a crate of milk in my hands delivering to a small 'huxters shop' past 'Mallens.' I delivered to Mallens as well, so I first thought that it might have been Mr Mallen speaking. I turned, and there was Horace getting out of this Austin sixteen van, in its cream livery, with red lettering on the side and back. I couldn't believe it, he was pulling my leg, I thought he must be the van boy, and his driver was inside the cooked meat shop. I put the crate down, and went over to Horace and shook his hand, just like us men did, and said "Blimey yove come up in the bleedin' world ain'tcha?" He gave me one of those big grins of his, and replied "Are it's a good job this is Ronnie, o get jus' ova three pounds a wick, mind jo o 'ave ta werk ova in the factry fer that, an' it's seven days a wick, but neva mind it's monnee innit? An' then there's the extras, a birra meat, an' pies 'ere an' there, an' on top o that there's allis a birra fiddle as well, so all in all it's a great job."

" 'ow did ja manige ta gerrout ta the dairy though 'orice?" I asked " an' w'er's ya' driva then?"

Horace burst into laughter at this remark "I am the bleedin' driva, an' thats 'ow o gorr ourra the dairy as well. Ya' see Ron o gorra mert w'o already werks fer these people in Green Lern, Small 'eath, an' o wuz gerrin' a bit browned orff wi that Welsh twat Davies, so 'e 'ad a word wi' 'im, 'is gaffa tharris, an' 'e ast 'ow old o wuz. O tol 'im seventeen an' 'e sez 'Leave it wi' mi, an'o'll be in touch.'

"Well it wuz on'y about three days afowa 'e got back ta mi, an' sez fer mi ta gu up ta there plerce in Green Lern an' see 'im. So orff o went, an' in no time, 'e sent mi out wi' a bloke in one o their vans, an' o passed mi test, an' 'e sezs, o cun start next Mundee."

"Bloody 'ell that wuz quick wornnit 'orice, w'at did ya' tell ol' Davies?"

"O' dain' 'ave ta tell 'im anythin', this bloke dunnit all fer mi. Ya' see Ron w'en yove gorra drivin' licence, which o gorron that day, yo' gerra birra spechul treatment, cuz that's 'ow it is wi the Gov'ment. This bloke at Bywata's musta rung Davies up an' tol' 'im tharr 'e'd gorra let mi gu cuz o wuz a driva now, an' it wuz issenchul werk. The next thing o 'new wuz they gid mi, mi cards that very Satdee w'en o come in orff mi roun', nothin' wuz sed, an' o' jus' started 'ere on the followin' Mundee."

We talked on for a while about things in general, and the War at large. Horace gave me a couple of pork pies, and went on his way. As he drove off I must admit that I was rather envious of him, for amongst other things I wanted to do in my life, I wanted to be able to drive. That was the very last I saw of Horace Kwi. He was, again, one of the better things to happen in my life.

I moved slightly due to a pain on the left hand side of my back. In a sleepy state I looked around the small dingy front room of Joe's Mother's and Father's house. I say dingy, it was, but it was still more enchanting than either 2/24 or 228. The row of houses, which looked more like country cottages, up Church Terrace, were neat and very tidy, in fact I thought that they represented a little bit of the countryside placed there by God, to help the 'townies' see that it wasn't all grime and dirt everywhere. Joe, Pat, and Danny were sound asleep; it was still dark and only the flickering of the dying flames of the coal fire brought any light on to this most placid scene. I smiled to myself thinking about these three very dear friends lying there in the arms of Morpheus, completely innocent of all the troubles of the world outside this lovely, though dingy little house. It was, to say the least, a most wonderful sensation to witness these MEN (?) lying there just like babes in arms. Mind you, having lived a good while, and being a bloke myself, I often wonder, do us MEN (?) ever really grow up? More to the point, I think the girls really like us this way, just big grown-up babies. I thought about going into the little kitchen at the rear of this room and brewing a cuppa, but changed my mind seeing the three of them sleeping so soundly. So I moved over onto my right side to alleviate the pain I was still experiencing to the left side. I closed my eyes once again and let the quietness of the night take me into its billowy arms.

"Watcha doin' ternight young un, d' ya' fancy a ride out an' gein' me a birrov an' 'and?"

"Ar-r-r ro don' mind, w'ere ya' guin'?"

"All roun' Shropshire, w'ere 'avin' ta do an extra run at night now cuz ov this milk glut the farma's are 'avin'; it's summat ta do wi' all this fine weatha weem 'avin', an' the cows am geein' us mowa milk than they normally do."

I had finished my round at about two o'clock, it was later than all the other roundsmen, but as I was now on a wholesale round it meant working longer hours to accommodate shops, cafes, and canteens. I had put 'Dick' my lovely big horse away, but having done that I had got nattering to Frank the stableman who had worked up at the West Bromwich depot, and before I knew it Frank had looked at his big watch and said "Bloody 'ell Nip, it's near fowa ra clock, o dain' think we'd bin talking that lung, o'll 'ave ta gerra bleedin' move on or o wunt finish this lot ternight an it's mo turn ta come back bloody fire watchin' ternight as well, so tarrar then, o'll see ya' tamarra okay?"

"Ar-r-r rokay Frank." With that I collected my bike from one of the empty stalls (the head stableman, Sid, had let me carry on putting it there after Horace Willetts had gone into the Navy.) I moved off out of the stable area, intending to go straight down the drive into Sandwell Road and off home to 'The Brook.' I remembered however that I had got some notes that I had forgotten to give to Jim the supervisor when I came in from the completion of the round originally, and as these notes were appertaining to tomorrow's load it was essential that he have them that day.

So it was that I went across the yard to the checking in point once again. I gave Jim the necessary papers, and was about to mount my faithful steed and go home when Frank, one of the new lorry drivers, posed the question of what I was doing that night.

"Ar-r-rokay Frank, I'll jus' gu an' put mi bike back in the sterbles agen then okay, an' o'll ge yarran nand loadin' them churns on then."

"Good on ya' Nip, o could do wi' yan nand mi bleedin' backs playin' mi yup summat 'orrible." With that statement he gave me a visible grimace which I took to be the pain he was experiencing. My thoughts on that were "Silly ol pratt, they should geus younger blokes the chance ta drive, an' then they wouldn' 'ave ta depend on these silly ol' sods ta do men's work." I smiled at these thoughts of mine as I took my bike back to the stables.

"Blimey that wuz quick Ronnie" Frank the stableman said when he saw me enter the stable area again in such a short time. "Yo' ain come ta start ta morra's werk early 'ave ya, an' 'ave the day orff tamorra." We both laughed and then I related the story to him, of why I had indeed returned. I also requested that it would be alright to put my 'Kingsway' back into the spare stall again until I returned from the journey to Shropshire. "Course yo' cun Ronnie, it'll bi yoright as well cuz az o tol' ya' rime on fire watchin' ternight so I'll be yable ta keep an' eye on it, so orff ya' gu, an' enjoy yaself."

"Ar-r-rokay Frank, an' thanks a lot fer lookin' arta mi bike, tarrar."

"Tarrar Ronnie."

I went back to the other Frank, and I set to loading the lorry, which incidentally was 'The Greehouse,' with great ardour, due to the fact I wanted to be on my way on this beautiful afternoon, driving around the countryside where Jack Pittaway and I had cycled through all those months ago. Although I must admit I doubted the durability of this old lorry to survive such a trip, it would be a lot of fun trying I supposed, but in my heart of hearts I didn't care a lot anyway.

At long last we climbed aboard this decrepit vehicle, and Frank got life into it after many attempts, and some not too nice words. We pulled out of the dairy into Island Road, and turned left up to Holyhead Road. Past the 'Baggies' ground we went, and straight on into West Bromwich, right through there we travelled to 'Farleys Tower' where we took the right hand turn towards Wednesbury. From there we went on into Wolverhampton via the Bilston Road. 'The Greenhouse' seemed to sound and behave better with all this travelling, which both Frank and I appreciated. She took the hill out of Tettenhall Road, called 'The Rock' quite well considering. Mind you, I was glad that the churns on the back were empty and not full, or it might have been a different story!

We travelled around this most pleasant area, stopping at the various farms picking up the full churns, and replacing them with the equal number of empty ones. Most of the farmers had built a wooden structure at the entrance to the farms on which to put these churns, so that when we pulled alongside, it was an easy task for us to roll one lot off and another lot on with comparative ease, but this was not always the case. A few just put the churns on the floor, so fortunately it was perhaps a good thing that I had gone with Frank to help. With much cursing, and heaving we managed to lift the full churns up onto the lorry, and were so relieved when we completed each one. Of course this was not the case during the normal pick up and drop off in the mornings, because one of the farm hands, or even the farmer himself, was always available to give the driver a helping hand with this rather laborious task.

At one of these farms we went right to the front door of the main building. We off loaded, and loaded, and on completion a big handsome woman came to the door. " 'allo Frank my yold love, 'ave ee done then?"

"Ar-r-r we've finished mar wench, mi bloody back's playin' mi yup a bit though, an' om glad o the 'elp young Ron's gein' me, real glad, o don' . . ."

At this point the lady interrupted and said "Oi bet ee've bin doin' some extra naughties, an' tha's w'at's givin' ee the back trouble, yo' naughty ol' lad." At this she burst into a most lovely laugh; it was just like the tinkling of several glass bells. I looked at her, not having a clue what she was on about, and thought to myself what a lovely lady she was. Oh she was big alright, but she was so beautiful, and somehow this large build suited her. I smiled at her, and she reciprocated, and then she turned to Frank and said "I 'ope 'e aren't teachin' this 'ansome young lad any of you're bad 'abit's Frank, my yold love-e-er?" and she burst into that lovely laugh again. Frank didn't reply for he was in the process of lighting yet another of his roll-ups, but he did look at the lady and gave her a big smile.

"Come on then mi two 'ansomes, oive got the soup ready for ee, an' plenty of home-made bread an' butter-r-r, to gu down with it." and she disappeared inside the farmhouse.

"Cum on then, Ron, we allis 'a sommat ta eat 'ere; she's a smashin' lady she is, an' no marra w'o the driver is, 'e'll allis get the serm welcome. Well I've tasted some soups in my time but I can honestly say that I've never tasted anything like that lady's soup since, it was a meal. We were really full when we left that farm. I didn't know where in Shropshire the farm was situated or even remotely how I could get to it, but one thing that will remain with me for ever was that kind lady's soup, it really was marvellous.

We drove through the Shropshire lanes, Frank and I, and I enjoyed every moment of it. I wouldn't have missed it for the world. it was in every aspect one of the more treasured times of my life.

On the return journey we picked up a cyclist who had run into trouble with his bike, just under the viaduct in Shifnal. I thought to myself "Yer-r-, this is w'ere I crossed on the return journey from Shrewsbury with Jack," which brought back some happy memories of that day. We dropped him off at the top of Island Road and he said that he would be alright from there, for he had only got to go to Smethwick, and he could easily walk that.

My dreams went from that to Jack Grady, and the few times I had been with him on local journeys to a couple of Handsworth Dairies' other depots, 'Grove Vale,' just off Newton Road, and Selly Oak, which was situated on Pershore Road. Jack was a very well known bloke around Handsworth. He did a bit of almost everything. Taxi work, bartending. I think it was all the beer he must have drunk through the years that made him so fat later on in life. When I knew him at the dairy however he was as slim as a reed. I liked all these trips with the drivers, for although I didn't get paid it gave me a lot of knowledge on driving itself, and any questions I asked, were always answered with great detail. It was payment of a kind, and one which I really appreciated.

* * * *

"A come on sleepin' beauty, come on werk up or we'll bi bloody lert fer the trern."

"Train, train, what train, what's that call for? I don't go on trains, I go on buses, and trams, what is it this voice telling me I'm going on a train?"

"Come on Ron, ov bought cha some tea, an' a piece a toast, burrif ya' don' 'urry up wi shan't catch the trern ta Bewdley, come on now ya' dozy ol' sod."

"Bewdley, oh God that's right, I'm at Joe's, not at home."

I roused myself, and thought "Blimey yo' musta gone orff inta a right deep un," although naturally I didn't remember a thing. I rubbed my eyes, and looked around the room, with the daylight now filtering through the gaps in the still closed curtains. The fire had long since died out, and I shivered slightly at the thought of this. Danny stood by the door, Pat was sat in the right-hand corner having a cigarette, and Joe I assumed, which was proved right seconds later when he emerged from that tiny place, was in the kitchen. " Mind 'ow ya' gu Ron. Joe's put cha tea an' toast by the side o ya' chair," said Pat.

"Ar-r-r thanks Pat," and I reached down and picked the cup of steaming tea up, and poured the sweet liquid down my dry throat. I finished the cup in one go, and thoroughly enjoyed it. At this point Joe came in from the kitchen, and I said "Gorreny mowa tea mate, I'm as dry as anythin'."

"Oh yove returned ta the land o the livin' then? Pat, Danny, an' me 'ave bin sat thaya laughin' at cha snorin' an' guin' on." They all laughed at this, and then he went on "Ge us sha cup Ron an' o'll gu an' fill it fer ya', although don' tek too much time drinkin' it or like o said ta ya' we'll bi lert fer the trern." I handed him the cup, and he disappeared into the other room again.

After I had finished the meal, thrown some water over my face, and straightened my hair, we all went out into the 'Terrace' on our way to Handsworth and Smethwick station on the corner of Crockets Road and Booth Street. The weather was terrible; it was one of those cold, drizzly times. It was misty, and it appeared to cling to you, and the cold it brought with it seemed to penetrate your very bones. Mind you, just coming out of that warm little house in Church Terrace didn't improve matters very much. We chatted and larked about, as we made our way up Holyhead Road turning left into St James Street, and then into Crockets Road, and before we reached our final destination we had all warmed up considerably, and in fact were in a better frame of mind about the forthcoming day by the Severn.

Joe, as usual, paid our fares at the booking hall at the top of the steep incline leading to the station itself from the road. We had long ago stopped arguing with him about this due to the fact that he just laughed at us, and completely ignored our protests. We didn't have to wait long for the train, and we were well pleased about that. Being higher than the road itself it appeared to us to be even more misty, and in the open of the station platform, with the cold wind coming round us as well didn't enhance matters. It was so miserable that we didn't even bother to light a fag. First we heard the clang as the signal dropped down, and then a bell rang somewhere, which was always a good indication that something was happening, although none knew for sure what all these things meant. At least with the trams you did know that the buzzing inside the tram poles meant that a tram was coming, you didn't know which way, but you knew a tram was coming. With trains, well that was another thing altogether.

"O' think it's comin'," Pat said.

"Ar-r-ran bleedin' Christmas is," I replied miserably, wishing that I was back in Joe's little house again. I had gone a bit 'off' again, but the others were having none of that.

"Ya' misrable sod Smithy," they all said as a man. "Wassa marra wi' ya', it ain' that wench ya' gorra see ternight is it? She ain' upset ya' ras she?"

This came from Danny. I'd forgotten the girl momentarily, but on hearing about her, I brightened up again. "Nah it's soright lads, it wuz jus' gerrin' up, from that luvly chair rin yowa rouse Joe, an' comin' out inta this bleedin' lot," and I nodded in an upward direction, to the drizzle all around us. Then I continued "burrime a'right now," and gave them a smile. it was a false smile, but I don't think that they saw through it. Well I hoped they wouldn't, for there's nothing worse than having a 'grouch' on your hands for even a short time, let alone having one all day.

We all looked in the direction of 'The Fanny Brown,' and eventually through the misty atmosphere we saw, first a grey shadow, which became darker as it approached, and then we watched as the billowey white smoke appeared coming from the funnel of our train, 'The Fisherman's Special.'

Finally the iron giant pulled into the station, and with much blowing of steam and screeching and squealing it stopped, and we heard the porter shout out " 'an'sworth an' Smerrick, 'an'sworth an' Smerrick." It was a non-corridor train, so we knew we'd have to hold our water, or if the compartment wasn't occupied by anyone but us, then we could 'do it' out of the window, when we were in a secluded part of our journey. A second alternative would be to rush out at one of the numerous stations and use their convenience, but this was always a risky business, due to other blokes wanting to do the same thing. Also you could miss the train if you were half way through the 'doin's.' Never the less we always managed. We found an empty compartment, which we thought lucky for us, and climbed aboard, hoping no one else would disturb us throughout the journey. Settling into the soft comfortable seats of the carriage, we prepared ourselves for the journey to our favourite Sunday outing - well most Sunday's that is. Pat shoved his Woodbines round, and after lighting up we all snuggled down deeper into the luxury of the Great Western Railway's superb coaches.

I thought about the journey the train had already taken to reach us at Handsworth and Smethwick stations, and the track it would take to reach our final destination. Snow Hill, Hockley, Benson Road, then Handsworth and Smethwick, after that would be Halfords Halt, but of course this was only used when 'The Baggies' were at home, and the trains stopped for the visiting fans. After Halfords Halt, we would veer off the main line to Wolverhampton, Shrewsbury and Wales. Turning left and southward to our next station, Smethwick West, just by Oldbury Road. On then to Oldbury and Langley Green in Western Road by the Titford canal. Next port of call Rowley Regis and Oldbury

Station in appropriately named Station Road. Old Hill, with its lovely Haden Hill Park, again in Station Road, on to Cradley Heath in Chester Road, Lye, and then Stourbridge Junction. From there we passed Hagley, Blakedown, and finally Kidderminster, where the two stations G.W.R. and L.M.S. lay alongside one another. At this point we knew we weren't far away from our lovely Bewdley, in fact it was the very next station. We started to get ready to alight as soon as the train started to leave 'Kiddy.' The lads and myself would get off at this point, but our faithful iron maiden didn't stay there, she took her band of happy followers on to either Arley, Highley, Hampton Loade, Eardington or Bridgnorth This journey took one through some of the dirtiest industrial scenery, miserable in its outlook, but essential to the world for its iron products. No doubt about it The Black Country produced some of the finest iron, and metal products in the world, and still does, but oh what misery it brought to most of its inhabitants. I can, however, assure anyone, from practical, not hypothetical, experience that 'The Black Country Man' is a match for anyone in the world. For the most, he is an honest, straight-speaking man, who is never afraid of hard work, and does this work with a fond reverence and loyalty to his employer whoever he, or she may be. In turn he played hard as well, and drank hard in lots of cases, which in many years brought about successful sportsmen, and businessmen. These are to numerous to name, but they have been written about by far better authors than I, so suffice to say, generalising " 'e wor' a bad un, wor the lad frum the Black Country."

Then after Stourbridge, approximately that is, the scenery changed drastically. The black dirty buildings, the heavy laden skies, not acquired by God's work, but by man putting filth into the pure air God had given us, and the almost blackened surroundings of everything, and everywhere, suddenly changed into rolling hills of greens of all shades. The sky showed through in its real colour, light blue, in fact you were to all intents and purposes in another world altogether. It was hard for a 'Brummie' like me to take it all in the first time I made this journey. I can understand the Black Country man going out there of a weekend when the week's toil was over, it was indeed 'A Breath of Spring' to all townies.

Danny, Pat, Joe, and I chatted about this and that as the train made its way steadily towards Bewdley. We smoked almost continuously, for as we put one out, one of the others would produce his packet, and the magic words "Gu on 'ave anutha" was to hard to resist, due to the excitement, and relaxed mood we were all in. Fortunately, no one else entered our carriage during the whole trip, and we got out at Bewdley's pretty station without having spoken to another soul, which we thought great anyway.

The day itself went much as usual. We stopped at a little shop in the main street and had our usual, hot sausages on rolls, and a nice hot cup of tea. We then moved on right through the town, up the steep hill which took us in a northerly direction. About half way up the hill there was a gap in the hedgerow on the left and we went, as we had done on several occasions before, through to gain access to the river bank. Having some 'donnuck' as we made our way. We then stood for a moment deciding what next. The river was fascinating to us; I mean, there weren't many rivers around Handsworth were there?, and Hockley certainly came last in that field. Of course we had got 'The Brook,' but it hardly compensated for this wonderful 'Severn.' Eventually we found a spot where we sat down, and for the umpteenth time lit up a fag again. It really wasn't the best of days, the drizzle was still around, although it wasn't quite as cold. Watching what little activity there was on the water itself, and the fishermen attempting to catch something - even if it was only an old boot - myself, I have never shown the slightest interest in the sport. I could never see any reason in taking something out of the water that was quite happy, evidently, swimming about in it, but then to qualify them doing that I suppose they could say the same thing about the sport I was interested in: soccer. Why would twenty-two fully grown men wish to chase a 'pig's bladder' around a field, trying to put it into a net at one end of the field or another?

After an hour or so we got up and went for a walk along the bank, then returned and slowly made our way back into the pretty little town, for a spot of window shopping, and possibly to eye up the wenches. At long last the sun broke through and we made a rush for the river bank again but this time in the town itself, where we knew there would be some wooden benches on which to sit. We made ourselves comfortable on one of these. After trying our luck with some 'Black Country' wenches, who rebuked us out of hand telling us in no uncertain terms: "Yome no bleedin' good to us ya' fartin' little squirts, we wan' some real men," before marching off in the opposite direction. We took no notice of this slight about our manhood, we just laughed, and shouted after them, "Wi' wuz on'y jokin' any road up, an' anyway yome too bleedin' ol' fer us, yome ol' enough ta bi yowaa motha's." Two fingers up from one of the bunch of girls was the final reply, and at this we all burst into a fit of titters.

We sat there in the warm sunshine still smoking and nattering on about this and that (what had we used to talk about? God knows!). Eventually, I pulled the sleeves of my jacket up, for it was getting quite warm. Pat said, "W'at med yarrave them purron yarr rarms Ron?" (He was referring to the two tattoos, one on each forearm.)

"O don' know really Pat, o jus' thought od 'ave 'em on o s'ppose. Mind yo', if o do gu in the nervy, which om gunna try an' do arta mi seventeenth birthday nex' January, it'll serve mi yavvin' any purron then wunnit?"

"W'ere did ja rave 'em purron then, Ron?," he persisted. By this time the other two were showing quite an interest, so I thought I'll tell them the whole story.

"Well, o met a mate a mine owra W'itmore Street, 'e wuz a birrolda than me, an' we palled it tup in St Georges School, mostly cuz we cudden un'erstan' why we lived in 'ockley, an' 'adta gu all the way up thaya, w'en 'e cudda gone ta Icknield Street, an' o cudda gone ta Burb'ry Street, w'ich wuz much neara. It wuz a lung time arta we 'ad lef' school, an' o met 'im w'ile 'e wuz drivin' a pop lorry fer ra plerce in Ninivah Road. 'e'd gorr all these tattoo's on, an' I ast 'm w'ere re gorrem purron, an' 'e tol' me."

" O neva thoughra bourrit until one day o tol' anutha mate o mine, Frankie Anderton, abourrit, an' 'e said, 'Are ya' gunna 'ave some on Ron,' an' o dain' say anythin'. Arta ra w'ile though o thought that Frank mighrave thoughttharr I wuz scared or summat, abourravin' 'em purron, or ron the otha rand 'e mirrave thought o'd med the w'ole story up. So o said ta Frank, well we ain' doin' anythin' now so let's gu an' 'ave some on, an' wi 'ad a birrove a laugh, an' orff wi went.

"On the way ta w'ere the bloke done the tattoo's o waz a bit worried about w'arr rowa Mom an' Dad would think, but then o thought, om a man now, an' o gurra werk, so o cun please miself, so bum ta the lorrov 'em.

160

" The bloke's plerce w'ere re done the tattoos wuz in Bracebridge Street, not far frum the Aston 'ippodrome, an' 'The 'ouse that Jack Built.' Well, o don' know if 'is plerce wuz in Bracebridge Street or Raston Brook Street, burrit wuz jus' roun' the bend frum Newtown Row. It wuz an' ord'n'ry 'ouse, an' o knocked on the door an' a wench come, so I just ast, 'Is this the plerce w'ere the bloke does the tattoos love?' Shi said 'are rit is', an' then shi shoutid ta somebody in the back o the 'ouse, 'Dad there's some blokes 'ere wan' some tattoos done,' an' then shi buzzed orff back w'ere shi come frum.

"Next thing this bloke come, an' ast us in ta the frunt room, an' ast us ta sit down, an' then 'e said, 'D' yarall wan' tattoos done?'

" 'Nah, jus' 'im', said Frank. 'e then brought lot's o pitchas of different designs, an' o picked these two, an' 'e purrem on, an' bleedin' 'ell it did 'urt. It dain' 'urt as much as owa Mom's bleedin' tongue though w'en o gorrome, shi wen' absolutly barmy, an' shi said shid tell Dad, an' 'e'd tattoo mi yarse fer mi, burre neva did, 'e neva said anythin' abourrit, but shi wen' on moanin' fer wicks arta, although in the finish w'en o gid 'er some mowa money ev'ry wick ta shurrer rup, o dain' 'eara nutha thing, norra peep." Mind yo' o did 'ave a birra trouble w' it artawards. O 'ad a boil or summat come up on the one on mi right arm, an' o dain' wanna gurra the Docta's wi' it in cerse 'e started ta moan on abourrit an' ev'rythin', burr owa Mom gorrit right fer mi in the finish." I turned to Pat and said "Bein' as ya' ast mi Pat, are yo' thinkin ov 'avin' any on, cuz o'll come wi' ya' an' show ya' w'ere the bloke is if ya' wanna?"

"Nah bleedin' fear" replied Pat "O don' wann any on mi." That finished the conversation about the tattoos. I assumed that the other two didn't fancy the idea of having any tattoos applied either.

Getting on towards the time for us to return to 'Brum' we always called into a little pub in the town, where Joe would purchase, from an old man there, a few rabbits, which we supposed the old man had nicked, or poached. Anyway, at a tanner apiece we didn't argue. Of course we were under age, but we looked much older than our respective sixteen and seventeen years, so we got away with it. We called as usual, had a couple of halves each, enough to make us quite merry. Joe purchased the rabbits, and we made our way to the station to board our train. After an uneventful journey back home, and feeling quite happy with the two halves of beer in us, we made our way down to 'Kelly's Coffee House', and to the girl from Belgrave Terrace.

She was there waiting, so I rushed up to her, put my arms around her, as though I had just come home on leave from the Navy, after spending a long period at sea, but I didn't kiss her; it just wasn't done. I cuddled up to her, and she didn't object; in fact I thought she rather enjoyed it. "I yaven't kep' ya' wertin' 'ave o love?" I whispered in her ear. We broke our embrace and she looked at me and said " Ya' 'aven't Ron, burr I wouldn' 'ave minded anyway, od 'ave werted fereva, 'onist o would 'ave." We snuggled up to one another again, I was really enjoying myself.

"A come on yo' two love birds, we'em 'ungry, so le's gu in an' get summat ta eat." This was Joe interrupting our great love scene. I didn't really want to go into Kelly's, I wanted to go straight to 'ansa' with my new found love; I wanted to remain cuddled up to her forever. But it wasn't to be. I replied, knowing I couldn't let my mates down, after all they had been with me all day, so a few more minutes wasn't going to make any difference.

"Ar-r-rokay Joe we'em comin' in now." So into the cafe we went, I sat the girl down and asked what she would like. She looked up at me and said "O on'y wan' yo' Ron." I started to feel uncomfortable, and I replied quickly "Nah, o dain' mean anythin' like that love although what 'that' was I had no idea, but I thought it would sound good at the time "O meant watcha wan' ta eat?" She looked up at me with big open eyes and burst into a singing laughter, which finally resulted in tears falling down her beautiful cheeks. I often wondered at a later date - much later - why she laughed. Was it because of my ignorance, and she suspected this to be the reason? Or did she think I purposely ignored the remark, because of my thoughts for her? Well, I can assure you right now, I was ignorant of anything, other than a confused mind, and my answer to that as always: IGNORE IT, pretend it never happened, just keep quiet, let it go away on its own.

At last she stopped laughing, and said quietly, "I'll 'ave a Spam sandwich please Ronnie." I went to the counter, where Joe was ordering for Danny and Pat. "Watcha want Ron?"

"Nah it's soright Joe, don' yo' think yove paid fer rinough terday, I'll gerrit, but thanks all the serm."

"Om already gerrin' these so o mirras well get yowas, so come on an' tell mi."

I gave him our order, for I knew, as I've already told you, that it was useless to argue with Joe, what he said he meant. The girl and I ate our meal quickly; we both wanted to get off and make as much of the rest of the evening together as possible. Getting up from the table we said our 'tarrars' to Danny, Pat, and Joe and moved off arm in arm towards the door.

"A, a, Ronnie?" It was Joe balling across the smoke-filled room of 'Kelly's'. "Ain' cha fergot summat?" and he'd got a grin as wide as the Mersey Tunnel. I turned to see what the 'chow row' was all about, and there was Joe with my rabbit, hung up for all to see in the cafe, in his right hand. "Yode berra tek 'im along wi' ya' ta keep an' eye on ya', an' w'at yome doin'," and he burst into a fit of laughter, which naturally caused the rest of the customers, including Danny and Pat to join him. So it was a very red-faced Ronnie Smith who returned to Joe to pick up my furry friend.

Off we went down Soho Road, the girl, the rabbit, and me!

We entered Handsworth Park via the Holly Road gate (well it would have been a gate if they hadn't taken it away for the 'War Effort). Once away from the busy Soho Road, and walking up Thornhill Road we were bathed in bright moonlight; it was almost like day. Frost had appeared on some of the roofs of the elegant houses of the road, which looked like the icing on top of a cake. Walking slowly down the path leading to the tennis courts it was like walking down the 'Yellow Brick Road' that Judy Garland took with 'Toto' in "The Wizard of Oz." The moon was so bright it reflected everything in this wonderful yellow glow. Both of us laughed and danced about as we took the path past the courts, and in the general direction of 'The Tea Rooms, and Bower' situated not far from the Grove Lane entrance, opposite Douglas Road. I thought briefly about Auntie Bertha, Uncle Alf, and Cousin Bertha. I had now got into the habit of calling each day to No 73 for a chat, and a cup of tea. My wholesale round took me down the road serving the shop on the corner of Linwood Road first. Then after my visit I served another two shops, one on the left, the other on the right, before pushing 'Dick' up to the big shop on the corner of Grove Lane right opposite the chemist on the left hand corner. They had settled back into Douglas Road now after being bombed out. They were moved to another house in Rookery Road just past 'The Rookery Cinema.' Naturally, I only saw Uncle Alf, and Cousin Bertha occasionally due to the fact that he would be out at work at 'The Mint' in Icknield Street, and she would be at the office at 'Joseph Lucas's' in Great King Street. Auntie Berth used to make a fuss of me, so much so that I would often stay a little longer than I should, making me a bit late for the deliveries. I remember vividly how she laughed when I told her about the 'dentist' incident.

What happened was, I was having a lot of trouble with one of my back, bottom teeth through decay, and believe me it was playin' mi yup a bit. So on my way home from the dairy one day I rode my bike past New John Street West and went straight up Hockley Hill to Mr Phillips, the dentist, whose surgery was just on the left-hand side of the 'Hill', past Great King Street. I parked my bike, and went up the stairs facing me. The entrance on the left-hand side of the small hall before the stairs was into a watch and clock repairers, and Mr Phillips' surgery was situated over the top. The dentist removed the offending molar, and within half hour I was back on my bike going home via Great King Street and Barr Street. Well, you might say "There's nothing significant in that," but you didn't know the SMITH FAMILY!

The rule of 'The Smith household' - being quite Victorian despite the poverty - was that no one went anywhere without an escort. The doctors, the dentist's, that is if anyone cared to go, which unfortunately, but for yours truly, no one did, and 'Our Mom' was very superstitious of any of these professions, including hospitals, chemist's, or indeed anything to do with the maintenance of the body. Forget it. 'Mrs Smith' was ANTI anything like that, and that's what she instilled into us kids and anyone else for that matter. If you went for a job, to the shop, to relatives, and so many other visits, you never, never went alone, you always took someone from the household with you. THAT WAS MOM'S LAW.

I entered 228 after the removal of my tooth. Mom was in her usual place, in the chair with her back to the window looking out of the back yard, which led to the garden. " 'allo" she said "Yer dinna's in the oven, o wunt bi ya minnit gerrin' it ya', so sit down an' powa yaself a cuppa tea."

Off she went into the kitchen, and I poured the tea, shoutin' to Mom "D'yo' want one Mom?"

"Ar-r" came the muffled reply. So I poured one out for her as well. She came back into the middleroom with my dinner just as I was wiping blood from my mouth, which had naturally come from the cavity left by the vacant tooth.

"Wassamarra wi' ya' mouth, ya' ain' bin bleedin' fightin' ag'in 'ave ya'?"

"Nah-h-h Mom, it's jus' some blood from w'ere ri 'ad mi tooth out, tha's sall."

She put the dinner down in front of me, and stood there with her hands on her large hips. "Yo' done bleedin' w'at?" she said. "Ov 'ad mi tooth out, it wuz bloody painin' mi, so o wen' an' 'ad it out just."

"W'y dain' ya' come 'um fust, an' wert fer somebody ta gu wi' ya', yo' shudda come 'um fust ya' little sod, ya' shudda 'ad somebody wi' ya', yo' wert till o tell ya' Fertha, 'e'll gu bleedin' barmy 'e will." She went on and on, and all the time she was ranting I had got stuck into my dinner. I was hungry, as usual. She finished eventually and said "Yo' ain' e't ya' bleedin' dinna 'rave ya', arta ravin' a tooth out?"

163

"This amused me, although even though I was as big as I was, I dare not laugh, because even at this stage in my life I still wasn't quite sure of what she might do.

I had completely cleaned the plate, and this obviously was plain for anyone to see. It was like looking at someone waving madly in the sea obviously in trouble, and shouting "Are you alright pal?"

"Ar-r-rit's soright Mom, ov on'y 'ad a tooth out, I ain' 'ad an' operachun or anythin.'

"Yo' shudda tol' mi w'at yo' wuz gunna do, yo' shudda tol' mi, o donna warrom om gunna do wi' yo' o don't, yome allis bleedin' well playin' mi yup yo' am, an' yome gerrin' wuss now yome bigga" and off she went on and on, until in the end, although I didn't want to particularly, I went out, leaving her still going on.

This incident was related not only to all members of 'The Smith' family, but to nearly all the other families in the street. Some laughed at it, some agreed with Mom, and still others accepted the incident, but thought that I should have told Mom first, but in all instances I either thought, or said 'Bum.'

At last we arrived at the little iron shelter we had been walking towards, and sat down. We were lucky, there wasn't another soul about. I placed our friend, the rabbit, on the wooden bench away from us, and then we cuddled up together. We kissed, and held one another close, and after a while I undid her coat, and then replaced my arms around her. No objection, so I thought, I'll give the Horace Willetts routine a final go. I ran my hands over her back, and then her midrift, and finally I put my right hand on her right breast. Still no objection!

I carried on, and on, and on. She was moaning softly, and clinging closer to me, and I must admit I experienced some funny feelings Well I say funny, they were very nice feelings, but never the less to me funny. This went on for some time, and I thought to myself, well what do I do now, and I couldn't come to any satisfactory conclusion. Eventually though my left leg went a bit numb being in one position too long so I moved it to relieve this numbness and in doing so my leg went over hers, and I thought "whoa tha's nice", so I left it there, but still not knowing what the hell I was doing. Now at this point the young lady must have had different ideas of what I was about to do, for she whispered into my ear " No Ron, no, not now, it's the wrong time of the month, I'm sorry love, sorry." I pulled away suddenly; I was completely alarmed, and needless to say confused by this statement: "Wrong time of the month." What could that possibly mean? I hadn't done anything

I don't think I'd kissed her too much, what was she on about?

"W'assa marra Ron, w'a' rav I done?"

"Oh, it's soright," I mumbled. I was completely confused, I didn't know what to say. Women were so complicated, why couldn't they be like us blokes. I suppose I could ask her what she meant by " It's the wrong time of the month ", but I'd look a right ignorant so and so then wouldn't I? I started to sweat, although it was a cold night, and I couldn't understand that either. So in my complete ignorance I said "Well, come on then, we'd berra gu 'um, okay?"

I realise now of course what an insult it was to the girl, but in retrospect, I didn't have a clue what was going on. I was bemused, I was ignorant of the facts of life. All that kind of talk was very much 'hush-hush' in 'The Smith household.'

Indeed, not only in the Smith's household but in a good many more houses as well.

She didn't say a word, she just got up off the bench, and started walking back towards the exit in Holly Road. I knew instinctively that something was wrong, and further I knew it was my doing, but I didn't know what it was, so I could hardly rectify it. I thought I'd better keep my mouth shut, so as not to put my foot in it any further.

So it was that we walked in complete silence back down Thornhill Road to Soho Road, where we turned left to Belgrave Terrace. She didn't even say "Goodnight" or anything, she just went up the slight incline of the terrace, and I never saw her again. A bus just happened to pull up at the stop by Handsworth station as I was walking back to 'The Brook,' I thought, "Sod it, bloody wimmin, that's it. No mowa." I boarded the bus to get back to my mates at 'Ma Davies's Herb Shop,' where I knew for certain that I would get a warmer reception, which at the moment I felt I needed. I went upstairs, after paying the conductor the tuppence fare, to save him coming upstairs just for me. I sat down, and lit a cigarette. Taking a deep drag, I felt a little better; still miserable, but as I smoked the cigarette and the bus got nearer 'The Brook' I did start to feel more myself. Suddenly I said "Sod it!" The few passengers around me looked at me in surprise. I stared back at them, and then started to laugh. "Om sorry" I said to all of them "burr I've jus' thought, ov lef' mi bloody rabbit on the park bench in 'answorth Park." They looked startled, and I suddenly realised the statement I had made, they thought I had left a live rabbit in the park. So I hurriedly explained the complete story to them, and we all had a good laugh.

In one night, I had not only lost my lovely girl friend, I'd lost my rabbit as well. At least that laugh with complete strangers on the bus made up for most everything, for at last there was laughter brought into my miserable world.

WOMEN, that was the problem: WOMEN! That was it, I was going to have nothing to do with them from now on. They were far too complicated; nice, but complicated. I would knock around with my mates, at least if they got complicated you could talk to and they would give you a reply in a no-nonsense manner. No frills, evasions, or anything just the plain truth. Those were my final thoughts on the matter that night I came home from Belgrave Terrace. My God how wrong I was, and how wrong you know I was, but those were the thoughts of a sixteen-year-old lad, brought up in poverty, but never the less in a most pure, Victorian fashion.

I did, however, have one adventure into the unknown, before eventually joining the Royal Navy. When I had adventures of all kinds in my travels abroad, and in this country. My second eldest sister, 'Vi', had a visit from her husband Ralph's (everyone called him Ron) two sisters from Ramsbottom in Lancashire, and whilst they were in Hockley they extended an invitation for me, and 'Our Kid' to go and visit them.

Now at the age of sixteen I was to say the least beginning to feel my feet a bit, and with the war, as I've said before, one had to grow up maybe a little sooner than one would normally do. This opportunity to visit Ron's sisters was then a once in a lifetime chance. Up until that moment of time the farthest I'd ever been was Barnt Green with the scouts. If you remember they took us kids from the mission hall in Farm Street via 'Midland Red,' to town, and then by train to this outpost beyond The Lickeys. I'd heard of The Lickeys, of course, and some of my school mates had been there on the tram from Navigation Street, but me - never. Then the other trip to Atcham, and finally to Shrewsbury with Jack Pittaway, but this trip to the farthest corners of England - well, that was something else altogether.

'Our Kid' and I set off for this journey of a lifetime full of excitement. We had never, neither of us, been allowed to travel to this extent without being 'mob handed.' We were to stay with Evelyn; I think that she was the younger of the two sisters. This staying with Evelyn however was of no great significance, it was just for convenience, there was more room. Cissie the elder sister only lived a couple of doors up from Ev', as she liked to be called.

Arthur and I caught a bus from 'The Brook' to the top of Livery Street, and alighted outside the main entrance to Snow Hill Station. We then walked through St Phillips Churchyard, down Temple Street to its junction with Stephenson Street and Navigation Street. Turning left we crossed over to the entrance to New Street Station. We entered the musty looking booking hall, with its wooden floor, and old gas lamps still evident, although I supposed that they might have changed to electric by now, but I didn't pursue this matter, I was far too excited about our journey to Ron's sisters. I went to the small window (one of many) and enquired the platform number of our train. Subsequently I booked tickets for two. Arthur and I then walked on through the dingy room to another set of doors which announced on a huge wooden board 'Way to the Platforms.' Through these we went, with me carrying the small 'Blackwells' carrier bag, containing all we required for the trip; well, I suppose really this is all we would need for any trip. All the bag contained was an extra pair of socks each, a towel, and a bit of soap, which was plenty for two chaps, plenty. We'd got fags and money in our pockets, so that was it, all we wanted, and needed. We came out of the booking hall to find the steps leading downwards to the platforms, again all wood. Over the one set of stairs was a wooden board telling all and sundry that this was indeed 'DOWN,' and the other set of stairs 'UP.' Naturally, I took the 'UP' stairs, and Arthur with his quiet nature followed the 'DOWN' sign.

"Wassa marra can' ya' bleedin' read, some bloody cheek."

This comment was from a bloke coming up from the platforms, whom I had dodged to get down the stairs before 'Our Kid.' "Nah om sorry mate, they dain' teach mi to read at the sc'ool I wen' to, cuz they wuz tryin' ta reform us, at that sc'ool," I shouted to him, still running down the wooden steps.

"Od bleedin' reform yarrif od gotcha ya' little bleeda," was the last comment from this bloke, and his family.

I beat 'Our Kid' easily. When he came to me eventually he said "Yo' wanna pack that lot in, our Ronnie, or yome gunna 'ave us in trouble afowa we gerr rourra Brummijam."

I looked at him for a moment. His face was serious, big brown eyes, like 'Our Mom's,' but thin, unlike 'Our Mom'. I immediately felt deeply sorry for what I'd done, for I didn't want to spoil everything for us before we'd even started. "Sorry our kid, o wuz on'y 'avin' a birra donnuck, tha's sall, burr I'll pack it up now, o wunt do anythin' else; we'll 'ave a good time, okay?"

"Ar-r-rokay Ron, now come on an' le' s look out fer the platform, cuz yo' said the train guz in a quarta rov an 'our, dain' ya'?"

"Ar-r-r tha's it Arth' an' wi don' wanna bi lert do we?"

"Nah-h-h, we don'."

We moved off along the wooden boards of the bridge spanning the whole of the platforms, the steam from trains waiting below, and the general dust rising from several porters brushing the wooden boards in an attempt - though hopelessly inadequate for this huge task, to keep the floor clean - sometimes obliterating the signs which were numbering the different platforms. Finally we found the sign indicating the steps leading down to our particular platform, and were about to descend when we heard a voice shout "A, A, yo' two come 'ere?"

We stopped, and turned, looking in the direction we had come from, and saw a rather fat man in a most resplendent uniform running towards us. Well, I say running, he was shuffling, and also sweating, and blowing hard. My first thoughts on seeing this bloke were "Silly ol' sod, 'e'll bleedin' well kill 'imself if 'e guz on like that." We waited until he reached us, and then we had to wait until he regained his breath. Finally he wiped his forehead with a spotless white handkerchief, and then started. "A bloke's jus' tol' mi yabout yo' two runnin' down the wrung side o' the stairs, now o' don' wan any bloody cheek frum ya', o want cha names, an' addresses, an' om gunna report cha, so come on then."

"Wai'ra minnit mate," I started, because I didn't think 'Our Kid' could handle this situation.

"I ain" ya' bleedin' mate, an' yo' call mi Sir ya' cheeky young bleeda," he replied, and he started to go redder, and redder.

"Oright SIR" I replied, having sorted out very quickly the story I was going to spin. My emphasis on SIR, didn't please this very unpleasant man over much, but he let that one slide. "In the fust plerce it worn't both on us that come down the wrung steps, it wuz me, tha's sall, jus' me, an' the reason o wuz rushin' was cuz that pratt in the bookin' office gid us the wrung time o the train, 'e tol' us one time, an' now wi' see it's anutha. O thought wid only gorra couple a minnits, so o took the wrung steps, but now o see" (I pointed to the board with the chalked time on it, just to the right of the entrance to the stairs leading down to the platform we required) " that the time wuz wrung, an' wi' gorra few more minnits, although not many. An' any 'ow," I gabbled on, "o said o wuz sorry ta the bloke, burr I didn't' 'ave time ta explain ev'rythin', cuz o' thought me an' our kid 'ere would miss the train, burr I'm sorry Sir', if we caused any botha, but wi' wuz on'y tryin' ta catch owa train, worn' wi Arth?" I turned to Arthur for confirmation of this lie I was spinning, and really he had no chance but to nod in agreement.

The bloke looked at us very hard, and then asked us where we were going. He confirmed that this was the right platform, and that the train was due out any minute. He just stood staring at us, not saying anything. I think he was debating whether we were telling the truth or not. I thought to myself, "od berra say summat or we'll miss this bleedin' train, an' also it'll ge 'im mowa time ta look in ta things, an' maybe fin' out we're lyin', or ratha I'm lyin', Cuz if it come to a put to, o wouldn' lerr owa rartha tek any blame". I suddenly said to this railway official "Look mate, if we don' catch this trern, we'em gunna miss the people tharr ar' wertin' fer rus the otha rend, an' it'll mek 'em anxious, an' more to it, they'll bi worri'd ourra their minds, so what's it ta be eh?"

"Gu on ya' little bleeda's, o'll ge ya' the benifit o' the doubt, burr I'll rememba ya' fercis, an' if yo' cause any mowa trouble, o'll rememba this incident, an' then yo'll really bi for rit, gu on now, afowa o chernge mi mind."

167

"We ain' done anythin', so o don' know watcha guin on about Mista Sir, so tarrar, we'em guin' now, or relse we'll miss owa trern, an' then it'll bi yowa turn ta be in trouble, cuz I'll rememba yowa ferce as well, an' we'll know w'o ta come to."

With that I picked up our carrier bag, grabbed Arthur's arm and we ran down down the stairs to the waiting train, ignoring this most horrible man's remarks, as we went further and further out of earshot.

"Ya' cheeky young bleeda, o'll 'ave ya' w'en yo' come back, o'll bi yon the look out fer ya', o'll getche rif it's the last thing o do."

I looked back up the flight of stairs, but only when we had reached the bottom, and knew that this fat man had no chance of dashing down the stairs to us, and saw him waving a big ham fist at us. I smiled at him, but thought "Christ, if 'e 'it me in the gob wi' that fist 'e'ed knock mi yead orff mi shoulda's." With that in mind we climbed into the nearest third-class compartment, and settled in for the coming journey. Believe me, we were both relieved, to hear the whistle to indicate to the driver that 'All was clear for him to move off.' After a lot of shouting, and the last minute banging of carriage doors, we heard a further whistle, and waited anxiously for the next stage of the operation to get this train off from New Street Station, or away from that irate railway official on its way to Ramsbottom via Manchester. Suddenly there was a couple of jerks which I assumed was the start of our journey. A roar of steam from the engine drawing the coaches in their original livery of maroon and gold lettering. Further spasmodic roars of steam, and a bellowing from the beautiful engine, as though it was having difficulty getting started, and slipping on the iron rails beneath its huge wheels. The jerking stopped, and we commenced to glide, as we heard the engine settle down to a strict tempo of steam being ejected from its funnel.

I watched from the window as we left the end of the platform, and then entered the tunnel that would take us under the city. Arthur had let me sit by the window whilst he settled down to a quiet smoke. The compartment was nearly full, not quite, but nearly. The rest of the passengers seemed to be together however, for they were nattering away 'ten to the dozen.' Obviously the window was closed as we went into the tunnel taking us first under Navigation Street. We came out into the open again briefly before entering the second tunnel, a much longer one. Under Swallow Street with the headquarters of The Royal Mail atop and the ever popular 'Golden Eagle' opposite, where " Jimmy Houghton played drums nightly. He was one of a thousand characters of Brummijam. No doubt about it Jimmy was a fine drummer, I know, I've heard him on more than one occasion.

On went our train heading in a north-westerly direction, settling down to an even running. Ticketty tick, ticketty tick, tickety tick the wheels of our carriages went. Listening to it, one could almost believe it to be a song, with slight interruptions to it's tempo, when it ran over junction-points. On we went, under Easy Row, Paradise Street, Broad Street, Baskervillle Place, King Alfreds Place, King Edwards Place, St Mary's Row, and Bingley Hall. Out into the open again running between Cambridge Street, and Sheepcote Street which housed the huge chimney stack with the white letters displayed, announcing to the world that the factory below it was indeed 'BAXTERS' and they made screws. Under St Vincent Street we went, and then alongside Shakespeare Road, where one of my aunts lived, another Sunday morning venue for us 'Smith Kids'. Also Anderton Street where my brother-in-law, one of six, lived. This was 'Our Stan', whom I worked with at Scribbans' when I got demobbed from The Royal Navy. Stan was someone very special to me; we were mates long before I introduced him to the family, and he started courting 'Our Ginge', finally marrying her. It was Stan who really taught me to drive a petrol van. Oh, I could, and did drive electric trucks, but a petrol vehicle was a different animal altogether.

Our transport to the north sped on, gaining momentum, the ticketty tick of the wheels becoming faster and faster. Under the bridge at Monument Road, passing Cope Street in a flash, then Northbrook Street on the left. Another bridge at Dudley Road just before we flashed through Winson Green Station, with its complex of Prison, Mental Hospital, Geriatric Hospital, Brookfields House, containing men of the streets looking for a 'night's kip'. Last but certainly not least, Dudley Road Hospital itself, a hospital I was to have a great deal to do with in later years. The line veered slightly to the right after the station going around the basin of The Birmingham Canal and bringing us quite close to Wellington Street, and at the junction with Vittoria Street, Smethwick, stood 'The Railway Inn', one of my many watering holes at a later part of my life.

We re-crossed The Birmingham Canal just past 'The Railway'. Veering to the left, this time taking us past Avery's scale works, of James Watt fame, and 'The Soap Hole', which had a signal box indicating on a board that this was not a joke, but the real name. I think that the name originated from a soap works thriving there some years earlier. Passing through shunting yards and Soho Station at quite 'a lick' we moved, through Rolfe Street Station. On we went close to the G.W.R. line after passing under Roebuck Lane, and the famous Galton Bridge, which I had good cause to remember when 'Dolly' ran away with me on my return to the dairy. Again, we were running alongside The Birmingham Canal until we reached Oldbury Station, in Bromford Road, where it veered off to the right. We carried on past Broadwell Lane which housed Triplex works, and then Fountain Lane where Cuxon and Gerrard, the pharmaceutical company of world renown had its head office, and works. After that we seemed to enter open countryside. Well, I say 'open countryside', in comparison with the 'Hockley Brook' area. Anything with more than a couple of trees in it was 'open countryside'. Through Dudley Port Station we steamed, and I never saw one ship - not one! (old joke, very old.) We flashed through Tipton, another area I was to have a lot to do with. Journeying to the right again we headed towards Coseley, passing through Deepfields and Coseley Station. Just after Anchor Bridge I saw The Birmingham and Wolverhampton Canal on the left, but it wasn't there for long. We journeyed straight on, whilst it went off to the right at Lanesfield, steaming on through Ettingshall Road and Bilston Station before the driver started to slow down for our entrance to Wolverhampton for the first stop of our journey. Just before entering this large station we saw a G.W.R. local train passing in the opposite direction, going under the bridge at Lower Horesley Fields.

'Our Kid' and me watched the activity on the station. A couple of the passengers from our compartment got out, but no one boarded. The porters were evident giving assistance to some of the travellers. Lots of shouting, laughing, hugging, and loving as people met people, and I thought to myself, "I wonda rif Cissie an' Evlyne will bi like that w'en we get ta Ramsbottom?"

After what seemed a lifetime, a whistle blew, doors were slammed, another whistle, and the first jerks of the carriage again. We were off on the second stage of this wonderful adventure - our next stop, Stafford. I dozed for some time after

169

Stoke, and could not recognise some of the countryside we were flashing through, but the next thing I knew was we were entering Manchester Station. We alighted from the train when it had come to a halt and made our way with the rest of the crowd, whom we assumed were heading in the direction of the exit. The station we entered from Birmingham was (I think) Piccadilly, and we had been instructed by Ron Holt, when we arrived there, to go across the city to Victoria Station, for the next part of our journey.

At last we arrived at the 'Way Out' sign, and joined the queue, which would take us on the next part of this adventure.

"W'ich way d' wi gu fer Vi'torea Sterchun mate?", we enquired of the railway official taking the tickets from the passengers.

"W'at d'us thee say lad?, o' can never understand you Brummies, so jus' say it a little slower, an' I'll be able to make out w'at thee are on about." I thought, he must be bloody thick or something, wanting me to say it slower, but never the less I thought I'd better comply with his request, or I might possibly finish up with another situation like the one at New Street Station. So I repeated very slowly: "W'ich, way .. d' .. wi', gu, fer, Vi'torea Sterchun .. mert?" then as an after thought I added "Please." The bloke looked at me briefly. I don't think he could make up his mind whether I was taking the micky out of him, or what. He didn't make anything of this, for in the next instance he gabbled the directions in his Lancashire accent. Although we didn't quite get the gist of all his words, we didn't argue, first, because the queue behind us were getting a little impatient, and secondly, we didn't want to upset another railway official.

We came out of the station at last 'Our Kid', Blackwells Carrier Bag and me. We headed in what I thought to be a northerly direction for Victoria Station. Naturally, through the gabbling of the railway official we had to ask on several occasions if we were indeed walking in the right direction, and to our surprise we were. Eventually we arrived at this most ornate station, and we asked the time of the next train to Ramsbottom, and on receiving this information we wended our way to the platform. Our train was not due for another half an hour, so I went off to try and get something to eat, whilst 'Our Kid' sat on one of the wooden benches to look after our suitcase. Eventually I found the station buffet, bought a few sandwiches, and returned to Arthur. We found the sandwiches quite good, despite all the puns about railway food. We stuffed 'em down owa 'odges and felt quite pleasantly sated. I offered Arthur a drink, but he declined, so we lit up a fag and sat there quietly waiting for our transport to Ronnie Holt's sisters.

The train arrived with much blowing, and puffing and other usual noises that these massive steam maidens make. In no time at all we were off to our final destination: Ramsbottom. It always brought to mind that song which was going the rounds then 'Enoch, Ramsbottom and me.'

'Our Kid' and I finally arrived at this quaint little station in a very short space of time after passing through Bury. We got off the train and walked along the beautifully clean platform towards the exit, when we suddenly heard a voice, " 'allo lads, I orp ya' journeys been or reet, I'm Evelyn." It was a lady to the left of us. On hearing this we went across to her and told her we were indeed Arthur and Ronnie. She kissed both of us, though I didn't like this very much; to me it was 'kinda cissie'. Blokes didn't do this in public, but as an after- thought, I didn't demonstrate my feelings, I thought perhaps it was these 'foreigner's' way of greeting us men from the great City of Birmingham.

The three of us walked out of the station, and turned left which I saw led us to a kind of main street. Off to the right of the station exit and entrance I saw big wooden gates across the road, and some cars waiting in a queue. Bear in mind I hadn't seen anything like this around Hockley, and neither had 'Our Kid' for that matter, so I automatically stood still to watch events. Evelyn did explain that it was a railway crossing, but I wanted to see what it was for myself, at that very moment my thoughts on the matter were that this scene reminded me of a western film. The film when they were pioneering the railways of America out west, and the train actually ran through the middle of the town. Both our kid and myself watched avidly, unable to take our eyes off the two long white gates, similar to those up All Saints Road in Hockley where we used to watch the trains of The Great Western Railway go by.

At long last we heard the now familiar whistle, and the banging of doors, then the whistle from the train driver. The blowing of steam, and the several short chugs before he settled down to a steady rhythm. The train that we had ridden on from Manchester suddenly came into view, chugging away merrily, crossing over the ' 'oss road'. We couldn't believe it, this was really something new to us 'ockley 'ites." A train actually crossing over a street, just wait until I got home to tell my mates about this. We were both very excited. We watched, much to the amusement of Evelyn, as every last coach passed by, and then the gates opened to let the street vehicles cross over the railway lines.

We were so happy as we made our way up to the main road, where we turned to the left and headed up a long steep hill. On the way up I asked Evelyn how far the train went on from Ramsbottom. She wasn't too sure, but she did think that it went on to Burnley, and Blackburn. Eventually, we reached the summit of this steep hill, where we turned left again, into a street, not dissimilar to Little King Street. Not quite as long, but it had a factory, just like 'Coopers Felt Works' on the right, and houses on the left. The factory I found out later was one of many Lancashire mills. The most significant difference, from Birmingham's Little King Street, was that all the buildings were built with large grey concrete blocks, as opposed to the small clay bricks used in the building of most houses in Birmingham, These buildings conjured up a wonderful thought of castles, and forts of days gone by. For me it was so different from 228. My immediate thoughts on the matter were the lovely time I was going to have exploring all these surroundings. I was by nature very inquisitive, and this would give me the material I required to satisfy my character.

Evelyn, Arthur and myself walked down the street to the last house, that was situated on a corner. It was 'L'-shaped, and as far as I could see the mill ran the whole length of this street on the right, and I supposed that there were houses on its left. The three of us stopped at the house. Evelyn entered, turning to us as she did, nodding her head to indicate us to follow.

We entered this room, for that's all it was, just like 2/24. It was just one room, and a little cubby hole, which served as a kitchen, a bathroom, and an entrance to the 'Bogey 'ole'. I smiled to myself, for this was an exact replica of Guest Street. (I wondered if there were ten people living in it as well.) Naturally, we were at home right away, for there was no difference either way. The Holt family represented the 'Smith' family quite adequately in the north. A fire was blazing away merrily, although it wasn't really that cold, and over on the left-hand side of this fireplace was Ronnie's other sister, Cissie. There were several other people in this small area, and 'Our Kid' and I were introduced to them. It was abit like our being 'royalty'.

"O bet thee would like a cuppa tea would'n thee lad's?" This was Cissie interrupting the general conversation.

"Ar' wi' would plese love", I replied, for I knew it was no good waiting for Arthur to reply. He was too shy even for that. She went off into the 'bogey 'ole' to attend to the mashing, and Evelyn said, "Would ya' lark ta see w'ere thall bi sleepin' lads, while Ciss is merkin' tea?"

"Ar' od like that please." So off we went up the wooden stairs, again just like 2/24, to the small landing at the top, but instead of turning right, as we did in Guest Street for our bedroom, Evelyn turned left. The room was very sparse, just a small bed, where presumably both Arthur and I were expected to sleep, and a big wooden dresser/cum wardrobe. Wooden floors with no lino, nor rugs. God, it was just like being home again, and I knew that I was going to really enjoy myself. I was, I must admit, a bit apprehensive about our new living quarters, and gave it a good deal of thought on our journey northwards. Now I had no worries at all; they were the "serm as us in 'ockley,' and this made me very happy - very happy indeed.I knew that Arthur had got to return home a day before I did, for he had to go to work on the Tuesday, but somehow or other I had got an extra day.

Evelyn and Cissie took us to a working man's club on the night time, and we had a nice time, with the usual activities taking place, a comedian, a singer etc. I had a half pint, and Arthur had a few more, he appeared to like the drink, but I'm afraid I wasn't too keen. I would have sooner had a cup of tea. I did however change my taste a little later, but that's another part of my story. On arrival back home that night the girls did us proud with the supper, it was great, and plenty of it. The first night was a good start to our short holiday with 'Our Ron's' two sisters. Consequently we were looking forward to the rest of it.

* * * *

Clump! Clump! Clump! "W'at the bleedin' 'ell's all that," I thought. It sounded like someone hitting a piece of slate against a piece of wood, and with this sound were voices in a language I couldn't quite comprehend, but it was never the less very pleasant to listen to. I stirred in the small bed, trying to rouse myself in these new surroundings. 'Our Arthur' was still sound asleep, so I slipped quietly out of bed, and put my trousers on, which I had thrown underneath it the night before. Well, I didn't want Evelyn or Cissie coming in and catching me with just my shirt on, did I? I crept over to the window, the only window facing into the street and peered down to see what was causing all the commotion. It wasn't light yet, but it was light enough for me to distinguish certain things. The morning was miserable. it wasn't raining, but it was a kind of drizzle, with a mist hanging about. Lights were flashing, just like fireflies, very small, with an orange and yellow flame. I rubbed my eyes, and eventually saw that the lights were indeed cigarettes; that the people below were either smoking, or holding them. There was the occasional flare of light as one bloke gave another a light, or a cascade of sparks as another man nipped his fag.

172

I looked at this scene for a while, and gradually it became clearer, as I became more awake, and the morning mist started to clear. What I had before me was the night shift coming off, and the morning shift coming on, and the 'clumps' were the women's and men's clogs, a thing I'd never seen, or for that matter heard before. This was something else new for me. I went back to the bed, and sat down. I didn't like to go down, for I had no idea what time it was, and more important, I didn't know what time this family got up in a morning. I felt at that moment as though I'd been imprisoned. I just couldn't go anywhere, or do anything. I picked up my fags off the floor, took one from the pack and put it into my mouth, and was just about to light it when I felt 'Our Kid' stir. Turning to face him I said "D' ya' wanna fag Arth?" He looked at me through sleep laden eyes and said "Watcho bleedin' doin' owa Nip, can' ya' sleep or summat?

"Nah o jus' bin watchin' them people down thaya comin' an' guin' ta werk, they bleedin' woke mi yup they did, so o thought od 'ave a drag, so d' ya' want one or not?"

"Ar-r-roright Ron, ge us one 'ere." I handed Arthur a cigarette, and we had just lit them when we heard a knock at our door. "Ar' yarra werk lads, ov brought tha a cuppa tea?"

"W-o-o, tha's great tharris," I replied quickly, whilst 'Our Kid' dived back under the bed clothes, fag and all, scared in case whoever it was with the tea came in, and saw him in his bed. I smiled to myself at this gesture, and then went to the door. It was Cissie stood there with a tray of tea, and surprise, surprise, biscuits as well. I thought "W'at a bloody treat, it's jus' like w'en we wuz kids on a Sundee mornin', on'y this worn't Sundee, it wuz Satdee, an' wi certainly worn't kids any mowa."

Cissie smiled at me and said " 'ave thee 'ad a good neets sleep Ronnie?" She was the plump one of the two sisters, and had Ron's looks about her. Pale face, and mousy hair down to her shoulders, whilst Evelyn had a very narrow face, with dark hair, and a very pointed nose, no doubt she followed some other members of the family, although I was not in a position to know which, not knowing that much about them.

"Are love, me an' owa kid 'ave slep' really good, 'e's still in the land o' nod" I lied, "burr 'e'll soon werken up w'en o' put this cuppa tea unda ris nose" and we both laughed at this comment.

"Don't thi bi long though lads, cuz owa Ev's gerrin' ya' brekfast ready fer ya', rokay?"

"Ar' rokay love, wi wunt bi lung, an' thanks eva sa much." With that she went back down the wooden stairs again, and I returned to 'Our Kid' who had resumed his sitting position, ready for the first cup of tea.

We had come down on the Friday (funny how we refer to going anywhere as coming up or down isn't it? Actually, as we had gone North I suppose it should have been gone up; still whatever, we'd arrived at Ramsbottom on the Friday). 'Our Kid' had got to return on the Monday, for Southall and Smith's resumed work on the Tuesday, but for reasons that I have forgotten now I hadn't got to return until the Wednesday, so we had arranged for me to stay an extra day on my own. Naturally this was another big step for me in proving that I was now indeed a Man. 'Our Mom' hadn't gone much on the idea, but we soon smoothed her over, promising I'd be a good lad, and on my best behaviour, and not to talk to any strangers, especially women. This perplexed me somewhat, but I didn't follow it through, due to the fact I would have shown my ignorance on the matter.

Arthur and I finished our tea, had another fag and then went downstairs to the one little room, which so represented the room we used to have at 2/24. The smell of bacon cooking really whet our appetites, and I said to 'Arth', "Bloody 'ell owa kid they don' do ta bad fer themselves do they, bercon on a Satadee?"

"Shurrup ya'silly sod, they'll bloody 'ear ya', an' if they tell owa rold lady, she wunt bi to pleased will she?"

"Ar ro dain' mean anythin' owa kid, yome too fussy yo' am, they don' mind they'm like owa Ron they yam, they'll jus' laugh, tha's sall, so shurrup yaself, an' get sat down." He made a playful punch at me, and I evaded it, saying "Yo' ain' quick enough fer me" but before I finished the sentence he'd dabbed me with the other fist, and this time it connected. I laughed and told him that he was getting a little quicker in his 'old age', and he just laughed right back at me.

Evelyn brought the breakfast in on two huge tin plates, and were these plates full! Bacon, sausage, and some kind of pastry, which I have never been able to define, but I kid you not, it was wonderful, and to prove my statement, when Evelyn asked if I wanted any more I just held my tin plate out, like Oliver, and never said anything.

Both Evelyn and Cissie made us welcome during our short stay, they couldn't do enough for us. Although this particular part of my life is slightly blurred, I do remember the Working Man's Club they took us to, with the usual routine of singer, comedian, etc. I wished with all my heart that Danny, Pat, and Joe had been there with me, for I did feel kind of lonely without them, although 'Our Arth' " tried to be like a mate to me, but at the end of the day he had got his friends, and I'd got mine, and we were really worlds apart.

Ramsbottom appeared to be one long street, and more or less nothing more, or was it that we didn't venture far enough to find out? Anyway our tour of the town didn't take long at all.

Finally Monday came and I went with Evelyn and Cissie down to the railway station to see 'Our Kid' off back to 'Brum.' I laughingly warned him, as 'Our Mom' had warned us, not to get talking to any strange women. Both Evelyn and Cissie thought this really funny, and 'killed' themselves laughing. We watched until the train disappeared out of sight, leaving nothing more that the wisps of smoke from its big funnel, and even that was swallowed up by the atmosphere eventually, and we walked back across the iron bridge over the track to go home. I wasn't lonely, however. I thought I might be, but I wasn't. I left the sisters when we were half way up the hill which led to their house telling them "O'm gunna 'ave a look at that up thaya, pointing in the direction of a monument way up the hill on the right-hand side of the main street, behind some houses, a considerable way behind.

"Well don't thee bi lung Ronnie, cuz we'll bi 'avin' tea soon, oright?"

"O wunt bi lung love, it wunt tek mi ya minnit or two ta gerrup thaya an' back," I replied, full of myself being a man. They both laughed at this, and said "It might tek thee a little longer than thy think Ronnie, still we'll wert on wunt wi 'Ciss?"

"I, we'll wert on fer thee lad, we'll wert on." Off they went home, and I went up between a long row of terraced houses over the cobbled bricks. The cobbles stopped when I reached the end of the houses. This wide street continued into a

174

narrow lane. It really surprised me how the environment changed so drastically in such a short space of time. One minute you were in a populated area, and the next you were, to all intent and purpose, right in the middle of the country. it was indeed very beautiful.

I walked, I walked, and I walked. I thought to myself "Bloody 'ell o'm neva gunna see this bleedin' lump a stone." It seemed to go for ages, and I now realised what the two girls were laughing at, this monument was indeed farther away than one could imagine. Never the less I was determined to reach it, whatever the cost. I finally came to it and I found that it was a monument to Robert Peel. I thought "God, ov walked all this bloody way ta see a lump a stone to a coppa." I looked at it for a moment, and then I thought, "Od soona bi yavin' mi tea, than bein' 'ere, still o cun allis tell mi merts abourit, it'll look good wunnit?" I reasoned with myself.

I certainly got back down quicker than I went up. I didn't want to miss my tea, also I wanted to gu ta the pitchers as well, for I had seen that it was a James Cagney film on, and I didn't want to miss that. The film was titled 'East of the Rising Sun'. Naturally, like most youngsters, we liked a good war film for it gave us a good feeling to know that we were 'the good guys' fighting all these 'bad guys' for principles far beyond our thoughts, but just thinking that what we were striving for was the everlasting PEACE.

I did enjoy the film, and I bought some chips on the way home. I enjoyed those as well, even though I knew perfectly well that the girls would have a nice supper waiting for me when I finally arrived home. My thoughts on the matter were that I would have chips now, and who knows what for supper, so it served me right when I got into the house to find that they had got 'fish and chips' for supper! Did that deter me? You have got to be joking. I just wolfed them down.

I got up the next morning, and found that I missed 'Our Kid', it was as though something had gone away from me personally. I know Arthur had gone physically but this was something else; something I couldn't understand, and being as ignorant, as I was, I really couldn't come to terms with it. So like so many more things throughout my life, I did the only thing possible: dismissed it all, and lit a fag.

Not being able to make up my mind what to do, on this my last day with these wonderful girls, I said to them "Is there any baths 'ere?" They looked at me in amazement, then Cissie said, "Nay love, but o tell thee w'at we'll do, we'll borra a tin tub frum this neighbour ov owas, an' we'll boil thee some water, an' w'en that's done we'll both gu out fer a w'ile, an' then thee can 'ave a bath in peace, 'ow's that suit ya' luv?" I looked at them in utter disbelief, what the hell were they talking about? Then it suddenly came to me, and I burst out laughing "Nah-h-h, o dain' mean o wannid a bath, o meant o wannid a swim, warr ri meant wuz, ar' there rany swimmin' baths near rere? They looked back at me for a while, and then they to burst out laughing until tears came to their eyes. Finally this abated, and they told me that the nearest swimming baths was at Bury. Then they gave me the times of the buses, and a rough idea of where the baths were. So off I went up the street, turned left at the main road to the the bus stop and caught the single deck bus which took me into the big city.

I hired a 'cossie', and had a lovely time. I also met a girl. I fixed a date with her which I had no intention of keeping. Well, with all the trouble I'd had with women to date I didn't want to start anything this far away from home. Anyway I was finished with women altogether after the 'Girl from Belgrave Terrace incident.

Cissie, Evelyn, some of their mates, and myself went to The Working Man's Club again, on this my last evening with them. This time I did have a few beers. I did enjoy them, well I was a man wasn't I, and I had got to start acting like a man hadn't I? I joined in the singing, and joking, and altogether had a lovely evening. Also I slept better than I had ever slept before, it was wonderful.

Of course, I felt it in the morning. I had an awful headache, but I soon got over it. I had my usual 'mornin' fag', then went down to a lovely breakfast. That last morning together we couldn't do much really, for the train I had to catch, was departing mid morning. It didn't take me long to pack, I hadn't got anything to pack. Arthur had taken the 'Blackwells' paper carrier, so I shoved the towel, the only one we had taken, down the front of my jacket, made sure that I had got my fags and what bit of money I had left safely in my pocket, and then in the other pocket I made sure that my return ticket for Birmingham was there. I didn't want any more trouble at New Street, I'd had enough on the journey up here.

The train came at last, a little late, but not much, and I got into an empty compartment. After a while I heard the now familiar whistle, and the shout from the guard to indicate to the engine driver that he was clear to move off. I again felt the jerk of the carriage as the spasmodic roar of the smoke came from the funnel starting the 'iron lady' off on her journey, the first part of my journey to Manchester.

As the train moved off from Ramsbottom station that Tuesday I witnessed two lovely ladies who had treated Arthur and myself so well during our short stay with them, weeping as though they were losing their son, instead of the brother of their brother's wife. I hung out of the window, and waved, and waved until both they, and Ramsbottom Station disappeared from view. I again had the most funny feeling come over me; my tummy felt upset - a thing which normally never happened to me. I still couldn't understand these feelings, but I knew that they must mean something, Again, I did the only thing I knew what to do: I sat back in the comfort of the compartment, and lit yet another cigarette. I wasn't to know it then of course, but the next time I was to see these wonderful ladies was at 'Our Dear Ronnie's' funeral in the Sixties.

The journey back home to Birmingham was uneventful. I enjoyed the quiet, after what had been quite an exciting few days. The train pulled into New Street, and I alighted. Ascending the wooden stairs up to the main passageway through the station itself I heard a voice " 'ey Ronnie, 'ave yarrad a nice time?" I looked around to ascertain where the voice had come from. I mean I wasn't expecting anyone to meet me this end. People were going up and down the main thoroughfare leading from Stephenson Street right through to Station Street. Most of these folk were, naturally, service women and men. Sailors going back to their ships, or shore bases; airmen returning to their airfields or administrative occupations, all important to one another.

Last but definitely not least, soldiers going back to their barracks~ or in all respects, they were going the other way, coming home on leave to their loved ones. The war itself at this time was going very well for the Allies, and I had serious doubts as to whether or not it would be over before I had reached the age of seventeen, and eligible to volunteer for the Royal Navy. I know these thoughts were terrible, but that was the way it was, with nearly all young men of my age.

176

We wanted to be in on the action - not realising the tragedy that might be in store for us, and more important, what had already happened to thousands of young men already. Like I've said many times, however, the thoughts of young people are so vastly different to those of people a little, and a lot older. Experience, that's what's lacking in younger people's thoughts, and actions, but you will never stop it, they think they are right, and the elders think they are wrong. I think that's the way it will always be, but on the other hand it's not a bad thing is it?

"Ova rere, ova rere Ronnie!" It was that voice again. I had started to walk towards the exit in Stephenson Street, and had momentarily, with my thoughts, forgotten the voice. Stopping and looking round, I suddenly spotted 'Our Vi' trying to catch up with me. it was quite apparent that I had been too quick for her when I had come up from the platform where the Manchester train had pulled in. She caught up with me, she was smiling, and I thought how pretty she looked at that particular moment. We didn't kiss; I'm afraid the Smith's " weren't into that kind of thing, not that we didn't love one another, we did, but we just didn't show our real emotions, that's all. We stood there in the middle of the thoroughfare just like two people meeting one another after one had been away for a very long time. It was for me a very nice feeling, and I let my thoughts run away with me once more.

I had been away for years, with my sweetheart not knowing where I was, and I wasn't able to contact her either. I was, of course, serving in The Royal Navy, and I had been at sea for long periods. Resplendent in my petty officer's uniform, like 'Our Joe's' I met my sweetheart. We had so many things to talk about, and so many things to do. Oh dear God, it was so nice to be home again.

" 'ow's Ev'lyn an' Cissie Ronnie?" I came back to reality with a bang! "Oh they're great, an' wiv 'ad a lovely time." I then went on to relate the time spent with 'Our Violet's' two very dear sisters-in-law. We chatted as we walked towards the bus terminus in Colmore Row. Across Stephenson Street into Lower Temple Street, Temple Street, and then through St Phillips Churchyard which brought us out right opposite the beautiful structure of Snow Hill Station.' The weather was so nice that we decided to walk home instead of going by bus. Off we went down Livery Street, still talking about the 'Ramsbottom Holiday,' and Evelyn and Cissie in particular. Along Great Hampton Street, passing 'Cannings,' 'Joseph Lucas's,' 'Hockleychem,' 'Davenports,' 'Swallow Raincoats,' 'Restalls,' then on into Hockley Hill itself with 'Smiths (Harry of course) the Ironmongers,' Dr Lyons in the house - the very mysterious house that lay back off the road behind huge trees, and bushes. Then we passed where 'Vi' worked, 'Howlets,' with the 'Florist' and 'Peter Blooms' on the right. 'The Gomm Manufacturing' and 'Collins' on the left, right opposite Guest Street. We turned right into Guest Street. I looked over at 'The Wold' and thought of the times I had been to 'Mr Wold' to make a small repair to my cycle, a repair which on most occasions he didn't even charge us kids.

Finally we entered the dim, dusty surrounds of the passage leading to the front door of 228. Never the less I was glad to be home, for it had seemed a lot longer than four days. It seemed to have lasted for four years. 'Our Mom' asked me if I'd had a nice time, but more important " 'ave ya' be'aved ya' bloody self?" I ignored this remark, thinking to myself "Om growed up now, an' I'll do warr I bleedin' well like." Naturally, I didn't let Mom ever know these kind of thoughts, because I really believe that she would have given me a 'back 'ander' even then. I had something to eat, and the inevitable several cups of tea, before announcing that "om guin' out ta see mi merts."

"Yove on'y jus' gorrin the bloody 'ouse, wassamarra ya' got bleedin' ants in ya' trousis or sommat?" This comment from 'You know who,' which I again totally ignored, I swept out of the house with only one thought on my mind, to get up to Handsworth to my mates. That's what I really wanted, I wanted to be with Danny, Pat, and Joe. We met and had a great time up 'The Monkey Run,' then as always I finished up at 'Ma Davies's,' with the story of my holiday at Ramsbottom changing all the time. The story of the girl in Bury, whom I met whilst swimming, changed all of a sudden. I did go back to Bury on the night time, and oh boy, did we have a wonderful time together.

"Tha's the way ta do it Ronnie," said Jackie Walford, "keep it orff yarown doorstep, an' leave it up thaya, ya' dai' tell 'er w'ere ya' lived did ya'?" I looked at Jackie with what I thought as a very knowledgeable look, and said "D' ya' think om bleedin' barmy or summat Jack, course o dain' ge 'er mi yaddress."

As usual I slept really well that night. I awoke early to return to work at Handsworth Dairies, after my wonderful break at Ramsbottom.

* * * *

Lancashire held some other wonderful memories for me also. Not Lancashire itself, but the people from that county. This lady was an exception to any rule; to me she was everything. Oh no she wasn't pretty, beautiful, had a lovely figure, voice, deportment or anything like that at all, but, 'BY GUM,' was she something She was small, very small, about five foot nothing, or maybe smaller, she was plump. A lovely pleasant face, with an everlasting smile, even better than 'The Mona Lisa.' She was so full of life, you just would not believe it. I can honestly say I never saw this wonderful lady without a smile; it was a fixture. Her husband was a very quiet man - well that was the impression I had on the very few occasions that I met him. He worked for 'Stotherts of Atherstone'. They were of 'Carters Little Liver Pills' fame. Not only were they in the pharmaceutical world, but they sold 'pop' as well; lovely old business, but like everything else time marches on. I think the gentleman was some type of representative for this wonderful old company. Then there was Valerie the daughter, she to was a very quiet girl, and very nice, like both her parents. Val had a certain aura about her; yes, she was quiet and intent, and although I never found out what she did, I would imagine that it would be something in the City. Taking it all round they were a very loving, close family, and their name was Keeling. This very lovely family had a shop in Junction Road, which was situated on the left-hand side looking down towards Crockets Road, in between Woodland Road and Station Road. (Harold Haynes lived in Station Road.)

I met this wonderful family whilst on the wholesale round, and I can remember Mrs Keeling's welcome to me every morning I entered the shop to deliver the daily supply of milk: " 'ellor Ronnie mar luvly lad, 'ow are thee this mornin'?" I would deliver the milk, take the empties away and put them on my flat cart. I would give 'Dick' his nose-bag, then re-enter the shop, but this time I would go into the back parlour, where a cup of tea would be waiting for me, whilst Mrs Keeling was cooking my breakfast. Naturally this didn't occur the first time

I delivered there, but it wasn't very many days, from the first day that it did happen. I couldn't have been treated better than if I had been Mrs Keeling's son. They were wonderful.

I remember inviting this lovely family one night down to the Y.W.C.A. to see a play some of the members were putting on, as it was the first time that they had been out with me, for it was always in the course of my job that we met. I thought I'd better make an effort. It was just about this time that I was going through the pipe smoking phase. Oh I'd seen Michael Dennison, Michael Redgrave, Michael Gregson, James Mason, Orson Welles, and oh so many other film stars smoking their various pipes, in as many various situations, so I thought no, this is it, this is me, quiet, soft spoken, and sophisticated. I got myself a pipe of sorts (which turned out to be a load of old rubbish) and some tobacco. The scene was set. I sat there all suave, and dressed in 'Mi Sundee best', on the end of one of the middle rows of the big room, saving three seats for my guests, and attempting to smoke this excuse for a pipe. All I achieved was a constant spasmodic run of choking, and burning to my tongue. Still, I stuck it out, until eventually I saw Mr and Mrs Keeling, and Val enter the room. I ran across to them, told the lady waiting by the entrance at the side of the stage that they were my guests, and that I had already bought the tickets. We went back to the row and I saw Mr and Mrs Keeling to their seats, then I sat next to Val, and we waited for the show to start. Mr Keeling lit his pipe up, and settled down puffing gently, so I tried to imitate him. What a disaster; I puffed for a few moments and then I felt so queer I stopped smoking, hoping it would go away, but it didn't. The show started, and everyone was enjoying it except 'yours truly'. I started to feel worse, and suddenly there was a new aroma on the scene, one of burning. Now this didn't enhance matters for me and my sickness. Everyone was looking around trying to ascertain where the burning was coming from, when suddenly I found out. "O' mi bloody leg!" were the first words I uttered. This certainly stopped the show. Well, not literally, but it did cause people in the close vicinity to stop looking and turn round to see what was going on. I soon found out for them. Whilst feeling sickly I had lowered the pipe and was holding it on my right thigh. What must have happened was the bowl of the pipe must have turned over and the hot tobacco had burnt a hole through to 'Mi Sundee best' trousers, and consequently burnt my leg too.

I went into immediate panic trying to put the smouldering trousers, and smouldering leg out, which in turn caused everyone around me, including the Keeling family, to dissolve into fits of laughter, although I couldn't for the life of me find anything funny to laugh at. In the finish out of shame I left the room, and went down to the toilets below. I threw the bloody pipe and tobacco into the metal ash can then I looked at 'Mi Sundee best' trousis. What a mess! If this wasn't enough, I suddenly I had to rush to the toilet bowl, and was violently sick. That then was the beginning, and the end of pipe smoking for me, film stars or no film stars, they could have it - have the lot! I did go back to the show, and Val whispered to me "Are you alright Ronnie?" I replied I was, although I was far from alright. I was glad when that particular evening came to a close. I might add, I did not repeat my story to the gang at 'Ma Davies's', where I went after seeing the Keeling family safely on the bus to take them back to their wonderful little shop in Junction Road.

Mrs Keeling had her little fling with the pipe smoking incident for sometime afterwards, and Val did too. On the few occasions that I saw Mr Keeling he used to say: " 'ow's the pipe smoking going Ronnie, any betta?" Eventually it died a natural death, of course; by then I could share in the joke, but in the first stages it used to 'burn me up a bit?'

It wasn't long after the pipe incident that Mr Davies called me into the office yet again. He informed me that Norman Hadley would be taking over my round with his motor vehicle. Apparently they had decided that it would be quicker for Norman with his lorry to do the two rounds, his and mine, and would prove more efficient. Nobody mentioned that Norman would be getting paid more for doing this, although I knew this to be a fact. The real reason for this transfer became apparent. Stan (I have forgotten his surname although we were good friends) on No 8 round had been accepted into the Royal Navy. He was to join on the following Monday, the Monday after Mr Davies had called me into the office, and informed me that I would be taking over his round.

Naturally I was very disappointed in being taken off the wholesale round, firstly because I would be losing contact with a lot of wonderful people, these people who ran the small shops around the Handsworth area, and most of all the Keelings. But, as I have already explained many times, I couldn't do a thing about it due to The Ministry of Works rulings.

I saw Stan, and he told me that it was a very good round, and the tips were good. Also he gave me a general run down on the round itself, for which I was very grateful. This change of rounds did prove to be successful in more than one way, however. The round itself started in Grafton Road, right by the dairy, and took in Antrobus Road, Grove Lane, Albert Road, Brunswick Road, Hinstock Road, Phillip Victor Road, and was a very good round. On the other hand I knew that I would be losing my Sunday's off, but that didn't worry me unduly. I knew that I would get back into the swing of things quickly. I would miss seeing my mates, Danny, Pat, and Joe, and our trips to Bewdley, although when I told them about the new round, and its implications, they shrugged it off saying "Thas soright Ron, we'll wert fer ya' ta finish, an' then we'll gu an' a' sum donnuck lerter ron, it wunt mek any diffrence ta us." This was most assuring to me in the circumstances.

Stan, the lad who was joining 'The Andrew,' was a little shorter than my five-foot eleven inches, although he made up for this by being a lot more stocky; he was very muscular. He was a very quiet lad, well for what I knew of him. I only ever saw him lose his temper once in the time that I knew him, and believe me it was not a pretty sight for the other bloke concerned. I knew on that occasion that Stan could use himself - use himself very well. As I have said, he was a stocky lad, with a broad face, which appeared to be continually sunburnt, brown eyes, spaced very widely, either side of a broad nose, and a very generous mouth below it. His teeth were white and strong, although not even, and on the left side of the top set, one of them was missing, which incidentally did not distract from an unusually attractive, handsome face - in fact if anything it added to it. On his cheeks he did have rather large type of pimples, which, in my opinion, gave him that 'rugged' look.

I waited for Stan on the Saturday. That was the only day I could meet him due to my being on a wholesale round I finished much later than the retail rounds during the week, but on a Saturday when the retail men had to collect their money in, we all finished around the same time. I stood in the 'tack room,' and after a while he arrived in the yard to unload his empties. I went over to him and said "If yove gorra minnit Stan praps yo' could ge us a bit mowa info on No 8."

"Ar' ro course o cun Ronnie." he replied, giving me the benefit of his missing tooth, with a broad smile, " O tell ya' w'at, Ronnie' he continued "W'y dotcha cum " um wi" mi, an' 'ave a cuppa tea, an' wi cun 'ave a real ole natta rabourit, eh?"

"Ar-r-rokay Stan, tha's great." I knew that he had got a bike, so I assumed that he didn't have to bother about buses or anything, but to make absolutely sure I said "Yowa're on ya' bike intcha Stan?"

"Ar-r-ro course I yam, Iyav ta 'ave a bike really cuz the buzzis ar' funny frum w'ere ri live, and the single decka Midland Red buzz ain' all that regla any road up."

He went through unloading, with me giving him a hand. Then I told him to go up and pay in whilst I put 'Danny' his horse away, and put the harness in the 'tack room'. He thanked me, and went off around the front to the entrance of the office whilst I led 'Danny' into the stables to put him to bed after his day's work.

I met Stan out front of the dairies building, having picked his bike up from 'Danny's' stall, and I said "W'ich way am wi guin' Stan?"

"D' ya' know 'The Blue Gert's' arall Ron?"

"Ov 'eard onnit, burr ri ain' sure."

"Well d' yal know Smerrick 'igh Street?" I thought for a minute, not being quite sure of my answer, then I said "Is it anyw'ere near Soho?" I knew that location for certain due to 'Our Gran' and 'Our Grandad' living there.

"Well," replied Stan thoughtfully, "it ain' exactly thaya, but yome on the right track, ya' know w'en yo' gu up Rabone Lane, tha's the road which guz on frum Booth Street."

"Ar-r-ro know that Stan" I replied enthusiastically, for this area I definitely knew, so I gained confidence from this.

"Well, yo' gu up Rabone Lane until yo' get ta the pub called 'The W'ite 'oss', tha's w'ere ya' turn orff left fer Soho."

"Ar-r-rum wi' ya' Stan." I knew that to be the turning for Gran's.

"Well ya' don' turn lef' thaya, ya' gu straight on down Rolfe Street."

"Ov neva bin down that way", I interrupted.

"Anyway Ron tha's the way wi' gu, an' if yo' don' know it now, yo' soon will wun ya'?"

"Ar-r-r yome right Stan, I'll soon pick it up."

"Yo' wun need it will ya' rif om guin' the bleedin' Nervy, cuz I'll bi'ya' lung way away frum Smerrick then, cuz o don" think thay'm bringin' bleedin' battleships up the cut yet, are they?" We both had a good laugh at this comment, and then mounted our steeds and set off for Stan's house.

We went down Sandwell Road into Crockets Road, turned right into Rabone Lane, the lane that I did not know the name of, although I had travelled it many times on my Sunday morning visits to 'Gran and Grandad Smith's' at 21 Market Street, Soho. Past the gas tanks on both corners of Foundry Lane, up the hill, over the Birmingham Canal, and 'George Burns' where 'Our Jack' worked as a furnaceman, and then we arrived at the junction with Soho Street and 'The

White Horse.' I looked up Soho Street, and thought "O'll 'ave ta gu an' si Gran an' Grandad one o these times. O ain' si 'em fer ages now." We swung off to the right, and travelled down Rolfe Street, all new territory to me. When going through a new area I always liked to note places down in my memory, just in case I ever did go that way again. 'The Staffordshire Knot' at the junction of Rabone Lane and Rolfe Street, 'The Star' on the corner of New Street, the Fire Station and the Post Office, on the right hand side, 'The Stamping Mills' on the left, between New Street and Hill Street, and occupying almost all that triangle. The bang, bang, bang of the huge stamping machines, which continued into the night, as well as all day, and could be heard for quite a distance around, they were that noisy. Further up on the left the Swimming Baths, where I spent some time in later years, not swimming, but dancing, then a little further still the Great Western Railway Station. Stan and I were chatting away merrily, not only about No 8 round, but the war, and how he was looking forward to going into The Royal Navy. I told him in confidence that after my seventeenth birthday which was the following 3rd of January, I too was going to attempt to join the 'Andrew.' Stan replied, "Well yo' shudden 'ave any trouble gerrin in Ron, yo' look bloody fit enough ta me."

Finally we reached the end of Rolfe Street at the traffic lights, which were green. We rode straight across, turning right, and in a short distance Stan said "There's the 'Blue Gerts' Ronnie, an' then ova on that side is 'The Ol' Toll 'ouse.' I looked across the road in the direction Stan had pointed and saw what l thought looked like a miniature windmill, without the sails. I was immediately impressed, and have been ever since. It's still there today, and so is 'The Blue Gates.' Stan and I turned left at the pub, rode up Stoney Lane, which, to me, initially looked a very long thoroughfare indeed, and my thoughts on that were "I yope wi yain' gorra gu all the way up thaya." I needn't have worried, however. We passed Church Hill Street on the left, Stony Street on the right, and as Stan hadn't said anything I prepared myself for a long journey up the lane. Suddenly Stan shot off to the left up Green Street, right opposite Bleak Street, whilst I went sailing on. He burst out laughing, and said "If yome wi' mi Ron, an' yome cumin' 'um wi' mi yome guin' the wrung way, cum on up 'ere." I turned my bike round without any comment, and Stan continued "Yo needen gerron ya' bike Ron, I yon'y live jus' up 'ere ron the right, so it wunt bi wuth it."

We pushed our cycles up Green Street, a little way on the right, then we turned up an entry. At the bottom of the entry we turned left where Stan propped his cycle under the window of the back house, which was like the house that we 'Smith's' lived in at Guest Street. I parked my cycle against his, and he said "Come on in Ron, an' oll gu an' mek us a cuppa tea okay?"

"Ar-r-rokay Stan, thanks" and into the house I went, following Stan. I entered this room, and oh how the memories of 2/24 came flooding back. The one difference however was that it was the opposite way around to Guest Street. The entrance door was on the left, the window on the right. Consequently the fireplace was situated on the right, and the 'bogey 'ole' was on the left, which left the entrance to the upstairs just past the fireplace. Red brick quarries on the floor, with an herden rug in front of the fireplace, a crude wooden table, and an assortment of chairs scattered around this 'duplication' of 2/24. Sitting on one of these chairs, I looked around the room again - yes this was Guest Street alright. I assumed that Stan was making the tea in the 'bogey 'ole' so I thought I'd have a closer look whilst he was out of the way (nosey bleeda)

One thing I had missed on closer examination was a door at the end of the room, which I could only presume led to another room beyond, or a closet. I was never to find out this particular mystery, but the next thing I noticed, Stan explained to me in full. On a shelf in the corner by the window was a speaker, well at first glance it looked like a wireless set. The shelf was painted brown (what wasn't those day's?), and this speaker-cum-wireless was as usual in grain, and polished, unlike anything at 2/24. I began to wonder however how such a delicate shelf could possibly hold a wireless set with its accumulator, and the various batteries that it would have required. Also there was only one knob, nothing else; just the round part where the yellow mesh was situated, and this one single knob? When Stan returned from the 'bogey 'ole' with two tin mugs of tea I was still looking in the direction of this contraption, practically unaware of this dear friend entering.

" 'ere yar Ron, 'ere's ya' tea."

"O' thanks, Stan." I was really still fascinated by this piece of equipment up on the shelf, so fascinated that I just had to ask what was most probably a question that had been asked several times before. Before I could ask, however, Stan started to smile and said "O' betcha gunna arsk mi w'at tharris up thaya on the shelf, ain' ya'?" He didn't wait for an answer he just went on: "Soright Ron, stacks a people arsk the serm question, yo' ain' on yarrown." which confirmed what I had thought earlier.

"That box up thaya is on'y a speaka, an' all ya' rave ta do is turn the knob. 'ere rile show ya'." With that he went across to the box, reached up and turned the knob clockwise. Immediately beautiful music came flowing over the room. I was certainly amazed; no accumulators, no batteries, how could all this happen? Stan started to laugh, and came back to the table, and sat down. He sipped at his tea before continuing what I thought was going to be an awe-inspiring tale, and smiled gently. There's a bloke up in Waterloo Road, just up the Cape, an' w'arr 'e's done, an' don' arsk mi cuz'onist o don' know, 'e's fixed up a big thing like a radio, well it looks like a radio, on'y it's much bigga. Ov on'y sin it once, burrit's a great big thing, wi' lot's wires cumin' frum it, an' it's inside a shop along Waterloo Road. Anyway warr re does is 'e chargis one an' a tanna a wick ta people, an' then 'e comes ta yarr rouse an' put's one o them speakers inta yarr rouse, an' then 'e does summat else, an' the next thing ya' know there's music comin' out ov it. The big radio up in 'is shop is playin' all the time, so I reckon that w'arr 'e does is lerr ev'rybody tune in on it, an' tha's awhy 'e chargis the one an' a tanna, an' 'e calls 'is shop 'The Smethwick Broadcasting Company.'

I wasn't any the wiser by Stan's explanation of this broadcasting system, but again I covered up by just nodding, and trying to look intelligent. Of course, in later years I did understand and I thought what an ingenious man this bloke must have been to give everyone (within a confined area I suppose) the benefit of having programmes on tap without the necessity of buying a wireless set, which you couldn't obtain during the war anyway. On top of that it saved you the expense of accumulators, or hiring them, and batteries. I thought this wonderful.

Stan went into the Navy, and I took over his round, and I was never to see him again, like so many other people in my life, but the friendship meant so much to me at the time, that I have never forgotten it.

The war itself at this time in my life was gradually coming to an end, although as I explained earlier this wasn't what I really wanted. Naturally, I apologise for this feeling, due to the immaturity of my thoughts at that time. Although in fairness to myself, I wasn't on my own, for thousands of youths were thinking along the same lines. We thought it was so glamourous, and exciting for all the men in the Army, Navy, and Air Force. The uniform, the freedom, the travel, which when you actually joined proved to be a different thing altogether.

The attitude of the people of Hockley at the time that I'm talking about now was one of happiness, light heartedness - in fact almost a party atmosphere. Yes, Christmas 1944, and the period either side of it was one of joy, real joy and good will towards man. Everyone appeared to be enjoying this new lease of life. Of course many were sad, due to the loss of loved ones, those reported missing, and in various prisoner-of-war camps, wondering whether they would make it home. Never the less these people still tried to enjoy this wonderful period. Hope stood out for many of them, hope for a much better life when the enemy was finally defeated.

* * * *

I go back to January the 7th 1944 for the start of this climb back to winning the war with Germany and Japan:

DAILY EXPRESS

Friday January 7th 1944

"BRITAIN HAS FIGHTER WITH NO PROPELLER" - THE JET PLANE ARRIVES - and goes into mass production.

All tests passed, speed is colossal. Driven by hot air.

Work began on the engines in 1933, by Group Captain Frank Whittle, the inventor, a pre-war R.A.F. man. Whittle was given one of Britain's greatest test pilots, Philip. E.G.Sayer to carry out experimental flights. After several attempts Sayer made the first successful jet propelled fighter flight, in May 1941. Flight Lieutenant Sayer was killed flying, in October 1942.

BERLIN FEARS MORE BIG RETREATS.

Russians take town 12 miles inside Poland. From E.D. Masterman. Stockholm, Thursday.

DAILY MAIL

Monday. January 17th 1944.

"EISENHOWER TAKES OVER AS INVASION
COMMANDER-IN-CHIEF.

"Supreme headquarters of the Allied Expeditionary Force - the Army to invade Europe issued its first communique last night. It stated that General Dwight

Eisenhower has taken over his post in Britain as the Supreme Commander-in-Chief.

"BIG RUSSIAN BREAKTHROUGH IN THE NORTH" 100,000,German dead in three weeks. 7000 prisoners taken

"DAILY MAIL"
Saturday, April 1st 1944.

"WINGATE KILLED IN AIR CRASH"
Young wife was told news a day before the world.
First man to outwit Japs, Major General Orde Wingate, who married in 1935 to Miss Paterson.

"NEWS CHRONICLE"
Monday June 5th 1944.

"ROME FALLS: ENEMY STREAM NORTH"
Bombers destroy 300 vehicles as Germans fight rear guard action. Allied tanks won fierce battle in suburbs. Allied troops have reached the centre of Rome.

* * * *

Did you Maclean your teeth today? That's easy to sea!
Maclean's toothpaste, one size during the war, 1/1d a tube.

"EVENING DESPATCH" 6.30 City.
Tuesday 6th June 1944.

"INVASION GOING WELL : TANKS ASHORE. ALLIES HAVE FOOTHOLD."

Slashing inland, all to plan, and what a plan.
11,000 planes, and 4,000 ships engaged.

Our invasion is "proceeding to plan - and what a plan." This is what a confident Mr Churchill told the House of Commons today in a brief review of the landings in Northern France which began soon after dawn.

BIRMINGHAM PRAYED.

Grey haired women with shopping bags, young office girls, workmen with oily hands, and business men were among the many who knelt in prayer in St Martins Church in Birmingham, at lunch time today.

Amusements in Birmingham on this wonderful "D DAY" read as follows:

DANCING:

Grand Casino, Mecca Dancing, Twice Daily at 2-30 and 6-30 Refreshments at popular prices Continuous dancing to: TEDDY FOSTER and his Broadcasting band. JACK GROOM and his band.

"THE MASQUE" Birminghams Best Ballroom. Dancing Daily. 3-6 and 6-30–10 JACK DALES BAND WALFORD ROAD SPARKBROOK. Tel: Vic 1397.

THEATRE:

ASTON HIPPODROME Box Office open 10am 7pm 6.0. TWICE NIGHTLY 8.0. ENORMOUS ATTRACTION!! Harry Benet Presents. "FLORADORA" WITH JAY LAURIER. First Class Company of Sixty.

BIRMINGHAM HIPPODROME Hurst Street MIDland 2576. 5.10.pm. TWICE DAILY. 7.25.pm. " This way for Laughter" ADALAIDE HALL. GEORGIE WOOD GEORGE MOON and BURTON BROWN. Eddie Ready and Joy. Pepino's Miniature Circus Peter Waring, Albert Saveen, The Three Red Heads, Len Williams. Box Office open 10am.- 8.pm.

CINEMA:

ODEON New Street. Birminghams Paramount Theatre. Doors open 10 O'Clock. A thrill a minute in Hitchcocks powerful production. " LIFEBOAT" With: TALLULAH BANKHEAD. WILLIAM.BENDIX. HENRY HULL Mary Anderson, Heather Angel. Six men and THREE WOMEN...At the mercy of the sea... and each other. Also, "GET GOING" (U) with Robert Paige, Grace McDonald A thrilling spy comedy.

Gaumont. Continuous from 12-15 Huge Double Feature Programme. MICHAEL O'SHEA, SUSAN HAYWOOD in JACK LONDON (A) Photographed in Sepia. NORTHWEST RANGERS (A) with James Craig, John Carradine. Patricia Dane, William Lundigan. Coming. "THE SULLIVANS" (U).

Scala Today, a Double Feature Programme. JACK HOLT in HOLT OF THE SECRET SERVICE (A). 1.57, 4.46, 7.35. Also. KENNY BAKER in. DOUGHBOYS IN IRELAND (U)

NEWS THEATRE. HIGH STREET. 10.30.Daily

Sundays 3pm. 10d and 1/8d Only. "GIVE TILL IT HURTS" (A) Crime Doesn't pay. "TREE TRIUMPHANT" Secrets of life nature study. "REASON AND EMOTION" (A) Disney's latest cartoon. VARIETY. WORLDS LATEST NEWS…

TATLER THEATRE. STATION STREET Continuous Daily. 10-15 am to 10.0.pm. Prices: 10d. and 1/8d. " VALLEY of the WIND RUSH." travel. "REASON AND EMOTION" Disney's latest (A). "CHOO CHOO, SWING." Musical. Also Latest News…

Albion. New Inns. Handsworth. 0433. "Journey into Fear." (A) Dolores Del Rio: "Cinerella Swings It" (U) Guy Kibbee.

Astoria. Aston (ABC) Ast. 2384. Robert Young, Dorothy McGuire in: Claudia (A): William Tracy, Marjorie Woolworth in "Yanks Ahoy" (U) News.

Beacon. Gt. Barr, (Opposite The Scott Arms) Robert Taylor, George Murphy. "Bataan" (A). 2.55, 5.25, 7.55. Full Sup. Thursday: Falcon in Danger. (A).

Birchfield. Perry Barr. BIR: 4333. "I Escaped from the Gestapo" (A). "Dean Jagger, John Carradine: also East Side Kids: Ghosts in the Night. (U).

Bristol. Bristol Road. (ABC) CAL. 1904. in colour: Betty Grable, Robert Young "SWEET ROSY O'GRADY" (U). Richard Dix "The Kansan" (U).

Clifton. Gt Barr. Tom Kelly and Walter Brennan. "The Adventures of Tom Sawyer (U) (Tech) 3.0, 5.50, 8.45. Jimmy Lydon: "Henry plays Cupid." (U).

Crown. Ladywood. (ABC) EDG:1122. George Sanders Marguerite Chapman: Appointment in Berlin. (U). Edmund Lowe. Dangerous Blondes (A).

Edgbaston. Monument Road. (ABC) EDG: 3273. Roy Rogers, Sheila Ryan in Song of Texas (U). Margaret Lockwood, Derek Farr Quiet Wedding. (A).

Elite. Handsworth: Diana Barrymore and Robert Paige in "Fired Wife" (A). Also "The Strange Death of Adolf Hitler. (A).

Empire. Smethwick. SME: 0757. Elsie and Doris Waters, Ernerst Butcher "It's in the Bag" (U). Bob Steele in "Brand of the Outlaws" (U).

Gaiety: Coleshill Street (ABC) CEN: 6649. Otto Kruger, Elissa Landi, in "Corregidor" (A). James Dunn, Florence Rice in "The Ghost and the Guest" (A).

Grand: Soho Road, Handsworth. "CONEY ISLAND" BETTY GRABLE, GEORGE MONTGOMERY. And Full Support. (Technicolour) (U).

Grove Cinema: Dudley Road. SME: 0343. VIVIEN LEIGH, ROBERT TAYLOR "WATERLOO BRIDGE." Screened at 3.5, 5.32, 7.59.

Lyric: Mickey Rooney, Judy Garland in "Girl Crazy" (U) also "Mrs Lady Bug (U). Thursday: "Sweet Rosy O'Grady" (U). (Technicolour)

Odeon: Kingstanding. SUT: 2551. THE MIRACLE OF MORGANS CREEK" (A). also "The Cat and the Canary."

Odeon: Perry Barr. BIR: 4453. Cot from 2.0. "Johnny Vagabond (U). "There's a Future in it" (U) Sun "Pittsburgh" (A) "Hi Buddy" (U).

Orient: Aston. (ABC) NOR: 1615. All Critics agree! Worlds Greatest Musical!!! "IRVING BERLIN'S" "THIS IS THE ARMY" (U) in Technicolour.

PALLADIUM: HOCKLEY. (ABC) NOR: 0380. MERLE OBERON, LAWRENCE OLIVIER, DAVID NIVEN "WUTHERING HEIGHTS" (A). MARSHA HUNT IN "THE LONG SHOT" (U).

REGAL: HANDSWORTH. (ABC) NOR: 1801. IRVING BERLIN'S WONDER SHOW IN TECHNICOLOUR. "THIS IS THE ARMY" GEO MURPHY, JOAN LESLIE.

VILLA. CROSS. (GB). NOR: 0607. CAROLE LOMBARD: "NOTHING SACRED" (A) ALSO "FARMYARD FOLLIES" (U). THURSDAY "TEXAS TO TOKYO" (U).

WINSON GREEN: NOR. 1790. "THE DESTROYER" (U). EDWARD G. ROBINSON. THURSDAY: "CRAZY TO KILL." (A).

Clifton: Stone Cross. STO: 2141. "New Moon" Jeanette McDonald. 2.54, 4.50, 8.13 also "Hitlers Madman" (A) Pat Morison. 1.30, 6.49.

Imperial: West Bromwich. WES: 0192. Orson Welles, Joan Fontaine in "Jane Eyre" (A) also Full Supporting Programme.

Palace Cinema: WES: 0358. Randolph Scott in "Nelson Touch" (U) with Andy Devine, Noah Beery Jnr: also "Get Going."

Plaza: West Bromwich. WES 0030. "Desert Rats" & "Doughboys in Tunisian Victory" also Tim McCoy, Susanna Kaaren "Phantom Ranger."

Queens Cinema: WES: 0351. Clive Brook, Morland Graham, "Brides of the Sea" (The Shipbuilders). Also "Jungle Scrap Book."

St Georges Cinema: Phone: 0737. Charles Laughton and Donna Reed in "The Man from Down Under." Also "It May Happen to You".

Tower (ABC). WES: 1210. James Mason, Carla Lehmann "Candlelight in Algeria (U); Sidney Toler, "Charlie Chan in the Secret Service." (U).

Plenty of jobs were available on this day too:

SITUATIONS VACANT

Foster Brothers. Clothing Company Ltd: Require services of several shop assistants (Male or Female) for Birmingham and District- Apply by letter only, giving fullest particulars to: Staff Manager, Foster Bros Clothing Co Ltd, 62 Albert Street, Birmingham

Handy Man or Bar Pot Man; Porter; full time: 'Golden Eagle' Hill Street.

Bread Bakers and Labourers for modern plant, good wages and conditions: Apply Mr. J.E Simnet, Bradfords Bakery, Norton Street, Hockley.

Youths required age 14,15,16,17 : rates 1s, 1s. 1d, 1s. 2d, 1s. 3d, per hour, plus bonuses: Supreme Laundries, Laundry Road, off Dudley Road, Smethwick.

1/6d per hour: Part time assistants are required for this easy form of Counter Service in Lyons Tea Shops in Birmingham. Also Staff to clean, and wash up. Evening duties 5-10pm. Good Wages, plus efficiency bonus, and excellent Staff meal facilities. Previous experience not necessary- Apply any day between 9am-4pm. 61 New Street, Birmingham.

Barmaid, experienced, good references essential- Apply in person to Manager, White Horse, Congreve Street.

B C.S. Ltd, Dairy Department, Vauxhall Road, Birmingham 7. Require Female Clerks. Apply letter or personally. 8,10,or 90, tram from City. City Circle Bus.

C.&.A. Modes Limited. Require Smart, Capable, Woman, for responsible full time position. Must be experienced in Fashion Trade. Good Salary. Apply Manager New Street.

Carter-Salesman. Urgently Required, permanent position for Capable Man. State Age, Wage and Experience. Box No L4, Ev'g Despatch.

Dairy Workers: Men not liable military service. Midland Counties Dairy Limited, Corporation Street, B'ham.

Milk Roundsmen: Not liable military service, for various districts. Midland Counties Dairy Ltd, Corporation Street, Birmingham.

Morning and Evening Cleaners required. Must be exempt. Apply Staff Office, Lewis's Ltd. any morning between 9.0. and 10.30.am.

Shop Porter: Required for General Duties; References; Exempt; Oswald Bailey Ltd, Bull Ring,B'ham.

Waitress required immediately. Apply: Arden Cafe, New Street.

Youth wanted age 15-16. Paragon Laundry Ltd, Hutton Road, off Westminster Road, Handsworth.

Youths; 14-16. Urgently required for several Departmental Offices. Excellent conditions, and prospects. Apply personally, Labour Office : W. Canning and Co. Ltd. Gt Hampton Street.

Although petrol was rationed, you couldn't get tyres, and you certainly couldn't get spares; there were still 'Used,' but obviously not 'New' cars, and commercials for sale: just look at these bargains:

COMMERCIAL VEHICLES: A.B.Fletcher, Birmingham's largest Car and Lorry Dismantlers, authorised buyers of Ministry of Transport condemned vehicles. Ring or write: A.B. Fletcher, 63 and 89 Dartmouth Street, Ashted, Birmingham. Aston Cross 3450 and 1801.

Fordson 5cwt van 1936. Recently completely overhauled, tyres as new. £95. Watsons Broad Street.

USED CAR BARGAINS : Ford Eight saloons. Two Special values. 1938 Saloon, engine recently overhauled; £97.10s. Saloon, re conditioned engine recently fitted £149. Both guaranteed.- Watsons Broad Street.

Morris 8hp-Sal. 1936. Two Seater Tourer. £50 or Deposit, £3. 3s. 9d. Monthly, Below. Morris 8hp. 1936-7. Saloon, £65. or Deposit £4 Monthly. Exchanges arranged. Below. Seen after 6pm. 12 Hazelhurst Road, Castle Bromwich. Also others in stock.

Two good Fourteens for sale, Hillman September 1938. Beautiful condition throughout; £295. Wolesley 1939. One Owner. First Class all round; £365. Both guaranteed. Watsons Broad Street.

... and then there was the MISCELLANEOUS COLUMN .

A RE-UPHOLSTERY OFFER: BRANSONS the Old Established Upholsterers, will re cover, and re upholster, your Suite, no matter what the condition. All new springing and hygienic fittings, and only the best materials used, Rexhides, Cowhides, uncut Moquettes and non crush Velvets. Expert Craftsmen will re make your Suite, and we guarantee every article to be as good, if-not better than new. No Suite too large, or too small. Moderate charges. Free collection, and Delivery. We have the finest selection of materials in Birmingham. No Coupons required. Send, phone, or write, for our traveller, who will call with patterns. BRANSONS UPHOLSTERY WORKS, 168 BEARWOOD ROAD. BEA. 2468.

Any Blacksmith work, general, bricklayers tools made, repaired, work for small power hammer. 281 Bordesley Green.

Beautiful Permanent Waves, and Curls, 21s and 25s etc. Reduced Price short period only. Satisfaction Guaranteed; Maison Ann, 19a Smallbrook Street, MIDland 4216.

HAIRDRESSING: Please note that: Hood Driers and Perm Heaters are still being repaired by Sullivan and Co, Helena Street, Parade, Birmingham 1. CEN. 3997. Twenty years of experience guarantees first class work. PLEASE NOTE: We have opened New Branch Showrooms at 11 St Mary's Row, Moseley Village, Birmingham 13. SOU. 0171.

HOW TO STOP SMOKING: Send stamp for booklet of World Famous remedy. Stanley Institute Ltd (B.E.) 265 Strand, London. WC.2.

INVASION DATES.

Here are the invasion dates.

GERMANY INVADED: Poland 1st September 1939, NORWAY and DENMARK, 9th April 1940, HOLLAND, BELGIUM, and LUXEMBOURG, 10th May 1940, JUGOSLAVIA and GREECE, 6th April 1941, CRETE, 20th May 1941, RUSSIA, 22nd June 1941.

ALLIES INVADED: French North Africa, 8th November 1942, Sicily, 10th July 1943, Italy, 3rd September 1943, France 6th June 1944.

BIRMINGHAM SOLDIER AWARDED THE M.M.

"What do you think about my being awarded the M.M.?" That was the casual way in which Sgt Douglas Plumley, aged 26, broke the news of his award half way through a letter to his wife, Helen, who lives at 11 Holly Road, Quinton, Birmingham. It was awarded him for gallantry on the Indo-Burma Frontier.

"WHITE HORSE WAS NEVER BETTER THAN IT IS TODAY"

It would be easier to buy White Horse Whisky as and when you like today if there were not so many people trying to do the same thing. Like so many of the comforts of peace-time, White Horse is scarcer because of the war. It takes long years to bring this famous whisky to ripeness and maturity It took forethought and provident care to provide the present regulated supply. And the same care and forethought are your assurance that today and in the years to come the quality of White Horse will be guarded as jealously as ever. More White Horse could not be released without broaching stocks still growing old and ripe for your future pleasure. And for no consideration will the good name of this great and famous blend be put in jeopardy.

MAXIMUM PRICES. Bottles: 25/9d; Half Bottles: 13/6d, as fixed by The Scotch Whisky Association.

"MODERN GIRLS" - PUBLIC OPINION
LETTERS TO THE EDITOR

EDITHA B C WAREING is quite wrong in thinking I live in "a world of my own" I've lived here since being bombed out, and I come into Birmingham every day, week-ends included, and see plenty of it. Her remarks certainly don't apply to me - it is just further evidence of her facility of jumping to conclusions.

It is usually people who have seen little of life who are most intolerant. Things are not always what they seem. I am not in the literal sense a "modern girl," as I am married and have a son. I just happen to be a broadminded woman who has seen a good deal of life in many cities, and I dislike people condemning all for the misbehaviour of a few. I like young people, and see no vice in the majority of them. It is usually only the high spirits of youth which makes them behave in a frivolous manner. I did not intend my previous remarks as an insult, but I could also say "If the cap fits." Editha B.C.Wareing certainly gave the impression in her previous letters of being unpopular, and it doesn't need much insight to guess why she professes to dislike modern girls.

If some people are unkind enough to laugh at her, I am sorry for her, but why let such trivialities bother her - and sneering at other girls won't help.

A really sensible person tries to be tolerant towards others' failings.

BARNT.GREEN.   P.L.

HOSPITAL VOLUNTEERS If "Puzzled Ann" will send her name to the Editor, it may be possible to help her, A.R. Anderson and others; We cannot publish letters that are not accompanied by the writers' full addresses.

THESE THEN WERE A FEW EXTRACTIONS FROM "EVENING DESPATCH" on Tuesday 6th June 1944.

No.16,504. Black Out 11.10.pm.to 5.2.am. Code Letter for tonight "A". Moon 10.0pm to 5.57am. 6.30 City. Cost: ONE PENNY

"THE EVENING NEWS"

No. 19,461 LONDON, Thursday, July 6th 1944.   One Penny.

"FLYING BOMBS KILL 2,752, INJURE 8,000; VERY HIGH TOLL IN LONDON - Premier."

"NEWS CHRONICLE"

No. 30,635.   Friday, July, 21st, 1944.   ONE PENNY

"HITLER: ASSASSINATION ATTEMPTED AT HIS HEADQUARTERS"

The Fuhrer escaped with slight burns, and concussion, says Berlin. 13 High ranking Officers injured in explosion.

"HIMMLER IS NOW THE DICTATOR IN GERMANY"

Heinrich Himmler, leader of the S.S. and Gestapo, is today, in practise dictator of Germany. In a few weeks time I understand, announcements will be made confirming his overriding authority in the Councils of The General Staff. HITLER, save as a figurehead, has become a cipher. STOCKHOLM Thursday.

"JAPAN FACES HER CRISIS"

Two men, an admiral, and a general, have been asked to form a new Japanese Government, to replace that of General Tojo.

"NAZI HAD NO DOUBT WAR WAS LOST."

(Normandy, Wednesday) In a prisoner of war camp a few miles from Caen front today I saw hundreds of Germans who had survived yesterday morning's greatest ever bombardment by the Allied Air Forces.

"We were amazed that the Allies had so many planes" a 21-year old Corporal said. "We knew you were strong, but after this we can have no doubt of the outcome of the war." The Corporal, born in New York, was a journalist before the war.

An interesting advertisement in "THE SUNDAY SUN" July 23 1944, brings home how prices have changed in the furniture trade :

CIVIL SERVICE FURNISHING DEPOT. 44 Clayton Street, Newcastle on Tyne. (Opposite Liptons) Phone 23805.

Monthly Terms Arranged. Second hand but First Rate Furniture and Pianos. No Permits required.

	£.	s.	d.
Bedroom Suite, Satin, and Walnut	25.	12.	6.
Bedroom Suite, Ash	35.	12.	6.
Bedroom Suite, Satin, Walnut	28.	12.	6.
Bedroom Suite, Oak	58.	15.	0.
Dining Set, Oak, Modern	50.	0.	0.
Dining Set, Oak, Modern	91.	0.	0.
Dining Set, Oak, Modern, with Buffet Sideboard	113.	16.	3.
3.Piece Suite in Blue Damask	38.	15.	0.

A short comparison table will show you what pounds, shillings, and pence, was all about

A Farthing was the lowest denomination, then a Halfpenny, a Penny, three penny bit (silver first and then metal) Sixpenny piece (A tanner), Shilling (A Bob.), Florin (Two Bob) Half a Crown (Half a Dollar) Ten Shilling Note (Ten Bob) and a Pound Note (Twenty Shillings), with finally the old big white Five Pound Note (One Hundred Shillings.). Now starting from the farthing will be the breakdown of this old system before decimalisation in 1971

Two Farthings.	=	One Halfpenny.
Four Farthings.	=	One Penny.
Two Halfpennies.	=	One Penny.
Three Pennies.	=	One Three Penny Piece.
Six Pennies.	=	One Sixpenny Piece.
Twelve Pennies.	=	One Shilling Piece.
Twenty Four Pennies.	=	A Florin.
Thirty Pennies.	=	A Half Crown.
One Hundred and Twenty Pennies.	=	One Ten Shilling Note.
Two Hundred and Forty Pennies.	=	One Pound Note.
One Thousand and Two Hundred Pennies.	=	One Five Pound Note.

The rough comparison between decimal currency and the old pounds, shillings, and pence is as follows.

£.s.d.		Decimal
One Farthing.	=	Nil.
One Halfpenny.	=	Nil.
One Penny.	=	1 Sixth of $2\frac{1}{2}$ Pence.
Three Penny Piece.	=	3 Sixths of $2\frac{1}{2}$ Pence.
Sixpenny Piece.	=	$2\frac{1}{2}$ Pence.
One Shilling Piece	=	5 Pence.
Two Shilling Piece	=	10 Pence.
A Half Crown.	=	$12\frac{1}{2}$ Pence.
One Ten Shilling Note.	=	50 Pence.
One Pound Note.	=	1 Pound Coin, or 100 Pence.
One Five Pound Note.	=	Same.

"THE DAILY TELEGRAPH."

No. 27,832. LONDON, Saturday, August 26th,1944. (and "The Morning Post") Price.1½ d.

"GENERAL de GAULLE ENTERS LIBERATED PARIS"

Last Germans surrender after ultimatum.

Allied tanks in day of street fighting. Great force reported on way to City.

"THE DAILY SKETCH."

No. 11,019.   Friday, September 8th 1944.   One Penny.

"THEY BEAT THE FLYING BOMBS"

Professor Sir Thomas Merton, named yesterday as the inventor of a 1s (5p) range finder which enabled night fighter pilots to destroy many flying bombs. "The idea for this gadget came to me suddenly," said Sir Thomas yesterday "and within a matter of hours I had made one up from odd scraps of material. Squadron Leader Joseph Berry, DFC, (won over Italy), and Bar, named as the RAF Tempest pilot who destroyed more than 60 flying bombs - all but three at night. Berry is 24, married, and his home is at Sunnydale Road, Nottingham. He was an income tax collector till he joined the RAF.

"DAILY MIRROR."

No. 12,719   Friday September 22nd 1944   One Penny
"DEMOBBING: FULL PLANS."

"Pay rises for long service."   "New Call-up of deferred men."

General demobilisation does not start until Japan is beaten, but piecemeal demobbing starts when Germany is beaten. Man (and Woman) power will have to be re-arranged between the services and the factories as the military situation develops, and the call up will continue, even while men are being released from the Forces to return to industry. The Fifty and Overs will be out first, if they want to go.

PAY: New long-service pay rates for the Forces come into operation as from September 3; Japanese campaign rates on November 1st. 7 shillings (35p) a week extra for those below Sergeant with three years service.

QUIET CORNER: By PATIENCE STRONG

"LOVE WILL SHOW THE WAY"

> There will be a bridge to gap when you come home to me
> After all the weary years, a strange thing it
> will be-to hear your voice, to see your face, to
> walk and talk with you-picking up the broken
> fragments; starting life anew.
> Will it be an easy task to build our world
> again? Yes, if to our vows and pledges faithful
> we remain...we shall have to gather up the threads
> of yesterday-But love will make us kind and wise,
> and Love will show the way.

"DAILY EXPRESS."

HITLER: We fight-until we get a Peace that safeguards Germany's future.

HIMMLER: We fight: in the houses, in the ditches, in the farms, round the trees.

No. 13,848. BIack-out 6.29.pm. to 7.2.am.
Thursday, October 19th 1944.   One Penny

RUNSTEDT WARNS: "THE FINAL HOUR."

"The armlet army: 16-60s get Home Guard call up. Berlin all yesterday sounded the alarm that the grand climax of the war is near.

"THE DAILY TELEGRAPH"
and Morning Post.
No. 27,900. London Tuesday November 14th 1944. Price. 1½d.

"TIRPITZ SUNK"

Tirpitz sunk by 29 Lancasters. Three direct hits by 12,000lb bombs Battleship capsizes : One plane lost.

Blasted by the terrific explosions of three RAF 12,000lb 'earthquake' bombs in a few minutes along her 790 feet of deck, the 45,000 ton battleship Tirpitz - last remaining pride of the German Navy since her sister ship, the Bismark, was sunk in May 1941, by The Royal Navy - lay capsized yesterday at the bottom of Tromsoe Fjord, in Northern Norway.

"CHRISTMAS PERIOD 1944.

"DAILY EXPRESS."

No. 13,899   Monday, December 18th, 1944   One Penny

Germans attack on 60-mile front, re-enter Belgium. Biggest Panzer blow since Battle of France. Black Parachute troops drop behind Allies.

197

From MONTAGUE LACEY. 1st US Army Sunday.

"RUNSTEDT STRIKE IN ONE LAST EFFORT"

German tanks since dawn have been thrusting into our lines at points over a 60 mile front from the River Roer to Luxemburg, and they have re-entered Belgium and Luxemburg. It seems that the Germans have decided to launch a counter offensive of some considerable strength. They are throwing in fresh divisions of infantry, and these men, with tanks, have overrun a number of villages and made several wedges on the Belgian-German and Luxemburg borders.

"DAILY MAIL"

No: 15,180.   One Penny.   For King and Empire.

Friday December 29 1944

"PATTON'S 3rd ARMY STRIKES AT 'BULGE' FROM SOUTH"

Spearheads withdrawn, Say the Germans : General Patton's Third Army is striking northwards against the southern flank of Runstedt's big bulge in Belgium, it was officially announced last night. His tanks raced to meet the Germans as they fanned out towards the City of Luxemburg. Runstedt's south-westward drive was halted, and Patton advanced 16 miles in six days to relieve Bastogne.

"1945"

"THE YEAR OF WAR AND PEACE"

"DAILY MAIL"

NO: 15,1980   One Penny.   For King and Empire.

Friday January 19th 1945.

"RED ARMY ARMY ENTER GERMANY."

Nazis Hurl in Volkssturm and Police. KONIEV'S tanks driving west from Czestochowa area, have smashed through the German border and were tonight engaged in bitter fighting with German battle groups flung into the line in a desperate endeavour to stem the advance while a defence is organised further back.

"DAILY EXPRESS"

No. 13,946   Dim Out 6.40 pm to 7.40 am.   One Penny
Tuesday, February 13th, 1945.

1.   Germany is doomed. It is hopeless to resist.
2.   Occupation by Britain, U.S.A, Russia, and France, in four zones.
3.   Compensation to limit of capacity.
4.   Polish Frontier will be the Curzon Line.

"BIG 3: GERMANY TO PAY."

"Victory and Peace plan drawn up in Crimea."

"FOUR POWER CONTROL OF GERMANY..."

World charter to be evolved at 'Frisco talks.

"Express Diplomatic Correspondent."

"NEWS CHRONICLE."

No: 30,849.   Saturday, March 31st 1945.   One Penny.

NEWS CHRONICLE WAR CORRESPONDENTS. ALL REPORT VICTORY NEAR.

S.L. SOLON.

THE MASTER PLAN IS SUCCEEDING.

COLIN WILLS.

ACROSS REICH FLOWS OUR QUICKSILVER.

NORMAN CLARK.

NOW FOR LARGE SCALE MOPPING UP.

STANLEY BARON.

GREATEST TURNING MOVEMENT IN HISTORY.

W. FORREST.

COLLAPSE FINDS WORKERS LEADERLESS

RONALD WALKER.

NO REAL LIFE IN DUISBURG FOR SIX MONTHS.

JAN YINDRICH.

VOLKSSTURM TO FIRST CHANCE TO GO HOME. ALL REICH IS BEING MOPPED UP. "V-DAY" WITHIN A WEEK.

"ANNIHILATION IS NOW AT HAND."

"Flood of Allied armour is loose in Germany"

FROM: S.L. SOLON. New Chronicle War Correspondent.

****

MONTGOMERY'S H.Q. Friday.

More than twenty armoured columns, pouring forth from the Allied Armies in the greatest flood of armour yet used in this War, are loose in Germany.

"INFANTRY CLEAR ONE TOWN AFTER ANOTHER"

From: Colin Wills. New Chronicle War Correspondent.

WITH THE SECOND ARMY FRIDAY:

Hundreds of miles of roads eastwards over the green Westphalian downlands are shaking day and night with the weight of British armoured columns rolling far into Germany.

Official statements speak of advances up to 40 miles, but official statements cannot keep pace with an affair like this.

It is as though Montgomery has pulled over the Rhine a great mass of quicksilver which is running out in all directions.

"DAILY MIRROR"

No. 12,890   Friday, April 13th, 1945.   One Penny

"ROOSEVELT DIES ON THE EVE OF ALLIED TRIUMPHS"

President Roosevelt died suddenly from a cerebral haemorrhage in his sleep at West Springs, Georgia, yesterday afternoon.

A White House statement said : Vice President Trueman had been notified. He was called to The White House and informed by Mrs Roosevelt.

The White House announcement added that a Cabinet Meeting had been called.

The four Roosevelt boys in the Services have been sent a message by their Mother which said that the President slipped away yesterday afternoon.

"He did his job to the end, as he would want to," the statement continued.

"END IN A FEW DAY'S, U.S.TOLD:
BRIDGE IS SIX MILES LONG OVER ELBE."

"Paratroops drop near Berlin, say reports . . ."

A HIGH AMERICAN GENERAL STAFF OFFICER told The U.S. Senate Military Committee last night, that the end of the organised fighting in Germany will probably come within a few days. As he spoke, Ninth Army troops who had crossed the Elbe fanned out across the Prussian plain towards the outer defences of Berlin. A midnight message disclosed that they hold a bridgehead six miles long and there was an unconfirmed report from French sources that paratroops have been dropped at Brandenburg, twenty miles from the Capitol.

"THIS IS RITA'S REBECCA."

Rebecca, the baby, starts life with a chance of
inheriting Columbia film star Rita Hayworth's
good look's and Pappa Orson Welles's zippy
genius as radio innovator, pep film producer,
and one man circus.
Rebecca arrived via caesarean operation
last December.
Mamma affects a kimono, and wears her
nails long, Chinese fashion, without varnish.

"LIGHTS O' LONDON SIGNAL."

"By your Political Correspondent . . ."

London is to celebrate V-E. Night, with a blaze
of light. The signal will be the switching on
of the light over Big Ben, which in Peace time
marks the fact that Parliment is sitting.
Seated in his chair at the House of Commons the
Speaker will press a button to switch on
the light, and this will signal to the world that
the six year black out is over.
Immediately the whole building will be
floodlit, and at the same time other public

201

buildings will become a mass of light.
This will be the signal to the public to
"light up" and from London the blaze will
spread all over the country- the signal may be
given by the BBC, according to one proposal
- and from there all over liberated Europe.
But it will be a one night only celebration.
We cannot afford the fuel for long illuminations.

"WORLD DEMANDS JUSTICE"

GERMAN PEOPLE FORCED TO SEE GERMAN CRIMES.

German women are forced to see the horrors of Buchenwald Camp. One of them is in tears. Others did not complete the tour. They fainted. Germans were made to bury the remains of helpless victims who died by slow torture.

Men and Women of the nearby town of Weimar are taken into the prison yard of Buchenwald Camp. Dangling from the scaffold is the body of a victim wearing the striped clothing of a political prisoner - a man guilty only of a desire to fight Nazism and hanged as American troops were advancing on the camp.

Prisoners at Buchenwald, emaciated as the result of slow starvation, sit listlessly while the townsfolk are forced to file through this Nazi torture mill. Do you think that bullet headed German in knickerbockers has learnt a lesson? (Picture of a most arrogant looking German filing past the prisoners.)

Nordhausen Camp where German civilians were conscripted from a nearby town, to carry for burial, the bodies of victims - 2,500 of them - left on an open field by the murderers who ran the place.

When American Forces captured Nordhausen they found hundreds of bodies. Hitler's political prisoners - French, Russian, Polish, Belgian, and a few Germans. The first order given by the Military Government Officer, Major David Poulette of Farmville, Va; was to the local burgomaster. It ordered him to summon immediately 600 of the town's leading citizens, dressed in their best clothes to bury the corpses with their own hands.

"THE BRITISH ARMY REPORTS . . ."

General Dempsey's senior medical officer, a Brigadier, said yesterday at Montgomery's H.Q. that the Belsen Horror Camp, near Bremen with its thousands of typhus, typhoid, and T.B. cases was "the most horrible, frightful place" he had ever seen. He stayed in this camp for forty eight hours, and yesterday gave an eye witness report of conditions. Here are some of the things he saw:-

There was a pile - between 60 to 80 yards long, 30 yards wide, and four feet high - of the unclothed bodies of women, all within sight of several hundred children.

Gutters were filled with rotting dead and men had come to the gutters to die, using the kerbstones as backrests.

There were 28,000 women and 11,000 men in two sections of the overcrowded camp and about 500 children.

There was bunk accommodation for only 474 women out of 1,704; acute typhus, typhoid, and T.B. cases. In addition, 18,600, women who should have been in hospital were lying on hard, bare, bug-ridden boards.

In the men's quarters there were 1,900 bunks for 2,242 acute cases.

Another 7,000 cases should have been in hospital.

"The prison Doctors tell me that cannibalism is going on the brigadier said. "There were five to seven births daily, but there was no water."

Already thousands of German prisoners have been paraded to the camp to see the conditions, the filth, disease and death of patients of all nationalities, including four British.

The first night, said the Brigadier, they had to guard the food supplies they brought to the camp with tanks to stop the starving prisoners killing themselves by over-eating, and British soldiers had to fire over their heads.

"Turnip soup was all that the Germans gave the prisoners.

"The next morning I drove round the camp with the German camp Commandant leading in a jeep. He was a typical German brute - a cruel, sadistical, heavy-featured Nazi. He was quite unashamed.

"We saw compounds filled with dead, and dying. One pit was choked with blackend bodies. There were several piles of unclothed dead.

"I saw women lying on bare boards, so weak they could hardly raise themselves on their arms to try and cheer as we went through.

"I am told that 30,000 prisoners died in the last few months and I can well believe the figure.

"One of the inmates I saw was a German Professor who had been put there for making rude remarks about Hitler.

"Naked men and women tried to keep themselves clean with dregs of coffee cups.

"Those who were too weak to fetch it had no food and died.

"Children were in comparatively good condition. The women had not spared themselves to see that the condition of the children was as comfortable as possible.

"Medical stores were quite inadequate - no vaccines, delousers, or drugs.

"THE CAMP COMMANDANT IS NOW UNDER

CLOSE ARREST."

"DAILY MIRROR"

No. 12,985. Thursday, April 19th, 1945 One Penny

"MAKE BUCHENWALD A TEMPLE OF SHAME,
AN M.P. DEMANDS."

Mr Churchill will be asked in the Commons today "whether he will take steps to ensure that the Allies come to a decision that the prison camp of Buchenwald shall be retained intact as a Memorial of German methods."

"NEWS CHRONICLE."

No. 30,873. Saturday, April 28th, 1945. One Penny

"LINK UP."

Secret is out: Americans and Russians meet at Torgau on Elbe at 4.20.pm on Wednesday. "Mussolini captured and Goering is reported shot dead."

"THE PEOPLE"

No. 3,313 64th Year. Sunday, April 29th, 1945.
  2d.

"Munich Revolt Reported, as Hitler's Empire Falls To Bits

"SURRENDER OFFER HERALDS END OF TOPPLING REICH."

Munich Revolt Mystery: Rebels seize Radio Station "Front Line Gone" - "Linked up on broad front." - "LAST HOURS IN BLAZING BERLIN."

"THEY'VE PLAYED THEIR LAST CARDS"

Goering, Goebbels, Hitler, Himmler, Mussolini: The men whose lives and actions have bequeathed to posterity a chapter of savagery and degradation without parallel in human history.

"SEARCHLIGHT ON SPORT."
by TOM MORGAN.

BRUCE WOODCOCK, England's heavyweight hope, fights Ken Shaw at Queensbury Club, London, on Wednesday.

FRANK SOO, Stoke City, and England, has been put on the transfer list, at his own request. He shouldn't be long without a club.

LEAGUE NORTH CUP.

(Third Round-Second Games.) (Aggregate scores in parentheses)

CARDIFF CITY... (2) 2.   WOLVES... (4) 1.
Hollyman,Carless.   Finch.
40,000. H.T. 2-0

CHESTERFIELD... (1) 1.   LIVERPOOL... (0) 0.
Collins.
27,000. H.T. 0-0.

MANCHESTER UNITED... (5) 3.   DONCASTER ROVERS... (2) 1.
Bodle. Wrigglesworth.(2).
30,000. H.T. 2-1

NEWCASTLE UNITED... (4) 4.   BOLTON... (5) 2.
Stubbins.(3) Milburn.   Hunt, Lofthouse.
45,000. H.T. 3-0 After extra time.

The draw for the Semi Finals of The League Cup North ties,to be played on the Home and Away principle with the first named clubs at Home on May 5th, and the return matches on May 12th was made in Preston last night. Pairings and forecast;

MANCHESTER.UNITED v Chesterfield.

WOLVERHAMPTON WANDERERS v Bolton Wanderers

"HITLER DEAD, GERMAN RADIO TELLS WORLD"

"DAILY MAIL."

No. 15,285.   One Penny   For King and Empire.   Wednesday, May 2nd 1945.

"ADMIRAL DOENITZ IS NEW FUHRER"

"THE BATTLE GOES ON."

"The Hater of Britain now rules. 1918... Insane.... 1945...Fuhrer.
By Daily Mail Reporter.

GRAND ADMIRAL KARL DOENITZ, hater of Britain, and Hitler "yes man" takes over from the man who raised him to the position of Commander in Chief of the German Navy. At one time during the last War [1914-18], Doenitz was a prisoner of war in Allied hands. We had to let him go because he was insane.

"DAILY EXPRESS"

No. 14,013   Thursday, May 3rd, 1945.   One Penny

"THE MOST TREMENDOUS NEWS NIGHT OF THE WAR."

ARMY OF 1,000,000 SURRENDERS. "HITLER AND GOEBBELS SUICIDE". HOLLAND, NORWAY END IS NEAR.

All through last night the most dramatic news of the war was pouring into "The Daily Express" office showing that the Nazi resistance is near its end;

1. The enemy army of 1,000,000 in Italy and Western Austria surrendered, yielding a vast area of the Southern Redoubt.

2. Berlin fell to the Russians. Hitler and Goebbels are reported to have committed suicide.

3. German resistance in Holland was reported over. An early surrender in Norway and Denmark is expected. 4 Large German forces seeking to escape into Denmark have been cut off by a British drive to the Baltic.

"THE DAILY SKETCH"

A Kemsley Newspaper

No. 11,223.   Tuesday, May 8th, 1945.   One Penny

THIS IS VE-DAY.

PREMIER IS TO BROADCAST AT 3.PM. TWO DAYS HOLIDAY.

An official announcement will be broadcast by the Prime Minister at three o'clock this afternoon. In view of this fact, today will be treated as VICTORY IN EUROPE DAY and will be regarded as a holiday. Tomorrow will also be a holiday.

The King will broadcast to the peoples of the British Empire and Commonwealth today at 9pm. D.B.S.T. Parliament will meet at the usual time today.

The Ministry of Information issued this pronouncement yesterday evening after a day of suspense and excitement as the world waited for the official end to the war in Europe.

JODL SIGNS AT EISENHOWER'S H.Q.

For Germany the war ended at 2.41 am yesterday when General Jodl, German Army Chief of Staff, signed the first instrument signifying his country's unconditional surrender at the little red school house in Rheims which is General Eisenhower's headquarters.

General Bedell Smith, Eisenhower's Chief of Staff, signed for the Supreme Allied Command, according to an account of the ceremony broadcast by New York Radio.

General Ivan Susloparov signed for Russia and General Francois Sevez for France.

The German emissaries were asked several times if they understood the significance of the seriousness of the terms, and each time said they did.

When the signing was completed General Jodl said:

"WITH THIS SIGNATURE THE GERMAN PEOPLE, FOR BETTER OR FOR WORSE, ARE DELIVERED INTO THE VICTOR'S HANDS.

"THE DAILY SKETCH."

A Kemsley Newspaper.

No. 11,224.   Wednesday, May 9th, 1945.   One Penny.

"THEY SHARED OUR ORDEALS - NOW THEY

REJOICE WITH US."

From a balcony at Buckingham Palace The King and Queen, accompanied by Princess Elizabeth and Princess Margaret, smile and wave at the cheering crowd, many thousands strong.

"AFTER THE SURRENDER."

On Monday, May 7th, at 2.41am, Germany surrendered unconditionally to the Allies at Rheims. Colonel General Gustav Jodl, the new German Army Chief of Staff, signed for Germany, and General Bedell Smith (U.S.A.), for the Supreme Allied Command. In attendance at the signing were: Col. Zikovitch (Russia.), Gen Suslaparov (Russia), Gen. Bedell Smith (U.S.A.), Gen. Eisenhower, Air Chief Marshal Tedder (U.K.), Admiral Burrow (U.K.), Gen. Spaatz (U.S.A., Gen Sevez (France).

"MONTY SAYS: Now Win the Peace"

"We have won the German War. Let us now Win the Peace." said Field Marshal Montgomery in a personal victory message issued last night to all ranks under his command. "We all have a great feeling of joy and thankfulness that we have been preserved to see this day." said the message. "We must remember to give the praise and thankfulness where it is due. This is The Lord's doing, and it is marvellous in our eyes."

"Let us never forget what we owe to our Russian and American Allies. This great Allied team has achieved much in the War. May it achieve even more in Peace.

"Without doubt, great problems lie ahead. The World will not recover quickly from the upheaval that has taken place. There is much work for each of us.

" It may be some difficult times lie ahead for our country, for each one of us personally.

"If it happens, then our discipline will pull us through. But we must remember that the best discipline implies the subordination of self for the benefit of the community.

"And so let us embark on what lies ahead full of joy and optimism. GOOD LUCK TO YOU ALL."

The War with Germany was over, finished, and so the whole might of the Allied Forces could now turn its attention to the War against

the Japanese.

Nobody in their wildest imagination could have suspected how soon after V-E Day would come V-J.Day?

"THE EVENING NEWS"

No. 19,752.   London. Wednesday May 23rd, 1945.   One Penny

"THE GOVERNMENT RESIGNS."

Mr Churchill gives the King his decision: Caretakers to be chosen in next few days. Nine major offices have to be filled.

In a 45 minute talk with the King at Buckingham Palace this afternoon, Mr Churchill tendered his resignation as Prime Minister and asked for the dissolution of Parliament.

U.S. GIVES JAPS A WARNING. "Quit or DEVASTATION."

Japan has now been solemnly warned that the only alternative to unconditional surrender is destruction on a greater scale than that which Germany brought on herself.

The U.S.Office of War Information is telling the Japanese people, "with the highest Government backing." says B.U.P, "that they must make peace on our terms or take the consequences.

At the same time a statement that Singapore and Japan itself lie open to Allied attacks was made by President Trueman in a report to Congress.

" Hard won victories have been paving the way for the final assault against the Japanese forces on the Asiatic mainland and the homeland of Japan." he said.

"NEWS CHRONICLE." 4am Edition.

No. 30,492.   Thursday, July 19th, 1945.   One Penny.

"TOKYO BAY FORTS ARE SHELLED BY ALLIED FLEET."
Carrier planes attack ships hidden in base.

"WASHINGTON DENIES JAP PEACE RUMOUR."

"DAILY EXPRESS."

NO: 14,094.   Tuesday, August 7th, 1945.   One Penny.
TOP SECRET.

24th JULY 1945.

MEMORANDUM FOR GENERAL ARNOLD.

SUBJECT: Groves Project.

1.   The following plan and schedule for initial attacks using special bombs have been worked out.

"DAILY EXPRESS."

No. 14,094   Tuesday, August 7th, 1945   One Penny

SMOKE HIDES CITY 16 HOURS AFTER GREATEST SECRET WEAPON STRIKES.

"THE BOMB THAT HAS CHANGED THE WORLD."

"JAPS TOLD NOW QUIT"

The Allies disclosed last night that they have used against Japan the most fearful device of War yet produced - an ATOMIC BOMB.

It was dropped at 20 minutes past midnight, London time, yesterday on the Japanese port of HIROSHIMA, 190 miles west of Kobe.

The City was blotted out by a cloud of dust and smoke. Sixteen hours later reconnaissance pilots were still waiting for the cloud to lift to let them see what had happened.

THE BOMB WAS A LAST WARNING. Now leaflets will tell the Japanese what to expect unless their Government surrenders.

So great will be the devastation if they do not surrender that Allied forces may be able to invade without opposition.

"20,000 TONS IN GOLF BALL."

One Atomic bomb has a destructive force equal to that of 20,000 tons of T.N.T., or five 1,000 plane raids. This terrific power is packed in a space of little more than golf ball size.

Experts estimate that the bomb can destroy anything on the surface in an area of at least two square miles - twice the size of The City of London.

When it was tested after being assembled in a farmhouse in the remote desert of New Mexico, a steel tower used for the experiment vapourised; two men standing nearly six miles away were blown down; blast effect was felt 300 miles away.

And, at Albuquerque, a hundred and twenty miles away a blind girl cried "What is that?" when the flash lightened the sky before the explosion could be heard.

"PLANE KIDNAPS SCIENTIST."

Snatched from the Nazis to help us.

A Dane who was smuggled into Britain and two Germans who were hounded out of their Country helped the Allies to perfect the Atom bomb.

PROFESSOR NIELS BOHR is the Dane; one of the men who isolated the rare form of uranium known as U.235. When the Nazis invaded Denmark they wanted him to carry on the atomic research that had won him the Nobel Prize. HIS ANSWER - he closed his laboratory and vanished "underground." The Gestapo hunted him. In October 1943 Resistance men whisked him past the Gestapo into Sweden. Twelve days he stayed in Sweden; protected by squads of Swedish police from the ever-hunting agents and the Gestapo. A Mosquito flew through the "German Air" over Norway to pick up the professor and bring him to England. Here, and later, in the U.S.A. Professor Bohr and his colleagues worked on the problems of the atom bomb, their whereabouts always secret, their laboratories always guarded. Professor Bohr is in Britain now; his whereabouts are no longer secret. He is in London.

TWO GERMANS

PROFESSOR RUDOLPH PEIRERLS and DR FRANZ EUGENSINON are the Germans; Berlin Jews who fled from Hitler's persecution and re-paid Britain for her sanctuary. Professor Peirerls has been Professor of Applied Mathematics at BIRMINGHAM UNIVERSITY since 1937. Other scientists who worked on the bomb were; SIR GEORGE PAGET THOMSON, 53,Professor of Physics, Imperial College of Science since 1930. A widower with two sons, two daughters; lives in Stanley Gardens, Notting Hill Gate, W, likes ski-ing and sailing. MR.WALLACE ALAN AKERS, 57, is a Director of I.C.I.; educated Lake House School, Bexhill, Aldenham School, and Christ Church, Oxford. A bachelor-yachtsman. Lives at the Royal Thames Yacht Club.

TWINS

SIR JAMES CHADWICK, Professor of Physics at Liverpool University. He started in science in 1932 by discovering an uncharged particle, the neutron, which completely changed conceptions of the constitution matter. He is a Nobel Prize Winner. Married 1925, has twin daughters.

PROFESSOR. J.D. COCKCROFT, Jacksonian Professor of Natural Philosophy, Cambridge. Thirteen years ago he broke up the atom by machinery, heralding the use of atomic energy for war. He is 48, married, and has a son and four daughters.

PROFESSOR NORMAN FEATHER of The Cavandish Laboratory, Cambridge, claims he split the oxygen atom; first man to do it, in 1932.

LORD CHERWELL, until 1941 Professor Frederick Alexander Lindemann, Professor of Experimental Philosophy at Oxford since 1919 and Mr Churchill's personal assistant in 1940.

"THIS ENDS WAR AS WE KNOW IT." The Allied discovery ends war as we know it, because not only bombs, but torpedoes, gun shells and infantry weapons can be filled with atomic explosive.

Here is the principal; when the atomic bomb strikes the ground a mechanism causes the uranium in it to disintegrate into millions of particles with enormous energy, moving at speeds like 186,000 miles a second. These bombarding particles coupled with the sudden liberation of terrific heat cause a catastrophic explosion,

The bomb probably contains less than an ounce of the rare metal uranium,which like radium,is constantly casting off high speed particles, but in small numbers.

What the scientists have done is to find a way of setting free all the locked up energy at once. The World's supply of uranium is very small. But using an apparatus called the cyclotron, scientists at Cambridge have been able to give to other substances the properties of the uranium. No battleship could stand a near miss from an atomic bomb. No plane could last in a sky of bursting atomic A.A. shells. Tank armour could never be made to withstand the impact of a Piat bomb filled with new explosive.

One ounce of atomic explosive probably liberates more energy in a flash than can be drawn from Niagara Falls in a week.

Surely, however, the most important newspapers of the world were the one's issued on SEPTEMBER 3rd 1945 which told the world that we were at PEACE at last after six years to the date of bitter fighting, bloodshed, atrocities, and trauma brought about by MAN'S BIGGEST ENEMY:GREED. Whether it be greed for MONEY, POWER, REVENGE, or so many other aspects of this horrible state, that's what all these conflict's, and wars are about. Oh they might conjure up all kinds of reasons, and some of them appear to be quite legitimate, but never the less it all concludes to that one word GREED! This very happy day for all humanity, both us and the enemy, because I never forget that all Germans, Japanese and Italians weren't in agreement with their particular dictators, or emperors or whatever government they were under, and so they were as relieved as we were to see their men come home, and to resume a peaceful life. I will complete this scant update of the 1939-1945 War with the headlines, and part report of the END with the cover the "Daily Mail" gave:

"DAILY MAIL."

NO:15,390.   ONE PENNY.   FOR.KING.and.EMPIRE.
MONDAY.SEPTEMBER.3rd.1945.

****

MACARTHUR.SIGNS.FOR.THE.VICTORS.WITHOUT.A.GLANCE.AT.HIS. ENEMIES.

****

END.OF.WAR. DAILY.MAIL.MAN.SEES.SURRENDER.

****

11.Japanese hand over Dead.Empire

****

From: GRAHAM.STANFORD.

Daily Mail Pacific Bureau Correspondent. Aboard U.S.S. Missouri, FLAGSHIP OF THE THIRD FLEET, Tokio Bay, Sunday.

As hundreds of American and British fighter planes roared over their heads,11 men of Japan stepped slowly down the gangway of this ship this morning to join an American destroyer and sail back to their shattered capital.

There were four soldiers without swords or sabres, three sailors who have lost their ships, and four frock-coated diplomats who are now without diplomatic rights.

They walked alone, and with them carried a document - their unconditional surrender to the Allies. It was a symbolic "curtain" to the surrender ceremony.

It was a curtain so drastically rung down that it brought gasps of surprise from scores of Allied generals, admirals, and other high ranking officers who had crowded on the veranda deck of Admiral Halsey's flagship to witness the ceremony.

WARNING IN THE SKY

As the ceremony closed and the words of General MacArthur's prayer for peace were dying away, squadrons of planes appeared in the sky, and as if in warning to all future warmakers passed over the ship as the Japanese delegates were leaving.

These 11 men - representing the Emperor of Japan, the Imperial Japanese Government, and the Japanese people of this beaten country - had stood lonely and uneasy on the deck of this battleship while the official ceremony of their surrender was carried out.

Before them wearing no decorations, but just a plain khaki uniform and his well-worn campaign hat, had stood General Douglas MacArthur, Supreme Allied Commander.

He had given orders where they should stand. He called them forward to sign the surrender document, and when it was over he dismissed them with scarcely a glance, and they went away, led by their elderly one-legged Foreign Minister, Mr. Mamoru Shigemitsu, and General Yoshijiro, Chief of the Japanese Staff.

With a broad smile Admiral Sir Bruce Fraser, C.in.C. British Pacific Fleet, came aboard with other officers who had been fighting side by side with the Third Fleet.

They all wore white shorts and short sleeved tunics, in contrast with the dark Army uniform of the Russian representatives.

As soon as he came aboard Vice-Admiral Sir Bernard Rawlings, Commander, British Task Force, asked what had happened to the Chippendale-style table which he had given for signing the surrender.

He had offered the table because there was no wooden furniture aboard U.S. ships.

At the last moment it was found that the table was too small, so a larger steel table was produced and covered with gold trimmed green baize.

JOKES, THEN

In half an hour more than one hundred high ranking officers of the United States, United Kingdom, Russia, China, Australia, Canada, France, New Zealand, and the Netherlands, were packed like sardines on a small veranda balcony. There was a lot of back slapping, and joking as on the deck below the ship's band played martial music.

Then, on the stroke of 8.30 the deck was cleared, a crowd of Allied Officers formed up in groups around the deck, and left in the middle was a small bare stretch for the surrender table and a microphone.

213

More than 100 Allied Army, Navy, and Air Force officers and 350 War Correspondents were gathered around this small "island of deck" and it was here that 11 men from Japan would stand.

The report by Graham Stanford went on in all its wonderful coverage to commemorate this most auspicious occasion, and it described in detail every aspect of this surrender by the Japanese, and marked the end of this terrible war. But, did it have the desired effect in later years? No, of course it didn't; everyone knows that without me telling them. On the front of one daily paper at the finish of the war was a drawing of a soldier, battered, weary, and bewildered, standing on a map of Europe, and he was handing the nation a piece of paper with these words on it: HERE YOU ARE, AND MAKE SURE YOU DON'T LOSE IT AGAIN.

Well I must admit that to date we have not in the strictest sense been in danger of losing Europe again, but just for the record, and a very scant record, let us go through what has happened since 3rd September 1945,on the Monday that Japan surrendered.

We had "The Suez" incident, Korea, Vietnam, Malaya, Cyprus, The Six Day War " between Israel and Egypt, the Cuba incident, the Falklands, the Gulf War, and so many other wars or conflicts which you the reader will probably remember. Man seems to stumble blindly through this precious life of ours, making one mistake after another, and it's always the innocent bystanders that appear to get the worst "end of the stick." Perhaps it's a great plan by the Almighty, but I don't really believe that. Anyway enough of my moaning. The World was rejoicing about the Peace we had all got, both enemy and victor. We had now got the vast task of rebuilding again.

Three dates of utmost significance at the end of the thirties, and the beginning of the forties: "The Day War Started, 3rd September 1939, Sunday", Victory over Europe Day, Tuesday May 8th 1945 and Victory over Japan Day, Monday 3rd September 1945; but in "The Smith Household there was another most significant date, the 20th August 1945. However, I won't jump the gun, so let's go back now that I've given you a scant run down on the procedure of the war, and its final conclusion.

Stan, my mate from Smethwick, joined the Royal Navy sometime in November 1944, and as instructed I was taken off my wholesale round and transferred onto No 8 round. The round itself caused no problems; in fact it was the best round I had been on so far. The tips were good, better than any other, and the customers were so kind in every aspect. They soon got used to me, and I certainly got used to them. Mind you, Stan was a hard act to follow, he was a real smashin' bloke. Never the less I felt as though I was being used by the dairy. These thoughts nagged at me constantly, until in the end just after my 17th Birthday in January 1945, which of course made me eligible to join the forces, I decided to do something about it - not necessarily the right thing, but I wanted to show Handsworth Dairies, and all who ran it that I was fed up with being shunted around, being "knocked from pillar to post", so I decided that first I would go and ask for a rise. I was still only getting 27/6d per week, and had all the responsibility of a much larger round, which in turn meant that I was working more hours, especially on a Saturday when I collected the customers' money in.

I came in on one of the week days, having had a pretty awful day. I started late, but that was my fault really I wouldn't get up when 'Our Mom' called me. Being late getting up caused further trouble when I went onto 'The Brook' to catch the bus. I wasn't going to work on my bike was I? It was bloody well pouring with rain. I got into the bus shelter outside 'The Watt' right opposite 'The Palladium' and found that the queue was a mile long, whereas I normally boarded the bus quite easily at my normal time.

Finally, I squeezed my way onto the crowded 'Leyland Cub' and we made slow progress up to 'The New Inns.' Of course this threw me late throughout the day, and I was not feeling in the best of moods when I arrived back at the dairy. Having put 'Danny' into his stall, and taking the harness into the tack room, I had definitely decided that this was the day for putting my plan into action.

Off I went in a pretty awful temper to the upper office, and I asked the girl behind the paying in desk if I could see someone about my wages. She informed me to wait and disappeared into another room. After a while, she came back, and opened a door at the side of the partition and invited me in. Now this action deterred me somewhat, because I had never been behind the paying in desk before, and consequently it gave me the feeling of attending the Doctor's, a thing which no-one liked those day's. I was nervous, and uneasy as I entered another small room beyond the front pay desk. There behind a huge desk was the portly but smartly dressed Mr. Arnold White. His cowgown was spotless white, his shirt and tie immaculate. I felt that I had violated the inner sanctum of a church. My belly rolled and made funny noises, and continued to do so when Mr. White spoke. "Now what's the problem son?" he started smiling at me; never asked me to sit down. It made me feel awkward standing there in front of him. I felt as though I had been summoned to see Mr. Locker or Mr. Margerrison, two of my headmasters. I didn't say anything for a moment, and he went on, in rather a sterner pitch, "Now come on lad, spit it out, what do you want? I haven't got all day you know."

This made me a little bit more angry, so I blurted out "Warr ri wan sir is mowa money, tha's warr ri want. I ain' 'ad a rise since o bin werkin' 'ere, an o wan' some mowa monee." I ran out of steam. I had said what I wanted to say, too quickly and in the wrong way. Never the less I had said it, and at that moment that was all I wanted to do, tell him.

He didn't say a word for quite a while; he just looked at me, with a sarcastic smile on his face - that's all, just this smile. After a few moments, which seemed like an eternity to me he suddenly leant forward and pulled open one of the drawers in the desk, and extracted a sheaf of well worn papers. Settling once more into his comfortable chair, he commenced to look through these papers, with me standing there like a complete 'nana'. Well I couldn't say anything could I? I think that I had said it all, already. I was however very uncomfortable.

"Ah, here we are." said Mr. Arnold, suddenly. He pushed a sheet of paper across to me from the bundle. "Read that son, and you will understand the reason why we can't give you any more money."

"Why can' ya tell mi, oi'll belive ya'?" I replied quickly, not wanting to read through a lot of paraphernalia. Another pause, and then, "Well son that's the direct orders from The Ministry of Works, which explains to both the Employer and the Employee, and part of these orders are that there is a scale for all workers of a particular age. It runs from 14 to 65, and that's the scale of pay, believe me son we are paying you the proper rate, alright?"

Well, what could I say, I had to believe him, but it didn't do anything for my anger at Handsworth Dairies. I thought "They were a bleedin' lorra twisters" - that's what my immediate thoughts were.

I mumbled a quick "thank ya'," and I left the office hurriedly, but not so quick that I didn't notice the smug grin on Mr. White's, face. I went down those wooden stairs in a blind rage, passing people who said " 'ello Ronnie" and ignoring them. I was so mad at the world in general, that I went to get my bike, only to realise that when I got to the stall where I kept it that I had indeed come to work on the bus.

It hadn't been a good day. On the way home, when I had settled down on top of the bus, and lit a cigarette, to calm my nerves, I suddenly decided what I would do. I smiled to myself and thought "I'll kill two birds wi' one stone, tha's warr I'll do." By the time I'd reached 228 I was feeling a whole lot better.

The following week after I had made some discreet enquiries, I went up to Dalton Street, just off Corporation Street, nearly opposite the Law Courts, and entered the Recruiting Office. I went in and talked to some bloke in Army uniform, and said "Is this the plerce were yo' cun join the Nervy mert?"

I don't think this bloke took too kindly to this request really, his face went a little red, just as if he'd had too much booze on the dinner time. He stared at me, and then informed me that this was The Army Recruiting Office, and made some unkind gesture about my eyesight, which I ignored, and went on, "Well mert w'ere cun o gu ta gerrin the Nervy then?"

I don't think he really wanted to tell me, for in the next instance he was trying to get me to join the army. I wasn't having any of this though, I'd had enough of Mr. Arnold White, telling me what to do, and I wasn't having any more of that nonsense.

"O don' wanna gu in the Army, an' it don' marra 'ow lung ya' gu on, yo' wun mek mi change mi mind." I said finally.

After much to-ing and fro-ing, he reluctantly gave me a leaflet on His Majesty's Royal Navy. On the front of the leaflet, stamped over a picture of a destroyer cutting swiftly through the water, were the words "Join the Royal Navy now, and see the World." was the address of the recruiting office. it was miles away from Dalton Street, right up Broad Street by Five Ways, in Bishopgate Street.

I walked out of the Army Recruiting Office and thought to myself, "Well they wun bi yopen now; bi the time ov gorrup thaya, so o wun' gu terday, o'll gu lerta." With that I wended my way home to 228.

Quite a few day's later - and need I say I was feeling a sight better than that day when I saw Mr. White, I was unloading my empties, and there was this tall lanky guy in front doing the same thing. I knew him but only by sight, not to speak to. "Warrow" he said to me, and I returned the greeting in much the same way but added nothing. After unloading, and putting our respective horses away, we met again in the tack room. Mrs Thomas was in there busy, and when I went in with 'Danny's' harness she said "Would you like a cuppa as well Ronnie, I am just making Bob a cup?"

"Whoa thanks eva sa much Mrs Thomas, O would please." I put Danny's harness up on its peg and returned to the wooden table where Mrs Thomas did the harness cleaning, and sat down by this lanky bloke, Bob.

We sat there and chatted about this and that, Mrs. Thomas, Bob, and myself, when eventually we ran out of things to talk about, and I think it was this that made me tell them of my deep secret. "Om thinkin' o guin in the Nervy." I blurted out, and then waited for the reaction. Mrs Thomas said "Oh Ron, not you as well, nearly all the young men have gone away now, are you sure that's what you want to do love?"

"Well om fed o werkin' 'ere, not cuz o the werk, o like that, burrive bin up an' sin Arnold forra rise, an' 'e wun gi mi one 'e sez it's through the gover'ment, burr ri think 'e don' wanna gi mi yenny mowa munnee, tha's warr I think."

"Ar rive bin thinkin' the serm," said Bob. "W'en ya' guin' ta see yabourrit mate?"

"Well ov got the address w'ere ta gu, an' o thought o might gu the sarta, an' see 'em."

"D' ya' mind if o cum wi' ya', Ron, tha's ya' nerm innit?"

"Ar-r-r tha's right, an yome Bob, narr, o don' mind ya' comin; shall wi' gu now?"

"Ar-r-rokay Ron, we'll gu now."

So it was that Bob Jones (I found out his surname whilst having a cigarette with him on the bus into town) and I went to the 'Fanny Brown' to join up. I had gone on my bike that morning, and I suggested that he (Bob) and I go to Bishopgate Street on our bikes, but unfortunately Bob hadn't got a bike, so that was out. What we did do however was, I walked home with Bob to his house in Church Terrace, and left my bike there. I found that he lived about two doors up from my pal Joe, and indeed Bob knew him well, and we had a bit of a natter about that. Bob's Mom was a small woman, beautiful and sparkling, the type that looked as if they were smiling constantly. We had a cup of tea, Bob didn't say where he was going, just that we were going out together that afternoon, so it was that we went by bus. The intention was that on completion of joining up - for we had no idea about the procedure; we could have been thrown into the Royal Navy that same day for all we knew about it - I would return to Church Terrace and retrieve my 'Kingsway,' and then travel back to 'The Brook.'

We arrived in town, then caught a No. 7 Portland Road bus from Colmore Row, which dropped us off at Five Ways. Bob and I then walked slowly back down from the bus stop to Bishopgate Street which was on the right-hand side coming from Hagley Road. Turning right we then commenced to search for the Recruiting Office. This didn't take long, for the notices outside this ornate building, that looked like, and probably was, an old church hall, were evident for anyone to see. Notices with ships of all types on, and sailors, resplendent in their different types of uniform, telling everyone how splendid it would be for you to join The Royal Navy. All the different types of jobs that you could apply for, all presented by skilled artists, making the most menial jobs in the Navy, seem like paradise.

We went up the few steps leading to the main reception area, where we met a man resplendent in uniform, but what a uniform. Forage cap with gold badge on the front, smartly pressed jacket and trousers, with gold buttons, and a further gold badge on either lapel, and round the sleeve of each arm were three golden buttons. On the left side of this man's chest, high up, were about three rows of medal ribbons. We were impressed. I don't know what Bob was thinking, but I could see myself walking into 'Ma Davies's' one dark night, with this bloke's beautiful uniform on, and telling all the mob in there all my adventures whilst at sea (?).

"Yes, lads, and what can we do for you then?" the uniformed man spoke up, looking at us with a broad grin on his face. "Wiv cum ta join the nervy mista," we both mumbled together.

"Come on then lads, just come on in here, and let's see what we can do for you eh?"

"Thanks mista" we still mumbled, completely in awe of this man, and the whole surroundings.

All three of us walked into a room at the rear of the reception area, the man went behind a big desk, and sat down, inviting us to do the same on a couple of chairs the other side of him. " Right lads, my name is Chief Petty Officer... (I've forgotten his name now.) so you want to join His Majesty's Royal Navy, eh?"

"Yes sir, please," we again both mumbled. We had also changed the 'mista' to 'sir', after he had mentioned the word 'officer'.

Altogether we spent about an hour with the 'chief' whilst he took particulars of what we were doing at present, what we did at school, and more to the point what we wanted to do once we gained entrance into the Royal Navy. On completion of these questions and answers, he gave us each a form with all our particulars on. handed us an additional card with an appointment for a medical examination.

Bob and I walked slowly from the Bishopgate Recruiting Office studying the forms the Chief Petty Officer had given us. To my surprise I found that I had got to go back to the recruiting office in Dalton Street for this medical examination, which I didn't fancy much due to my first visit there, and the look the bloke behind the counter had given me. But on the other hand I wanted to join the navy so much that I put this thought into the back of my mind very quickly.

"W'at dert 'ave yo' got fer yarr rappointment with the Doc Ron?" Bob enquired. I looked at the little card that was given to me last and found to my surprise that I wasn't due to see the medical board until early March, which to me seemed an eternity away. I wasn't too happy about that; still, on the other hand I thought, at least I have got an appointment. I told Bob the date, and he was a bit choked for his wasn't until after mine, and mentally I smiled to myself in a smug way. So we had no option but to wait.

As you know the war was going very well for the Allies, and I began to wonder if I would get into the 'Andrew' whilst it was still on. Obviously I had told Danny, Pat, and Joe, and they all enthused over it, but at the same time expressed that they were going to miss me. It was however Danny who it would hit the most for we had set up a kind of deep friendship between us, and we talked long and deep after we had parted from the other two one night. It had been 'man's talk,' and how he wished that he was coming into the navy with me, but wondered if he would make it due to a defect in one of his ears.

Eventually the date for my medical arrived, so I donned 'mi Sundee best' with 'you know who' looking on a little curiously, due to it only being in the middle of the week. "W'ere yo' guin' all bloody poshed up our Ronnie," she asked. I just smiled and replied, "Ov gorra wench ta see Mom, an' she 'as We'nsdee artanoon orff, so we thought wid gu up ta the club (the Y.W.C.A. in Soho Hill) an' 'ave a dance, okay?" I lied easily, for I was now so determined to join the navy, that I found that I could do anything I wanted. "Ar-r-r, but chow bi carefull owa Ronnie guin' out wi' all them wenchis, don' yo' gu gerrin inta any trouble now will ya'?"

I naturally hadn't got a clue as to what she was talking about, but the answer came natural, "Cor's o wunt Mom, I'll bi yoright, 'onist o will, so don' worry, right?" and with that I departed rather quickly, ran down to 'The Brook' and caught the bus to town.

I looked around this large room, which reminded me of rather a large 'gent's toilet.' Along both sides were partitions, similar to those we use for horses up at the dairy, but in my mind I scaled them down to look like the partitions used for men to urinate in. I smiled at this thought, and considered what a smart chap I was.

"Yes, what can I do for you ?" She was a very pretty and pleasant lady who made this enquiry. She sat behind a rather large wooden desk in a partitioned area at the front of this large urinal. I had, had my first view of this through the large glass windows immediately behind this lady's desk. Also in view were several white coated men, coming out of one cubicle into another also blokes, in varying stages of undress, were walking from one cubicle to another. Again I thought to myself, this will give me a chance to show off my 'muscular body.' This, of course, was the period in my life when I had begun to really fancy my chances, and consequently thought I really was 'the cat's whiskers.' Don't we all go through this period?

"Ov come fer ra medicul examinachun ma'am," I replied, and handed her the card, which I had kept in my cowgown, since it was originally handed to me by the 'Chief.' Consequently it was a little grubby, to say the least, but the lady behind the desk didn't refer to the state of the card, she just went ahead, and put the particulars down on yet another piece of paper. Then she asked me a few more questions about my own doctor etc, and finally bade me to sit down on a long wooden bench, which had already got one or two other occupants. I sat down, and naturally started to natter to the other blokes, asking what we intended to go in, and what we wanted to do - the usual type of conversation people had when waiting their turn for something of the unknown to happen. I suppose this kind of conversation was to bolster one's courage for this unknown thing really. We sat there for what seemed an eternity when all of a sudden a most distinguished looking gentleman in an immaculate white coat opened the door leading to 'the toilets' (as I'd decided to name the area for examinations), and said in a very posh, and quiet voice, "Mr Smith - Mr. Ronald William James Smith?"

This surprised me quite a lot, due to the fact that these other guys had been sitting there when I came in, so consequently I didn't think it fair for me to go before them, and I gave them a facial expression to prove what my thoughts were. They gave a silent shrug of their shoulders, to intimate I suppose: "Well they must know what they are doing."

I got up from the bench, and said "Yes Sir, I'm Ron Smith." He looked at me, and continued "Come with me Mr. Smith," and I followed him along the middle of the cubicles until he stopped and indicated the one he wanted me to go into. "Just take your clothes off in there, and I will be back in a moment." he told me.

Now to tell me to take all my clothes of was tantamount to telling a conductor on the Birmingham Corporation Omnibus and Tramway's to conduct the Birmingham Symphony Orchestra. This was the first time that anyone, other than the Friday night bath in Guest Street, had requested me to do this.

"All ov them, sir?" I asked the gentleman, as he was about to depart to some other part of the toilets. He smiled and replied "Yes, all of them, now don't be shy, no-one is going to come in there who isn't entitled to, and we have to examine you if you want to go into the services, don't we?"

"Well, yes sir, o suppose yo' 'ave burr I dain 'spect ta 'ave ta tek all mi clo'se orff, still, never mind…"

The man left me to get on with what he had requested, and needless to say I didn't like this part of the procedure one bit. No-one, but no-one, had ever seen me in the 'nod,' except 'Our Mom' of course an' she dain' count did she?,I thought. I felt myself going hot and cold as I first removed my outer garments, and arranged them carefully on the chair, which was situated besides a small table. I had never worn underwear in my life, and naturally didn't feel the necessity for it. Like I said when I went to school, "on'y cissies wore clo'se unda their trousis."

I had removed everything but my trousers, and at this point I wondered whether going into the Royal Navy was worth all of these sacrifices, I thought at one time, I know, I'll put all my clothes back on and run out of here, and forget all about it. I was in the midst of these thoughts when all of a sudden a screech brought me out of my reverie. The screech proved to be the curtain of the cubicle being drawn back, and in came the original gentleman, with another man, who looked equally as distinguished.

"Right lad get the rest of your clothes off, and then get onto the bed," the first gentleman said. I was, I must admit, in awe of anyone like this so off came the trousers, and my shyness was completely forgotten. I threw the trousers on top of the neat pile I had made of my other clothes, and hopped quickly onto the stiff beautifully white sheet, that covered the hardness of the bed itself.

Then it all started, with first the man, and then the other, poking here and poking there, and saying things like "Breath in, and out. cough, bend your knee over the other one," and then hitting it with what I could only describe as the tom tom stick of a set of drums.

This all went on for a while and then the first gentleman said, "Alright, Mr Smith, we have finished with you now, so get dressed." They then started to write something down on another form of some sort. I did as the gentleman had told me, and when finished I waited for him to complete the form, and when this was done he handed it to me and then took me out of the cubicle, and pointed to another, instructing me to go in there and wait.

This I did, and some other gentleman came, and examined my teeth, then this procedure went on, with men in white coats examining every part, and crevice of my body. This went quite well until I came to the eyesight test. The man placed me on a high chair, similar to that one would put a new baby into, and then he dimmed the lights in the area. He then messed around a bit first putting this light on, and then dimming that one, until at last he seemed satisfied with his efforts.

"Right lad, now tell me what you can see on that board over there," and he pointed in the direction of the far wall. Now I've heard jokes told by several comedians, exactly the same as I'm going to relate now, but with one vast difference, and that difference was, simply, that this was the whole truth!

"What board?" I replied.

"That board over there, look."

"I can't see any board," I went on innocently. (I bet he re-told that comment a few times to his colleagues.) "You cannot see the board lad?" he went on.

"No, I'm sorry sir, I can't."

I knew that something was radically wrong, and I had a funny feeling come over me; thoughts of not being able to go into the Royal Navy after all, just because I couldn't see some silly board. The gentleman, now convinced that I really couldn't see the board, came across to me and fitted a heavy frame on my nose, and then attached two arms over my ears, and I really panicked then. "On'y cissies wore glasses" was my first thought, and then I thought "Ov neva sin a sailor in glasses, burr I ain guin' in anythin' else, so there." The gentleman then fitted some glass into the front of the frames and kept asking if I could see anything. At first it was very difficult for me, first it went blurred more, and then it seemed to clear. All of a sudden, everything became so crystal clear I could not believe my eyes. It was impossible, I thought, that this man could put a piece of glass in front of my eyes and "Hey presto!" everything became alive. For the first time that I can ever remember I could see every little item.

"I can see!" I shouted out, "I can see!"

"That's good," the man replied, ignoring my loud exclamation. Now let's see what we can do to make it a little more permanent, shall we?"

He messed around with these glasses for a while and then he asked me again to read the board. I looked across at it and not only could I see it, but I could read the last line. I thought that I had come across a miracle. I just couldn't believe that I'd gone through life so far without the aid of these magic lenses.

The gentleman who had performed this miracle, put me through several other tests and seemed to be happy regarding those. Again papers were filled in, and I moved onto the next man in white.

On completion of the examinations I again returned to the lady in the foyer. She asked my name, and then said that she had made an appointment for me to visit an optician in Newhall Street for a date in early May, which I again thought to be an eternity away. Still I couldn't grumble I suppose, I reasoned with myself that they wouldn't go to all this trouble if they weren't going to accept me into the service. Never the less, I still worried.

I didn't see Bob Jones around, which I was glad of, due to the fact that it would save me explaining to him the business with the "glassis bloke." However, before I'd had the opportunity of going to the optician's in Newhall Street the war in Europe was over - and what a time Danny, Pat, Joe, and myself had on the night of the 8th May 1945. I went to work as usual (when didn't Handsworth Dairies work?), but throughout my deliveries I witnessed people preparing their particular roads, and streets for the forthcoming celebrations. Barrels of beer became evident, and food appeared as though there had never been a shortage.

As I went round Grafton Road, Hollycroft Road, Astley Road, Aylsford Road, Antrobus Road, Grove Lane, Grove Hill Road, Phillip Victor Road, Hinstock Road, Brunswick Road, Brunswick Gardens, Albert Road, Herbert Road, which were all the roads on No 8 round, there was not a thoroughfare that wasn't preparing for a good 'knees up' that night. in some cases when I arrived with the milk, they were - and this was evident too - already starting the celebrations.

It was,without doubt the most wonderful day I have ever in my life witnessed.

Everybody, and I mean everybody was in a party mood; it was the most wonderful day ever. Naturally, alcoholic drinks were offered to me, but I didn't drink them. Never the less I shared the mood of the people on this most glorious day with a cup of tea here, and a cup of tea there, so by the time I'd finished my round on Tuesday the 8th of May 1945, my cup runneth over, and the toilet was in much demand.

I met Danny, Pat and Joe on the evening, and we went 'walk abouts' around the Handsworth district, and I assure you, that if we had taken a drink in those days we could have got drunk a dozen times over. The people throughout Gt Britain must have been so confident of us winning the war from the very start by the mere fact that so much food was produced, and drinks as well that they must have been storing it for a very long time, expecting this day to arrive.

Musicians suddenly appeared to make up small bands, which the people, not necessarily from their particular road, or street, could dance to. Piano's had been dragged out of houses by the score,and everywhere us four went that night we were invited to dance, and take part in the merriment. One lady I remember very well, was dancing in the middle of Victoria Road, Handsworth, in between Queens Head Road and Babington Road. She was dancing alone, and had a huge frying pan situated down the front of her frock, and presumably her drawers, but I was never to find out was inviting all and sundry to have a kick at it, whatever 'it' was.

Yes, everybody was so happy that night, it was such a wonderful time for all the peoples of the oppressed nations, and the end of Hitler and Mussolini. We had only got Tojo to dispense with, and the peace that we had been looking forward to for so long would be complete. Yes, that's one night that I - and I hope Danny, Pat, and Joe, wherever they may be - enjoyed to the full. It was well past midnight - in fact it was nearly dawn - when I finally arrived back at 228, exhausted, but very happy. Happy to have taken part on such an auspicious occasion.

My appointment came for me to attend the optician in Newhall Street. I was, to say the least, slightly disinterested about the whole thing now. Oh I know it was wicked of me to think such things, but as I've said before they were the thoughts of immaturity. Like all other young men I had seen too many Errol Flynn, John Wayne, Leslie Howard, Jack Hawkins, and John Mills films, and that's how we thought the war was. We desperately wanted to be in on the action, not realising of course what the real action was.

As I approached Newhall Street my feet dragged somewhat. I took the card with my appointment out of my pocket to check the exact address, and in doing so I noticed words that I hadn't noticed before, which made me think again about the possibility of just turning around going home and forgetting the whole thing. Right at the bottom of the card it stated: 'It is an offence not to keep the above appointment unless such urgent reasons occur, when it is yours, or others duty if you are ill, to inform the office. If you ignore this appointment for no reason, and you do not inform the office then you will be liable to be prosecuted, and either fined or sent to prison."

My footsteps to the optician increased. I found the correct address very quickly indeed, for the last thing I wanted then was to be involved with courts, and the police.The gentleman I saw was a different man whom I had seen on the last occasion. We went through more or less the same routine, but with one difference, this time he showed me a selection of frames for me to choose from. Naturally I wasn't happy with the wearing of glasses situation at all, but I thought if I have to wear them I might as well pick the frames of my liking. I eventually settled for a pair of 'Glenn Miller' type frames, not exactly the same, but very similar, which I thought if I'd got to wear them I might as well look as nice as I could. Anyway Glenn Miller and his music were definitely the 'in thing' at that time.

On completion of the examination the optician told me to sit down, then telephoned someone, somewhere. He laughed at something the other person had said, and replied "Well yes, I know it might be a little late, but it's got to be done until we are told differently." This conversation went on for some time. I was, to be honest, getting a little bored with the whole thing, and indeed wishing that I'd never been anywhere near a recruiting office. Eventually the gentleman put the telephone down, and looked at me saying "I won't be a moment now Mr Smith, I've just got to sort an appointment out for you, and then you can get on your way, alright?"

"Yer, tha's sokay, I ain' in any 'urry," I lied, wishing that he would get a move on. I looked at the small brown card the optician had given to me, once outside in Newhall Street again, and I found that I had got to return to the recruiting office in Bishopgate Street on Wednesday the 8th August 1945, at 2-30pm. My thoughts on the matter at that moment were "Bleedin' 'ell, they've got time ta finish this bloody war, an' start anutha bleeda by then." This time however I did take the time to study the card with a little more care, and sure enough there was the same warning telling me what would happen if I did not attend at the time given.

I met Danny, Pat, and Joe that evening and gave them a run on the events to date, but naturally I didn't tell them about the glasses. They were more excited about the whole thing than I was.

Time dragged by so slowly, of course I told nearly all my customers on No 8 round that it was imminent that I would be going into the navy shortly. They were very sympathetic about the whole thing, for we had by this time got used to one another. I obviously didn't tell the management, for who knows what they might do. Funny thing as well, I didn't see Bob Jones either, so I assumed that he was having problems, that proved to be completely unfounded later.

June came and went, then July, and then on Monday the 6th August 1945, at twenty minutes past midnight THE ATOM BOMB was dropped on Hiroshima, with a warning from the U.S.A. for the Japanese to surrender. So the war was virtually over, and I still hadn't got into the Royal Navy, although I had volunteered my services. One thing that happened, however, that re-kindled my desire to join the navy was that Handsworth Dairies were now becoming intolerable. There were rumours of the younger men doing more work, for no more pay. My thoughts on the matter were: let's get away from here, and start afresh. It will all be new; new friends, new places, and who knows, I might even go abroad. What a lovely thought that was. I had been depressed by the whole situation I must admit, but I didn't stay that way for long, for one thing I'm not that type of person anyway. As time went by I was really looking forward to going into the navy, that is if my eyesight problem didn't stop me.

I still hadn't told any of the family what was going on, and furthermore I didn't intend to, due to the fact they still might not accept me, so there was no point at that time. Little did I know however the events that were to come, and what serious events they were as well.

At long last Wednesday the 8th of August arrived, and off I went to the recruiting office in Bishopgate Street to keep my appointment. Obviously I went on my own, for I hadn't seen Bob Jones to converse with. On arrival I found the same Chief Petty Officer who had seen both Bob and I on our first visit. We exchanged greetings, I handed him the card,and then he went off somewhere to collect some other documents. Returning after a few minutes, he placed several of these pieces of paper in front of him on the desk, and commenced to study them.

"Alright son," he said after a couple of minutes, "Everything seems to be in order,so all I've got to do is to give you another card, which roughly explains that if you do not hear from us within a month then you will have to return here for me to make you another card out for a further month. I will, however, save you the trouble of keep coming back here,so I'll cross the Month out, and make it Three Months how's that suit you?"

"Well o wuz 'opin' ta gerrin the nervy pretty quick, sir, burr I serpose I'll 'ave ta wert now, still neva mind." I must have looked pretty much like I spoke for the 'Chief's' next words were, I'm almost sure, meant as a consolation. "Look son, I know it's your aim to get into the Royal Navy, and by the look of your records so far, the Royal Navy could do with a fellow like you, but with the war being nearly over, they naturally won't need the amount of men now, so please try and understand won't you?"

"Ar-r-rokay sir, an' thank ya' eva sa much, fer rall yove done." Then shook hands with him, and left the office.

I was so miserable, I looked at the brown card, and saw that he had crossed out 'one month' and replaced it with 'three months' in a very neat hand. Consequently, I thought - as I had done all my life 'til now - "Sod it then!"

That was Wednesday the 8th of August 1945, the day that I had more or less been told that I was surplus to requirements, so off home to 228 I went not wishing to talk to anyone, about anything. By the Saturday however I had forgotten all about the navy and everything. I was, as always, back to normal. I had accepted the situation, but I still didn't let on to any of my mates, and boy, was I glad I hadn't told any of the family.

I went about my business with almost a carefree attitude for the days leading up to Saturday, 18th August, 1945, and then... ?

"An' w'at the bleedin' 'ell's this then?"

This was 'you know who' addressing me on my return from work on Saturday evening at around 6 o'clock, the day when I was naturally a lot later than in the week due to the collection of money from the customers.

I had, had quite a good day on that Saturday; the tips had come in more than usual, and the day seemed to go very pleasantly indeed. Of course, it had been very hot, which was weather that I personally loved, much better than the cold, harsh winter. I finished a little earlier than usual as well, for there's no doubt about it, you tend to work a lot better in the sun than you would if it were, say, raining, or something. I put 'Danny' into his stall, and took the harness back to the tack room. Then I went up to the office and paid in, picked up my wages, which I didn't even bother to look at, for I knew exactly what the contents were, about 25/-d, with deductions, and I gave all of it to Mom anyway. You can bet that if there had been anything short,she would have let me know in no uncertain manner.

I rode home down Holyhead Road in the pleasant sunshine looking up Church Terrace as I passed. It was strange, me doing that, but I suppose I was wondering if Bob had heard anything from the navy yet. Just thought association, I presumed.

Arriving home, I put my 'Kingsway' into the hall and went into the middle room. Mom as usual was in her chair with her back to the window, as the sun always set, or rather was completing its daily arc in that direction, its rays coming into the middle room, it made it hard to distinguish anybody's features. In fact 'Our Mom' always looked like a big black blob.

In the room also were 'Our Kid', and I think Hilda, Violet, and the three little wenches, Audrey, Dorothy, and 'The Babby.' Apparently they knew what was going on, because as soon as I entered the room and wished everybody "warro", they all immediately went quiet on me. This I did find strange, but ignored it, as I did anything I couldn't understand.

"Am yo' bleedin' deaf, or summat, I ast ya',w'at the bleedin' 'ell's this?"

I could vaguely see, although the ray's from the sun were blinding me, that she was waving something about in the air. " 'ow the bleedin' 'ell am I serposed ta know w'at it is if I ain' sin it Mom?" - Pause. "Yo'll bi the bleedin' death on me yo' will," she carried on. And I still didn't have a clue what she was on about.

"Well, let's 'ave a look at w'at cha got an' then I'll be erble ta tell ya' w'arrit's all about wun I?" All of a sudden the rest of them started, "Yo' shoulda tol' us w'at yo' wuz doin' our Ronnie. Yo' wert till owa Dad get's up yo'll bi forrit then. W'y did ya' 'ave ta gu an' do it Ron,ya' dain' 'ave ta do it did ya'?"

All of a sudden my lights came on. I'd found the twopence short of a bob. I'd found the proverbial nine bob note. This was something to do with me joining the navy, but what? I wasn't expecting anyone to write to me. It was me who had got to go back to Bishopgate Street in three month's time,or rather three months less ten day's if we were going to be accurate.

I went round the table and took the card Mom had in her hand, and started to read it. I read it. Read it again. Then I read it slowly for the third time. NO, THERE WAS NO MISTAKE:

———————

ON HIS MAJESTY'S SERVICE.

—

I HAVE TO INFORM YOU: Ronald William James Smith OF :
228 New John Street West, Hockley, Birmingham 19. THAT

YOU HAVE BEEN ACCEPTED INTO H.M. FORCES
BRANCH: Royal Navy.
YOU ARE TO REPORT TO: (the stamp of the recruiting
office in Bishopgate Street was in evidence) AND
ACCORDINGLY YOU ARE TO BE TRANSFERRED
FROM THERE TO H.M.S Royal Arthur, Skegness.
YOU SHOULD PRESENT YOURSELF AT THE PLACE
STATED AT 9.am.

Signed . . . .

On the rear of this card was a list of what I had to take with me, and what not to bring, but I was much too impatient to read all that, at that very moment. All I could thing of right then, was, I was going to be in the Royal Navy on Monday the 20th of August,1945. I would no longer be just another milk roundsman; I would be a sailor. Think of the uniform, and how it would enhance my chances with the girls. Also how my mates would envy me. Oh God I was so happy, I didn't know what to do with myself.

"O serppose yome bleedin' 'appy wi' yaself, ain' ya', now yove gonnan upset all the bleedin' 'ouse?" This was Mom continuing where she had left off. Later, of course, I did realise what I had actually done, much later in life, and I did talk to Mom and Dad about it, and they did understand then, but now?

"Mom, o dain' mean ta upset ya' 'onist o dain't, but o couldn't tell ya, cuzo dain' know w'etha o wuz gunna gerrin the nervy until the larst minnit, an' this 'as come as a real surprise,o dain' 'spect it ta come, this quick, 'onist o dain't."

"Yo' knew w'at yo' wuz doin' w'en yo' w'en an' joined the nervy, din ya'? Ya' bloody knew tharr rall right, so w'y dain' yal tell us then, eh, gu on gerrout o that if yo' cun then." She had started to cry. I hadn't seen Mom do this too many times before in my short life so far, but worse still, I just hadn't got a clue how to deal with it either. The Smith family weren't much for kissing and showing signs of affection, although, may I hasten to add, the love was there, definitely there, and I can assure anyone of that.

I stood immobile, I didn't know what to do. Mom was crying and one of the big wenches was trying to console her. I felt so ashamed at what I'd done, but at the same time I wanted to get out of this house and go and tell the world and his wife that I was now, or would be in a couple of day's time, a member of His Majesty's Royal Navy.

The situation was saved when I heard the door leading from the hall into the middle room open. I turned to see who was coming in, and I had another chill run through my veins when I saw it was 'Our Dad.' He looked bleary eyed, and very tired, although he had only just got out of bed for his tea, and then to prepare for the evening session down at 'The Turk.' He stopped in the doorway, his blue eyes watering, his face tired from the long hours he worked at 'Bradfords,' and worked bloody hard too I witnessed this myself when I worked at 'Rowlands Bakery' first, and then 'Bradfords Bakery' years later.

He had his empty cup in his one hand, and his 'Gold Flake' and 'Swan Vestas' in the other. Dad stared for a minute, not saying a word, and then his face lit up with a most wonderful smile, a smile that only 'My Dad' could smile, and he said in his deep husky voice, "So, wiv gorranutha serlor in the family, besides our Joe then?"

The smile turned into a chuckle, and he went on, after giving a casual glance towards Mom, who was still crying. "Yo' shudda lerrus know though Son, it's a birrov a serprise ta anybody ta find that their Son 'as gorra gu away in jus' two days; it's a bit much innit?" It worn't like tharrat all Dad, an' ov 'splained ta Mom as best as o could. Look I'll show ya', an' then p'r'aps ya'll believe me."

With that I took the original brown card the 'Chief' had given me with the word MONTH crossed out, and the words THREE MONTHS written in, from out of the top pocket of my cowgown, a place I kept all my worldly documentation, and handed it to Dad.

He looked at it for a while, then he said, looking across at 'Our Mom,' "The lad's right Lil, it's gorrit tall 'ere, 'e dain' expect ta bi called up sa quick, 'e wuz expectin' ta bi tol' in about three months, not ten days, so come on now love an' dry ya' tears. 'e's gorra gu out inta the world sometime Motha, an' now is as good as any time." He then went across to Mom, and took over from the big wench that had been consoling her.

Dad looked across at me, and I saw that he too had now got tears' running down his cheeks, and he said in a broken voice, "Son, 'adn't ya' berra gu an' tell ya' gaffa about this, cuz o don' expect they know do they?" An' don' ferget ta tell 'im that ya' ain' guin' in tamorra, cuz yove gorr 'ave one day orff, afowa ya' gu away on Mundee, an' if 'e sez anythin' yo' tell 'im ya' Dad's told ya' ta tell 'm yo' ain' guin' in, an' let that be an' end to it, alright?"

I'd forgotten all about Handsworth Dairies in my excitement. Of course I'd got to go and tell them, and I'd got to go and tell them NOW.

"Thanks Dad," I replied, "I'll tell 'im don' worry, an' it'll be a pleasure ta do it as well." I didn't make any further observations regarding what I meant by that last statement. I wasn't quite certain whether Mom and Dad would understand. Obviously what I did mean, was that this quickness of call up would put the dairy in all kinds of predicaments, due to the already vast shortage of staff. Little was I to know what extra delight regarding this nasty thought I was to be given when I arrived back at the dairy on this Saturday, the 18th August, 1945.

I pulled my 'Kingsway' back out of the hall again straight away, even forgetting to have my dinner, which was the favourite meal of the day, and re-traced my steps to Handsworth Dairies in Island Road.

Arriving back in the yard rather breathless due to me riding like mad to inform my employers of the situation, I was amazed to find Bob Jones waiting outside the supervisor's office when I went through the main entrance. I couldn't believe it. Had Bob had his call up papers as well? No that would be impossible, it just couldn't be, not two of us going on the same day; no, fate couldn't be that cruel to the management of Handsworth Dairies. So, I wondered why I was starting to laugh at this morbid situation. As I approached Bob he started to laugh as well, so I thought, it's got to be true, he has, he's been called up as well. As if to confirm my very thoughts, Bob raised his right hand with the little brown card in it. Propping my bike up against the supervisor's shed, I approached Bob with a grin on my face like a Cheshire cat. By this time I was almost certain that Bob was there for the same reason as myself, to tell whoever management were there that we had worked our last day for Handsworth Dairies.

" 'ave yo' gotcha perpers as well?" This wasn't Bob, as I had expected to ask the question, but Jim who was the duty supervisor that afternoon. "Ar-r-r yome right Jim, our Mom 'ad gorrem fer me w'en o gorrome terday, an' wuz she bloody mad, she dain' 'arf gi' me the rung side ov 'er tongue as well, cuz I 'adden told a tha ri wuz guin'."

"Yo' dain' did ja Ronnie?" Jim said with a broad grin on his face, " 'as she come roun' ta yowa thinkin' now, or not?"

"Well it don' marra now does it, cuz there ain' much anybody cun do abourrit now is tha?" I gave a rather hysterical laugh. I suddenly realised what I had just said: "There wasn't much anybody could do about it now," and momentarily - but only momentarily - did I think about what I really had done? I don't know why, but all of a sudden I remembered George, the driver at Handsworth Dairies, who drove 'The Greenhouse' before Ron. He joined the army, and was eventually put into the Paratroop Regiment.

He came down to the dairy to see some of his old mates, and have a natter, He wasn't a mate of mine, due to the fact that he was slightly older than me, but never the less I did go over to him and have a natter as well. Apparently he had taken part in the 'Arnham Battle' and unfortunately he was wounded, which resulted in him losing his left forearm. He was, of course, invalided out, and he was now doing an insurance round.

"What are you doing here Smith?"

My thoughts were rudely interrupted by this command. It was, and I knew for certain, by the accent, Mr.Cyril Davies, who had uttered these words. I turned slowly, and stared him straight in the face, feeling a little angry at the way he had addressed me.

"W'arram I doin' 'ere Mr Davies, I'll tell ya warrime doin' 'ere, ov come ta tell ya' tha' ri wunt be yin tamorra, an' o wunt bi comin' 'ere ragen, cuz ov bin called up fer the nervy, tha's warrime doin' 'ere."

With that caustic comment, which was certainly not the usual me, I pushed the brown card at him. He stared at me for a while not saying anything. His large blue eyes literally bulging from his small, thin, and what I thought, evil face. Mr Davies was already a pale complexioned man, but I thought right there and then he had gone a shade, quite a shade, paler.

"They can't do this to me, I won't allow it. You two come into work tomorrow as usual, I'll get this sorted out with the Labour Exchange on Monday. I'll have this stopped, so off you go now, and come into work tomorrow as usual, do you understand?" I piped up before Bob had a chance to. I could see out of the corner of my eye that Jim the supervisor was enjoying every minute of this.

"Om sorry Mr Davies, burr I don' think that yo' cun do anythin' abourrit, ya' see Bob an' me 'ave volunteered to gu in the nervy we ain' bin called up like the othas so o don' think that yo' cun stop it, cuz it's diff'rent innit?" I really hadn't got a clue whether or not the statement I had made was in fact legitimate, but it certainly seemed to have worked. In the next instance, Mr Davies's face went blood red, and he said "Alright then sod off, sod off in the navy, but don't come asking for your job's back when you come out, go on then both of you." With that he stormed off in the direction of his house. That was the very last time I was to see Mr. Cyril Davies.

We all three had a good laugh when he had turned the corner, and disappeared. We said our goodbyes to Jim, and asked him to convey these to everyone else when he could. Jim promised to do so. We also promised that when we had leave we would come up to the dairy to see him. I did personally, but whether Bob did I've no idea.

Later on in years I did realise what a mess we had left poor Mr. Davies in, and indeed I would have been in the same frame of mind, had I been him. I didn't fortunately have to face the embarrassment of asking for a job there when I came out of the navy. By the time I came out, I had the pick of hundreds of jobs, and the last place I wanted to work was Handsworth Dairies, after the way they had treated not only me, but other young men who worked there at that time. They were indeed one the firms that legally exploited the work force, within the jurisdiction of the Ministry of Labour.

After collecting our P.45s and other relevant documents Bob and I left the dairy. I walked with him as far as Church Terrace, in fact I went up and saw his mother. She wished me all the best for the future, and laughingly asked me to look after 'her Bob.' Of course the real reason I went up the terrace was to break the news to Joe first. As I have mentioned he lived only a couple of doors away from Bob Then afterwards it was my intention to call on Pat and Danny, before going home to change, and get ready for the evening.

Bob and I had compared cards on the way from the dairy to his house, and found out that we had been consigned to the same ship H.M.S. Royal Arthur, so I wouldn't be alone on this big adventure after all. I left Bob promising to see him outside the recruiting office at 8-45. on Monday. He had his friends he wanted to say goodbye to, and I had mine.

I called at Joe's but his Mother told me that he wasn't in, so I asked her to pass my wonderful news on to him, and tell him I would see him later. She agreed, and wished me all the best. Then I intended to go up Brewery Street to tell Pat, but then I thought, "What if he's out? so I changed my mind and went straight to Danny's house at the back of the shoeshop.

"W'arrow Artha" (I had to call him by his proper name in front of his Mother.)

"Warrow Ronnie, w'at brings yo' 'ere sa early, yo' ain' 'ad the sack 'ave ya'?" he said laughingly, and then took me through to the one room situated behind the shop. On the way through I gave him the answer to his question, but, may I add not the one he expected.

"Well, Arth, I ain' 'ad the sack, burr rive packed 'an'sworth Dairies in, an' got miself anutha job." By the time I'd finished this statement we were in the room. I said " 'ello Mrs Jones" to his Mother, then Arthur interrupted quickly, knowing that I'd got something to tell him, he must have seen it in my face that things were not as they should be. "What's sall the myst'ry Ron, yove packed 'an'sworth Dairies in, o dain' think yo' could pack a job in wi'out guin' through all kinds a red tape, so w'atcha goin' on about then?" I couldn't hold it back any longer. I couldn't keep my best mate in any further suspense. I took the brown card out of my cowgown, handed it to him, then stood back and watched his face.

Suddenly a big grin spread across his face. He said "Oh great Ron, absolutely great, I'm eva sa pleased fer ya', I really yam, burr at the serm time om gunna miss ya', ya' will write wuntcha?"

"Course o will, any road up, od berra gerrorff now, an' change me, so that we cun gu an' 'ave a birra donnuck ternight, an' then tamorra night as well, cuz it'll bi the last fer some time I spect wun it?"

"Ar-r-rokay Ron, see yarrin a bit then."

Mrs Jones wished me all the best, and Arthur, or should I say Danny, promised to spread the news to Pat after I'd gone home to change.

I returned home, and found that Mom was now in a better mood. I supposed that Dad had had a talk with her, and soothed her down a bit. She got my dinner from the oven, and it was burnt, just how I liked it fortunately. Then she went off to get changed to go down to 'The Turk' for her evening out with Dad. Feeling sorry for her I gave her her money, and another quid out of my tips, to have a drink on me, promising to send her some money home whilst I was away in the navy. This seemed to comfort her for the moment, and she even managed to say "Thank ya' Ronnie, yome a good lad really."

Danny, Pat, Joe, and myself had a real good time that Saturday night. We even allowed ourselves a special treat: we went into 'The Nelson' in Booth Street, and had a quick 'half.' The landlord looked a bit suspicious at us, but when Danny explained that I was to go into the navy on the Monday he warmed to us considerably.

I managed to get through Sunday without too many hiccups. As the hours ticked by I was getting more excited about this new, and big adventure. Something that I had not done before, I was going to be away from home, not for one night, nor two, but for a time only determined by the Royal Navy.

At last the great day arrived: Monday 20th August, 1945. I awoke early, very early indeed, which when you think about it, was perfectly natural, due to these exciting circumstances. On awakening I thought how pleasant it was, not having to go to work. I couldn't quite grasp this sudden freedom that I had attained. It was just like having a holiday whilst others carried on working. Immediately coming to mind was the time had off from 'Rowlands Bakery,' when I went on the cycling trip to Atcham with Jack Pittaway.

I got out of bed, with 'Our Kid' still snoring his head off. I hadn't got a clue what time it was. Looking through the window I saw that the sun was already well up, not by the actual sight of it, this was impossible unless you went down into the street, and looked west towards Summer Lane where you could actually see the sun coming up. Looking out of our bedroom however was slightly different, for this room was facing a northerly direction. No, I could tell the sun was well up by the very bright light of the morning.

Thinking to myself w'arra wonderful day ta be guin' inta the Navy I thanked God mentally for giving me this wonderful life. Donning my 'Sunday Best' - well I couldn't go into the navy with my working day clothes could I? - I went down the wooden stairs, the last time for a while anyway, and into the middle room. I was amazed to see 'Our Dad' sat in Mom's chair over by the window leading into the garden. A fire burning brightly in the hearth. (As I've said before, don't matter how hot it was outside, 228 was always a cold house, which under some circumstances was very good.)

" 'ello Dad, yome 'um early aintcha?" Dad stared at me for a moment, and then said slowly "Ya' dain' think od let cho gu away wi' out sayin' tarrar did ja?"

Right at that moment I felt that Dad wanted to say an awful lot more to me, but either he couldn't find the words, or more probably, he did know the words, but emotion wouldn't let them flow. I too was equally at a loss for words, so I just said "Oh, thanks Dad, thanks a lot, o wudden 'ave liked ta 'ave gone wi' out seein' yo' eitha."

I sat down opposite Dad, and poured myself a cup of tea, asking him if he wanted one as well, He replied, "No thanks Son, I'll wert till Motha brings mi breckfust in."

"Ar-r-rokay Dad." I had got half way down my first cuppa, when 'Our Mom' came through from the back kitchen.

"Oh, yome up then, o thought ya' might be wi' yo' guin' away an all."

"Now Motha, remember w'at wi said, the lad's explained w'at 'appened, now leave 'im alone, 'e'll 'ave enough ta contend wi' in the months a'ead, so 'e don' wan' rem indin' ov all that, so leave 'im be, there's a good wench."

"Yo' ain' 'ad the little bugga like I yave Artha,'e's bin a bugga all 'is life, an' 'e ain' changin' now. Fancy 'im guin' an' doin' this on us, arta the way we've looked arta rim all 'is life."

"Motha, ov told ya' once or twice, now pack it in an' leave the lad alone yo'll on'y worry ya'self needlessly, cuz at the end o the day it ain' gunna mek an' 'erpath a diff'rance, so let the lad be, an' o don' wann 'ear anutha word."

She looked first at me, then across at Dad, then back to me. She didn't say a word, she just put Dad's breakfast in front of him, then went off into the back again. I was to say the least bemused by the whole situation. I mean in the films, when a bloke was going off to war, all the family, and the street for that matter, were there kissing and hugging, and laughing and crying, but here was I, Mom was balling me out, for something I hadn't really been responsible for. Oh I know, I hadn't told her that I had volunteered for the navy, but I did intend telling her when the call-up papers came, well, before they came really, because I would have probably have had to go up to the recruiting centre anyway. I really was at a loss with the situation this lovely morning of the 20th August, 1945.

Mom eventually returned with my breakfast, and what a breakfast; it looked as though she was going to feed the five thousand. As I've already told you cooked breakfasts were only evident on a Sunday morning, but here we were with the biggest cooked breakfast I'd seen for a long time, and on a Monday Morning, too. There were four rashers of bacon, the same number of sausages, a couple of fried eggs, all swimming in lovely fat laden fried tomatoes and, as usual all the bread and butter I could possibly manage

"There ya' are ya' little bugga, ya' don' deserve it, but chove gorra lung journey in front on ya', an' o don' suppose the food 'll bi as good, or plentiful w'ere yome guin, so gu on an' gerrit down ya'."

I looked at Mom, and was about to say "Thank ya' Mom," but didn't get the chance, for she turned quickly and returned to the back kitchen. I looked at the meal, and couldn't quite understand all this attention from 'You Know Who.' Dad coughed, it was a cough to draw my attention to him, more than one of his deep throated coughs through dragging on his 'Gold Flake.'

I looked over at him, and he whispered to me "It's ya' Motha's way ov sayin' she's forgive ya' Son, she don' know any otha way. Believe me I know 'er, so gu on an' get stuck inta ya' breckfust, an' enjoy it, cuz if the nervy is anythin' like the army I wuz in, in the 1914-1918 War, then ya' Motha's right, the food wunt bi good, an' it certainly wunt bi plentiful, but yo'll enjoy it any road up." He then started to laugh in his good humoured gruff manner.

Mom didn't return from the kitchen whilst I was eating this enormous meal. I naturally didn't think anything about that, but what I did think about whilst chobblin? It was Dad's words: "It's ya' Motha's way ov sayin' she's forgive ya' Son, she don' know any otha way, believe me, o know 'er."

I thought about those words with an intensity I had never experienced before. Obviously I hadn't the least bit of knowledge of how to deal with anything like this, well not in a way that a person with a little bit 'up top' would have done anyway. I thought, how can I tell Mom without appearing a big 'cissie' how I feel about this most emotional situation… ?

At last I had reached a decision, the only one my limited knowledge would allow at this most important time in my life. Here I was in a few minutes time, going to go God knows where. I hadn't got the slightest idea where this Skegness was; it might as well have been in Australia for all I knew. More important however this was the first time that one of 'The Smith's' (barring 'Our Kid' when he was a 'Bevin Boy,' he came home nearly every weekend, and sometimes wouldn't go back, as I told you earlier) was actually going to be away from home for an indefinite period. Oh of course there was Joe, Jack, and Ronnie, they were away in the Navy, Air Force, and Army respectively, but then they weren't really one of 'The Smith's' were they? Don't get me wrong however, to us lot they were family in every respect but for the name. In fact we never ever referred to them as 'brother-in-Law,' it was always 'Our Kid.' and it was really meant. We never thought of them as 'Langmaid,' 'Collins' or 'Holt,' to us they were 'Smiths' in every way.

My decision after careful thought was to give Mom what she liked most - MONEY! Oh I know it may sound crude, but you must understand that that is the way emotions between us 'Smith's' were passed. Not only 'The Smiths' practised this method of 'Love and Devotion,' so too did lots of other people in Hockley. How many times have I heard this expression from someone's wife, girl friend, husband or boy friend: "We 'ad a terrible row larst night, an' wi' nearly finisht up fightin', but wi' med it up this mornin' (artanoon, or ev'nin' as the case may be), an' 'e (she) bought me ya lov'ly present (gi' mi ya quid ta gu an' buy miself sommat with, or some such present). It was prevalent in the Hockley area, and I'm equally sure in a good many more places as well. I knew that I had got just over three pounds in my pocket, which was more than enough to last me for a while. I thought Mom will be bound to miss my 27/6d each week, for up till this moment I didn't know how much the navy paid. I hadn't bothered to give that a thought.

I finished my huge breakfast, had another two cups of tea, and whilst drinking these 'Our Kid' had come down from his bed. I looked at the clock on the mantlepiece when he entered the room, for I knew that unlike me he really didn't like getting up in the morning. He was due at 'Southall and Smith's' at 8 o'clock, and he was, according to Mom, never downstairs much before 7-35. This allowed him a quick cup of tea, a little bit of bread and butter, then a quick dash down

Guest Street into Villa Street to the factory, just past 'The Angel' public house on the left-hand side. I found to my relief that it was only 7-20, early for 'Our Kid,' but getting on a bit for me this morning. The last thing I wanted to do was turn up at the recruiting office late.

Getting up from the table, I pulled the money I had from my pocket, and sorted a pound note from the other three, then as an after thought I looked at the coins in my pocket. I had two half crowns, one florin, a couple of sixpences, and a little copper. I looked at this change then extracted the two half crowns from it, and added it to the pound note I'd already transferred to the left hand, from my right. "Mom," I shouted to her, she was still in the back kitchen. "Om guin' now, oright?" She came through to the middle room, and I noticed that she had been crying. On reaching me she said "Now yo' bi careful owa Ronnie, an' don' ferget ta write will ya', ov pu ya' some ink, an' a pen an' some perpa, an' that, as well as some san'witches, an' don' gu gerrin' inta any trouble will ya'?"

"Nah course o wunt Mom, o wunt gerrin ta any trouble, 'onist, an' 'ere ya' ar', 'ave this until o find out w'at's guin' on," and I handed her the pound note and two half crowns.

Mom looked at the money for a moment, then she reached into her pinnie and extracted her well-worn brown purse, placed the cash inside, then she handed me a brown-paper carrier bag with 'Bartram's Butcher's,' 8 Hunters Road, Hockley, Birmingham 19. Families and Businesses catered for.' printed on the side. "Now yo' bi careful owa Ronnie wun ya'?" Before I could answer she rushed back into the kitchen again. I made to go after her, but Dad intervened. "Nah leave a alone Son," he said in a very soft, and gentle voice "She'll be youright, yo come on in the front wi' me, an' I'll si ta ya' Motha w'en ov sin yarroff. Come on now." With that Dad, Arthur, and I went into the front room. All the wenches were upstairs. I rather think now that they kept out of the way, not knowing what our Mom might,or might not, do on this very emotional parting.

There we stood in the front room, which smelt of mansion polish and dust; the three of us. First Arthur said "Tarrar rour kid, look arta yaself, an' don' ferget ta write like owa Mom sez." We shook hands, and then Dad said "Son, o can' gi ya' munnee, or ranythin' like that, but w'at o will ge ya' is a bit of advice an' yo' remember this an' at least yo'll be strert in yar mind, oright? I stared at Dad not knowing what was coming. I could feel myself near to tears, but I held them back. Well a bloke just guin' inta the nervy din' cry did 'e? Dad stared back at me, then in a firm voice, but such a sincere voice he said:

"SON, WHATEVER YOU DO - AND WHEREVER YOU GO ALWAYS TELL THE TRUTH. IT MAY AT TIMES GET YOU INTO TROUBLE BY DOING SO. BUT TELL THE TRUTH BECAUSE YOUR CONSCIENCE WILL BE CLEAR AT ALL TIMES, AND YOU WILL FIND OUT IN YOUR LIFE THAT A CLEAR CONSCIENCE IS WORTH MORE THAN A POT OF GOLD." (All this in good old Brummijam accent though.)

Everything in the room went very quiet for a moment, then Dad continued, now in a different vein altogether "Gu on now Ron, an' do ya' best, as yo' allis do, an' enjoy yaself in the nervy, an' we'll 'ave a couple la drinks w'en yo' cum 'um on leave eh?" He started to laugh, with that lovely chuckle again, put out his hand for me to shake. He put his arm around my shoulders and gently moved me towards the hall, and then out into the entry. He stopped in the hall and said quietly "Gu on now Son, wi' don' wanna upset yer Motha any mowa do we, so off ya' gu, an' don' ferget warr I told ya'. Tarrar Son, an' God Bless Ya'."

"Tarrar Dad, an' say tarrar ta ev'rybody fer me will ya', it wunt bi lung befowa rime 'um agen okay?"

"Ar-rroright Son, now yo' gerrorff or yo'll bi lert." With that he closed the door. I felt hurt at this, Dad closing the door on me, but I did understand later, he had to, because he wanted to get to Mom and console her at this moment of grief.

Off I went down New John Street West looking forward to my new life. It seemed as though everyone in the street knew: Mrs Shaw, Mrs Beddoes, Mrs Bedford, Mrs Belcher, Mrs Nash, Mrs Bull, and oh so many others all stood on their respective doorsteps saying "All the best Ronnie, mind 'ow ya' gu." "Don' do anythin' I wudden do." "Ya' know all the nice girls love a saila, so yo' bi careful." Was my face red, by the time I'd got to the bottom of the street. I turned the corner onto 'The Brook' glad to be out of sight, it was so embarrassing for me.

I walked past 'Coleman's,' 'Higgs,' 'Butlers' 'The Hardware Shop,' 'Bendalls,' 'C.V. Bull's,' 'Hardy's.' I had a quick look in there, just in case Joan might be inside, but no luck. "I wunda riff she knows om guin' in the nervy," I thought. "I yope shi does." On past 'The Shoe Shop,' 'Izon's the Chemist,' 'Cockrams,' and finally on that side, 'The Benyon.' On reaching the pub, I spotted a bus coming past the 'Palladium,'so I rushed across the junction to Tippers' and arrived at the bus stop just in time to meet it. I got on board after the passengers for 'Hockley Brook' got off, and went upstairs. As I did when I was younger, I made a bee-line for the seat situated over the driver's head; it was empty. Settling into the seat, I managed to light a 'Senior Service' (well, what other cigarette could one smoke?) before the bus moved off from 'The Brook."

I stared intently at every building, trying to memorise every nook and cranny of each one, so that I wouldn't forget them on my journey into the unknown. I knew that it would be some time before I saw my 'Hockley Brook' again, and through these thoughts my tummy began to feel funny again, so I decided enough was enough, and then looked forward to concentrate on what lay ahead, and not what was behind.

Never the less when the 'Leyland Cub' reached the top of Hockley Hill by 'The Duke of York,' I couldn't resist one last look at the place I'd lived all my life so far. So I stood up, and turned around gazing down the gangway of the bus to look longingly down Hockley Hill towards 'The Brook,' thinking "I wonder how long it will be before I see you again?"

A REAL LANDLUBBER ENTERS THE SERVICE OF
HIS MAJESTY'S ROYAL NAVY - 20th AUGUST 1945.
"Floating away from 'THE BROOK' out to the open SEA."
20th August 1945 to 16th December 1947.

My journey from Hockley to town in this cream and dark-blue bus was a journey of complete nostalgia for me. Monday, 20th August 1945 was the day that started my biggest adventure in life so far. I was going on a journey from which I would not return to 228 on the same day, indeed I had no knowledge when I would return to 228. This was an adventure which most men would give their hind teeth for a journey into the unknown; well that's how I thought of it. No one had prepared me for this, it was something that I had got to face for myself. Never the less I was looking forward to it, in fact I was excited about it. I had made up my mind that I was going to try my hardest at whatever the Royal Navy had to offer, to achieve some sort of end, and hopefully a successful one. I looked out of the windows of the bus, looked intently for the very first time, trying to take in every aspect of these home surroundings. I wished that I could take all of what I looked at, and wanted, put them into a box so that whenever I felt the need, I could take them out of that box and rekindle the flame of what they were; thereby holding my life as it had been so far and never letting it go. I saw all the following buildings, some of which had housed lovely people. These were naturally more precious to me than buildings, but the buildings themselves held the key to that magic moment. 'Ma Davies's Herb Shop,' 'Collins,' 'The Wold,' 'Howletts,'

'The Post Office,' with which I was to become involved in later, 'Dr Lyons,' 'Dingleys the Tailors,' 'Harry Smith's,' 'Joseph Lucas's,' in Gt King Street, 'The Duke of York,' another place I was to become involved in later, 'Mrs Cope's Cafe,' 'The Trees,' 'Hockleychem,' 'Clewley's,' in Vyse Street, 'Swallow Raincoats, Fine in the Rain,' 'P. Law Car Sales,' 'Davenports,' 'Restalls,' 'Adolph Scott,' 'Joseph Lucas's,' in Gt Hampton Street, 'Cannings,' on the corner of Hall Street, and Gt Hampton Row, and so many more, that I could probably fill a book. Yes, I wanted to hold all these places, and many, many, more so close to me, so that I would never forget my beloved home, HOCKLEY.

The bus sped down Livery Street, and then up the steep climb to the terminus outside Snow Hill Station. It pulled up eventually, I alighted, but unlike my fellow passengers, who were rushing off to their places of employment, I stood still on the pavement. I watched these people rushing about like herds of wild animals. I was absolutely fascinated by it, for up until now I had never experienced this way of life due to my work, and the early hours it involved. I had to be at Rowlands at 5-30,am and I had to be at Handsworth Dairies at a much similar time, so I didn't have to witness all these people rushing about at that time of day. I could imagine these same people, however, going to the East, West, and North of our wonderful characteristic City, catching further buses, or trams, to convey them to their eventual destination, some, perhaps, staying right here in the City itself. Hearing the whistle of a train, the blowing of steam, the whistle of the guard's signal that it was clear for the driver to proceed, brought All Saints Road, and Saturday morning's back to me. I heard the departure of that train with a series of shunting noises, knowing that eventually it would settle down to a steady rhythm as it picked up speed, for its journey to wherever.

It was a lovely sunny morning, but just a little cold at that time, but one anticipated that it would be quite warm later, as indeed it turned out to be. I breathed in what I personally thought was a pleasant smell, although I must admit others wouldn't find it so. This smell of steam, oil, and petrol, mixed with the wonderful aroma of bread being cooked somewhere, and not only bread, but other food as well. Wonderful snatches of first one, and then another tickled my nostrils with delight. I stood there momentarily enjoying, no, savouring these smells, somehow trying to hold them forever. At this moment I had closed my eyes letting all this come over me. Eventually I opened them, and looked at what was going on around me. The people rushing from Snow Hill Station from the

Livery Street exit. Taxis going in and out, shining beautifully in their black coats. It was lovely really to see how these drivers of the taxis looked after their vehicles, polishing them with loving care, every minute that they weren't out for hire.

I saw horse-drawn vehicles of all kinds, 'Great Western Railway,' 'London Midland and Scottish Railway,' the network which I found out later would be taking me to my 'Stone Class Frigate' at Skegness. 'Hawley's Bakery,' 'Scribbans' Bakery, I even saw the girl who delivered around town for 'Handsworth Dairies.' Ann her name was, but unfortunately she was too far away for me to say "Hello." Yes, I watched all this activity with great enthusiasm, knowing that it would be some time before I saw it all again. Suddenly I came out of this reverie, and thought I won't be going anywhere at this rate, I'd better get a move on or I was going to be late. I don't suppose that that would go down well with the representatives of His Majesty's Royal Navy. Clutching my carrier bag, I crossed the road, and made my way up to Colmore Row. Once there I walked steadily along intending to catch either a No. 7 Portland Road bus, or a No. 9 Quinton bus, which would drop me off just past Bishopgate Street at Five Ways, but my intentions were not to be fulfiled.

I looked at the metal and glass structures which formed the shelter for people intending to board these buses. To my dismay I found that in both cases people were indeed overflowing from them for quite a long way, so I could visualise a very long wait, for neither of these routes' buses had arrived yet. I made my mind up rather quickly; the best thing to do would be to walk the distance from Colmore Row to Bishopgate Street. Having made up my mind to to do this I quickened my steps along the Row, in fact I almost broke out into a run. Although I was in a rush I still looked around me, taking in all the places I probably wouldn't see again for a while. 'St Phillips Cathedral and churchyard,' 'The Grand Hotel,' The Kardomah,' 'J.Lyons Tea Shop,' Galloways Corner,' 'The Town Hall,' 'The Council House.' I didn't go past all of these buildings, for I turned into Eden Place which housed 'The Stock Exchange,' and the old man who painted, or crayoned, wonderful pictures on the pavement at the bottom of the place on the left-hand side. He just sat there with his old dog each day, until I suppose he just didn't turn up any more. I wonder if anyone enquired after him, when he stopped habitating this pitch?

At the bottom of Eden Place I turned left into Edmund Street passing under the ornate bridge, and buildings, and the old tram terminus, which now served as the new bus stops. I crossed over Congreve Street, had a quick glance at 'The White Horse,' into Chamberlain Square, going by the ornate fountain, and town hall, before I went by the offices of Births, Marriages, and Deaths on the right. Stopping for the traffic outside O.H.M.S. shop, and crossing Easy Row, when it had subsided sufficiently into Broad Street. On passing the sports outfitters, 'Lilleywhite and Frowds,' I caught sight of a gentleman standing just inside the doorway. From his waistcoat I saw a watch chain hanging, so I went to him to ascertain the exact time, for by this moment I was getting a little worried.

" 'scuse mi sir, but could ya' gi mi the time please?" He was a most distinguished looking man and I was, to say the least, in awe of him. He had a 'billy cock' on his head, at what I thought a nice rakish angle, which gave him a 'Mississippi Gambler' look. Beneath this hard hat was an equally hard face, nicely featured, but hard. Brown eyes, sparkling, with little lines under them, but

236

enhancing them somehow, a crooked nose, which I thought might have experienced a 'bit in the ring,' wide but nice mouth, with a grey handlebar moustache just over the top. A white starched collar, and neat tie, with a brilliantly white shirt. He wore a black suit and shoes, in fact he might have been something to do with funeral directors, but needless to say I didn't ask, and he wasn't about to tell me, was he?

"Certainly my boy," he answered in ever such a posh voice; posh but definitely not 'cissie.' He removed the watch, a gold watch, the same as his chain, and looked at it for a moment, then said "It's just parst twenty minutes after eight."

I thought to myself "Whoo-oo-oo, gerra load ov 'im, it's just parst twenty minnit's harfter height. Blimey 'e musta swallad 'a bloody dicchunary 'e must,' but of course I didn't reveal these thoughts. If I had have done I could have seen, and felt a bloody 'bang up the earole' off this nice, but very hard looking gentleman. All I did say was "Thank ya' sir, thank ya' very much," and moved on my way up Broad Street. However, it did surprise me, it only being 8-20, because it was only an hour ago that 'Our Kid' had come downstairs into the middle room prior to me leaving home. I thought well, that's how time must go when you are happy. I continued along Broad Street at a much more leisurely pace, knowing that I had got pretty well of time to get me to Bishopgate Street for 8-45.

At long last I took the left-hand turn into Bishopgate Street and to my surprise I found that Bob was already there. He was amongst some other blokes, and nattering away ten to the dozen.

"Hiya Bob," I called, when I was quite some distance from him. He stopped talking to these other blokes, and turned around, shouting back a similar kind of greeting. When I reached him he said, pointing to a skinny looking bloke, with buck teeth, blonde curly hair, and the biggest blue eyes. "This is Fred Rainey, Ron, an' 'e comes from 'erbe't Road, Small 'eath." Then he turned to the other bloke, who was older than us. He must have been twenty odd, but God, was he handsome in a swarthy kind of way, with black hair, black as night, and plenty of it, groomed immaculately. His complexion was dark, as if he had been in the sun constantly for a good many years, black eyebrows above intent staring brown eyes, and a nicely fashioned nose, thin lips, but again nice, that revealed, when he spoke to me, white even teeth, with just a bit of a wide gap between the two upper middle teeth, like 'Terry Thomas,' but not quite so pronounced.

"This is Sid Green, Ron, an' 'e's from Wa'sall, 'e is." We exchanged greetings, chatted on for a while, and finished up by agreeing to stay with one another, well as much as we could anyway, throughout what was to come. I did say to Bob, however, "Crikey Bob, yo' gorr 'ere pretty sharpish din ya', watcha do camp out 'ere all bleedin' night?" We all had a laugh at this comment, then Bob said "Nah Ron, o thought about coppin' the 74 or some otha buzz that come down So'o Road, but then o thought o bet they don' 'ave trams in Skegness,so w'arr ri did wuz, o caught the Outa Circle buzz from Rookery Road, an' dropped orff at Dudley Road, an' then o went inta Icknield Port Road, ya' know where Joannie Boulton lives?" (He gave one of those know-it-all looks and smiled, when he said this, which I totally ignored) "an' o caught the thirty-three tram up ta Five Ways, an' then jus' walked down Broad Street 'ere, an' it seemed quicka any road up."

"Ar-r-ro neva thoughronnit that way Bob" I replied. "Any road up it'd bi quicka fer yo' from yowa rend wouldn't it. O wish o cud a gone on a tram, burr they all finisht w'en the war started, well in March afowa the war started anyway."

237

Bob didn't answer me on any aspect of what I had just said, he just turned and continued with the conversation I suppose they were having when I arrived, so I had no alternative but to close in on the conversation.

There we were then, stood outside the recruiting office, chatting away to one another, at peace with the world. Suddenly the doors to the office were opened, and another man, in much the same uniform as 'The Chief,' stood there surveying this happy little band. The uniform itself was exactly the same as 'The-Chief's' but there were no three buttons around the sleeves, just two small ones attached to the seam. On the left arm of this man's uniform above the elbow were two cross anchors, and a crown situated in the middle at the top of the anchors. Below these cross anchors were three stripes, just like a seargent's in the army. On the right, arm again just above the elbow, were two sticks, well that's what they looked like to me, at that moment, and these two were crossed. All these badges were made of some kind of gold thread, and looked very impressive. To complete this man's uniform were six gold buttons, and a huge array of medal ribbons displayed high up on his left chest. God, was I impressed, and so were the others in the crowd. He was so smart and upright, you just couldn't believe your eyes. I Learned later of course that this man was indeed a 'Three Badge Gunnery Petty Officer.' The stripes were not rank, but service in the Royal Navy, and amounted to some sixteen years. We looked at this representative of His Majesty's Royal Navy, an oh, how I envied him all his smartness, cleanliness, and upstanding figure. I rather supposed that the others were too. I've no doubt in my mind that we could all see ourselves looking like this within a very short time of us entering the service. What I didn't realise however was all the hard work that had got to go into the final make up of this resplendent figure of a man. The years he had spent in the navy, and the work he had got to complete, both practical and theoretical, to first attain his leading hand status, and then even harder work to attain his present position. We could only see the finished product. All we were thinking about, well assuming that the others stood there on that Monday morning were thinking the same thoughts as myself, was the smartness of the uniform, and the very beautiful decorations that went with it, and not the hard work that it entailed to attain this position.

I could just imagine myself walking into the Y.W.C.A. club, with Billy Dipple and his cronies there, and watching as they looked me over. They wouldn't be able to believe their eyes, at my resplendent figure - all the gold badges, and the medal ribbons. Oh I would tell them a thing or two about the seven seas, and all my escapades. How I had been torpedoed, and saved all the other blokes, and got them home safely. Oh what a thrill it would... "Oright lads, come on, let's 'ave ya rinside, an' smart abourrit."

This was the resplendent figure of a man telling us lot to 'move it' and get our bodies inside the office. I went right off him from that moment on - "Sod 'im, an' 'is bleedin' posh uniform, an' badgis, an' ev'rythin'," but despite these thoughts, I still scurried up the steps with the others into the recruiting office.

Entering the building, we quickly passed the area where we had met 'The Chief' for our first interview, and went into a far larger room. All that was in this room as far as I could see was a table, and another gentleman, beside 'The Chief,' who like these other two, was dressed in naval uniform, but this one was far different than theirs. The uniform was first a much better quality, it looked to be a much heavier material than the first uniforms, and as I was to find out much later this material was indeed doeskin. This gentleman had no badges on his uniform, oh, he had medal ribbons galore, again well up on his left chest, in fact they were nearly on his shoulder. He had eight gold buttons on his coat, as opposed to the six on 'The Chief''s' and the 'Petty Officer's,' and then on the bottom of his sleeves, about three inches up from the cuff were two gold wavy bands (Lieutenant, Royal Navy Voluntary Reserve). Above these two bands, twining into them was a square band.

The Petty Officer marched smartly up to this other gentleman, and then coming to an abrupt halt, saluted him and said "All new recruits aboard and counted for Sir."

"Thank you, Petty Officer." The Petty Officer saluted again did a smart about turn, and then marched back to us.

The Lieutenant looked at us for a moment, then slowly walked towards this line of civilians. "Gentlemen," he started, "You are about to embark on a new, and hopefully, wonderful career. Obviously it is up to you how you conduct yourselves in whatever you choose to do in His Majesty's Royal Navy. In a moment the petty officer will call your names out, and as he does you march up to me at this table and sign a document, you will then receive the King's shilling, which is a token of payment to you from the Government to seal the agreement that you have signed. On completion of this declaration, you will then deem yourselves to be members of the aforesaid His Majesty's Royal Navy. Consequently you will from that moment forward consider yourselves under the direct command of all senior ranks to yourselves as new recruits, and will obey all orders from them, from then on. Now do you all understand me?" There was a chorus of "Yes Sir " to this question. The petty officer then started to read our names out, and we did exactly what this gentleman ordered, we were all so in awe of what he had told us. Having completed this phase of the operation, we just stood around waiting for the next move by these splendidly uniformed men. The officer, and the petty officer eventually left us, and went into another room. We lit up our cigarettes, and started to have a chat to one another. The four of us: Fred Rainey, Sid Green, Bob Jones, and myself more or less stuck with one another, and this was to be for a few months during our initial training. "Right oh you lads, let's 'ave ya' then." This intrusion into our rather cosy little 'mothers' meeting' took us all by surprise. We did not respond as quickly as the speaker of this command apparently wanted, so he then went on: "As I said, let's 'ave ya, an' yo'll 'ave ta bi quicka than that w'en yome aboard ship or yo'll bi fer the 'igh jump, all on ya'. So, now jump to it, an' getcha selves into a line o' some sort, come on now."

All of us to a man quickly formed a line, and I thought to myself "Bleedin' 'ell, I ain't 'ardly bin in the bleedin' Navy a minnit, an' om in trouble, so od berra watch miself cuz o' don' wanna gerron the wrung side o' this bloke, 'e looks as though 'e cud tek the lorron us on single 'anded and win.

This bloke was about six foot odd, high and had the build of 'Charles Atlas'. He was dressed smartly in what I call 'real matelot's rig.' Everything about this bloke was absolutely 'ticketty boo.' His hat was square on, and collar, faded blue, with the three white lines going around was immaculate, the lanyard was as white as snow, the black silk lay perfectly. Seven creases in his bell bottoms sharp as a razor, he was in fact the epitome of a 'Royal Naval Rating.' His boots, well you could definitely see your face in them and, as we were to learn later, he must have 'boned' them every day. On his left arm were three red stripes, but nothing else. (A three badge nothing, I can't put down the right terminology for his rating, the publisher just wouldn't print it!) Looking at him put memories of 'Our Joe' into my mind, not the build of course, for Joe was of slight build, but very wiry. Thinking of Joe however put my mind at ease to the situation for the moment, I thought he is just another bloke, like 'Our Joe,' in fact he isn't as good as 'Our Joe' for he had got an anchor over the one stripe he had on his left arm, so 'e must 'ave bin berra. Anyway this new bloke stood in front of us, and held a board in his right hand. Slowly looking along the line, he said "Now, om gunna read yoa nerms out, jus' ta mek shure ov gotch rall, an' w'en ov read ya' nerms out, o wantcha ta move ova thaya, by the dowa, d' ya' un'erstan' mi?" Very quickly we again replied in chorus "Yes Sir." He looked at us with the look of someone who had just discovered he had trod in some 'dog poo' up to his thighs, and said "l ain't a Sir, an' o don' wanna be. Now that yome in the Navy the fust thing yove gorra learn is, that yo' on'y call officers Sir, an' ta ev'rybody else Aye Aye will be enough. Now 'ave ya' got that?"

"Aye, Aye!" we all shouted in unison.

"Tha's berra," he replied. He then commenced to read our names out, and each one replied "Aye, Aye!" and went over to the door until the roll call was completed. He then marched over to us, and in a quieter tone said "Right lads, we're gunna gu down ta New Street Sterchun, now o' can't march ya' down thaya, cuz we ain' gorra band in the fust plerce, an' in the secon' plerce yo' ain' gorreny uniforms on, so om gunna 'ave ta trust ya' ta walk down wi' me in an' orderly fashion, okay?"

"Aye, Aye!" we chimed, like a lot of sheep.

"Right," he continued, "let's gu then."

Off we went up Bishopgate Street, turning right into Broad Street, on the next step of our journey, in what I thought as a new, and exciting adventure in my life. As we walked down Broad Street I looked around intently at all, the buildings, somehow trying to hold the picture that I saw, putting it into a kind of mental album. I dearly wanted to get this album out, and recapture these moments at a later date, when I reached heaven knows where in this new turn in my life.

Fred, Sid, Bob and myself chatted away merrily, and also the three-badge bloke seemed to have changed, once outside the recruiting office. I thought about this for a short while. It wasn't so rare for a person to adopt one kind of character whilst in view of others in a superior position, but once outside their control, adopt another. Obviously enough he was in the fore front of this contingent, but we could see and hear his change of attitude towards us new blokes coming into the navy, when probably he was on the verge of coming out. This change in his attitude made me, at least, feel a good deal better to whatever might be in store for us when we reached this place named SKEGNESS.

Past the 'Orthopaedic Hospital' on the corner of Sheepcote Street.

Looking down this street I could see the high chimney stack with 'Baxters Screws' in metal letters running up the whole height of it. The steam from the various trains travelling either through, or shunting up and down the yards quite evident.

Past Granville Street, Berkley Street, onto Gas Street, with 'The Midland Education' shop on the corner. 'Edwards' the plumbers merchants, at the junction of King Edwards Place, and St Peters Place. On we walked, past 'The Hall of Memory' by Easy Row, with its row of beautiful Georgian Style houses (now offices). The lovely 'Cresent Theatre' at the rear in Crescent Wharf. Lilley White and Frowds, and opposite the O.H.M.S. shop on the corner of Easy Row and Edmund Street. Obviously, the nearer to New Street station we got, the more excited we were. I don't know how the others felt at this point, they probably took it all in their stride, having been on trains, and visited far off places before. For me, however, prior to this great adventure, my visits to far away places were: Handsworth (Victoria Park), Perry Hall Park (I shan't forget that visit in a hurry), see 'Love All' at Perry Hall. 'A Paddle in Hockley Brook'), Barnt Green, with the other mob from St Saviours Church Hall in Farm Street and donated by the local Boy Scout movement.

Then there was the trip to 'Ramsbottom' with 'Owa Kid' to stay with my brother-in-law's sister; that was indeed the farthest I had travelled from Hockley. Not forgetting, however, our cycle ride from Hockley to Shrewsbury, by me and Jack Pittaway. Just like a bunch of school kids, nattering away with our school teacher, in the form of this very smart 'three-badge' nothing, we moved on down Easy Row, then turning left into Paradise Street, past Ratcliff Place which housed the main library of Birmingham, and situated at the side of the Town Hall. Into Victoria Square, where we turned right into Hill Street. Red Vans of the Royal Mail flitting about like ants round a honey pot, they were everywhere (little realising that in a few years time I would be driving one of those ants). We descended the steep incline passing The Golden Eagle " on the corner of Swallow Street (the pub of Jimmy Houghton fame),then crossing over to bring us to the junction of Navigation Street. At this point we could see the object of our walk from Bishopgate Street, New Street Station, which to me, not being able to speak for the others, and to ask would have been a slight on my life to date, meant the means to be transported away from the life and surroundings I had been so used to for over seventeen years now. I could see the steam from the trains already in the station, rising to the clear blue sky, just like puffy balloons, having been let loose by their owners.

We waited for the busy traffic to clear, and then made our way over to Queen's Drive. One or two of the blokes, after asking permission from the 'three badger', of course, broke away to buy a newspaper, and/or cigarettes from the kiosk on the right-hand side of Queens Drive. On completion of this the 'three-badger' got us round him, and said, "Now lads, w'en we gerron the platform I gorra gu an' see the Regulatin' Offica, an' gerr all the gen, an' perpa werk fer rowa trip, so om gunna trust ya' not ta do anythin bloody silly like wunderin' orff, or, wus still, skid arsin' back 'um, cuz remba this, although yo' ain't gorreny uniforms yet, yome now in 'is Majisti's Royal Navy, an' subject to the laws in that service. Now don' yo' ferget that, if yove gorreny questions yo' wanna ask, nows the time, cuz we wunt 'ave a lorra time arta, oright?"

"Aye, Aye!" was the full response, but no questions. So we filed down the drive, turning left at the two entrances in the dip, and onto the platform which the 'three-badger' assured us was ours. He then departed with a last "Now don' ferget warr I told ya', an' don' move till o get back, oright?"

"Aye, Aye" again.

After he had gone, we smoked, and nattered to one another about what we wanted to do in 'The Andrew'.

Eventually, the train emerged from the long tunnel to our left, coming into the sunshine from the dark interior like some huge monster, black in colour, belching steam from its one nostril. As it passed us the whole platform seemed to shake; we stood back not wishing to get the steam - which was now blanketing the whole area in a thick fog - on to us. It stopped eventually, with lots of shouting, and whistle blowing, and a voice over the tannoy system which no one could possibly decipher. Looking around us we were at a loss what to do. We weren't sure this was our train, and the 'three-badger' was nowhere in sight. One or two lads, suggested that we go and find out about this train, but on the advice of the majority did not follow this through, remembering the words of our master, "Don' move till o get back." Suddenly he appeared almost as if out of nowhere, walking quite casually, towards the waiting train. We gathered round him quickly, not wanting to offend him in any way.

"Right lads, we'em all 'ere ain' we?" Silence. "O' said we'em all bloody 'ere ain' we?, buck up an' bloody ansa mi, or we'll miss the bloody train."

"Aye, Aye," we answered. It was getting to be a bit of a record now for us. "Right folla me, the compartments wi got am down 'ere."

Walking down the platform towards the bridge the train had come out of, we came to a carriage with the notice 'RESERVED' on about three or four windows. " 'ere we am lads, 'is Majisty 'as kep' these aside fer yo' lot, so think ya'selves lucky; yo'll bi trav'lin' in style, now gerr aboard, an' don' ferget one pierce by the winda fer yours truly, come now 'op to it."

We all clambered onto the train, and quickly sought our particular compartment, obviously with the group we had joined at the start. Fred, Sid, Bob, and myself stuck together in the one place, with some others, but never the less kept to ourselves. I obtained a place by the window, and half listened to what the other three were saying, and half observing what was going on on the platform. People rushing about finding a place on the train, others saying goodbye to their loved ones. Shouting by the railway staff, and the rumbling of heavy, man-handled flat carts with bags of all sorts of goods, and mail on. Some of these people in uniform, land army girls, sailors (like warr I wuz gunna be), airmen, army, Wrens, A.T.S. and a host of others. Seeing all these uniforms made me feel so good, knowing that it would not be long now before I would be joining them. Suddenly there was a long blast on a whistle, and everything seemed to quieten down. After this short lull, the rhythmic banging of doors, it was of course one of the porters walking along the train making sure that all the doors were securely closed. It went quiet again, and then..., another blast on the whistle. Then a sound like a dog with a deep bark going off at short intervals. The carriage shook, stopped, shook again, stopped, and then shook once more, before settling into a smooth tempo. The bark of the dog became quieter, and somehow nicer, until the two seemed to harmonise into one, as our transport to another stage in our lives moved out of New Street Station, Birmingham.

Each one of us in that compartment suddenly went quiet, as if a magical sign had swept over us, demanding that we reflect on the moment. I thought of Mom, Dad, Lily, Violet, Hilda, Arthur, Dorothy, Audrey, and last but not least, 'The Babby', our Betty. These thoughts continued with Jack, Ronnie, Joe my three brothers-in-law, then onto my friends, who I knew I would not see for sometime to come.

I had that queer sensation in my stomach I had witnessed before. I felt that I wanted to cry, (but grown men don't cry do they?) I looked outside seeing unfamiliar buildings passing as the train gathered speed, pulling farther and

242

farther away from the only life I had known up until this moment. Tonight I would be sleeping in a strange bed, along with people I did not really know. It was tormenting. I began to wonder if I had done the right thing. Then I let my mind go blank for a while, trying not to think of anything.

"Hey Ron, 'ave ya' gone bloody deaf or summat? Ov bin 'oldin' this fag out fer yo' so long now it's grown 'alf an inch."

I looked round to find that Sid was offering me a cigarette with the biggest smile on his face.

It was at that precise moment that I realised that I was moving on in my life, not finishing it at this stage. As the train moved into the countryside, it was as if God had said "Come on Son this is all meant for you, and your mates, so don't be down hearted."

I smiled back at Sid, thanked him for the fag, lit it, and snuggled back into my seat and thought "I'm flowing like a river to see what's out there in the world for me, in fact, I'm OVERFLOWING FROM HOCKLEY BROOK into a far bigger Brook."